THE
NAME OF
THIS BAND IS
R.E.M.

The
Name of
This Band Is
R.E.M.

A BIOGRAPHY

Peter Ames Carlin

DOUBLEDAY
New York

Jacket photograph © Tom Sheehan
Jacket design by Oliver Munday
Book design by Cassandra J. Pappas

Library of Congress Cataloging-in-Publication Data
Names: Carlin, Peter Ames, author.
Title: The name of this band is R.E.M. : a biography / Peter Ames Carlin.
Description: First edition. | New York : Doubleday, 2024. |
Includes bibliographical references and index.
Identifiers: LCCN 2023058685 (print) | LCCN 2023058686 (ebook) |
ISBN 9780385546942 (hardcover) | ISBN 9780385546973 (ebook)
Subjects: LCSH: R.E.M. (Musical group) | Rock musicians—
United States—Biography. | LCGFT: Biographies.
Classification: LCC ML421.R22 C37 2024 (print) |
LCC ML421.R22 (ebook) | DDC 782.42166092/2 [B]—dc23/eng/20231220
LC record available at https://lccn.loc.gov/2023058685
LC ebook record available at https://lccn.loc.gov/2023058686

MANUFACTURED IN THE UNITED STATES OF AMERICA
1st Printing

First Edition

For Claire, extremely much.

Contents

PART V
The Name of This Band Is R.E.M. and This Is What We Do

THE
NAME OF
THIS BAND IS
R.E.M.

Introduction

The Things They Wouldn't Do

Even from the start you would know them by the things they wouldn't do.

The refusals began before they got together, when Peter Buck, a rock 'n' roll obsessive who loved playing guitar, resolved never to join a band. Guys in bands were assholes, he said, and he wanted no part of it. When they were teenagers, drummer Bill Berry nearly walked out of a jam session because he had taken an instant dislike to his schoolmate Mike Mills, who he just discovered was about to play bass with him. Young Mike and Bill wound up becoming best friends anyway, which helped Bill talk singer Michael Stipe out of *his* initial refusal to make music with Mike, who was falling-down drunk when they first met. When the quartet came together in the college town of Athens, Georgia, in the winter of 1980, they at first refused to perform at the birthday party where they made their famous debut. Soon they would be known by their name, R.E.M., and by the other things they wouldn't do.

They also established themselves as a uniquely artful band, impressive enough to win bookings in Athens clubs that spring. Those led to gigs in other college towns, in Atlanta, and then all over the Southeast. It took only two years for the band to get signed by the prominent independent label I.R.S. Records, becoming recording artists with a new litany of options and opportunities they could rebuff.

It was a key part of R.E.M.'s identity and their philosophy of music, art, and life. The things people wanted them to do or expected them to do or insisted they do, that they would have no part of. None. Not happening. Nope. Not that they weren't capable of changing their minds, because they were. But on their own time, in their own way, when they were ready. Which is why they allowed themselves to be talked into opening for the Police at New York's Shea Stadium in August 1983. It wasn't something they felt comfortable doing, and they didn't enjoy it one bit, they said. But it did lead to their getting a shot on a national television show that fall.

Peter Buck and Mike Mills appeared on the local New York talk show *Live at Five* the day before the Shea concert and bumped into staffers from NBC's *Late Night with David Letterman*, a talk show that taped in the studio across the hall. The staffers turned out to be R.E.M. fans and asked if the band might be interested in coming on their program. "We said yes, as long as we didn't have to lip-synch and all that," Peter told a writer from *Athens Night Life* a few months later. "So we gave them the names of the people to call."[1] The official request came through their record company a few weeks later.

The musicians were thrilled. In the fall of 1983 their band had been together for just three years. Their first full-length album, *Murmur*, had been out for only a few months. They were spending the vast majority of their time on the road in a used Dodge Tradesman van, hauling from one rock 'n' roll club to another. *Late Night* was not just the hippest talk show on network television; it was also a conduit to millions of young, music-loving viewers. For R.E.M., a post-punk quartet from a tiny college town in northeast Georgia, it was an enormous opportunity. It was also a surprising time for their lead singer to decide that he didn't want to answer any questions from *Late Night*'s popular host, David Letterman.

As they became full-fledged recording artists, the band focused on the new array of expectations they couldn't tolerate. They wouldn't write songs with traditional structures, or craft lyrics that could be parsed for literal meaning. Assuming you could pick out what was being said, which you probably couldn't, because R.E.M. wouldn't mix the vocals above the instruments, and also wouldn't include a lyric sheet with their records. They wouldn't work with a producer who wanted to make their songs more radio-friendly. When the time came to promote their records on the road, the band refused to tour as an opener for most of the successful bands that offered them a shot at their larger audiences. They made occasional exceptions, as when they spent a week playing short sets in arenas and stadiums on the Police's 1983 tour. But they'd disliked the experience so intensely that they vowed never to do it again. Other acts asked; the executives at I.R.S., who understood the promotional possibilities, keened for a yes. R.E.M. held firm: no, no, and no.

When they started making promotional videos for their records, Michael Stipe wouldn't lip-synch his vocals for the camera, though that was the standard practice in virtually all popular videos. When the former art student turned singer started overseeing the production of their music videos, he refused to make clips that resembled anything else being aired on MTV, opting instead to make avant-garde art films, often abstract to the point of formlessness, all but guaranteeing they would never be broadcast. A refusal of another sort, but a refusal just the same.

David Letterman was a music fan who enjoyed chatting on the air with the artists he brought onto his show. Ordinarily a band's singer serves as the front man in interviews as well as onstage, so the *Late Night* staff assumed the host would address his questions to R.E.M.'s singer. But then Michael resolved that he didn't want to speak on the show. The singer was feeling shy; he didn't have anything to say that wasn't in his lyrics. The *Late Night* producers found this surprising, but told that the band's guitarist would be happy to step in, they said *Okay, fine.* When their song was over, Peter could join Letterman at the desk where he sat for the bulk of the show. But wait, because Peter didn't want to sit down all on his own. Couldn't bassist Mike Mills come with him? Well, no, because Letterman hated trying to interview two people at once. It made him nervous, not knowing where to look. The show's staffers worked out a compromise: when the time came to chat, Letterman would walk over to where the band was set up and ask his questions there. Peter said that would be acceptable.

They had their reasons for being so stubborn. Rock music, like the rest of the culture, was in an ebb tide in the early 1980s. Synthetic sounds, corrupt ideals, a catalog of gestures and poses designed to signal rebellion while actually enforcing the rigid conformity brought to bear by the various industrial, political, and social authorities. R.E.M. wanted nothing to do with any of it. They were too smart, too confident, too in love with what they did to want to change it in order to get ahead. That's what their litany of refusals signaled, anyway, and for the people who got it, who knew why saying no to the prevailing culture was so important, it mattered.

The day of the Letterman show, the members of R.E.M. were incredibly nervous. Once they did their run-through for the cameras, they went back to the dressing room and felt the pressure of the moment slap them in the face. They were going to be on national television! For a band from a small town with only one album and one EP on an indie label and a sum total of zero hit songs to their credit, it was a big leap. *An audience in the millions.* They had some friends in their dressing room, and a couple of cases of beer, so they cracked those open and started drinking, figuring that would calm them down. At one point the door swung open and David Letterman peered in, wanting to say hi and figure out what they could talk about when he came over to chat on the show. He was friendly and welcoming, which settled them down a little. But when Bill got up to find the men's room and saw the super-glamorous Italian actress Sophia Loren sitting by herself in a dressing room smoking a cigarette, he felt his heart leap into his mouth. When she looked back at him, he recalled a few months later, "I just lost it. I almost threw up on the spot."[2]

During the taping a couple of hours later, Letterman looked into the camera and started talking about the band from the tiny town of Athens, Georgia. He hoisted a copy of their new album, *Murmur.* The *Los Angeles Times* had just named it one of the five best records of the year, he told his audience. "We're happy to have them making their national television debut with us tonight," he continued. "Please welcome R.E.M." The crowd whooped excitedly, and the band launched into "Radio Free Europe," the closest thing they had to a hit song. Like the musicians, the song was lean, fast, and ardent. Four whacks on the drum and then the instrumentalists came in at full throttle, Peter bouncing like a jack-in-the-box as he strummed and picked at his black-and-white Rickenbacker and Mike flailing at his bass. Both musicians in constant motion while Michael stood nearly still, hands on the microphone, face shielded by a curtain of chestnut curls, as if the prospect of having his voice and image beamed into millions of television sets across the United States made him want to disappear.

You didn't have to be on television to want to vanish from sight in 1983. For a lot of young people in the United States, the early 1980s was as dispiriting as it got, not just for the toothless rock 'n' roll and *Lifestyles of the Rich and Famous*–style fetishization of wealth that spread across the culture, but also for what it all signified. President Ronald Reagan led a government that was actively shredding the social safety net, that scapegoated the disadvantaged and the different, that ignored the spread of AIDS, except to the extent it could justify treating gay people as a scourge. If you were poor or gay or even just different—arty, offbeat, angry, beset by visions of what should be, even given the allure of what was—you felt awfully alone. The music on the radio didn't speak to you. You had to look for special outposts where people like you could speak freely in your native tongue. If you were lucky, you'd live somewhere close to a college or a community that supported a fringe radio station. Some cities had specialty record stores, or there might be bookstores, a coffeehouse, a bar with a cool jukebox and a clientele who didn't want to watch sports or thump you for looking a particular way.

For television viewers, *Late Night with David Letterman* offered one kind of respite. A nightly dose of elevator races, monkey cams, and freak show characters like the dwarfish, four-eyed oldster Larry "Bud" Melman, whose inability to function on camera provided ironic commentary on the slick celebrity suck jobs taking place on literally every other talk show. And maybe *Late Night* was just a different kind of media bullshit, but Letterman, a gap-toothed midwestern comedian in his mid-thirties, couldn't resist making acidic asides or just glancing to the camera with a little smile to make sure you knew he knew how ridiculous it all was. *It's all bullshit*, was the subtext. *But at least we know it, so let's have some fun while the network is still letting us play with their toys.*

When the first song ended, Letterman stepped over and shook Michael's hand, then cut to a commercial. When the break ended, Michael had vanished and Letterman addressed his questions to Peter. To start, the guitarist denied that R.E.M., a well-known acronym for *rapid eye movement*, was in this case an acronym for *rapid eye movement*. "It can mean anything you want it to mean," he said. Next, Letterman asked about the Athens music scene; it was full of new bands, wasn't it? Peter nodded and rattled off a short list of their friends' bands, Pylon, Love Tractor, the Method Actors, and explained why so much music was coming out of that one small town: "There's a lack of anything else to do." Letterman turned to Mike to converse about how *Murmur* retailed for two dollars less than most albums. "Why don't they make 'em all cheaper?" the host wondered, and the bassist rubbed his thumb against his index and middle fingers, the international sign for cash on the barrelhead. "Money talks, folks," Letterman said dryly.

They got to play a second song. This would have been extraordinary enough for an unknown band on a national talk show, but what made it even more so was that the song they chose to perform wasn't from their new album, or even from the EP they'd released the previous year. It was a new song—so new, in fact, that when Letterman asked about the title Mike said, "It doesn't have one; it's too new," and Letterman chuckled. "Too new to be named. All right." The host stepped away and they went right into it, thudding drums leading into a midtempo ballad. Michael stepped back to the microphone, hair draped over his face, avoiding the camera's unblinking eye as he started to sing. *Did you never call? I waited for your call.* As in the previous song, his lyrics were all images and allusions, phrases that implied more than they actually said. Something about storms and disconnection, floods and fallen wires. The music sparkled and jangled, the bass pushing through the guitar, asserting a countermelody that fell away just as the next verse began, the instrumentalists in perfect synchrony while the singer continued the fretful tale they would eventually name "So. Central Rain (I'm Sorry)." *These rivers of suggestion are driving me away*, he sang through his hair.

Going on television may not change you, but it can have a dramatic effect on the way people see you. Peter discovered this a few weeks after the Letterman show, when he was back in Athens walking past a Coca-Cola bottling plant whose workers used to shout abuse when they spied him walking by. A new wave kid with a trench coat, sunglasses, and a funny haircut, the young musician made a tempting target for ridicule. "They'd be like, 'Hey faggot, blow me, faggot,'" Peter recalled to the writer Anthony DeCurtis. But that ended once he'd been on *Late Night*. "The same guys who'd been going, 'Hey, faggot,' were like *Hey, I saw you on David Letterman! Way to go man!*" Peter wasn't moved by that kind of praise. "I liked it better when they were yelling 'Hey fag.'"[3] But the magical powers of the mainstream media were not lost on him, or on his bandmates.

Despite or perhaps because of the things they wouldn't do, R.E.M.'s audience grew throughout the 1980s. Michael said in 1986 that neither he nor his bandmates were the least bit interested in making records that would appeal to mainstream radio. "I don't think radio deserves me. Yet,"[4] he told MTV, though it was that last word, *yet*, that would prove crucial. R.E.M.'s audience continued to grow, and by 1986 they had to start refusing to perform in sports arenas, or any venue that removed them too far from their audience. And the crowds kept growing. In 1987 the band released "The One I Love," a seething breakup song with an indelible guitar hook that catapulted them into *Billboard*'s top ten and carried *Document*, their final album for I.R.S., to sales of more than a million copies. Thinking that radio might deserve them after all, and that there was nothing wrong with getting their music into the ears of as many people as possible, they signed on with the mega-major label Warner Bros. Records and released *Green*, which sold twice as many copies as its predecessor, powered both by its own smash single ("Stand") and a world tour that, owing to R.E.M.'s rapidly expanding audience, played almost exclusively in the same sports arenas in which they had once refused to perform. They were just getting started.

Eventually the things they couldn't abide were eclipsed by the things they wanted. To be heard. To be seen. To have their music filling the air, and to cannonball their way into the middle of the mainstream and see how big a splash they could make. Because their music was an animation of values and ideals that stood in opposition to all the assumptions and rules brought to bear by the prevailing culture. By the dawn of the 1990s they had enough momentum to say yes to all sorts of things they'd never imagined doing. And they saw their success, and their fame, expand by factors.

Their first album of the new decade, 1991's *Out of Time*, catapulted the band to superstardom. The single "Losing My Religion" jumped into the top five and stayed near the top of the charts for most of the summer, selling more than a million copies. Album sales rocketed as a result, and stayed hot when the next single, "Shiny Happy People," also hit the top ten. Feeling burned out from the year they'd spent on the road promoting *Green*, the band had decided not to tour to promote the new album. Fortunately, the pair of hit singles spurred so much interest in *Out of Time* that its global sales leaped to nearly twenty million copies. The band's follow-up album, *Automatic for the People*, released just nineteen months after its predecessor, sold in similarly mammoth quantities. Then 1994's *Monster* all but equaled each of those albums' sales, and the long-awaited concert tour set for 1995 was booked into the largest venues in Europe, Asia, and the United States.

Some of their fans, followers, and friends thought R.E.M.'s move into the mainstream was a mistake. A violation, even, of the values they'd once shared. Once, they'd all been in it together, living, working, and singing in opposition to the dominant culture. All shouting *No!* together. What happened to the spunky alternative band whose singer spoke in riddles and wouldn't even look America in the eye?

They decided to take over, was what. To make music powerful enough to force the mainstream to say yes to them. They made that happen, then set out to do even more, albeit with some well-placed fears about the fate of ambitious people who fly a little too close to the sun. But when they had their instruments in hand, there was only one thing to do: turn up the amps, count in the next song, and make some noise.

Ready, everyone? As Michael would come to say at the start of their live shows: The name of this band is R.E.M., and this is what we do.

PART I

The Music of Dissent

1

___

Super Fucking Famous

few things that make perfect sense in retrospect, after everything he's done and the way he did it:

Of course the teenage Michael Stipe was a *Rocky Horror
Picture Show* guy.

Of course he was one of the cultists who attended the satiric
horror-slash-musical movie's weekly midnight showings at the Varsity Theater, right there among St. Louis's other young outsiders, the
arty and theatrical and socially dispossessed, the glams and nerds and
punks. Anyone an adolescent jock of the late 1970s might refer to,
with a derisive snort, as a *fag*.

And it goes without saying that the young Stipe dressed for the
showings in the most outlandish fashion, dolled up as the film's main
hero/villain, the sweet transvestite from Transsexual, Transylva-
nia, Dr. Frank-N-Furter, clad in a leather jacket, bustier, stockings,
and one of his mom's strands of pearls, with dark red lipstick and
extremely heavy and artfully applied mascara.

And also a button featuring the male/female logo of the lightly
transgressive '70s rock band Blue Öyster Cult.

A TV news crew came to see the *Rocky Horror* gang that spring,
to report a feature story about the bizarre goings-on taking place at
the university district theater's midnight screenings each week. Who
knew there could be all these kids dressed up and dancing around,

week after week, chorusing key lines of dialogue back at the screen in perfect synchrony, singing along to the songs, leaping to their feet to do the Time Warp again, and again?

Mike Stipe, a senior at Collinsville High School, was in the thick of it, and when the TV news showed up, lights, camera, and all, he beelined right over to see what was going on.

A bunch of kids were standing there, as people do when a portal to fame slides open, but the reporter was focused on one young woman who was excitedly explaining why she was about to see the movie for the sixty-first time. The reporter, expert at drollery, was making gentle but pointed sport of her. "Devotion has its limits," he was saying. "*Sixty* is enough. But one more time?"

Mike Stipe was eighteen years old and already impatient. He wasn't going to be a bystander to this. Not when *The Rocky Horror Picture Show* was being discussed. So he spoke up. Interrupted interviewer and interviewee in mid-discourse, and grasped the moment.

"This is an excellent movie. It really is," Mike declared. "And we're all quite normal, really."

The reporter was incredulous. How, he wondered, gesturing to the be-dragged, bewigged gaggle of teens, could they even begin to seem *normal*?

Mike mused for a moment. What were the usual signifiers for standard-issue St. Louis teens? Well, nearly every lunkhead patrolling the hallway at school came wearing the same T-shirts for the same mainstream rock radio station, so . . . He spoke in quick bursts, thinking aloud about how a normal-seeming teen would behave:

"Show up . . . tomorrow afternoon . . . dressed up in our little KSHE pig shirts and our blue jeans."

Around him, a burst of knowing laughter as the reporter continued. "That'd be normal?"

Mike, amid more laughs: "I guess . . . for the normal St. Louis KSHE fan, yes, it would."

The laughter, gaining force, became something else: applause.

They applauded him. Or maybe they were applauding themselves.

Mike's eyes shifted away from the TV reporter to focus on something else. Something that wasn't visible yet but was out there, somewhere. Maybe closer than it seemed.

—————

Speaking to another reporter decades later, Michael Stipe remembered how it felt to be so young. How much he had surging inside him, how desperate he was to express it, and how determined he was for people to hear him. To see so much, to feel so much, to want so much, to know it was right, and necessary, for so many reasons. To be a voice. To be *the* voice. For the right people, for the right reasons. And maybe for a couple of the wrong reasons too.

"I really wanted to be super fucking famous."[1]

2

Birdland

Many years later, nearing the end of yet another concert in front of yet another packed hall, Michael Stipe noticed a pair of school-aged boys standing in front of his stage. His band had just finished one song and he was about to set up the next, but first he pointed into the crowd. "Kiddo! Hey, kiddo, come on up. You too. Come on up."

R.E.M. was taping a show for the *Austin City Limits* public television series. The stage was low, and the boys, one about eleven years old, the other maybe thirteen, came bouncing up the stairs to stand there and beam excitedly at the singer. After asking their names (Simon and Elliott), Michael shook their hands and asked if they were seeing their first R.E.M. concert. They both said yes, so he asked what they thought. The smaller boy, Simon, who was not the least bit shy in front of a thousand concertgoers, a bank of television cameras, and the millions of viewers watching from afar, didn't hesitate. "I think you're awesome," he declared, and Elliott agreed. "That just about sums it up." This was in 2008, nearly thirty years into a career that had elevated him far above an ordinary person's experience of life and hero worship. But the singer seemed not just surprised but actually a little stunned by the boys' compliments. His eyes sparkled, and he laughed. "I like you guys a lot!" he said, taking a moment to shake both their hands one more time. The boys hopped back down into the crowd and he stood at the microphone, still gig-gling with happiness. "I don't know," he said. "I feel *awesome*."

Everyone carries their childhood with them throughout their adult lives, and though being part of a military family meant being per-petually on the move, Michael recalled his earliest years as extraor-dinarily warm and fulfilling. Asked in 2001 where he first felt like he really belonged, he didn't hesitate: as a child. "My entire childhood," he said, "I felt I really belonged to a strong family."

Born on January 4, 1960, John Michael Stipe was the son of John Wesley Mobley Stipe Jr., a rising officer in the U.S. Army, and the former Marianne Hatch, both from small towns in Georgia.

John, a square-jawed young man, came from Augusta, Georgia, and attended North Georgia College, a military institution where he regularly made the dean's list while earning degrees in physics and mathematics. Ambitious and energetic, he also played intramu-ral sports and served in straight-arrow organizations including the Scabbard and Blade military honor society, the Forensic Senate, the Officer's Club, the NCO Club, the Radio Club, and the Physics Club. John was still a student at North Georgia College when he met Marianne Hatch, a schoolmate who came from Hapeville, Georgia, a small town just south of Atlanta. The couple married in 1956 and settled in Decatur, Georgia, near Bainbridge Air Base, where John went to flight school. There John learned how to pilot helicopters and used his math skills to help compute the ebb and flow of goods and weaponry in the Army's supply chain. Cyndy, the couple's first child, arrived in 1958. Michael came two years later, and the baby of the family, Lynda, was born in 1962, just before John was assigned to a new post on a base in Texas.

From there the Stipe family rotated from one military base to the next as John's career grew and his duties expanded. From Texas to Alabama to Germany and then back to Texas, where Marianne and the children lived while John served in Vietnam, flying reconnais-sance missions in search of enemy positions. The helicopters flew low over the jungle, and when they located the Vietcong embattlements, the air outside the plastic bubble encasing Major Stipe and his crew would erupt with bullets, rocket-propelled grenades, and anti-aircraft weapons. Recon helicopter squads faced near-daily battle, were often hit, and regularly got shot down. The pilots who survived the six months of hazardous duty usually went home or switched to less dangerous duty as soon as possible. A few found something transcendent in battle: the heightened consciousness of living on the edge of death. When Major Stipe's hitch in recon was over, he signed up for six more months at the front.

At home in Texas, Marianne and her young kids focused on their days. Breakfasts, school bells, classes, picture books, episodes of the animated Stone Age sitcom *The Flintstones*, the comic adventures of the pretend-gone-real pop band the Monkees, and whatever cartoons they could catch after school. Being close in age, and by necessity, Cyndy, Mike, and Lynda were one another's best playmates. When Cyndy got a transistor radio around her tenth birthday, in 1967, they all tuned in to the Top 40 and country stations that crackled across the Texas airwaves. At seven years old, Mike fixed on the poppier songs: "Sugar, Sugar," as performed by the Archies, a group of musicians masquerading as characters from the *Archie* comics, along with the hits of the Monkees and the songs performed on the *Banana Splits* Saturday morning show.

The country music they heard was nearly as cartoonish, the airwaves overflowing with the likes of Johnny Cash's oddball "A Boy Named Sue," Merle Haggard's grumbling hippie takedown "Okie from Muskogee," and Tammy Wynette's pre-feminist anthem "Stand by Your Man." A chorus of oddball voices, serious and silly, celebratory and mournful, all of them blowing around the heads of children whose family was defined by the absence of a father whose days they couldn't imagine.

Major Stipe's tour of duty ended in 1972 and he received a new assignment at an army base near St. Louis, Missouri. This time the family moved off-base, buying a home in the suburban town of Collinsville, Illinois, just fifteen miles from the center of St. Louis. The house, a split-level, four-bedroom home at 408 Camelot Drive, stood on a street of midcentury homes not far from Interstate 55. It had a long, sloping front lawn and a backyard separated by a short fence from the Town & Country pool, a neighborhood club that was a magnet for Collinsville youth in the warmer months. Mike was thirteen years old when they got there, an incoming eighth grader in a new town with a new school full of unfamiliar kids and a dad he had barely seen since he was a grade schooler.

To connect with his son and help him meet other boys in their new home, John Stipe signed them both up for the Boy Scouts, Mike as a Tenderfoot Scout and John as the troop's scoutmaster. Bill Dorman, who befriended Mike when both of their troops were at scout camp in Missouri, was struck instantly by the Stipes, father and son. Dorman recalls the elder Stipe, by then a lieutenant colonel in the Army, as a near caricature of a military man. From the broad-brimmed cavalry hat that accentuated his six-foot-four frame to his prominent mustache, the pipe in his mouth, and the red flight suit he always wore, he looked as though he'd just stepped out of a helicopter. When Dorman saw *Apocalypse Now* a few years later, he wondered if Robert Duvall's character, the bluff warrior Lieutenant Colonel Bill Kilgore, with his broad-brimmed cavalry hat and hyper-macho posture, had been based on Lieutenant Colonel Stipe, who was a ringer in every way except for the bluster. On the rare occasion when the elder Stipe did speak, he did it so quietly you'd miss it if you weren't right next to him.

Mike Stipe had no problem speaking up. When he and Dorman shared a tent at a retreat, he terrified his bunkmate one rainy night by talking about the nuclear arms race between the United States and the Soviet Union and the theory of mutually assured destruction, that neither side would ever start a nuclear war when they both knew the other had enough weapons to obliterate them. Dorman didn't find the principle the least bit comforting, but soon he had more pressing concerns. A gust of wind knocked the boys' tent down, and they had to lug their backpacks to the Stipes' station wagon to get out of the storm. When Dorman started pulling off his jeans before climbing into his sleeping bag, Mike recoiled. "Whoa! Don't take your pants off—people will think we're homosexuals!" Mike was full of information about gay culture. As they settled in for the night, he told Dorman about life in ancient Greece, where some older men would take on a younger man as a combination protégé and sex partner. "That's pretty vanilla for today, but back in 1974 it was a big deal," Dorman says. "It just kind of blew my thirteen-year-old mind."[1]

As Michael got older, he got a charge from making his schoolmates shake their heads. He got two pairs of differently colored Converse sneakers and wore them mismatched. When conversation with the other boys bored him, he'd take a few steps away and start conversing with a tree. If another boy stepped up to hear what he was saying, Michael would lean in and start whispering. "He was off in his own little world and he really didn't give a fuck about what anyone thought of him," Dorman says.[2]

When Craig Franklin first saw Mike Stipe, it was the summer of 1975 and he was standing with some friends near the pool at the Town & Country club. The new kid made a distinctive entrance by strolling out of his house and hopping the fence that separated the properties. He wore a swimsuit with a long-sleeved button-up shirt, its dangling shirttails rolled up and tied around his midriff. A popular look at the time, but for women. Noticing a guy he knew from his Boy Scout troop, one of the kids Franklin was standing with, Mike gave a big wave and headed their way, a smile on his face. His friend, however, wasn't feeling especially friendly. "Let's get out of here," he muttered. "This kid is kinda weird." A few of the kids, including Franklin, stayed put. They got to talking, mostly about music, and became friends.[3]

In high school Mike followed his own sense of style, perching a fedora atop his shoulder-length curls and accessorizing his button-up shirts and jeans with a vest, a bandanna flowing from a pocket, and/or a line of safety pins. Joining the cast of a high school production of the Cold War satire *The Mouse That Roared*, in which he played Benter, the opposition leader portrayed by Leo McKern in the 1959 film, Mike made friends with Melanie Herrold, a vaguely androgynous girl who shared his off-center perspective on school and life in general. Their schoolmates noticed and did not approve. "We were both typical high school outcasts," she recalls. "You don't fit in and they have to label you. I was always a dyke or a slut, and he was either gay or just weird."[4]

The two outsiders bonded quickly, especially when it turned out that they had the same passion for music and a fervent desire to become rock stars. After school they spent hours in one another's room listening to records by Aerosmith, Led Zeppelin, and Pink Floyd, flipping through magazines and debating which one would end up featured in the pages of *Creem* first. For one of Herrold's birthdays Michael got them both matching kimono tops, the sort of silky, belted shirts Robert Plant wore onstage, and they took turns pairing them with some shiny silver pants Herrold's mother had made for her, posing for the camera just like the stars in the magazines. "We were both so androgynous," she says. "We always wore each other's clothes."

Herrold later got a job at the Varsity movie theater, in St. Louis, and she immediately alerted Mike when the midnight showings of *Rocky Horror* turned into costume parties for young outcasts with a penchant for group singing, dancing, and noisy inside jokes. Mike became an instant convert, taking on the guise of the movie's most louche character, the charismatic singing and dancing transvestite from outer space, Dr. Frank-N-Furter, played by Tim Curry. On his way out to the theater one night, Mike sauntered past Lieutenant Colonel Stipe, who looked up from his newspaper to see his son in a red bustier, leather jacket, and fishnet stockings, his face garish with mascara, eyeliner, powder, and rouge. "You're not going out like that, son, are you?" Mike grinned at his dad. Yes, he was. The elder Stipe, still wearing his Army uniform, had seen too much on the battlefields of Vietnam to get fussed about his son's choice of evening wear. Shrugging, he went back to his newspaper. "Okay, then. Have a good night."[5]

Lieutenant Colonel Stipe did his best to interest Mike in more traditional pursuits. One Christmas he gave his son a few Foxfire books, the popular series of titles that described old-fashioned Appalachian homesteading skills, such as hog slaughtering, furniture building, and possum cooking. It was a sweet gesture, but Mike was far more interested in modern urban life, particularly the bohemian demimonde in modern New York City.

The conduit opened when Cyndy found one of those Publishers Clearing House offers to subscribe to a dozen magazines for a penny. Mike signed up for *The Village Voice*, the weekly journal of downtown arts and culture. Every week he'd carry the newspaper down to his basement bedroom and marvel. The stories about up-and-coming artists and writers, the reviews of exhibitions at the Guggenheim, the Whitney, the Museum of Modern Art, and the palatial Metropolitan Museum, the listings for the downtown galleries, the art-house movie theaters, the nightly haul of plays taking place on Broadway, off-Broadway, and so far off-Broadway they were staged in alleys . . . Mike was enthralled. The personal ads were just as thrilling; the endless churn of people looking for jobs, roommates, friends, even lovers. The pages of movie ads featured *The Towering Inferno*, *The Exorcist*, and Woody Allen's *Love and Death* next to displays for *Kyoto in Bondage* and *Heavy Leather*, whose ad noted the "four great S&M features" that came with it.

When he showed it all to Craig Franklin, his friend gaped. "I said, 'What's all this gay stuff?'"[6] Mike just shrugged and pointed him toward the music pages. He didn't have to hear a note; the band names and photos alone sent his imagination reeling. The Ramones, Television, Talking Heads, the Cramps, Richard Hell, the New York Dolls—artists who were both wild and artistically daring, who pushed against the boundaries of rock 'n' roll, who not only ignored but actively undermined the rules about propriety, gender, and sex.

Mike had always been drawn to the music that gestured to rock 'n' roll's more transgressive impulses. The mini wave of glam-rock hits that washed across the Top 40 in 1972 and 1973—T. Rex's "Get It On," Mott the Hoople's "All the Young Dudes," David Essex's "Rock On," and the Sweet's "Ballroom Blitz"—coincided with the dawn of his adolescence, and the music, amplified by the looks and attitudes of the artists behind it, resonated in his imagination. Not that you had to venture out of rock 'n' roll's mainstream to see men testing the limits of gender. A decade earlier, the mop-topped Beatles had sparked fury among conservatives for their androgynous locks . . .

hanging all the way to their *ears*! By the end of the 1960s shoulder-length hair was nearly de rigueur for pop musicians, and Mick Jagger showed up for the Rolling Stones' vast Hyde Park concert in a filmy cloak that hung like a virginal white dress. He peeled it off to reveal tight white pants and a sleeveless T-shirt that emphasized his biceps. David Bowie took androgyny to a whole other level, and Led Zeppelin's Robert Plant split the difference, pairing feminine blouses with denim tight enough to make his maleness obvious even to fans sitting in the back of the arena.

Transgression, or at least the appearance of it, was stylish. But Mike had an appetite for the real thing, and with *The Village Voice* serving as a weekly dispatch from the front lines, he started recognizing names and tracking their stories and exploits. In 1975, one name that kept coming up was Patti Smith. Her photos, showing a slim, waifish woman who wore her dark hair in a Keith Richards-esque shag, appealed to his eye for androgyny. And the breadth of her work, which encompassed literature, rock 'n' roll, performance art, and, through the lens of her similarly androgynous and sexually divergent photographer boyfriend, Robert Mapplethorpe, visual art, stretched across the artistic horizon. But it was her music, or what people said about her music, that catalyzed Michael's imagination. Greil Marcus's review of Smith's first album, *Horses*, describing the record's themes and influences—old-fashioned rock 'n' roll raves, the New York avant-garde, early-twentieth-century surrealism, beatnik poetry, punk rock—riveted Mike from the start. The words on the page made it sound like the rock 'n' roll of his dreams: the music raw and spare, the words closer to poetry than pop lyrics, the narratives fracturing into dreamlike scenes that drew more from the free verse of the romantic nineteenth-century French poet Arthur Rimbaud than from anything in the rock/pop canon.

The release of *Horses* was a watershed moment for Michael Stipe. The tale he tells, years later, of buying and listening to *Horses* is as emotionally vivid and phantasmagorical as the songs on the album. He's said that he had to beg the owner of a local record store to order the album for him, and also that he bought it the day it came out. "I sat up all night with my headphones on, listening to it over and over again while eating a giant bowl of cherries," he told *Interview* in 2011. "In the morning I threw up and went to school."[7]

The chronology of the story doesn't quite add up. *Horses* was released on November 10, 1975. Greil Marcus's review of the album didn't appear in the *Voice* until the November 24 issue. And Melanie Herrold recalls Michael getting *Horses* as a Christmas present from one of his sisters, received in the same haul as the Foxfire book from his father. Plus, the summer crop of cherries would have likely vanished from the shelves of St. Louis grocery stores by November. But the literal truth of his account matters less than the emotional truth of the experience: the black of night, the music filling his ears, and the sense of overwhelm. The vomited cherries symbolize a kind of rebirth, then the return of the daylight and ordinary life, his transformation complete.

Mike took up the record like a signpost, a talisman, a divining rod. All of his friends recall having the same exchange with him: *Do you know who Patti Smith is? Have you heard* Horses *yet?* He called Craig Franklin and told him to come over as soon as possible and just listen. Franklin had his mom take him to Camelot Drive, where he found his friend waiting for him in the front yard, eating one of those nut-covered balls of cheese, holding it in his hand like an apple. That was the first odd thing that happened. They went inside and Michael took the record out of its sleeve and placed it on the turntable, set the needle on the vinyl, and sat down to measure his friend's response. Franklin, who was used to the sleek hard rock of Styx, Kansas, and the rest of the album-oriented rock bands, was flummoxed by the bare instrumentation and flights of unsettling poetry. "I was like, 'What *is* this?'" Michael found a more flexible pair of ears when he carted the record over to Michael Edson's house. "It was like *wow, a whole different world*," Edson recalls.[8]

One song in particular wouldn't let him go. "Birdland," a nine-minute epic inspired by a memoir Peter Reich wrote that described a dream he'd had soon after his father, the psychoanalyst Wilhelm Reich, died. In the dream the elder Reich returns to his son in a spaceship. Reich père invites Reich fils to come aboard, and the boy is overcome with joy: he's reunited with his lost father and they're going to go off into the stars, together for eternity. Except then he's back on Earth and his dad is soaring off without him, leaving Peter to cry out, in Patti's words:

> Take me up, daddy, to the belly of your ship,
> Let the ship slide open and I'll go inside of it
> Where you're not human, you are not human.

It's a powerful moment, and it's easy to imagine how it resonated for a teenager still processing the fear he felt as a boy, imagining the fate his father might meet in his helicopter in Vietnam. Lieutenant Colonel Stipe didn't talk about the war when he got home, but his silence echoed through Michael's experience of "Birdland." It fueled his connection to the music, and his understanding of how poetry could function within the confines of a pop song. It made him feel airborne. And it made him fantasize about the life he wanted to lead in the future.

"It was like the ground didn't exist," he would later say. "And at that moment I decided what I would do with my life, with all the arrogance of a 15-year-old who'd never written a song."[9]

Whenever Mike and Melanie Herrold were together, they'd end up singing. Driving in the car, belting along with the radio, walking home from school. They pooled their money to buy books of sheet music for their favorite albums, then rushed back to one or the other's house and cranked up the music so they could follow along and learn all the words and phrasing, working out the harmony parts as they went. Led Zeppelin, the Who, Aerosmith. Sometimes they'd pull out a cassette player and record themselves to see how they sounded. Herrold still has a tape of them doing "Fistful of Love," as performed by Jim Dandy and Ruby Starr on Black Oak Arkansas's *Live! Reading '76* album. Their tastes evolved as they got older, and the songs did too, to Patti Smith's "Pissing in a River" and "Radio Ethiopia" and favorites off of records by New York artists like Television and Talking Heads. But the teenagers' growing interest in punk and new wave music didn't supplant their taste for commercial rock 'n' roll, and when a few school friends invited Melanie to sing in their cover band, she dove in eagerly. Avatar, as they called themselves, stuck with the favorites: Led Zeppelin, Rush, Deep Purple, one or two by Bob Seger, and a few originals that didn't meander very far from the songs everyone knew.

At first Mike could only marvel at his friend's courage. He'd go with Melanie to rehearsals, and then to the parties and talent shows where they played, and be transfixed by it all: the interplay of the musicians, the way his friend let the music carry her past her self-consciousness. Melanie had a real voice, throaty and full of fire, and was able to not just hit the right notes but also deliver the words with a passion that projected the songs right into your chest. Mike was less sure about his voice, though he wasn't shy about belting along to songs on the radio. One night he was in a car with some friends when Aerosmith's "Dream On" came on the radio. Somebody cranked the volume and they all sang along, right up until the point near the end when Steven Tyler's repeated *Dream onnn, dream onnn, dream onnn*s climb up an octave to the very top of his range. Nobody else bothered trying to keep up, but Mike made the leap into falsetto easily, much to his friends' surprise. *Jeez, you can really sing!* Mike shrugged: no big deal. But it stuck with him. Not that he had the guts to go audition for a band . . . no matter how much Melanie urged him to give it a try.

3

Bad Habits

T hen a band came looking for him. It was early spring of 1978, Mike Stipe's senior year, and he got to talking with one of the other *Rocky Horror* fans, another Frank-N-Furter impersonator who, like Stipe, kept his hair long and shaggy enough for rock 'n' roll. Joe Haynes was a few years older and had already played guitar in a couple of neighborhood bands. Now he was putting together a new group and was looking for a singer: Would Mike want to try out? *Umm . . . maybe?* He consulted with Herrold, who urged him to go for it. *You gotta! You'll be great!* Mike went back to Haynes. *Sure, let's see what happens.* Haynes, for his part, was already sure it was going to be terrific. "He called me one day and said, 'I met this guy, he's the coolest, he's the best, we gotta get together with this guy,'" says Jim Warchol, the band's other member, who played the drums. Haynes set up a meeting at a nearby burger place, and the three of them spent an hour or two talking about music and what kind of band they wanted to make. "Mike didn't have a lot of experience," Warchol says. "But he was definitely a rock 'n' roller, definitely a singer, and he had the attitude and determination."[1]

The group they envisioned would play other bands' tunes, but, unlike all the other cover bands in St. Louis in 1978, they would focus on playing punk and new wave songs. They didn't have a bassist yet, but the three band members started rehearsing anyway, gathering one or two nights a week to play in the basement of an old house where Warchol's uncle ran an insurance company. Together they worked out a list of favorites they figured they could master. The Clash's arrangement of "I Fought the Law," the Who's version of Johnny Kidd's "Shakin' All Over," Alice Cooper's "I'm Eighteen," and tunes by the Sex Pistols, Tuff Darts, the Damned, and a few others. Finding a bassist proved tough. Warchol figured he and Haynes ran through at least a dozen without finding one who seemed to fit.

They still hadn't settled on anyone when they got their first engagement: a sweet sixteen party for the daughter of one of Haynes's neighbors. They set up in the living room, Haynes cranking up the bass setting on his amplifier and doing his best to keep up a propulsive low end while they ran through about an hour's worth of material. The kids, Warchol recalls, did not seem terribly impressed. "I don't remember anyone caring about us."[2] No matter; it was a start. They found a bass player soon after that, a mustached, fast-fingered guy named Buddy Weber, and got back to practicing.

Meanwhile, Craig Franklin and a few friends were putting together a group to play at Collinsville High's annual talent show. Franklin played guitar, and a pair of brothers, Andrew and Danny Gruber, played bass and drums, respectively. But none of them sang or could think of anyone at school who could. Desperate to find a front man, Franklin thought of Mike Stipe. Specifically, he thought of how he looked: the shoulder-length curls, the bandannas that dangled from the pockets of his bell-bottom pants, and the shirts he wore open to reveal his impressively hairy teenage chest. Finding his friend by his locker in the hallway one afternoon, Franklin posed the question: *Want to be the singer in our band?* Mike, who had kept his musical adventures separate from his life at school, shrugged. *I don't really sing*, he said. But Franklin, who didn't know about his friend's extracurricular band, bucked him up. "Well, you *look* like a rock 'n' roll guy." That made Mike laugh, and once he took a moment to contemplate the prospect of making like a rock star in front of all of his high school classmates, he nodded. *Yeah, let's do it.*[3]

Mike went over to Franklin's house a day or two later, carrying a couple of his sheet music books, collections of songs by the Rolling Stones and the Who. They kicked around some ideas. Franklin and the Gruber brothers had already jammed on a couple of Rush songs and had settled on the grinding "Working Man." Mike opened his Stones book and pointed to "Gimme Shelter." Could they learn how to do that one, too? The chords weren't too hard, Franklin decided, so sure.

They practiced a handful of times, and as the show got closer Michael started proposing some band names. The Dirty Habits? The Bad Habits? That sounded rock 'n' roll to him, but the other guys shrugged. Michael kept trying: How about the Jotz? That came from the world of cartoons. Jot was this childlike thing, a sort of smiling dot that learned simple lessons about life and morality courtesy of the Southern Baptists. They all agreed that'd be a funny name for a band, so sure. But just as they were about to take the stage the evening of the show, someone grabbed Franklin to ask for the band's name, and in a moment of panic he spaced out: "Just call us the Band," he said. Apparently Franklin forgot there was another, quite famous rock group with the same name, but nobody seemed to notice or care. The Grubers, Franklin, and Mike earned enthusiastic applause for their two songs, and the judges, a panel of teachers, rated the Jotz/the Band as the second best of the four group acts on the bill, giving the trophy to a dance group who called themselves Dancing Shoes.

Rehearsals with his other band kept on going too. The now four-piece band worked up a set of mostly punk and new wave covers with a few offbeat choices from more mainstream acts they liked. Dubbing themselves the Bad Habits, one of the names Michael had suggested for the Jotz, they posed for a photo comically demonstrating common vices—Haynes gnawing on his fingernails, bassist Buddy Weber puffing on a cigarette, Warchol clutching a beer, and Mike grinning mischievously with a finger jammed up his nose.

To get some pre-summer exposure, Mike signed them up to play a pair of songs at Collinsville High's year-end assembly for the class of 1978. The setup had them at one end of the gym, with another band on the far side, the bands trading off songs while their classmates hung out, signed one another's yearbooks, said their goodbyes. The prospect of departing high school singing rock 'n' roll in front of his own band felt almost irresistible to Mike, but when Melanie Herrold asked if she could handle the vocals for "Eighteen," he was happy to share his moment. They launched with the Alice Cooper. Herrold spat out the song with gritty resolve, then stepped aside as the other band launched into their song. Mike took his place at the microphone, waiting for the other band to finish their song, and could only keep standing there as they segued immediately into a second song, and then a third, and kept right on going until a teacher pulled the plug and declared the music segment of the assembly finished. Herrold came up to Mike looking horrified. She'd taken his chance for the big kiss-off! But he laughed it off. Fuck high school, right? *Let's get out of here.*

Just when things started to come together for Mike in Collinsville, it happened again. Having hit the end of his current term of enlistment, and now at retirement age, Lieutenant Colonel Stipe decided to end his career with the Army. No longer tied to a military base, he and Marianne decided to go back to where they had started, in rural Georgia. Lynda, who was still in high school, and Cyndi, who had graduated, would move with them to Athens, a small town about seventy miles east of Atlanta. They figured Mike would want to go with them too, since he'd just graduated from high school and Athens was the home of the University of Georgia. He could live at home and attend classes during the day. The timing was perfect. They would move in the summer, once the Collinsville school year ended. Except Mike didn't want to go. When he got the news, he went to Melanie Herrold's house looking gloomy.

"He was petrified to go to Athens," Herrold says. "He didn't want to live in the South. He didn't want to get a southern accent."[4] As sleepy as Collinsville was, he told his friend Michael Edson, at least it was next to St. Louis, a city with theaters, nightclubs, an actual cultural life.

So Mike wouldn't go. Instead he registered at Southern Illinois University, a commuter school in Edwardsville, about twenty minutes north of Collinsville. That was fine, John and Marianne said, as long as he found, and paid for, a place to live. Mike found a room in a house close to school rented by the members of the Laughing Heels, a punk band he'd met.

Mike's last few months in Collinsville were full of music, independence, and a slowly dawning understanding that it couldn't last. His classes were interesting enough, and the Bad Habits landed a few bookings here and there, mostly short sets at parties and a high school dance or two. But Joe Haynes was a more than solid guitarist, Jimmy Warchol and Buddy Weber had found a nice groove in the rhythm section, and Mike loved to hear his voice coming through the speakers.

The Bad Habits landed their first real show at the J.B. Annex nightclub, a small down-market venue in Columbia, Illinois, near the foot of the Jefferson Barracks Bridge, on August 21. They played a few other shows that fall and gained enough momentum to land a big break: an opening slot for Rockpile, the British new wave supergroup featuring Dave Edmunds and Nick Lowe. It was a Monday night show at Mississippi Nights, a thousand-capacity nightclub near the Mississippi River in downtown St. Louis. Haynes had pulled every string he could grasp to get his band onto the bill, and they did their best, opening with a hard-edged cover of the Boomtown Rats' "Lookin' After No. 1," and ran through energetic covers of the Yardbirds' "Heart Full of Soul," the Bobby Fuller Four's "I Fought the Law," the Rolling Stones' "(I Can't Get No) Satisfaction," and "Shakin' All Over." Mike, dressed sharp in snug Levi's 501s, a striped button-down shirt, and a blue knit tie, really ripped into that last one, singing the a cappella recitation of the song's title so that it sounded like *Shakin' . . . awwwwwlllll . . . overrrrr,* his voice hanging for a long moment before the band kicked back in. "Mike was a good singer," Warchol recalls. "A lot of it was about his attitude and determination."[5] And about something else that was less definable but just as important. Jim Roehm, who saw the show, recalls that the young singer drew so much attention from two female fans that the men they were with decided to follow the band out to where they were loading up their gear after the show and teach him a lesson. Another friend or two stepped between them to protect the musicians and a fight started. By the time it was over, one friend of Roehm's had been stabbed with a broken beer bottle and had to be rushed to a nearby emergency room. Mike and his bandmates escaped safely, but it was the last show they'd ever play.

———————

When his family left for Georgia, Mike knew he only had enough money to pay for two months of rent. He barely earned any money from the band, and the part-time job he'd found in a restaurant didn't come close to covering his expenses. When he couldn't afford his end of the rent at the band house, he packed his things and went back to Collinsville, where he moved in with his high school friend Michael Edson and his family. But he couldn't stay with them forever, and as the fall term of 1978 came to an end, Mike realized he had no choice but to head south. To his parents and sisters, to the University of Georgia, to whatever waited for him in tiny little Athens, Georgia. He got there in time for Christmas, and after a few days of exploring he reported to Edson that it was just as bad as he'd feared. "I don't want to live in this fuckin town," he wrote to his friend. "It's a hippie cow town. I hate it, I hate it, I hate it."[6]

4

An Oasis for Artists and Misfits

Mike Stipe moved into his parents' house just outside Athens and came to the University of Georgia like he'd always come to new schools in new towns: eyes open, mouth shut, noticing everything. There was a lot to keep him busy. Registering for classes, finding his way around the campus and then around the business district to its northwest, a blocks-long grid of shops, theaters, restaurants, and bars, most catering to the interests and budgets of students: T-shirts, all-day breakfasts, happy hours with fifty-cent drafts, textbooks, sandwiches and chips, blazers and khaki pants. More than a few storefronts were empty, dark windows testifying to the magnetic pull of the nearby suburban malls, which had been drawing businesses away from the center of town since the mid-'70s. But the telephone poles bristled with life: flyers for parties and bands, two-for-one drink nights, new wave night at Tyrone's.

He signed up for classes in the university's art department, projecting a major in photo design. It was one of the more pre-professional courses of study in the department, preparing students for careers in advertising and graphic design. But, as his parents reminded him, it was important to find a focus. They didn't mind if he studied art, but having a practical application for his passion was the smart thing to do. He took the other intro-level art classes too, the basics of drawing, color, and photography. Slowly his resistance to his new home (*I hate it, I hate it, I hate it*) began to ebb. Inspired by his changed circumstances, feeling nothing like the high schooler he'd been in Collinsville, the new student presented himself with a revised name. No longer Mike, he'd now be Michael Stipe.

Tucked into a ramshackle building away from the main campus, the art department existed on a different plane from the rest of the University of Georgia. While most of the school was defined by the usual big southern university institutions, the football team, the fraternities and sororities, and the teaching of solid mainstream values, the art department tilted toward subversion. The shift in the art school's sensibility started in the 1960s, when longtime chairman Lamar Dodd, an accomplished naturalist painter who had joined the department in 1937, launched a staffing initiative. In pursuit of practicing artists with degrees from impressive schools, Dodd wound up hiring a legion of well-trained but bohemian artists. Jim Herbert, a painter and video artist, made experimental films that featured nude models, many of whom were his students, a move that would have been pilloried today. Judith McWillie's ideals were informed by vernacular art. Robert Croker took a radical approach to teaching drawing and painting, compelling students to finish a drawing in as little as five seconds. Or else he'd have them work on an elaborate piece for two hours, only to instruct them to toss it on the floor; then he'd put on some music and tell them to dance on the much labored-upon work until it was in tatters. "Some of the kids would be like, *What do you mean?!*, like really freaking out," says former student Mark Cline. "But he was teaching us to think differently, that the act of creating was more important than the work itself. They wanted to shock us out of normalcy."[1]

For a certain kind of southern kid, the ones who didn't like sports and had no interest in studying agriculture or law or business, finding the University of Georgia's art school was like discovering a utopia. Sam Seawright, a preacher's kid who grew up in northern Georgia, recalls visiting his older brother John on campus one weekend, going from a screening of Jim Herbert's art films to an outdoor lecture by Truman Capote and then to parties full of young people exactly like him: small-town kids just learning that they weren't the only weird people around, and that their dreams and ambitions weren't so outlandish after all. "If you were different in your tiny town in Georgia, you'd fantasize about going to school in Athens," Seawright says. "It was an oasis for misfits and artists. If you didn't toe the line in Elberton, Georgia, or wherever, Dalton or Bainbridge, you'd come to Athens and find like-minded people. There was support; people lifted each other up and made everybody feel important and worthwhile. And there were just beautiful souls here."[2]

Now Michael dressed like a college student. Tennis shoes, shredded jeans, a T-shirt beneath a hooded sweatshirt. In classes he seemed to shrink into his hoodie, a silent presence shrouded in chestnut curls and layers of cotton. Other students tried to connect with him and had better luck when they were away from the crowd. In the hallway, somewhere on campus, in a restaurant. He had a way of drawing attention, even when he didn't say a word. Armistead Wellford, a painting student who sat near Michael in a color theory class, noticed that his quiet classmate didn't transport his art supplies in a satchel or one of the multicompartment carriers the other students had. Michael toted a child's lunch box from the *Munsters* TV sitcom. "I was taken with him immediately," Wellford says. "I knew he was cool."[3] At one point Michael dyed his hair green and cut it into eccentric shapes, curls piled high one week, then razored off the next, the sides out of balance. It was impossible to ignore, and so was he.

Judith McWillie, who taught the color theory class where Wellford encountered him, came from Memphis, and when Michael's hair took on a tight-in-back, floppy-in-the-front shape that reminded her of Jerry Lee Lewis, she took note. After he found Athens's vintage stores, Michael's look evolved in other ways. He started coming to class in fuchsia velvet pants and mismatched patterned shirts, and the loudness of his wardrobe and its contrast with his quiet demeanor gave him a kind of quirky gravitas among his fellow students. When McWillie told her students to make hyperrealistic paintings of something that's impossible to paint, she noticed that Michael's initial frustration with the assignment led him to create an image that bridged realism and abstraction in a strikingly unique way. "He got the gist and applied it in a different way."[4]

Painting professor Scott Belville saw the same thing in his entry-level class and was so struck by how Michael combined elements of a landscape and a still life on one canvas, he kept it to show other students who could benefit from seeing something so unusual. Later in the term Belville pulled Michael aside to ask about his plans for his future. Michael told him he wanted to major in photo design, and the professor, a talented painter in his own right, urged him to think about focusing his energies in another direction. "I told him, 'You may want to think about painting. I think you've got something here.'"[5]

Beneath the roof of the art department's little building, boundaries and limitations faded. The list of guest lecturers and resident artists included the likes of Elaine de Kooning, Alice Neel, and Philip Guston. "You could walk down the hall and take a class with Willem de Kooning's wife," Cline recalls. "And Alice Neel. I mean, fuck! Philip Guston walked in one day, a year before he died, and there he'd be, teaching painting and blowing people's minds. Taking us out of ourselves. So when it comes to the overriding aesthetic, that's what was really important: get out of yourself, get away from these structures of how it was supposed to be."[6]

Andy Nasisse, a ceramics professor who specialized in vernacular folk art, brought in Howard Finster, the folk artist, musician, and preacher, who made rustic, almost childlike paintings and sculptures. Finster was a real southern eccentric, a charismatic visionary whose work featured religious symbols, saints, space aliens, and Elvis Presley. Finster's spirit of inclusivity—from the subjects he chose to incorporate into his paintings to his openhearted approach to the students—reflected the spirit the department's teachers tried to impart to their students. "You saw people like him, you knew you could just do it," says Curtis Crowe, who studied painting. "You don't need credentials or training, just enthusiasm and getting up and doing it. We were like, *We can do it too! Anyone can!*"[7] Sitting in a chair not far from Crowe, Michael came to Finster's presentation with an air of skepticism, leaning back in his chair, arms crossed and brow knit together. But after an hour of the artist's stories, songs, and tales of the visions that had led him to take up art as an expression of the Holy Spirit, the young student was leaning forward, eyes alight. "He was knocked out and went up to visit Finster" in his Paradise

Garden home/studio/exhibition grounds, professor Art Rosenbaum recalled to me in 2021.[8]

Finster wrote songs to accompany his art, and strummed a banjo as he told stories about his life and art. It all came bathed in the same light that flooded his dreams and visions. Finster was extraordinary, but he wasn't alone: the weave of art and music was everywhere. Rosenbaum was as celebrated for his folk music archivalism as he was for his painting, and he used musicians as models, having his students paint them while they played. Robert Croker blasted the Ramones and the Velvet Underground in class while his students painted and had them bring their drawing pads to a nightclub to make sketches while bands performed and people danced. Students who could play brought their instruments to school, found collaborators, moved into empty rooms and staircases to see what kind of sound they could make. To Judith McWillie, it all went together. "You had to play music in order to be heard. Art takes a long time, and it's silent and needs a place to hang. That segued into performance art, where it all merged. And the vernacular vision came out because, *Fuck that, I want to* explode. *I* need *to do this!*"[9]

McWillie also recognized the connection between vernacular art, which emphasized feeling and expression over craft, and the visceral punch of punk rock. The students liked to listen to music and chat while they were painting in class, and when McWillie drifted past to look in on their work, she'd drift into their conversations. When an Eric Clapton song came on one day, she edged into a conversation Michael was having with another student. While Clapton blazed away on the radio, he posed the question to her: Was virtuosity really the mark of a great rock guitarist? McWillie shrugged. "I said, 'If you can't play it on a $50 guitar from Sears, it ain't rock 'n' roll.'"[10]

Something about art schools makes kids want to rock. For just as the art college at Leeds Polytechnic was serving as a spawning ground for British post-punk bands, the University of Georgia's art school would soon become a hub in America's independent music scene.

By the time Melanie Herrold came for a visit, in the midst of a road trip to see family in Alabama, Michael greeted his old friend happily and showed her everything he had found in his new home: the art department building, the cafés and bars where the art students hung out, and a multilevel record store Michael was so excited to show Melanie that he missed a step near the front and took a tumble, landing with a thud near the counter. The guy sitting there, tall and dark haired, cradling an unplugged Fender Telecaster guitar, looked up and smiled. *You okay?* Michael hopped up, smiled, grabbed Melanie's arm, and whispered into her ear. *That's Richard, he's kind of an expert.* His name wasn't Richard, but Michael would figure that out soon enough.

5

Dance This Mess Around

few years before the members of R.E.M. came to town, another Athens band got its start at a party. It was Valentine's Day 1977, at a rental house on Milledge Avenue, across the street from the Taco Stand, maybe a mile from the edge of campus. The tenants were art students, and the crowd that showed up, predominantly university types, bohemians, a few hip townies and curious neighbors, dressed for the moment. Some women in sky-high wigs, others in spangles, still others in denim coveralls. There were men in dresses, their faces bedecked with mascara and rouge, and women with mustaches painted over their upper lips. It was chilly outside, and the air inside the house was thick: with smoke, alcohol, chatter. And also, though you wouldn't have guessed it at the time, the first stirrings of the 1980s.

You could argue that February 1977 was as '70s as it ever got. Former Georgia governor Jimmy Carter smiling and quoting Dylan in the White House; the radio equal parts easy listening (Mary Mac-Gregor's "Torn Between Two Lovers"), freon-cooled L.A. rock (the Eagles' "New Kid in Town"), and sleek dance music (the Jacksons' "Enjoy Yourself"); the evening TV a shiny mix of featherweight nostalgia (*Happy Days, Laverne and Shirley*), fresh-scrubbed sexbots (*Three's Company, Charlie's Angels*), and techno-futuristic action (*The Six Million Dollar Man, The Bionic Woman*). The culture just like the hair: fluffy, shiny, lighter than air.

But some people were starting to have other ideas, including five musicians in Athens who had just decided to call themselves the B-52's. As they gathered around their instruments, which included a tape player, a thrift store electric guitar, bongos, but no bass, it was clear that this was a different kind of group. And it wasn't just the odd instruments. The two women, Kate Pierson and Cindy Wilson, wore enormous white bouffant wigs that made them look like poodles in sunglasses. Keith Strickland, who played the bongos, also wore a wig, an eye-popping shade of purple that matched his dress. The guitarist, Cindy's brother Ricky, looked nearly clean-cut. But it was Fred Schneider, standing at the other microphone in a sleek white jacket over a T-shirt, who started the show, making Morse code–like beeps with a child's walkie-talkie to launch "Planet Claire." This was the first of the six songs they had written, all featuring lean guitar riffs, cheesy two-finger organ, Schneider's unhinged auctioneer vocals, and otherworldly peals from the women, who harmonized, chanted, and made unsettling ululations that landed somewhere between Yoko Ono and angry cats. The tunes were simple but danceable, and the strangeness of it all—*Boys in bikinis!* Schneider brayed in "Rock Lobster," *girls in surfboards / Everybody's rockin'!*—electrified the crowd, making them dance so hard the floor started to bounce like a trampoline.

It came together in the most unlikely way. The bizarro wigs, the gender-bender clothes, the infectiously silly songs, and the musical limitations they leapfrogged in the most inventive ways. They had never played in public before, but somehow the B-52's—a name they took from the '50s beehive hairdos they sported—arrived fully formed. They played another party or two around Athens in the next few months, road-tripped up to New York City at the end of 1977 to check out the clubs, and scored a slot opening a Monday night show at the Max's Kansas City nightclub. They did well enough, got invited back, and scraped together a couple of other gigs opening shows at CBGB. This band of quirky, largely gay young southerners, with their wigs, walkie-talkies, dime-store instruments, and silly songs about lobsters, killer bees, and girls from outer space, hit the city like a warm southern breeze. Lou Reed came to one show. Members of Patti Smith's band came too, and soon the critics followed—*The New York Times'* John Rockwell, *The Village Voice*'s Robert Christgau—and their write-ups glowed. By mid-1978 the freaky Georgians were back in New York as headliners, playing multiple nights at Max's and CBGB, along with stand-alone shows at the Mudd Club and Hurrah. Danny Beard, who owned record stores in Atlanta and Athens, started his own record company, DB Records, to release a single of "Rock Lobster," backed by another original, "52 Girls." The record quickly sold out in New York (Beard pressed only a few thousand) and triggered a small bidding war between major labels. By the spring of 1979 they'd agreed to a deal with the Burbank-based Warner Bros. Records, which released their album that fall. A fizzy tonic amid the ponderous company of Pink Floyd's *The Wall,* the Eagles' *The Long Run,* and Led Zeppelin's *In Through the Out Door,* the self-titled *The B-52's* sold more than a million copies, launching the band and their wildly inventive and uniquely queer perspective into the upper reaches of the pop music stratosphere.

Could it really be that easy? Apparently so. It had taken less than three years for the B-52's to go from musical neophytes to critically beloved, platinum-selling pop stars. All it had taken was an original idea—combine high camp with the rudimentary riffs of punk rock, make it funny and danceable—and the guts to step up onstage and start playing. And now they weren't just successful; they were acclaimed as innovators. *Artists.*

This had not gone unnoticed at the University of Georgia art school.

Randy Bewley and Michael Lachowski first got the idea just as the B-52's were shuttling between Athens and New York, not just drawing crowds to the clubs but winning raves in the rock media. Both were art students and music fans, both drawn to the artier punk and new wave bands—Cabaret Voltaire, Suicide, the Ramones. The minimalism of punk, and the success of the B-52's, whom they'd both seen perform at parties in town, was instructive, and inspiring. Neither owned nor played an instrument. In the spirit of the moment, it didn't seem to matter. Bewley decided to take on the guitar. Lachowski, noting that the bass had two fewer strings, opted for what struck him as the easier instrument. Bewley purchased both, along with amplifiers, at a nearby pawnshop and the pair set to work. It helped to view the instruments as raw tools, Lachowski explains. "You could make a sound on them with or without any training, so that's how we approached it."[1] Another art student, Curtis Crowe, lived upstairs from Bewley's apartment and, after listening to the duo, offered to pitch in on drums. They were happy to have Crowe join, and as Bewley and Lachowski improved their songs, a sound began to take shape. In search of a singer, they went to Vanessa Briscoe, another art school classmate. She had no experience, but of course that was exactly what they were after.

The foursome wasn't supposed to be a band per se. They weren't really musicians, even if they'd learned their instruments well enough. The entire point of the enterprise was to experience what it felt like to go onstage, become good enough to land a club show in New York, and get written up in *New York Rocker.* Once they'd achieved that, they'd be done. They weren't a rock band as much as an art installation *about* a rock band.

They called themselves Pylon, after the orange traffic cones, and in the winter of 1979 they played their first show in a space above Chapter 3 Records. Next they played a show in the studio Crowe and his friend Bill Tabor had rented above a sandwich shop and named after its sole source of light: a forty-watt bulb hanging down from the ceiling. They got the same reaction both nights. "People mostly just stood there looking at us," Briscoe (now Briscoe Hay) recalls.[2] Then some friends asked them to play a party in a house just outside town.

The members of the B-52's were hanging out there, and when Pylon started playing, the other Athens band stormed the dance floor. After the music was finished, the Bs showered the new band with praise and told them they had to get themselves to New York—they knew people, they could help. True to their word, Fred Schneider and Kate Pierson handed Pylon's demo tape to the manager at Hurrah's nightclub. Soon Lachowski got a call from the club's booker: Did Pylon want to open a show for Gang of Four? Dates in Boston and Philadelphia materialized, thanks to their booking in New York. The Philadelphia show was rough going. The audience didn't connect with the repetitious, circular groove of their songs. But when they got to New York, and the packed-in house awaiting Gang of Four at Hurrah, Pylon connected. "They had a very distinctive sound," says the writer and critic Anthony DeCurtis, who saw Pylon soon after that first New York show. "They were very consciously an art band. And Michael Lachowski would look at his watch onstage, to make you conscious that he wasn't living to be onstage." That they came from Athens mattered, too. "New Yorkers, in their ridiculous way, had adopted the B-52's, and everyone fell in love with Athens," DeCurtis says. "So the media came to them easily."[3]

Indeed, the write-up of the Gang of Four show that appeared in Andy Warhol's *Interview* magazine a few weeks later played up Pylon and their place of origin as prime attractions. The B-52's, it read, were "a tough act to follow—but Pylon is also a credit to their community."[4]

And the community of Athens music was about to erupt.

6

Let's Make a Band

For Michael Stipe, the Wuxtry record store was a revelation. Outside of the art school it was his favorite place in Athens, like a dream he'd had back in Collinsville, made real just a few blocks from school. Music played constantly, most of it stuff he either knew or wanted to know about. The walls bristled with posters of the bands he'd been reading about in *The Village Voice* and *Creem*. And the clerk he usually found behind the counter, the guitar-strumming guy he'd told Melanie was named Richard but was actually named Peter, was like a rock magazine come to life. He seemed to know about every band that ever existed, especially the obscure ones. And if he didn't have their records on the shelves, he knew where to find them. Sometimes they'd already be in his own collection, and he was always happy to bring them in so Michael could borrow whatever he wanted to hear.

When he was in high school it had all seemed so distant. Michael could read about the new music in the *Voice*, he could gape at the pictures of the Ramones, the Damned, and Iggy Pop in *Creem*, but the records themselves . . . the essential sound . . . had largely been unavailable to him. That started to change in the spring of his senior year, when he fell in with the *Rocky Horror* crowd, met Joe Haynes and the other Bad Habits, and moved to the Laughing Heels' band house in Edwardsville. But the music, and the sort of people who got it, who understood what made that edgy, abrasive sound so exciting, and why it was so important for music to transgress mainstream society's demands, was only now coming into focus. In Athens, Georgia, of all places.

Echoes of the Bad Habits, and especially that electrifying night in front of the Mississippi Nights crowd, stayed in Michael's mind. He kept his eye on the classified ads and the bulletin boards around campus, and when he saw a listing from a cover band looking for a singer, he auditioned and won the job. Musically, it was a step backward: the band, known as Gangster, played popular songs by exactly the sort of mainstream rock bands he and Joe Haynes had vowed to avoid when they were establishing the Bad Habits just a few months earlier. But singing mediocre rock 'n' roll songs with an uninspired cover band was a lot better than not singing at all, so Michael joined in happily, buying himself a vintage suit to fit in with the group's 1930s gangster stage look. To complete the stage image, and protect his own, he took a stage name—Michael Valentine, as in the notorious gangland Valentine's Day Massacre—and when the band performed, he did most of his singing with the brim of his fedora pulled low over his eyes.

A reliable cover band now equipped with a strong singer, Gangster did well in the cover-hungry bars around Athens. For Michael the group's success was a mixed blessing. He enjoyed the singing, and he even made a little money for his trouble, but his art classes were pulling him in another direction. The tension was immediately apparent to Terry Allen when he happened upon Gangster at the Last Resort bar, on West Clayton Street in downtown Athens. Allen, a young photographer with an ear for pop music, came in for a drink near closing time one night and was captivated by what he heard from the bandstand. Most of the cover bands he'd seen tilted heavily toward southern rock—Lynyrd Skynyrd, the Allman Brothers Band, the hit redneck sound. But Gangster played older, cooler stuff. Songs by the Animals, the Doors . . . not the usual playlist for a bar band in Georgia in 1979. Allen carried his beer closer and focused on the singer, whose sonorous, textured voice kept demanding his attention, no matter how intently he tried to disappear, facing the drums and keeping the brim of his hat so low it was nearly impossible to see his face. When they finished, Allen went up to greet him. "I told him I liked it and he said, 'Oh my God, that was so embarrassing. I hate this band.'" Allen knew the scene, there were certainly other bands he could look into. Michael nodded. "That's what I gotta do," he said. "Do you know anyone who plays guitar?"[1]

Actually, Michael had already met one.

Peter Buck had settled in Athens just a few months before Michael, moving from Atlanta to take a job at the smaller of Wuxtry's two Athens outlets, a combination records-and-comics shop near campus on Baxter Street. Peter was tall and broad-shouldered, with shiny brown hair that fell across his forehead and over his ears. He wore jeans and button-up shirts and scuffed sneakers, as appropriate for record store work as for slouching in the back of a high school class-room. He could seem taciturn when you first met him, peering down silently from behind those dark bangs. But his eyes were sharp, and as Michael discovered, once Peter spied a compatriot, he could talk at length. Michael first drew his attention when he started asking for the sort of punk and new wave records that Peter liked. Television, the New York Dolls, the Heartbreakers. Some of the really obscure stuff, too: Suicide, Richard Hell and the Voidoids. When Michael started buying records Peter had stocked for his own enjoyment, the clerk started a conversation. They mostly stuck to bands and records at first, but in those days being drawn to those records signified a lot of things that had nothing to do with music.

Once they got to talking, they realized how much they had in common. Peter had also come from the suburbs and been introduced to New York punk rock by *The Village Voice*—he was a few years older than Michael but had also subscribed when he was a high schooler. He'd been entranced by the same articles about Patti Smith in 1975, bought *Horses* soon after its release, and been transported by how the artist's poetry played against the visceral wallop of the music. That juxtaposition, the outer limits of both literature and music, was where Peter's consciousness lived. He read constantly, and widely, and almost always kept a book within reach in case he got bored. When he wasn't reading, or even when he was, he'd play his guitar, another near-constant presence in his life. Often when Michael came into Wuxtry he'd find Peter behind the counter, leaning back on the stool idly strumming along to whatever was playing on the shop speakers, or working out something else entirely. His prized possession at the time was his Fender Telecaster, an electric he played without an amplifier when he was at work. This drew Michael's attention.

He had questions. *You're probably in a band, right?* Peter shrugged. Nope, no band. He'd thought about joining a band, but as much as he liked playing on his own, it seemed like a bad idea. *Guys in bands are usually assholes,* he said. *And I don't want to become an asshole.* This made Michael laugh. *He* was in a band . . . not a very good band, but that wasn't because the other guys were assholes. They just wanted to play dumb songs for dumb people. And even that could be fun, he had to admit, because playing music is fun, even when the songs kinda suck. Peter shrugged. Well, maybe. They could try writing some songs first. They could hang out, listen to some records, have a few beers, see where it took them. That sounded like fun to both of them. And something began.

They started getting together. Peter would play his acoustic guitar, come up with a song Michael also knew, and they'd give it a go. Peter was an interesting player. He didn't whip off lead parts between the verses, or attempt any solos, even for fun. He stuck to the chords, keeping the rhythm going, giving Michael something to sing to. They liked playing together and did it regularly, sometimes spinning off into ideas for songs of their own. Peter playing some changes, Michael humming a scrap of melody, maybe scatting some words over the top. When they ran out of gas they talked about the kind of songs they wanted to write. First they laid out everything they hated about most rock 'n' roll songs. The clichéd lyrics, the predictable chord patterns. Why did everything have to sound alike? They thought it would be fun to subvert all the expectations, taking standard lyrical tropes and twisting the familiar words in new and unlikely ways until they said something completely different and totally unexpected.

If Peter had resisted the impulse to join a band, playing with Michael had changed his mind. More than a few of his regular customers at Wuxtry were students who either were in bands or said they wanted to be in one, and he began feeling out some of them, figuring out what music they liked, what they'd be like to play with. Paul Butchart played drums and was talking about getting a band going, and Peter floated it by him. "He said he had a friend who could really sing," Butchart recalls. "They had a few songs they'd written, and we should get together and see what we can do."[2] Butchart was certainly game, and then Peter brought it up to Butchart's friend Kit Swartz, who was just as eager to start a band. Swartz hadn't started playing any instruments yet, but in the wake of the B-52's and Pylon, that hardly seemed to matter. Peter had a perfect place for them to play: he'd just moved into a disused church someone had converted into apartments, and most of the sanctuary was empty, a perfect place to rehearse. So it was agreed. They just needed to find a time they could all meet. Somehow they never could. But a lot of young people around Athens were up for joining bands then, and soon Peter met another drummer, a fun-focused pre-law student at the university who had a friend he said was a killer bass player. They had gone to high school in Macon and played in a couple of bands there. It had been a while since they'd played, but they'd come to Athens together and brought their instruments, just in case.

7

Don't Rock 'n' Roll, No!

They met at a house party, in one of the crumbling old bunga-
lows students rented around the kudzu-hung corner of Barber
Street and Nantahala Avenue, maybe a mile away from campus.
There were beers, music playing, the usual chatter. Bill Berry would
have recognized Peter Buck from behind the counter at Wuxtry,
assuming he'd been there. Which seems like a safe assumption, given
his friends and his interests, and his lack of interest in his classes. Bill
was dark-haired, heavy-browed, and mordantly funny. They talked
about bands, of course, and if Peter's knowledge of the British punk
scene was hard to beat, Bill knew who managed them, when and
where they had toured in America, and in some cases how well they
had drawn. He'd spent a few months working in a concert booking
agency in Macon, and the one guy he'd gotten to know there had
come from England with a lot of connections. He'd turned Bill on
to all these bands, including the one his brother was in. *You know the
Police? Sure, of course.* "*Roxanne.*" Everybody knew the Police. Well,
their drummer was this guy's brother.

Bill played drums, too. He'd been in a couple of bands in high
school. Nothing that great, but they had fun for a while—played a
bunch of parties, even made a little money here and there. Then
the singer had gone to college, the next version of the band hadn't
worked out, and Bill put his drums away. His best friend had played
bass in the group and was just as dispirited. Still, neither of them had

been ready to go to college just yet, so they got an apartment together in Macon and tried to find jobs. Bill was the one who scored, finding the booking agency job. It seemed like a good way to stay close to music, even if he wasn't playing.

It was fun for a year or so but running errands and driving rock stars around Macon got old after a while, and he and his buddy, who got stuck working at Sears, decided to go to college. The University of Georgia seemed as good a place as any, and Bill thought he might try to become a lawyer and get into the music business that way. He hadn't really focused on his studies just yet. The temptations of dormitory life and the opportunity to have fun around the clock had proven a bit of a distraction, ha-ha, but he did get a spot on the school's concert committee and he was learning some useful stuff there.

Did he ever think about joining another band? Bill shrugged, that dry chuckle. Well. Actually, he'd brought his drums to school, just in case someone wanted to jam or whatever, and wound up playing with this weird outfit . . . you've heard of the Wuoggerz? That was a total goof, a bunch of DJs from the campus radio station WUOG-FM had gotten drunk and decided to form a band. They pronounced it *Wugg-ers*, and one or two of them could actually play. They had a decent guitar player who could sing, a bassist and a keyboard player, a few people who played percussion, a guy who strummed a big plastic fish—sometimes he played percussion on a bong—and a bunch of girls who sang backup. Bill didn't work at the station, but he had a few friends who did, and they knew he played the drums, so when they asked him to sit in on a bunch of cover songs and one or two of their originals, he figured it would be fun. They didn't play much, they barely ever rehearsed, and the truly ridiculous thing was that they'd actually played some real shows—opening for the Brains on campus and then for the Police at the Georgia Theatre downtown.

That last one was particularly absurd, playing on a real stage with a real band from England. But the Wuoggerz were just silly enough, and had enough friends in the audience, to go over with the Athens crowd. He didn't mention this part, but they'd done so well opening for the Police that drummer Stewart Copeland, whose brother Ian had worked with Bill at the booking agency in Macon, asked them to come with the Police to play the rest of the shows on their swing through the Southeast, starting just a few days from then. Unfortunately, the timing couldn't have been worse: the show in Athens had been on Tuesday, May 1; finals week started three days later, the same day the Police wanted the Wuoggerz to open the show at the Fat Cats club, in Hollywood, Florida. Johnny Pride, the Wuoggerz's guitarist, shrugged it off like this: "We couldn't be rock stars because we had to take algebra tests." Oh, well. Easy come, easy go.[1]

Still, being in a band again, even a silly one, had reminded Bill Berry of how much fun it was to play rock 'n' roll. It even made him think about starting a real band. Maybe they'd just play parties, but wouldn't that be fun? He'd thought about a name. The Corvettes, maybe the Corvairs. One of those dangerous sports cars from the '60s. Man, that could be fun. Peter was nodding. *Well, I know this guy who sings. He's good and we've been writing some songs . . . Maybe we should get together.* Bill nodded. He had that friend who played the bass; he'd definitely be up for something, too.

They all had a friend in common. Kathleen O'Brien had lived in Reed Hall, the big, loud dormitory where Bill spent his freshman year drinking and partying and staying up far too late to wake up in time for his classes the next morning. O'Brien moved off campus in the fall of 1979, winding up in one of these crackpot apartments built into St. Mary's, the small, crumbling old Episcopal church at the bottom of Oconee Street, near the Oconee River.

O'Brien had heard about the church through Dan Wall, the co-owner of the Wuxtry Records stores, who had been living there but was recruiting new tenants so he could move out. Ken Buck, the older brother of his employee Peter Buck, came in first. Peter joined his brother a month or two later, and O'Brien moved in somewhere around then, too. She heard Peter practicing his guitar in his room and remembered that Bill played the drums. Those two would get along, she figured, and having Bill around the church wouldn't be bad, either. He was a sweet guy with a cockeyed sense of fun, and that epic unibrow that somehow made him strikingly handsome. She had sensed some sparkles between them in the midst of the Reed

Hall chaos and, as she put it, "I basically did whatever I could to throw us in the same situation."[2] So Kathleen pulled Peter and Bill together at the party, and she was there when Peter introduced his singer friend Michael Stipe to Bill, and also at Tyrone's O.C. nightclub a few nights later when Bill waved over his bass-playing friend from Macon. Michael saw him coming and had an immediate, overwhelming reaction: "I said, '*No fucking way*,'" he recalled to journalist Rodger Lyle Brown.[3]

Mike Mills had the slim build and sweet face of a teenager and, when Bill called him over to greet his new friends, the watery smile and cloddish feet of a stumbling drunk. Michael looked him over silently, icily. The bell-bottom pants. The short, dorky hair. The nimrod glasses. He slurred a hello, belched alcohol, laughed at a joke nobody else heard, and nearly toppled over with the effort. Bill smiled, shook his head, and waved him off. He'd met Mills in high school and hated him at first too; he'd figured him for a pencil-neck show-off back then. An A student, a do-gooder, a dork. But Mike could really play the bass. Then they'd wound up at the same jam session, and that changed everything. Also he turned out to be a cool guy. So Bill felt confident reassuring Michael and Peter about his extremely drunk friend. *He'll sober up, then you'll like him.* Peter nodded, Michael sighed and shrugged. *Sure, fine. Let's get together and see what happens.*

Michael was ready for something to happen. It was early 1980 and he'd been in Athens for more than a year. He'd been meeting people, impressing them with his creativity, his quirkiness, the way his artistry seemed to move in every direction at once. He drew, he painted, he made photographs, he found images he liked, cut them out, and made collages he hand-colored and compiled into four-by-four-inch pages, which he copied on a color Xerox machine and stapled into a 'zine he called *Momo* and handed to friends around campus. He struck his teachers as a talented artist, and they took him seriously, seeing a future waiting for him in photography, in design, in painting, in whatever their own discipline happened to be. Michael appreciated the encouragement but had another idea. Scott Belville, the painting professor who had urged Michael to pursue his talents in that direction, would see him step away from his canvas in class, go to his locker at the side of the room, take out a notebook, and start scribbling. He was not sketching or drawing something. "He'd be writing lyrics," Belville says.[4]

The professor knew Michael had to follow his muse wherever it pulled him. But he also felt obligated to caution him: music careers rarely last more than five years.[5] And he had the talent to paint for the rest of his life. Michael took it on, and his dedication to his classes never seemed to waver. But the praise he was earning, and the confidence it gave him, only fired his musical ambitions. "He'd say, 'I want to be a singer, a great rock singer,'" recalls Mark Cline, another art student who also felt the allure of making music. "He was single-mindedly focused on that."[6]

Michael was still a member of the band Gangster, but he couldn't reconcile his artistic ambitions with the evenings he spent singing lumpen rock 'n' roll with them. At first it had seemed satisfying to project himself into Michael Valentine, the rock-singing gangster, shielding his own identity in an alter ego who wasn't really Michael Stipe. Not entirely, anyway. But this Michael Valentine character wasn't like one of David Bowie's alter egos; he wasn't alien like Ziggy Stardust or tragically stylish like the Thin White Duke. And he certainly didn't push the boundaries of gender or sexuality like the galaxy of superstars surrounding Andy Warhol. If music was going to be his art, then everything about his music had to be artful. And nobody else in Gangster was interested in that. But Peter Buck was. And if these other guys could play too, that began to feel like a band he could believe in. He resigned his position with Gangster and never spoke of them again.

St. Mary's Church became the center of band operations. Michael moved into Peter's room for a bit. Then, floated by the money he'd earned working as a busboy at the Steak and Ale restaurant downtown, he took over one of the other church apartments that winter. It was a strange but convivial place to live. St. Mary's Episcopal Church had been built in the early 1870s by the owner of a nearby textile factory for the laborers to worship in, but it lost its flock when the business closed around the end of the century. Soon after that it had been deconsecrated and repurposed. The Red Cross took over the building in 1946, then handed it off to the city, which used it as a historical museum until the mid-1960s, when bits of the walls and ceiling started falling off. The former church sat empty until 1968, when a young real estate investor named Marion Cartwright bought the place with an eye toward transforming it into residential space for students. Working quickly and on the cheap, he hired some builders to construct a kind of modular, five-bedroom apartment within the church structure, filling in the entryway and the front of the sanctuary. A quartet of law students became the first tenants of the mahogany-veneered, shag-carpeted rooms in 1968, and generations of post- and undergraduates followed over the next eleven years. By the time Peter joined Dan Wall and his brother in the church, he found, in his words, "a rotten, dumpy little shithole"[7] that only impoverished students could tolerate entering, let alone living in.

Still, the church came with a great asset for residents who wanted to play music. The crawl space in the back of Kathleen O'Brien's closet led to what remained of the sanctuary: a vaulted stone-and-wood chamber whose ceiling rose to the bottom of the steeple. The pews had vanished, but the altar remained, making a perfect stage upon which the musicians could set up. You just wanted to make sure you didn't step off the far side, where rain dripping from a gash on one side of the steeple had eaten away the floor. It was murky in there, the air thick with the smell of rotten wood and crumbled stone. When Berry and Mills came over with their gear, they set up on the altar, running extension cords from the apartments to power the gear and the battered lamps and clip lights they used to throw some shadowy light around the room.

They started like all bands do, figuring out which songs they all knew, settling on a key, and then diving in. From the go, the parts seemed to click together. Easy songs at first, three or four chords, basic structure. The Velvet Underground's "There She Goes Again," the Monkees' "(I'm Not Your) Steppin' Stone." Peter, the least experienced of the musicians, stuck to simple parts, alternating staccato stabs with chords he'd let ring. Mike helped establish the basic groove with his bass, and let his fingers leap into the upper frets for runs that played against the song's central melody. Bill kept the rhythm taut, with an occasional snare shot to emphasize an upbeat. Michael's vocals played out across the top, and as the smiles between Bill and Mike seemed to indicate, Peter's assertion that the guy could really sing had been correct. He had range and power, and a kind of vocal texture that could go from velvety to gravelly in the space of a single line. He also had a catalog of hiccups, yelps, and asides that were part Elvis Presley, part Buddy Holly, and, the way he did them, all art-rock weirdness. One song after another. Johnny Rivers's "Secret Agent Man" (recently revived by a Devo cover), the Sex Pistols' "Anarchy in the UK." Their faces glowed against the dim yellow light, a little sweat mixed with a growing excitement. Peter and Michael introduced one or two of their originals. The others listened for a moment, found their way in, and then, immediately, the songs had more depth, more drive. They felt real.

Now they got together to play regularly. Two or three times a week, at least, working through those first songs, adding others as they came up. Mike worked out harmonies, some with Bill pitching in in a lower voice, sometimes just the bassist's smooth tenor finding a countermelody to weave in with Michael's lead. *How about a Buddy Holly song? Do you guys like Television?* The guys started piecing together new originals, starting with someone's riff, hooking it to another guy's chord progression, which might pivot into another set of changes, while Michael sang along, trying out melodies and words, phrases that seemed to go together. *I've been walking alone now for a long, long time / Don't wanna hang out with the friends who just aren't mine* . . . Spiky thoughts matched with hurtling rhythms and herky-jerky chords. Youth, confusion, frustration, crash bang boom. *I can't see, I'm so young!* Then back to the Monkees or the Velvet Underground or—*turn it up!*—the Sex Pistols. The sound came right through the two-by-four beams, insulation, and drywall that separated the sanctuary from the apartments, so O'Brien and the others could hear every thud and note. When the band really got going, the other housemates and their friends would duck in through the crawl space, handing through their beers and bongs, and start dancing. A spontaneous party with a live band! Rehearsals with a cheering section!

O'Brien began to think about having a real party. Her birthday was coming on April 5, and since that would be a Saturday and they had access to such an incredible party space, she figured she'd do it up big. Throw herself a big party with a couple of kegs, all of her friends, maybe a couple of bands. She and Bill had paired off by then—having him around the church so regularly had worked out just like she hoped it would—so it made sense for the new band to debut on her big night. They were reluctant at first. *C'mon, man, no way. We've only been doing this for a few weeks, we're not even close to ready* . . . blah-blah-blah. But O'Brien was charming, supportive, and also willful. When she wanted something, it was nearly impossible to say no. She kept asking. They kept saying no, at first. Then maybe. *Okay, we'll think about it.*

Meanwhile, Kit Swartz and Paul Butchart had figured out their band, with Butchart on the drums, Swartz picking up the guitar, and Jimmy Ellison, the soon-to-be-ex-husband of Pylon singer Valerie Briscoe, taking up the bass in a three-man combo they called the Side Effects. That they had declared themselves a band and come up with a name before two-thirds of the members had become conversant with their instruments was not a problem. It was, in many ways, the point. Because formal knowledge meant following rules, and rules were limiting. Rules stanched creativity. Rules made you more like everyone else. And the whole point of art, at least the way it was taught, practiced, and admired in Athens, was to be only like yourself. To describe the world the way you saw it, felt it, and tasted it. Like the B-52's could only be the B-52's. Like Pylon could only play Pylon songs—except for the *Batman* theme, which they played exactly like Pylon would play it, mostly because they weren't capable of playing it any other way. But they'd been creative enough to transform their limitations into something so unique that they'd impressed the critics in New York City, the very epicenter of American art and music, as the harbingers of something dynamic and new.

The combined influence of the Bs and Pylon spurred a flood of new art-forward bands in Athens. A pair of philosophy students named Vic Varney and David Gamble formed a duo they called the

Method Actors, with the former on guitar and vocals and the latter on the drums. Art students Mark Cline and Armistead Wellford teamed up with a Navy veteran/UGA student named Mike Richmond to form the instrumental group Love Tractor, with Cline and Richmond on guitar, Wellford on bass, and a rhythm machine keeping time until the always-eager-to-learn Kit Swartz volunteered to take up the drums. The Tone Tones had been at it for a year or two already, Turtle Bay and Men in Trees were just starting up. Suddenly you couldn't walk a block in Athens without hearing guitars tangling with the thrum of a bass and the thumping drums of another band trying to find a sound.

So many bands, so many friends. O'Brien was at the center of it all, so she had plenty of options for her party. The Side Effects had never performed in public before, but of course they'd be happy to play. Men in Trees might have been on the list, too. O'Brien went back to Bill, Peter, Michael, and Mike and laid it on a little thicker. She'd been listening to them, they were more than ready to play in public! And because they lived in the church and played there, they could go last, which would make them headliners and make the crowd that much more drunk by the time they got going. If they made any mistakes, nobody would notice. Finally her entreaties, and their growing eagerness to face a crowd, won them over. Yes, okay, they'd do it. They didn't have a band name yet, but they'd work on it.

They rehearsed regularly until the third week in March, when the foursome split in half for UGA's spring break. Mike and Bill stayed in Georgia while Michael and Peter climbed into a van with Butchart, Swartz, and a WUOG disc jockey named Kurt Wood for a road trip to New York City. Pylon was playing two shows at Hurrah that week, one night as the headliners and another opening for Lene Lovich, and that was enough of reason to make the trip, particularly for Peter and Michael, who had never seen the city before. They had no idea what else they'd do, or what punishments the big city might exact on a vanful of college kids meandering north in 1980 with next to no money in their pockets and no idea where to go or what to do when they got there. They had more faith than common sense, and a naive confidence that things would break their way. It could have led to disaster. Instead it was like Dorothy's visit to the Land of Oz: a dreamlike adventure filled with fortuitous meetings, unexpected invitations, and revelations that would resonate for decades.

The first night Michael, Peter, Butchart, and Wood pooled their money to get a room at the Iroquois hotel. It cost $50, which was far too much to afford for a second night, so they parked the van on a side street near Hurrah and used that as their home base. During the days they roamed the city, visiting museums, scouring record stores, riding the subways, getting lost, finding their way back. They couldn't shower, they barely had money to eat, it didn't matter. They saw Alan Vega, half of Suicide, play a solo show in a basement. They saw the German singer/performance artist Klaus Nomi perform. They bumped into Chosei Funahara, the bassist for the Plasmatics, and Michael was so starstruck, he told him they'd come all the way from Athens to see them, a story he made up on the spot. A woman named Karen Moline, a friend of Pylon, invited them to a party for the band, which also turned out to be a celebration of another friend's birthday. The starving young tourists feasted on jelly beans and cheesecake, and when Peter said hello to Lester Bangs, the famously gonzo critic glared unsteadily and called him a rotten cocksucker. It was the greatest vacation ever.

This was Pylon's third run through New York; they'd played Hurrah again in January, this time as headliners, to a smaller but more focused crowd of people who'd happened to see their set at the Gang of Four show the previous summer, or knew someone who had, or read about it in *Interview*. The January show sparked even more buzz from the likes of *The Village Voice*'s eminent critic Robert Christgau, and they left the city with a handful of bookings for March: two more shows at Hurrah, a night at the Mudd Club, sets at Tier 3 (TR3), in Tribeca, and at Maxwell's, just across the river in Hoboken, and as headliners at the epicenter of the punk/new wave scene, CBGB.

One new song, "Stop It," became a favorite at Hurrah, and maybe a statement of purpose, showcasing all of the band's spiky energy, its razored wit, its . . . can this even be possible . . . anti-music musicality. The drums thump, Curtis Crowe snug in the mechanized pocket, and Randy Bewley, his strings pegged to some self-invented tuning he came up with because he had no idea how to set them correctly, slides his fingers up and down the neck of his guitar, a harsh yet somehow tuneful melody Michael Lachowski mirrors on his bass while Vanessa Briscoe, standing upright and wide-eyed at her microphone, arms linked behind her back, sounds like she's conducting raw voltage.

Don't rock 'n' roll, no!

Don't rock 'n' roll, no, no, no, no, no!

This is the sound, the feeling, the world cracking open. Peter Buck, Michael Stipe, and their friends on the dance floor, moving with everyone else, the whole city, the real city, the only city.

Don't rock 'n' roll, no!

Don't rock 'n' roll, no, no, no, no, no!

It was electric, and electrifying. Everything Michael had read about in *The Village Voice*, his dream of New York City, made real.

I see the city rise up tall / The opportunities and possibilities!

This is how Michael would describe that trip to New York many years later, his eyes still alight with the memory of his younger self, discovering New York and his future in one hectic, unshowered, underfed, and magical week.

I have never felt so called!

8

A Party in the Church

The road to the party led away from campus, down Broad, over to Oconee Street, and then down. Down and down. Descending from town and heading toward the river, where the mills were, where the industrial buildings hunkered low in the early-spring night. Where the old red-brick church nestled beneath the bare branches of the white oaks. This was St. Mary's Episcopal. Or that's what they christened it when its heavy wooden doors swung open for the first time in 1871. Now the doors opened to a cheap, avocado-green kitchen, where cups were stacked on one counter and Kathleen O'Brien stood with a sheet cake, cutting slices onto paper plates. The living room was to the left, a nightmare in fake wood paneling and avocado shag carpet. A hallway led to Kathleen's room and to her closet, where you'd find your way to the other side.

A hole in the wall, maybe four feet by four feet, that started around your ankles. You had to hunker down, nearly crawl your way in, and once you were inside it was a whole other world. Dark wood, exposed brick, stone and shadows. The sharp waft of beer, cigarette smoke, the sweet funk of weed and rot. Music pumping. Extension cords snaking to the speakers, drums set up beneath a bedsheet, voices, laughter, college kids standing around with bellies full of beer, maybe some pills, definitely that frisson of being in the right place, with the right people, maybe even at the right time.

Ingrid Schorr was there, waiting her turn at the keg, everyone chattering and laughing in the murky light. Clip lights reached up through the smoke to the arching church ceiling. She'd heard about the party at the offices of the student newspaper, *The Red & Black*; people there had been talking about it. Schorr hadn't been on campus very long, and she was always up for a new band, a party, a new scene. And this ruined church was definitely a scene. The stone and wood and dirty, cobwebbed windows. The first person Schorr recognized, a girl she hadn't seen since high school in Atlanta, knew the singer in one of the groups. His name was Michael; they both worked in the Steak and Ale and he'd invited everyone there to come see his new band. The girl didn't know the band's name; Michael said they hadn't figured it out yet. This was their first show, she said. Michael said he was terrified, so he was guzzling as much beer as possible.

Peter Buck, Schorr recognized him from Wuxtry Records, was standing by the keg, a cup of beer in his hand. He was dressed much sharper than usual, in a striped shirt he buttoned to the neck, beneath a tight-cut blazer he wore new wave style, the sleeves pushed up his forearms. A stud glimmered in one of his ears and he gulped from his beer, craning his neck, a young man very much on edge. He drained his cup, stepped to the keg for a refill, took a big swallow, nodded at whoever he was talking to and strode toward the entryway, folding himself in half to squeeze back into O'Brien's closet and back into the apartments. On his way through he brushed up against Armistead Wellford, the painting student, who was just finding the party side. Nearly colliding with Buck, Wellford noticed that the stud in Peter's ear was shaped like an electric guitar. A Fender Telecaster. "I remember thinking, *Man, that guy's a* star!" he says. "He already had mystique. They *all* had mystique."[1]

More bodies through the hole, then more, and more. It got crowded and hot, and even smokier than before. Pylon drummer Curtis Crowe was there too, and so was his band's singer, Vanessa Briscoe, who knew O'Brien from the Wuoggerz and a hundred other parties. Art students, music people, more. Kit Swartz, Paul Butchart. Mark Cline came with Davy Stevenson, the two of them pinwheeling through the crowd thanks to the ministrations of Jeremy Ayers, Davy's boyfriend at the time, who pressed LSD onto their tongues just as they were setting out for the church.[2] Gay kids and art kids. Boys who wore skirts and girls who came in short hair and coveralls. The sort of kids a car of frat boys would greet, through the window of a Corvette speeding down Milledge Avenue, with a homophobic curse. All of them passing bottles, handing around joints, trading pills, pieces of birthday cake. You would think of *Alice in Wonderland* and the looking glass, the portal from one realm to another. Shedding the limitations of one, exulting in the possibilities and pondering the muddles of the next.

Kathleen O'Brien and her cake stood at the threshold. She was all too familiar with the muddles of life, and the darkness, but she also had a way of knowing things. That Bill Berry would be a good and important friend. That he should meet Peter Buck, that they would get along, and probably know other cool people, and if they decided to get together and play music it'd be worth hearing. She'd heard their first attempt to jam, and the rehearsals that had followed, then set up a party in large part to compel them to play in public. She put the word out across her sprawling network, procured the beer, recruited another new band, talked Bill's band out of their shyness, then emptied her closet to clear the way to the other side. She knew they could fill that dark place with life and light, and make the night, and her birthday, incandesce.

At 10:30 p.m. a ripple went through the throng. From the back you could see a few heads rise above the others. Guys turning on amplifiers, pulling the sheet off the drums, switching on microphones. Kit Swartz strapped on a cheap copy of a Fender Jaguar, fiddling with knobs while Paul Butchart plunked down behind the drums. Jimmy Ellison plucked at an orange violin-shaped bass, the notes reverberating as he turned it up. This was the evening's first band, this trio that called themselves the Side Effects. They had come together in the manner of Pylon, the members first deciding to form a band, then working out who was going to learn which instrument. Their first rehearsals were cacophonous affairs, the musicians trading off bass, guitar, and drumsticks to see who was best at what. Once Swartz picked up a few chords, they started coming up with songs—simple, angular progressions they played with a choppy, driving rhythm that got the lubricated church crowd bopping. O'Brien was in the middle of it all, dancing and laughing with everyone else, their faces glowing with the effort.

The throng danced through the Side Effects' set, sticking with them even when the groove fractured and Swartz, sinking into a sparkle-eyed LSD trance,[3] lost his grip on the neck of his guitar. They finished to a cheerful ovation, shrugged off their instruments, and loaded them into their cases, coiling cords, kicking aside their drained beer cups, clearing the stage for the next guys. Two of whom had done such a good job of warding off their nerves at the keg that they could barely stand up. As their starting time drew near, it got worse. Michael, who had downed his share of beer, felt the excitement sharpen his senses while Peter, lurking outside, careened into the shadows and threw up into a bush.[4] Bill and Mike might have been a little nervous, and had certainly enjoyed their own share of social lubricants. But the new band's rhythm section had also been playing together in public since they were fifteen years old. They'd performed at dozens of parties just like this one and had become accustomed to the weight of the eyeballs, everyone watching as they pull together into the moment when someone counts to four, the sticks spank the snare, the air fills with sound, and the anxiety combusts into energy.

And they were pretty sure they were good. Good enough, at least. Even from the start, when it was just them in the empty church, they could hear how it was all coming together. How Bill and Mike clicked in together like musical Legos, and how Peter's spare, rhythmic approach to the guitar left room for Mike to fill with countermelodies that played against Michael's vocal lines, his honeyed Elvis slides embellished with rockabilly hiccups and stutters. All the hand waving and head shaking that greeted Kathleen's first requests for them to play her party, the insisting that they just weren't ready, that they were months away from anything like a full public performance, was half-hearted at best. The truth was, all stage fright aside, they were raring to go.

———

Weeks before the party, chatting aimlessly in the midst of some classroom project in their color theory course, Armistead Wellford started quizzing Michael on his new band. In the midst of a downpour of art department bands, Wellford was looking to get in on the action himself. So what did it take? Who was in Michael's band, and what were they like? Michael flashed a crooked smile and nodded excitedly. He was happy to share! "And he said, 'There's Peter on guitar and he's really great, and Bill's on drums and he's really great, and Mike plays bass and he's really great, and I sing and *I'm* really great.'"[5] Michael was kidding, but also not, which is what made Wellford laugh so much then, and now. "It was just so funny. He didn't mean to be stuck-up. He was just telling the truth."[6] Wellford began to understand this for himself the night before the party, when he came by the church in time to see the two new bands work through their sets. The Side Effects were fun in that high-spirited, low-expertise way, but the Twisted Kites, the placeholder name the foursome came up with when they couldn't settle on an even halfway decent name, were on another level. The three Side Effects, along with Wellford, Mark Cline, and a couple of other friends, could only listen and gape at one another. "They were just clowning around, working their thing out, but it sounded so great," Wellford says.[7] Paul Butchart knew exactly what the difference was between his band and this other newly formed group. "They'd play cover songs and you could recognize what they were," he says. "They sounded like a real band."[8]

Finally it was time to play. Peter rinsed the taste of puke from his mouth with another swig of beer, Michael standing up on his own two feet, Bill and Mike only slightly distorted by their indulgences. Getting to the stage was a trick. The church, which had been cozy even before a third of the sanctuary was taken up by that crackpot apartment setup, was jammed with partiers. Curtis Crowe had gone outside at some point, and when he realized he'd never be able to squeeze back inside, he went around the outside until he found a window he could peer through. Vanessa Briscoe found a way to climb to the church's rafters and made herself a perch up there. When the four musicians stepped onto the stage, took up their instruments, and started tuning, Briscoe heard shrieks. "Girls actually screamed and ran to the front of the stage," she says. "I was like, *Oh, wow.*"[9]

Then they started playing, alternating the originals they'd been honing with their quirky array of cover songs. Which ran the gamut, from the Velvet Underground ("There She Goes Again") to the Monkees ("I'm Not Your Steppin' Stone") to Johnny Rivers ("Secret Agent Man") to the Sex Pistols ("God Save the Queen"). The original songs moved like panthers: sure-footed, muscular, agile on the corners. Mike and Bill made a solid, soul-tinged foundation, locked together but swinging, while Peter's studied guitar parts gave the bassist room to move, climbing, looping, and tumbling around the sure-handed guitarist's rhythmic chord swipes. Stipe's lyrics aimed for big adolescent feelings and blasted away with both barrels. *I just don't want you anymore*, he proclaimed to a dismissed lover at the end of "All the Right Friends." *You feel so old / I feel so new*, he wailed in "Mystery to Me." Even the most nuanced song, the gimlet view of Elvis Presley's death, rocketed to a head-spinning conclusion: *I can't see . . . I'm so goddamn young!*

Michael borrowed that last line from Patti Smith's "Privilege (Set Me Free)," but the implications, the heady blend of inexperience, wildness, and endless promise, were as true for his new band as it had been for his idol a few years earlier. They had just gotten started, right here and right now, and were already on their way.

PART II

"We're Still Laughing.
It's a Real Shock."

9

Picture James Brown Fronting the Dave Clark Five

Kathleen O'Brien buttonholed Mike Hobbs and let him have it. *You hear that? Pretty great, huh? You should book them.* The music was still going, the place was jumping, the dancing and shouting, the air steaming, full of smoke and sweat, the band still up there cooking away. *Imagine how they'll do in a real club. C'mon, Mike, give 'em a chance, Mike.* Hobbs held up his hands in surrender. He'd mixed the sound at Tyrone's long enough to know a solid band when he heard one. He wasn't a big music guy per se, mostly a jack-of-all-trades who figured out how to run a soundboard and could tell a punk/new wave band from a frat rock band, which was important, since the club had started filling midweek slots with edgier acts. Their audience tended to be skinny kids with eccentric clothes and weird hair. They didn't drink as much as the old-school rock fans, but none of the other clubs in Athens booked the bands they liked and they'd been doing okay with the new wavers on these weeknights. They had the Brains coming up from Atlanta in early May and could use an opener for them, so, sure, these guys could work. Hobbs, operating in good-sport mode, went up to where the band was standing after their set, gulping beers and wiping the sweat from their faces, and pitched it to them. Would they be up for an opening slot? It wouldn't pay much, but they didn't care—of course they'd do it! But what was their name again? Hobbs realized he hadn't caught it when they came out. They laughed and shook their heads. They'd have to get back to him.

The night ended in a blur: so much beer, so many pills, so many joints, so much music and motion. Word of the new bands crackled through their members' networks of friends and classmates and the other bands, people talking in various shades of excitement, good cheer, competition, and, for the people in the other bands, maybe a little foreboding. That last part wasn't about the Side Effects, though. Nobody had a cross word for the inventive way Paul, Jimmy, and Kit had spun their limited chops into fun, danceable songs. That was the sweet spot for these punky art bands, the confluence of impulse, amateurism, and pure expression. Like the B-52's and Pylon, they played whatever they felt, however they could. Those other guys, though . . . well. Huh.

It was the old songs that set them off. The Monkees and the Sex Pistols and even the Velvet Underground songs. Cool selections, sure, but hadn't they already been done? "For us snobbier aficionados the cover songs were a bad sign," says Pylon drummer Curtis Crowe. "Now you're a frat rock band, or a cover band. Not a *new* act."[1] Still, the fact that their original songs blended so well with the covers was . . . intriguing. "When they played their own songs, you didn't feel like they were shifting gears; it was all one continual show." And as Crowe admits, that's where the foreboding came from. "They were a real band with real songs with real chord progressions. At the end, everyone knew something had happened."[2]

The Tyrone's O.C. booking came even as the final notes of the set were still reverberating in the church eaves. A day or two later they got another show offer, this time from the proprietors of the Koffee Klub, a new, informal coffeehouse tucked into an empty storefront on West Clayton Street, not far from the north side of campus. Dennis Greenia and Rick Hawkins were socially and politically conscious guys who liked the idea of making a communal space where customers would help paint and decorate the walls, bring in entertainment, and help clean up at the end of the evening, too. "Remember that this is YOUR place and it will be whatever YOU make it," declared a poster on one of the not-quite-painted walls. Hawkins was best known around town as Rick the Printer, since he ran the print shop next door to St. Mary's Church, the go-to producer of handbills and posters for Athens's bands, arts groups, and other entertainment concerns. Word of the new band practicing at the church got to the printers and they extended an invitation to the musicians to play their second-ever show at their new coffeehouse on April 19. The foursome took the show eagerly, figuring it would give them a chance to run through their set in a low-profile but still public setting before their big shot at Tyrone's in early May. The Koffee Klub show also gave them a reason to come up with a suitable band name so Rick the Printer would have something to promote on the show poster.

Distilling the essence of a band, particularly one built from four distinct personalities, is always a challenge. What word or short phrase could summarize a punk-and-pop band from the South whose influences ranged from the Velvet Underground to the Sex Pistols to the *Monkees*? The first set of options tilted toward the outrageous. Negro Wives. Negro Eyes. Slut Bank. No, no, and no. Third Wives? No. Cans of Piss? Right, try to imagine explaining that one to your parents. Also: *gross.* Michael picked up a dictionary, flipped open a page, and saw: R.E.M. An abbreviation for *rapid eye movement,* the deep state of sleep in which dreaming occurs. Michael wasn't thinking about sleeping or dreaming when he saw it, he would later insist. He just liked the term. What he really liked the most, he'd say, was the dots: the periods indicating that the *R, E,* and *M* were short for something else. It could mean anything, he decided. Anything, everything, and nothing. That was his favorite kind of name. The others agreed and that was that. They'd be R.E.M.

Word about the new band had gotten around, and as the evening of April 19 slipped into the wee hours of the 20th, the tables in the Koffee Klub's front room filled, then overflowed into the larger back room, where the band had set up their instruments, first with knots of friends, then a small crowd, then a light mob, then a dense one. The club didn't have a license to serve beer, so folks brought their own. At 1 a.m., when the show was supposed to start, more than a hundred people filled the back room. When the band came out forty-five minutes later, the throng that greeted them was closer to 150, significantly larger than the throng at the church.

Once again they came out rocking, alternating cover songs with punchy originals that kept the room moving. Again, the danceability came courtesy of the rhythm section, Bill's propulsive drumming locked in with Mike's bass, which anchored the deep end while also leaping upward to embroider Peter's economical rhythm guitar. All of which served as a foundation for Michael's vocals, which scrambled Elvis's smoothness with Patti Smith's poetic urgency, while the backing harmonies by Bill and Mike added a delicious pop shimmer. Watching from the side of the room, Bertis Downs, a law school student nearing the end of his second year in UGA's program, had a hard time telling the originals from the cover songs, given the band's quirky tastes. The friend he'd come with, a third-year law student and music nut named Russell Carter, filled in some of the gaps— *That's "Shake Some Action" by the Flamin' Groovies, that's the Monkees, "Steppin' Stone," maybe this one is one of theirs? Never heard it before . . .* Years later Downs wouldn't be able to summon the specifics, but he'd never forget the electricity of the moment, of being in the room as the band played for nearly the first time, already channeling the sound that would come to mean so much to so many people, and send him down a road he could never have imagined traveling until he was there, moving so fast the rest of the world was reduced to a smear.

But first it was just this night, in this room, for forty-five minutes. The whirling, pounding drums and pulsing, melodic bass, the chiming guitar, and the singer whose sonorous voice anchored the music even as his performance, stock-still one minute, erupting in movement the next, animated the band's spirit. The room was alive with the music. Bodies moving, heads bobbing, hands in the air, feet and shoulders, a happy tangle of youth in all their sweaty exultation and . . . uh-oh.

Badges, caps, uniforms. Handcuffs, clubs, sidearms. Notepads. Cameras.

At the above date and time the above officers (Pritchett, Evans, Deramus) entered the incident location and observed approximately 150 people, a live band, numerous cups, beer cans and bottles. Some of the bottles still contained what smelled like beer in them.[3]

The cops put it all in their incident report. Apparently there had been a complaint about the music. Something to do with a lot of noise in the middle of the night. Who was in charge here? Dennis Greenia (*W M, 28 Yrs, 6′1″, 190 lbs*) stepped up and spoke to one officer while another took notes and a third snapped photos of the attendees, seemingly to let them know they were now among the usual suspects; troublemakers; headed for a fall. In the front of the room the band segued, wittily, into Johnny Rivers's "Secret Agent Man." The cops weren't tickled. Greenia was served with a summons for running a discotheque without a license, while two or three of Downs's law-school mates, lightly soused and heavily aggrieved, made slightly slurred inquiries about all this searching and seizing in light of the Fourth Amendment, which officers Pritchett, Evans, and Deramus pretended not to hear.[4]

That ended that show.

The sun rose on Sunday, the next week passed, then the one after that. Then it was May 6, the day of the Tyrone's show, and Peter woke up smelling disaster on the late-morning breeze. It reeked of humiliation. His humiliation. Onstage, under the lights. Because he . . . wasn't very good. On guitar. He was self-taught, and never bothered to learn much in the way of scales or theory or anything formal. Mike Mills knew all that stuff and could play solos and complex jazz chords Peter couldn't begin to wrap his fingers around. Mike had shaken off Peter's offer to let him take over the guitar—he liked the chemistry he and Bill had in the rhythm section, for one thing. And Peter had developed an economical way of playing that sounded like nobody Mike had ever heard before.

But of course Peter didn't hear it like that, particularly when he had to play in public. Which was hard enough at the church and at the Koffee Klub, though those were more like parties than proper shows. Even so, he'd been terrified on both of those nights. Anticipating the moment his mind would go blank, his fingers freezing in place as the rest of the band shot off without him, leaving him to the staring eyes, the confused titters giving way to laughter when the other guys turned to face him. The music trailing off, the silence growing, looming, swallowing him whole.

This was the nightmare that played across Peter's imagination when he let his mind wander. He'd channel the anxiety into action most days, playing his parts over and over and over, making sure he had every note, pause, and nuance wired down so cold he could play them backward, forward, eyes closed, standing on his head. But somehow that didn't help on show days. He'd do his best to keep it at bay, slugging down beers, trying to find a place on the inebriation scale that was just on the right side of the line dividing pleasantly numb from completely out of it. But the sight of the empty stage, amp lights glowing red, the crowd pressing close, faces turned up and expectant, would freak him the fuck out. Too many eyes. Too many ears. Too much expectation. Too much attention. He couldn't stand it. But he also couldn't resist it.

So he kept coming back. Kept strapping on his guitar and plugging in, hoping that his instrument would be enough. He could focus on the fretboard, on the motion of his fingers, on the sound of the music, the heartbeat rhythm that tied him to the other guys, that kept him from getting sucked off the stage and hurled through the crust of the earth.

When he woke up the day of a show, it would already be boiling up inside of him, this restless, rootless terror. He had a buddy from Emory University, Ken Fechtner. They'd met in the dorms not long after Peter got to campus in the fall of '75 and spent the next couple of years in an endless rolling conversation about bands, records, books, shows, all of Peter's favorite things. Peter had told him about his band in Athens, so Fechtner drove up for the church show, only to be met outside by an apologetic but firm Bill Berry: *Peter doesn't want you to come . . . He'll be too nervous if you're there.*[5] Sigh. Sure, fine, whatever. Fechtner backed off that time, but then Peter was exultant on the phone the next day. It had gone so great . . . they'd already scored a gig at Tyrone's, opening for the Brains, a real pro band from Atlanta! So there was no way he was going to miss that one. Tuesday night, May 6, Fechtner drove back from Atlanta and got to Tyrone's with enough time before the show to find his friend hanging out backstage, pale and sweaty, unable to stand in one place, let alone sit still, wondering aloud if he should just puke now and get it over with. Christ, what a mess.

Maybe he puked, maybe he didn't. Maybe he slugged down enough beer to stop caring. When the lights went out and the crowd pushed to the front, the four members of R.E.M. stepped onstage, the musicians locked eyes, and Peter launched into the opening riff of "Shakin' All Over." The other guys came blasting in after him and the crowd went *Ooooob!* "The Athens foursome exploded with energy in only their third public performance," William Haines wrote in a rave review published two days later in *The Red & Black*. "This was dance music impossible to resist." Haines might have carried a teeny bit of bias in favor of the hometown band. The review's headline termed R.E.M. the "underdogs," and Haines's lead noted that the Atlanta group, who had a deal with Mercury Records and were behind the popular pop-punk anthem "Money Changes Everything," had also been blown off the stage in their previous Athens appearance by the Wuoggerz. Still, Haines paints a vivid portrait of a blistering performance by R.E.M., whose original songs, he continued, were "even more amazing than their excellent cover choices."[6]

Peter, only just fending off the terrors, strutted through some songs doing all his guitar hero moves, Telecaster held low across his body, machine gun style, slashing at the strings while he spun and jumped to emphasize the beat, only to anticipate a tough passage and, *whoops!*, ducking away to play it in the safe harbor behind his amp. No matter; Haines singled the guitarist out for praise: "A crackshot 'Secret Agent Man' showcased Buck's guitar talent. He looked like a hired gun, peeling off ancient riffs as if they had just been learned last week. And they could have been." And Peter was just one quarter of a band that, in Haines's eyes, had found a way to alchemize pop music's most magical properties. "Picture James Brown fronting the Dave Clark Five and you only begin to get a handle on the excitement this band causes."[7]

Of course, Peter hadn't heard it the way Haines had. Once his excitement had ebbed after their set, Peter made a point of apologizing, first to soundman/stage manager Sean Bourne for the amount of time it had taken R.E.M. to clear their gear off the stage,[8] then to Ken Fechtner for the band's amateurish performance.[9] They were still working out the kinks, he said; they'd be better soon. But if he was on his way to apologize to anyone else, he was stopped short when the B-52's' Cindy Wilson buttonholed him. Their set had been wonderful, she shouted at him. The band was so great, and their songs were so cool! Peter had been agog after that, grabbing Fechtner's arm and pulling him aside to recount the whole conversation. "I can't believe Cindy Wilson thinks we're good,"[10] he crowed. By the end of the evening Tyrone's' management had booked R.E.M. to headline a show the next week, and representatives from the student union hired them to open for the Brains at an all-campus event scheduled for the university's Legion Field two days later.

They were all thrilled, but for Peter, to find himself playing guitar in a rock band, and a good one that was blowing people away enough to score two new gigs for every gig they played, was living a dream he'd been having since he started listening to rock 'n' roll radio in grade school. Now if he could only figure out how to do it without puking before the shows, he'd really be happy.

10

We Weren't Really Close
in a Lot of Ways

At Crestwood High School he kept his distance from the crowd. The 1975 *Arsenal* yearbook reveals a single glimpse of the teenage Pete Buck. In his senior portrait, he wears the required tuxedo jacket and formal black bow tie, along with his silky shoulder-length hair and cool, unsmiling detachment. Elsewhere his classmates beam at the camera or look thoughtful, even studious. They disport on the fields, work together to produce the school newspaper and yearbook. They perform in debates, plays, and musicals, serve in student council offices and on advisory committees, or goof with friends in the cafeteria or lounge in groups on the lush green lawn outside the school. Pete is nowhere to be found.

It's not like he was unwelcome. By the standards of adolescent society, Pete presented well. He was tall and handsome, his eyes sharp and clear, his carriage relaxed. His silence seemed rooted in confidence rather than fear. He never went anywhere without a book, and if he got bored with class he'd prop whatever he had inside the assigned text and read it while the teacher carried on, unaware. Most days he dressed like the other boys, casual but neat in jeans and a T-shirt or button-up. Then one day he'd walk into class in his pajamas and bathrobe and act like nothing was out of the ordinary, sitting back and propping a slippered foot on an empty desk. Pete did well enough in his classes, but his test scores were said to be off the charts. When the junior class's SAT results came back in early 1975, word spread that Pete Buck had notched the highest score in the entire state of Georgia. It might not have been true, but hardly anyone doubted it. "Everyone knew he had a lot going on up there," his classmate Joe Craven says.[1]

Craven was smart too, but he had a lot going on everywhere. Designated an Outstanding Senior, Craven had a half page in the 1975 *Arsenal* listing his contributions to theater, journalism, student leadership, and the yearbook staff. On that level, he and Pete couldn't have been more different. But the thing they had in common made them nearly inseparable: they both played guitar. Most days after school, Craven would beeline to the Bucks' two-story colonial. They'd thump down the stairs to the basement, grab their instruments, and start strumming. They didn't know enough chords to worry about learning other people's songs, Craven says. But the absence of mastery freed them to do everything else. "We didn't have any goals. There were no tunes we wanted to learn, no body of work we wanted to perform. We just had our lab coats on—there we were in the castle and here comes the storm. *Let's see if we can bring anything to life!*"[2]

Peter Lawrence Buck was born on December 6, 1956, to parents Peter and Violet Buck, a pair of well-educated professionals living near Los Angeles. The elder Peter's career with the Simmons Mattress Company soon took them to Richmond, north of Berkeley, where younger son Ken was born in 1958. The family was still in Richmond in February 1964 when Peter, at seven years old, saw the Beatles' epochal performance on Ed Sullivan's popular Sunday night variety show on CBS. The music was exciting enough on its own, but the sight of the band on the stage, their shaggy hair and matching suits, and the hysterical reaction of the audience made the boy's heart hammer in his little chest. As he told author Brett Milano for his book *Vinyl Junkies*, Peter had already been drawn to the family's hi-fi system—a Heathkit record player his dad built from a kit—particularly when his father played records by his favorite artist: Ray Charles. Mrs. Buck preferred the pop-folk work of Burl Ives, which her older son came to despise, as he told Milano: "That scarred me for life."

Young Peter spent so much time pawing at his father's hi-fi, his parents bought him his own record player, an inexpensive close-and-play model that spun the 45 rpm singles that were the core of the pop music industry at the time. His first purchase, Peter said to Milano, was the Beatles' "A Hard Day's Night," in its original picture sleeve. Whenever he had a little pocket money, the first place Peter wanted to go was the neighborhood record store. He developed a schoolboy crush on a woman who worked there, a siren in go-go-boots who steered him away from hit singles by Tom Jones and the Seekers and toward the grittier, cooler likes of the Animals and the Rolling Stones. The pull to music and the early stirrings of romantic longing set the grade schooler's head spinning. "It was very influential to me that you tied those two things together—that kind of inchoate sexual urge and buying records," he told Milano. "And I was already obsessed."[3]

As pop music evolved in the mid- and late 1960s, Peter's tastes changed too. The Bucks followed the elder Peter's career to a Simmons factory in Munster, Indiana, where the nighttime skies glowed orange from the steel factories just over the horizon in Gary. The family moved back to California in late 1968, settling in Montrose, a suburb near Glendale, north of Los Angeles. Living in the staid, upper-middle-class suburbs gave the young adolescent an appetite for music that was smarter, and often weirder, than what could be found on the Top 40 stations he'd tuned in to as a boy. When he found a cool record store in Glendale that was staffed entirely by freaky guys with long hair and beards, Peter started hanging out, eavesdropping on their conversations while he flipped through the bins. Determined to spend as much time there as possible, he screwed up his courage and approached the hippie standing behind the register. "I'd do anything to work here,"[4] he declared. The guy thought about it for a bit and offered a deal: They couldn't pay him, but if Peter wanted to sweep the floors a couple of days a week, they'd give him a discount on anything he wanted to buy. Peter jumped at the chance.

He was thirteen years old. The months he spent at the shop were a revelation, a conduit into a realm of adulthood that was as beguiling as it was mysterious. Music, culture, politics, drugs, sex, history, freedom—all of it was in the record bins. Most of it went over his head; he was only starting to piece it together, sifting for clues on the album covers, listening for the messages encoded in the songs. The longhairs behind the counter nudged him in the right direction. *You should check out this band, this new record . . . This is older, but you can't understand the new stuff until you hear it . . . This looks good, but isn't. That one there, get that.* Peter pushed his broom, stayed out of the way, and watched it all go down. The other workers treated him like an adult, even if they made him leave the room when they wanted to smoke a joint. "And I'm like, 'Wow, man! I heard about that! Can I smoke some pot, too?' "[5]

He got hip. When the new thing came, Peter had already read about it, heard it, had bought it, and knew it front to back before it had a chance to become the big new thing. He bought James Taylor's *Sweet Baby James* the day it came out in February 1970, seven months before "Fire and Rain" hit the radio. He picked up Black Sabbath's debut album on its release day too. What he didn't hear from the hippies he could glean in the magazines and underground newspapers they kept on their racks. *Rolling Stone, Crawdaddy, Cheetah,* the *Los Angeles Free Press.* A language, a philosophy, a world, all of it woven into music.

The Bucks upped sticks again in 1971, heading this time to Martin's Landing, Georgia, a small community within Roswell, Georgia, a suburb of Atlanta. A suburb inside another suburb. This time the crucial record store was farther away, more than ten miles, but Peter made friends with the guy there. He remembered him as a kind of hippie-music Paul Bunyan, close to three hundred pounds, hair to his waist, beard to his chest, perpetually stoned and eager to share. When something caught his ear he'd call the Bucks' house and urge his young friend to get over there, now. "He'd call me up and say something like [in a conspiratorial whisper], 'Hey, that new Stones album, *Exile on Main Street*, it's coming out tonight,'" Peter recalled to Milano, and he'd be out of the house, down to the highway to thumb a ride and risk the abuse a kid with shoulder-length hair could get from a shitkicker driving through the Georgia 'burbs in the dregs of the hippie years, 1972. But *Exile*, man! He nabbed his copy, took a gander at the literal freaks gawping back among the blurry shots of Mick, Keith, and the others on the cover, and held it tight to his chest as he headed back to his record player at home.

New records, new languages, new worlds. John Coltrane, *A Love Supreme*. Van Dyke Parks, *Song Cycle*. Skip Spence, *Oar*. He held on to the old ones, too: the Beatles, the Monkees, the Beach Boys. It all fit together. Heard in the right moment, in the right mood, it was perfect. Peter would spin his records constantly, listening again and again while he pored over the lyrics, the liner notes and credits, absorbing all the names: the musicians, the producers, the arrangers, the engineers, the second engineers and art directors, the managers and road managers. The recording studios and mixing studios, the names and locations of the theaters where live shows went down. He could imagine being there. He could imagine making the music . . . wielding the guitar. It was always a guitar in his imagination. Always the guitar.

His younger brother, Ken, was the first to pick one up. He got a nylon-string guitar and started classical guitar lessons, mastering the theory and technique in the formal way required of serious musicians. Pete had no interest in conventional instruction; he didn't want to listen to someone else telling him how to learn, let alone what to play. If he couldn't play the music he wanted to hear—rock 'n' roll—he wanted nothing to do with it. So right around the time he got to high school, Pete got a steel-string guitar, picked up a few songbooks and instructional books with the basic chords and fingering, and set to figuring it out on his own. It was painstaking work, slow, with plenty of flubbed notes, but it came. Chords, melodies, songs. Sometimes he'd get Ken to play with him, and the brothers would gamely try to make some music together. When he got to talking to Joe Craven about music, they discovered how much they had in common. A passion for music, but also a way of thinking. "He was a soft-spoken, quiet guy, but I could look at him and tell his brain was racing," Craven says. "He was thinking about lots of things. I think he and I in our own ways were both experimenting, liberating ourselves from the tyranny of common sense."[6]

For all his good cheer and good grades, his student-body-president, lead-in-the-school-play, editor-of-the-yearbook ways, Craven was a breed apart from the other suburban achievers. There was sand on his tongue, a dissonant buzz that led him to the same outsider music Pete loved. Stuff from Frank Zappa and Captain Beefheart that blended form and chaos in ways that could make even the freakiest hippie back away. It was the incongruities that appealed to them. "Pete loved being paradoxical, mixing and matching things mentally and in appearance. I think he enjoyed experimenting with things that were contradictory. Seemingly contradictory emotions and ideas."[7]

The afternoon music sessions in the basement of Peter's two-story colonial were free-form. Both boys were new to their instruments, both still learning the fundamental chords and progressions. Neither had played long enough to develop relative pitch, the visceral comprehension that allows you to figure out a song as you listen to it, playing by ear, so they made up their own songs as they went. "We'd try to find a groove and play on it," Craven says. "A lot of it was instrumental. We played around with singing a little, but most of it was pretty experimental." Peter focused on the rhythm part, strumming chords while Craven plucked out a melody. Sometimes Ken would play with them, adding another guitar into the mix.

Eventually Pete got an electric guitar, then more instruments found their way into the Bucks' basement: a bass, amplifiers, a set of drums. A schoolmate named Bobby Jenkins brought over a Farfisa organ and added some keyboard parts. Some days the boys would play a kind of musical chairs, starting on one instrument, riffing for a while, then trading off and starting again. Sometimes they'd find a compelling new groove, sometimes it would collapse into a formless racket. "We did a lot of laughing," Craven recalls. "Pete had a great laugh. He'd laugh at everything, including himself."[8]

Eventually they mastered enough real songs to take their guitars to a party or two and play for their friends. That was fun, Craven recalls. Once they even played a few songs at a school assembly. What they played there, what the assembly was about, and how it went no longer feature in his memory, for reasons Craven isn't sure he understands. Maybe because it was, in Pete's words, a mess. If so, the problem would have been some combination of nerves and inexperience. They didn't smoke weed or do any of those other hippie-era drugs, but alcohol, on the other hand, was easily found and widely enjoyed by the teenage set in and around Dunwoody, Georgia. Kids would get a case of beer or raid their parents' liquor cabinet on a Saturday night and head down to the banks of the Chattahoochee River to get blasted. Or there'd be liquor-soaked parties, drunken racing through the neighborhood streets, endless opportunities to create your own catastrophe. Craven's parents were divorced, and he envied the domestic stability he saw in the Buck family's home. Pete didn't have a lot to say to his dad, but he was a teenage boy, it was the early 1970s—what else was new? Two parents, two kids, quiet evenings at home.

The silence told its own stories. And despite what appeared to be happy and prosperous childhoods, both of the Buck parents had long since learned that some stories were best left untold.

The elder Peter Buck was born in Los Angeles in 1923 to George and Eunice Buck. George was a salesman who died of pneumonia in 1927. This seems to have had a devastating impact on Eunice. She stayed in L.A., but Peter and his elder sister, Marguerite, were sent to a foster family in rural Canada, where they were put to work in the fields. It was a raw and difficult life until, blessedly, Eunice called them back. She'd fallen in love with and married a new husband, a kind and prosperous butcher named Stephen Picelich, who lived in Eagle Rock, a leafy suburb near Pasadena.[9]

Back in the sunshine, Marguerite and Peter prospered. Both were popular and successful at school and in Eagle Rock's youth societies. Peter was a star tackle on the Eagle Rock High School football team and made the All-Valley squad during the fall of 1941. He spent three years with the U.S. Marines during World War II and saw gruesome action on the island of Bougainville. "We made the initial landings and fought the Japs up there," he wrote to his parents in late 1943. "We were hit out there one night when we were about four miles in front of our lines . . . we pulled out in a hurry leaving about ten dead Japs. Earlier when we got hit was the 'scaredest' I've ever been!" The letter goes on. Hip-deep mud, nonstop rain, incoming mortar fire, outgoing machine gun fire, dense enough to leave the hill knee-deep in dead Japanese soldiers.[10] Later, Peter was injured in a hand grenade attack.[11] He came home after the war and studied journalism at the University of California, Berkeley, on the G.I. Bill and pursued graduate work at the University of Florence, in Italy. He married a hometown girl, Violet Lorenson, a UCLA grad pursuing a master's degree in history, in 1953.[12]

Violet's family came with their own extraordinary story. Her father, Harry Lorenson, was a high-ranking captain with the Los Angeles Police Department who was very close to Mayor Fletcher Bowron, whose administration had what you might call a working relationship with the city's reigning mobster, Mickey Cohen. According to Cohen's memoir, *Mickey Cohen: In My Own Words*, the mob boss was called to a meeting with Lorenson, who passed on the mayor's request that he exact some street justice on an electronics shop owner who had not only filed scores of nuisance suits against the city but also managed to claim ownership of a customer's home because she had an unpaid repair bill of $8.90. As Cohen wrote in his memoir, "In fact, what Lorenson said is, 'The Mayor wants this guy banged up so bad that he's sent to a hospital. But that's all!' "[13]

The mayor arranged to clear the shop owner's neighborhood of police for an hour the next Saturday. The crooked shop owner was busted up, and all would have gone according to plan if not for a pair of rookie cops who hadn't gotten the memo about turning a blind eye to the assault. Cohen's boys were arrested, Lorenson helped spring them before charges could be filed, and when the newspapers got wind of the scheme it all blew up.[14]

Lorenson and two other police officers were suspended from the force and then indicted on criminal charges, launching a scandal that played out in the front pages of all the Los Angeles newspapers for more than a year. But the prosecutors' case was shaky and Lorenson was eventually cleared of the charges and reinstated to the force. Nevertheless, he retired soon after, and eventually had to sue the city to receive the year of back pay he'd lost when he was suspended.[15]

Peter and Violet's wedding rated a long feature in the March 5, 1953, edition of the *Eagle Rock Sentinel*, which noted that the happy couple, following a brief honeymoon in Mexico, would move to Las Vegas, where Peter was working as an investigator for the federal government.[16] Their son Peter was born in L.A. in 1956, and the family moved north to the Bay Area, where the elder Peter started his career with the Simmons Mattress Company. Younger son Ken was born in 1958, and the family stayed put until 1965, when Simmons moved Peter to oversee a factory in Munster, Indiana. The family returned to California in 1968 then, when Peter was promoted to the company's Atlanta headquarters in 1971, moved to Georgia and into a comfortable two-story house in Martin's Landing, near the suburb of Roswell.

The elder Peter Buck stayed at Simmons for the rest of his career, which ended with his death, at sixty-two, in 1986. In marked contrast with the exploits he packed into the first twenty-five years of his life, the elder Buck's passing occasioned no published obituaries anywhere. His son has rarely spoken of his father in public, barely acknowledging either his parents or his relationship with them in any of the hundreds of interviews he has given in the past forty-plus years. None of his bandmates or friends who have discussed their relationship with Peter the musician ever mentioned his family, except in the most abstract way: that his parents, who both had graduate degrees, expected both of their sons to get college degrees, at the very least. Peter, for all his obvious intelligence and endless appetite for books and information of every sort, had no interest in doing that.

Father and son had never had much to talk about. The younger Peter Buck's rejection of education and his disinterest in continuing the family's journey from the working class to the educated white-collar sector aggravated his father no end. The boy's consuming interest in music struck his father as frivolous. Peter's dedication to his guitar and the discipline with which he pursued it didn't change the old man's mind. Neither did the fame, the critical acclaim, or even the financial rewards when they started to accrue. He tried to swallow his disappointment but never really could. Talking to a reporter in 1987, Peter recalled one thing his father had recently told him. "We weren't really close in a lot of ways, but the last thing he said to me before he died was, 'Make sure you make a million because there's nothing else on earth that you are able to do.' He was trying to kind of say 'stick with it,' but he was saying it in the nastiest possible way."[17]

11

Hey, He Really Knows His Shit!

I t was his clothes that Ken Fechtner noticed first. A junior at Emory University, the pre-med student had seen a couple of waves of incoming freshmen at the school. One of the few major colleges in the Southeast to not have a varsity sports program, Emory appealed to the region's more serious high schoolers. The ones who could already anticipate the postgrad programs that lay beyond their undergraduate years, and the careers that would follow after that. Sure, the place had its share of longhairs and party animals; it was still a college, still full of adolescents freshly liberated from home, parents and all the rules that had held them in place throughout their lives. But none of those eager young subversives had seemed remotely original to Fechtner, until he came across Peter Buck, lurking on the fringe of a dorm party.

The tall, dark-haired boy was positively electric in a pink ruffled tux shirt, a paisley smoking jacket, and red Converse high-tops. In a time and place where thrift-store shopping was not the rage, the guy looked like some kind of color-blind hobo. Fechtner walked up and introduced himself, and once they got to talking, the two students discovered an array of common enthusiasms. Raised near New York City in New Jersey, Fechtner knew all about the shadowy downtown bands like the New York Dolls and the Velvet Underground. Both were into Johnny Burnette and '50s rockabilly and were also unabashed fans of the ultra-bubblegum Scottish pop stars the Bay

City Rollers and the critically beloved, if little-known, power-pop band Big Star. Fechtner didn't get as much of a charge from the Grateful Dead as Peter did, but he chalked that up to his new friend's fixation on the guitar.

Music consumed the better part of Peter Buck's attention in college. He pledged the Delta Tau Delta fraternity and sometimes played with some of the other members in the frat house, and could also be seen strumming in his dorm room or outside on the grass. He did most of his playing on his own—he knew a lot of Monkees songs, a friend remembers—and almost always stuck to strumming the chords, which led some of the others to assume he wasn't good enough to attempt a lead guitar part. It didn't seem to bother him or diminish his interest in playing, particularly when a song got under his skin and he could sit with his guitar and stereo and play with what he heard, following along until he got to a sticky spot, when he'd pick up the needle and move it back, constantly picking up and dropping the needle, listening again. Repeating the process over and over until he'd figured out exactly how the song went.

Sometime in the spring term of his sophomore year, he had enough. Thinking of the beatniks, Jack Kerouac, and, perhaps, the music-above-all subculture surrounding the Grateful Dead, whose music he still adored, Peter packed a bag, picked up his guitar, and hitch-hiked to California, settling in San Luis Obispo, a small town near the Central California coast. Getting a room in a house full of hip-pies, he found a job washing dishes and spent a few months living the dropout life. The freedom agreed with him, but then his new roommates began to get on his nerves. All that weed smoking and the jam-band shit they played grated against his sensibilities, and when they reacted badly to his import copy of the Sex Pistols' single "God Save the Queen," he figured it was time to hit the road again. Back in Atlanta in the fall of 1977, Peter resumed classes at Emory, but he cushioned the blow by taking a job as a clerk at Doo Dah Records, a shop he'd frequented near Emory. He realized quickly that being on the other side of the counter, counseling kids who thought they wanted Judas Priest that they'd actually be more into the Ramones, felt like a calling.

Going to concerts had come to mean nearly as much to him as the records that had defined his childhood and adolescence. Peter saw his first show in 1971, when he caught Leon Russell and his band at Atlanta's Municipal Auditorium.[1] From that point onward, the sound of live music invigorated him so much, he'd see nearly anything that came to town. Southern rock, mainstream rock, folk, jazz, anything. He found something to love about nearly all of it. But the real revelation had come when he saw the New York Dolls opening for Mott the Hoople in 1973 at the Atlanta Municipal Auditorium.

An early precursor to both punk and glam rock, the all-male Dolls wore androgynous clothes and caked their faces with women's makeup while playing blistering rock songs about drugs, sex, and the variety of weird characters they encountered on the trashiest streets of New York City. Onstage they were a train wreck: stoned, stumbling, rarely in sync, perpetually on the verge of exploding into ruin. And for Peter, gaping from the center of the restive crowd, it was *thrilling*. The power of the performance coming not from professionalism or musicality, but from the complete absence of those things. What it proved, beyond an eyeshadow of a doubt, was that every word of their songs—"Pills," "Trash," "Personality Crisis," on and on—had been absolutely fucking *real*. The Dolls were just as fucked up as the people they sang about. "They weren't stars," Peter said later. "They staggered around and missed chords. But the magic was there."[2]

The shambolic but incandescent opening set the New York Dolls played that night, Peter reflected later, gave him a shove in an entirely new direction. He bought the band's just-released first album, then a few months later got a subscription to *The Village Voice*, the same New York newspaper that would soon be filling Michael Stipe's imagination with the new artier, harder-edged artists.

———

Real, gob-stained British punk rock came to Atlanta on January 5, 1978, when the Sex Pistols came to play the Great Southeast Music Hall, a five-hundred-capacity club located in, of all places, a shopping mall. It was the controversial British band's first American show, the start of a hotly anticipated tour that would also prove to be the final act of the group's brief, explosive career. Excited by the prospect of not just seeing the world's most notorious punk band but also being among the first Americans to have the privilege, Peter reserved a pair of tickets. He got to the venue just before the show was set to begin, only to be told that the management had underestimated the number of reporters, photographers, and other media folk who needed to get inside and had been forced to give Peter's tickets to one of the professionals. Peter's angry protestations didn't have much of an impact, but when the friend he'd brought with him, a fellow he recalled as both large and rambunctious, bowled over the doorman and dashed inside, Peter saw his opportunity and followed close on his heels.

He made it inside just as the Pistols came onstage. "Unhh, my name's John an' this is the Sex Pistols," declared lead singer Johnny Rotten, by way of introduction. After a moment they launched into "God Save the Queen," a song nearly unrivaled in their catalog for both outrage and, surprisingly enough, catchiness, with Rotten's snarls—*God save the queen / This fascist regime!*—coming over Steve Jones's crunchy but tuneful guitar.

Peter kept in motion, one eye on the stage, the other on the pair of bouncers who had tailed him into the club, determined to chase down the gate-crashers and drag them back out again. After everything he'd read about the Pistols, how wild they were, how dangerous, what Peter saw onstage seemed like just another rock 'n' roll show. Johnny Rotten was an electric front man and knew how to rile up the crowd. "Forget about starin' at us, just fuckin' *dance*," he said after the opening song. "We're all ugly an' we know it." But so what? Peter had read how the band's manager, the morally neutral provocateur Malcolm McLaren, had hatched the Sex Pistols as an idea before finding the performers to animate his concept. "The angry Monkees,"[3] Peter called them later.[4] Which didn't bother him, exactly—Peter *loved* the Monkees—but by the time the bouncers caught up with him, dragging him out of the club and hurling him indelicately onto the pavement, he felt less disappointed about missing the rest of the show.

Peter made it through the fall quarter at Emory, then dropped out again to devote himself to the record store. His parents weren't happy about his abandoning school, seemingly forever, but when his bosses at Doo Dah's offered him a bigger job with their record distribution business, he took it, thinking that being on the path to some kind of career would at least make him seem like a young man with a direction in life. Thus began Peter's short career as a rack jobber—the guy who lugs boxes of records from the warehouse to the record stores, collects the unsold albums, and then hauls them back to the warehouse.

If Peter imagined that working anywhere in the record business would be as much fun as what he had already been doing, he soon realized he'd been mistaken. Rather than spending his days listening to music and talking about records, now he was living behind the wheel of Doo Dah's delivery wagon, crawling through traffic on the freeways, getting lost on the city streets, and dealing with crabby employees in small-town department stores that kept just a few racks for that moment's biggest hits. Worse, he had nothing for entertainment except what he could find on the radio dial. What he began to realize, after not very long, was that he hated it. After a particularly stultifying day on the road, he resigned his position in typical Buckian fashion, by pulling the company car into its space in the warehouse parking lot, leaving the keys inside, locking the door, and walking away, never to return.

Peter had long since gotten to know the clerks at the nearby record stores, and when the owner of the Wax 'n' Facts shop, a recent University of Georgia graduate named Danny Beard, asked if he'd help reserve a room on the Emory campus for a band from Athens to perform in, Peter was happy to help. Beard knew the band—the B-52's—from his UGA days, and though they had played only a few parties and one or two public engagements, they already had booked a few shows in New York and wanted to get a little more experience before taking their shot in Gotham. Peter helped reserve the Coke

Room, in the Alumni Memorial University Center, a function room with space for a midsize party, and programmed the pre-show music with favorites from the Jam and Gene Vincent. The Bs showed up in all their eccentric finery, the wigs and bargain-basement instruments, trailing a flock of UGA students and other friends from Athens, and with the doors flung open and word of a party afoot, the place filled up with collegiate revelers who greeted the band with cheers, then danced happily to their joyously eccentric songs.

The crowd from Athens melded easily with the Emory students. Peter stood out, due in part to his being a sort of host for the event. He was also taller than most everyone and radiated . . . something . . . that drew the eye and stuck in the memory. "He looked like he always does," recalls Mark Cline, the UGA art student who would eventually cofound Love Tractor. "A leather jacket, jeans, T-shirt, Converse, his hair below his ears. And that's how we met. We started talking to him, and he knew his rock 'n' roll, though he hadn't been in a band yet. I came with Sam Seawright, and I told him, 'Hey, he really knows his shit!' Next thing I knew, Peter was in Athens. And he fit with everybody else."[5]

After Peter quit his job with Doo Dah's distribution outfit, he went down the street to Wuxtry Records, another cornucopia of new and used records, music magazines, music books, posters, T-shirts, everything that mattered, and asked co-owner Mark Methe if he had any openings. They had met before: Methe knew exactly who Peter was, knew *what* he was, which is to say, one of them. A record store guy. He didn't have any openings at this store, but had Peter ever been to Athens, where UGA is? Because they had two stores there and he could definitely use him, if he didn't mind moving. Peter didn't mind at all and took the job. When could he start? His brother, Ken, was already in Athens, so he'd have somewhere to crash till he found his own place. He packed his records and books into boxes, lugged them into his car, tossed in his guitar and amp, jumped into the driver's seat, and off he went. Ninety minutes later he was in downtown Athens, where his future awaited.

12

A Certain Amount of Chaos

ichael Stipe dances feverishly at the microphone, arms all over the place, hair flopping wildly, spitting out his lyrics like urgent messages: *Baby, I, I, I—don't wanna hang around with yewwwww / Baby, I, I, I—got better things to dewwww* . . . Mike Mills is also in constant motion just to Stipe's right, fingering his bass, bobbing his shoulders, then bopping back toward the drums to catch the eye of Bill Berry, who flails his arms to keep the beat. Meanwhile, Peter Buck performs the rituals of the rock guitarist, ducking here, sliding there, pausing during the song's middle section to focus on the arpeggiated chords. The song's "Baby I," one of the new originals they've been cranking out, and when it ends Bill rolls thunder on his floor tom to launch into an overdrive version of "Route 66" and the music erupts again. It ends slightly more than two minutes later, and they pause long enough for Michael to shout that the next song is for Cindy, and then they're off into "Scheherazade," another new original. *You say you make her feel all right / She says she wants you, but not tonight* . . . This is followed by another new original, also played at breakneck speed, and then another and another.

It's the late spring of 1980, only weeks since the church party in April, but suddenly this new band, only recently dubbed R.E.M., is the talk of the town. It happened that quickly. R.E.M.'s first headlining show at Tyrone's, on May 13, 1980, drew a bigger crowd to the club than they had played to a week earlier opening for the Brains. An even larger audience came to see both bands play a UGA student event at the Memorial Hall Ballroom on campus (the show was relocated from the school's Legion Field due to rain) on May 15, and R.E.M. returned to Tyrone's on the 21st to do another headlining set, to an even more packed club. When they played their first show at the 40 Watt, the do-it-yourself venue Curtis Crowe had launched above a sandwich shop downtown (which had since moved to a larger location a few doors down College Avenue), on May 30, they filled the place.

When R.E.M. headlined the Mad Hatter, a larger, more mainstream nightclub close to campus in downtown Athens, on June 3, the place filled up with people nobody had ever seen at an Athens art-rock band show. Jocks, preppies, guys in T-shirts branded with the Greek characters from fraternity row. All of them dancing and cheering and pumping their fists in the air like they were at an REO Speedwagon concert. The shows began to draw throngs, not just inside the clubs but on the street outside, too. A whole scene: some people waiting to get in, others hoping to catch some music through an open window, others just seeing the crowd, wondering what was going on. The excitement about the new band was palpable and, to some members of the scene, infuriating. When Pylon's Randy Bewley and Michael Lachowski got to the 40 Watt show at the end of May and saw how jammed it was, they stood on the street, sputtering to the photographer Terry Allen. The last time their band had played the 40 Watt, it wasn't anything like this! *Why are all these people going to see R.E.M. and not us?* "Pylon would get fifty people and R.E.M. would get two hundred–plus," Allen recalls. "You couldn't even fit inside. We were standing on the street hearing it echoing."[1]

Word of the hot new band began to echo beyond Athens. Three days after the Mad Hatter show, they ventured to Atlanta to make their big-city debut at the Warehouse, at the bottom of a bill supporting a band called the Space Heaters. Back in Athens the next day, the band went to the WUOG radio studios for a four-way on-air interview, then performed again that night at an outdoor show in nearby High Shoals, Georgia, opening for the southern boogie band Stillwater. They took most of June off, reuniting for a set at the Mad Hatter on the 30th, then launching into an ambitious July with a show at Atlanta's Agora Ballroom, another 40 Watt appearance back home, then three more shows in Atlanta, starting with a lightly attended set at Hedgens Tavern, in the Buckhead neighborhood, then a pair of dates opening for the British political punk band Gang of Four at the 688 Club, a recently opened venue focused on punk and new wave bands. Given a capacity of about five hundred, it was a relatively small place, a tube-shaped room with bleachers on the side and an open floor where fans could crowd the stage, dance, and, if the mood took them, smash into one another in a southern approximation of slam dancing.

The club's core audience divided into three distinct tribes: an art-music crowd, a neo-rockabilly contingent, and a smaller number of hardcore fans. All shared the same animus toward mainstream rock and the local bands that played that sort of shit, so R.E.M.'s pair of opening sets raised eyebrows all around the room. Wasn't that just a *Monkees* song, for fuck's sake? But then again, the band drew from an intriguingly diverse, and cool, array of sources—not just the Monkees but also the Velvet Underground, Johnny Rivers, and Johnny Kidd & the Pirates. And there was a spirit to their renditions, a wild, joyous energy that separated them from all the other bands in Athens, in Atlanta, and everywhere else they went.

Maybe it began with the rhythm section, the tight-but-flexible connection between Bill's drums and Mike's bass, the way they clicked together so naturally. And they played *fast*, ripping through the tunes at a high velocity that somehow didn't blur their precision: the drums and bass in lockstep, the guitar chords and notes in place, Michael belting his vocal across the top with a kind of rockabilly inflection, all hiccups and gulps, that made him seem electrified, and all the more spellbinding.

And as Mark Williams, the club's newly hired disc jockey, noticed, it didn't take long for the Athens band to start attracting an audience that went beyond the 688's usual punky crowd. By the time R.E.M. got back to the club for a pair of headlining shows at the end of the summer, Williams saw a wide array of new faces, not just the UGA gang who came down from Athens but also clean-cut collegiate types from Atlanta and mainstream rock fans who'd heard about the group from friends who had either been at an earlier show or seen them somewhere else. Pylon, the Side Effects, and Love Tractor had also done well at the club, but, Williams recalls, R.E.M. was on another level. "Their ascension was pretty rapid compared to other bands," he says.[2]

Bertis Downs IV, the law student who came to the Koffee Klub show in mid-April, had been drawn largely by his friendships with Bill Berry, whom he'd gotten to know when they were both on the UGA concert production committee, and Peter Buck, with whom he'd traded fanboy talk about Neil Young albums over the Wuxtry shop counter. Having two friends in a band was enough to draw Downs to the show late on a slow Saturday night, but what he heard in the forty-five minutes before the Athens police shut the place down excited him more than any live music he'd ever seen anyone play. Downs became a fixture at the shows around Athens, and once he'd gotten to know the other band members, he became comfortable enough to tell them how much promise he thought they had. *You guys could be bigger than the Beatles,* he said, with only a moderate amount of overstatement. Downs also had an offer. Though he was only a second-year law student and hadn't studied entertainment law in a formal way, he knew the basics of contracts and business law. He didn't have any ambitions to get into the music business, but if they ever had questions about a contract or other business arrangement someone wanted them to sign, he'd be happy to look it over, for free.

Other fans found ways to help, and became friends, too. When the photographer Terry Allen saw Peter or Mike lugging an amp up a deserted street at 2 a.m., he'd pull over, toss the thing into the back seat, and drive the tired musician home. Sandra-Lee Phipps and Carol Levy took band photographs, and Patton Biddle and Woody Nuss, who engineered sound at Tyrone's and the other clubs in town, could be called upon to procure and run PA systems when needed for parties and other venues that didn't have their own equipment. Kathleen O'Brien, who was now Bill's girlfriend, helped work the phones to land shows, which was particularly handy, since the drummer had the most interest, and experience, in the business end of the music industry. He'd paid attention and asked questions during his months as Paragon Booking Agency's office boy back in Macon and made friends among the agents and other staffers.

Don Braxley, who worked as an agent, remembered Bill as a nice high school kid who liked to have his buddy Mike come and hang out during slow afternoons in the office. Bill had called Braxley to get the Wuoggerz an opening slot with the Police when they played Athens in 1979, and he called on him again when R.E.M. started picking up steam during the summer of 1980. This time, Bill told him, he wanted to come down to Macon and meet with him in person. Bill brought Mike with him, and they had big news. They had formed a real band in Athens, with original songs, and things were really starting to happen for them. "He said they were going to be big, and he wanted me to help."[3]

Braxley was happy to listen and help however he could. As he told Bill, he wasn't in a position to sign R.E.M. as a client; they'd have to go speak with Ian Copeland, the former Paragon booker who had moved to New York to work more closely with his brother Miles, the founder and president of the independent record label I.R.S. But Braxley did spend a couple of hours with the boys, digging into his address book to give them the names and telephone numbers of dozens of clubs, universities, and other venues in the Southeast, along with the names of the promoters, bookers, and managers who booked the talent. He offered a few tips on which venues would let them play original music, rather than Top 40 or hard rock covers, and how starting with small places in out-of-the-way towns could lead to bigger and better venues and towns, especially if they played well and made a point of connecting with the people who came to see them. Playing music was fun, but they needed to approach it like work. A job, which required dedication and focus. Was this something they were all prepared to do?

Bill certainly was. Mike, too. Peter, . . . it was all anyone could do to pry the guitar out of his hands, so obviously. Michael was nearly as engaged in his art classes, he actually enjoyed going to school most days. But put a microphone in front of him, a band behind, and an audience at his feet and he came alive in a completely different way. His professors saw it too: Judy McWillie, whose color theory class included Pylon's Vanessa Briscoe and Love Tractor's Mark Cline and Armistead Wellford, among other Athens art-band members, realized it the first time she and her colleague Bill Marriott took up Michael's invitation to see his new band perform.

It was the May 15 set opening for the Brains, just six weeks since R.E.M.'s first show in the church. McWillie, whose research included a detailed study of the art and culture of evangelical faiths in the Deep South, was struck immediately by the passion of Michael's performance onstage. "He'd be singing and holding the microphone, standing there. But then at a certain point, if it was a fast song, he'd like snap and go into this dance," she says. "The only thing I'd seen before like that happens at tent revivals, when someone falls out into a trance. So when he did that, and he did moves like I'd never seen before, it was kind of this sideways shake thing. My God, you talk about incredible. My colleague and I looked at each other and said, 'Oh, my God, these people are real good. They're going to go some-where.'"[4]

They didn't have to use their new list of contacts to get the band's first out-of-state bookings that summer. The three North Carolina dates, back-to-back weekend shows at the Station nightclub, in Carrboro, and a Monday evening appearance at the Pier in nearby Raleigh, were originally set to feature Pylon, but the band backed out in order to prepare for the recording sessions for the *Gyrate* album. The Method Actors had gotten the first call to fill in, but they couldn't make the trip and referred the promoter to another new, largely unheard-of Athens band. When the phone rang at the apartment Bill shared with O'Brien, the drummer checked his calendar and saw that the prof-fered dates fit perfectly between the two Gang of Four openers in Atlanta and a headlining set at Tyrone's on July 22. They took the shows happily, packed their gear into the beat-up van they had just bought, and set out on the five-hour drive up I-85.

When they arrived they met the promoter, a twenty-seven-year-old record store manager who had recently started making some extra money by putting on shows in local clubs. His name was Jefferson Holt, the son of two attorneys. His mom, Bertha, was an influential Democratic state legislator with bracingly progressive social politics. Jefferson was tall and rail thin, with steel-rimmed glasses and the same combination of intelligence, rock 'n' roll passion, and good-time spirit the R.E.M. guys brought with them from Athens. They all hit it off immediately, and when the band stepped onstage at the Station and launched into their set, he was thrilled by what he heard. "The show was incredible," he said a few years later. "The greatest thing I'd ever seen in my life. They had so much fun, and they didn't seem to care about anything . . . It was what I would have imagined seeing from the Who before they signed a record contract . . . A certain amount of chaos."[5]

The fun continued after the Friday night show, when Holt joined the band for their post-show celebration at their hotel, and took them into Saturday, which they spent listening to records and goofing around with their new friend until that night's show. They had Sunday off and partied their way to the Monday evening appearance in Raleigh, which ended with Stipe inviting the entire crowd, about two dozen people in a town where the band was unknown, onto the stage to sing while the band (minus Bill, tethered to his drums) cheered them on from the dance floor.

The band headed back to Athens for the next evening's set at Tyrone's, but the buzz from the weekend, what he'd heard the band play onstage and the fun they'd had hanging around between shows, stayed with Holt. He was smart and ambitious; working at a record store by day and promoting the occasional club show wasn't nearly enough to occupy him, particularly in the sleepy corner of North Carolina where he lived. He kept in touch with his new friends and brought them back to the Station for another pair of dates in September. That made them even closer, and eventually Holt and Bill hatched a plan. Holt would quit his job, pack his things, and move to Athens, where he could spend his days working in a record store and his evenings serving as R.E.M.'s roadie or road manager, whatever they wanted to call him.

Holt rolled into town in October and turned his hand to doing whatever the band needed done. He drove the van, he carried equipment, he collected money from the club owners and doled it out to the guys at the end of the evening. When it turned out the band wasn't making enough money at their shows to pay him a proper salary, they came up with another arrangement. Holt would be their manager, taking responsibility for everything they had to do that wasn't musical. For this they'd pay him an equal share of everything they earned, meaning that from here on out R.E.M. would be a quintet: Mike Mills, Bill Berry, Peter Buck, Michael Stipe, and one equal, nonperforming member, Jefferson Holt.

13

Sit and Try for the Big Kill

Peter and Michael had scratched out a few original songs when they were first playing together, and Bill and Mike came in with a few tunes from their own experiments, all unperformed except for Bill's song "Narrator," which was a regular part of R.E.M.'s early sets, though it was almost unbelievably silly: sung in the voice of a guy who dreams of doing the voice-overs for Jacques Cousteau's TV specials about the magical world under the surface of the ocean. It all leads to a climactic punch line: the aspiring narrator can't swim. A ridiculous subject for a song, but, performed in double time, with Bill's drums going full tilt, Peter's guitar drenched in surf twang, Mike's bass rocketing to and fro, and Michael doing his best Elvis impression, it didn't sound completely out of place caroming around Tyrone's or the 40 Watt.

Once they started playing more shows, the four band members started banging out originals at a faster pace, and by the end of the spring of 1980 they were premiering new songs almost every time they performed. Most were musically spare: basic chords snapped together into simple constructions that leaned hard on repetition and hurtling momentum. The lyrics also betray the adolescent perspective of their authors, who were still in their early twenties and not shy about expressing the casual misogyny prone to young and sexually inexperienced men. "Baby I" was a kiss-off to a faithless lover, albeit with regrets (*Baby, I blew it when I never learned how to dance*). "All the

Right Friends" dismissed another paramour, this one a social climber who sucks up to all the wrong people. In "Scheherazade" the titular character is just another fast-talking, two-timing girl: *She'll tell you stories, you can bet / You know the girl, she's telling lies.* So many wicked women, so much deceit. Other songs cast a gimlet eye toward society and politics. "Dangerous Times" bemoaned shallow times that offered *nothing to care or die for.* "Chappaquiddick" made caustic sport of Senator Ted Kennedy's alcohol-drenched car accident in the summer of 1969 that resulted in the death of former Robert F. Kennedy campaign worker Mary Jo Kopechne, while "Body Count" tore into heedless young Americans who assumed their comfortable lives would never be interrupted by war. *And they won't let you wear your khakis / And your Izods anymore,* Stipe sang before chanting the name of the war his father had fought just ten years earlier: *Body count . . . Vietnam.*

"Mystery to Me," "A Girl Like You," "A Different Girl," and "Mediocrity" presented variations on the same theme, all performed to a driving, danceable beat, with a throbbing bass and abrupt guitar riffs. Nothing memorable, let alone distinctive. But they were learning and doing it quickly. As the bookings for summer stacked up in June, the growing confidence radiated into the band's songwriting. Where the earlier songs were flinty and one-dimensional, there appeared new songs that explored real and often complex feelings. The first came almost entirely from Mike, responding to the prospect of spending the summer apart from Ingrid Schorr, a friend of Michael's who had recently become Mike's girlfriend. Unfortunately, they'd discovered each other just before her departure for her family's home in suburban Maryland. Feeling bereft at the prospect of a summer without her, Mike sat down with his guitar and poured his heart into a straightforward lament sung to a catchy folk-country melody: "(Don't Go Back to) Rockville."

The foursome's group compositions took on even greater sophistication. Not long after Mike unveiled "Rockville," they worked together to come up with "Gardening at Night," which felt like an even bigger breakthrough: An archetype for a song on which all four members' unique strengths wove together into an entirely original kind of tune. Starting with a taut two-note guitar riff from Peter, the song blossomed almost instantly. They added Mike's bass and Bill's drums to a set of ringing open chords, which descended chromatically toward a quick drum break that kicked off a verse built around a slightly different descending pattern. Here Michael stepped up, singing urgently about money tossed on the floor, feelings that weren't quite real, and a yard so desolate there's only a fence and a glaring, blinding sun.

It must be time for penitence / gardening at night is never where.

The words came rattling out, an indistinct blur. Images, characters, and thoughts linked only by the urgency of Michael's delivery. Neighbors intrude, early sleepers who call a prayer line for guidance, for which they pay dearly. An older sister wags a censorious finger, but she's hiding her own sins, and there's nothing about this scene that isn't topsy-turvy, upside-down, day-for-night, leading to that same thought about penitence and the futility of growing crops beneath the moonlight: *Gardening at night, it's never where.*

Gardening at night is never . . . *where*, exactly? Michael doesn't complete the thought, but it doesn't matter, because everything else speaks so clearly: Peter arpeggiates the chords so they chime like bells; Mike's super-fluid bass fills in the open space beneath the guitar; and Bill keeps his drumming fast and economical, pushing the rhythm without intruding on the feeling in Michael's voice, which communicates so much more than the words of his tale could convey on their own.

"Sitting Still" starts with a different but equally tuneful descending chord pattern, then settles into an easier groove, Peter's guitar alternating between strums and arpeggios while Mike's bass thrums against the drums and Michael pieces syllables and phrases into a mosaic of words:

> *Up to par and Katie bars*
> *The kitchen signs but not me in*

Words on top of words. Again the narrative is murky, nearly abstract, but the feeling of the song comes through loud and clear, in the warmth in Michael's voice, in the tuneful jangle of Peter's guitar, which dandles notes above the foundational thrum and snap of the rhythm section, then most movingly in the chorus, a bloom of guitars and backing voices over which a single phrase circles. *I-I-I can hear, I-I-I can hear, I-I-I . . . can hear.* And as the four members of R.E.M. were fast discovering, it was in that space, in the blur between obscurity and tenderness, that the heart of the band resided.

By early 1981 R.E.M.'s performances consisted almost entirely of original songs, including a growing array of the newer, more imaginative compositions. "Shaking Through," "Ages of You," "Windout," and "Get on Their Way" all premiered in or around January 1981, as did another new high-water mark, "Radio Free Europe." Skittering and upbeat, the song was a showcase for Michael's growing skill not just as a lyricist but also a writer of melodies that were as memorable as they were unexpected. The vocal line in "Radio Free Europe," strung across chords provided by Peter, Bill, and Mike, follows the texture of the song, skipping quickly around the simple changes in the verse. Then, as the guitar shifts to an unresolved suspended chord, it stays on one note for several beats, like a dancer hanging in midair. It's the transformative moment in the song, the point where a simple three-chord rock tune becomes something else entirely, and Michael's ability to isolate and amplify the emotion in the music stopped his bandmates in their tracks.

"I'll never forget the time . . . I heard the melody Michael put over it," Mike said to reporters from a British fanzine a few years later, capturing his surprise in confused yelps: "Where? How? Why? When?" Michael's lyrics, which tangled a media critique into stray thoughts about immigration and, it seems, nationalism, flowed as easily and enigmatically as his other newer compositions, and the song was an instant crowd favorite when they introduced it at Tyrone's at the end of January.

Eager to move beyond the narrow circuit they'd been traversing between Athens, Atlanta, and the college towns of North Carolina, the band decided to take their best songs into a recording studio and make a promotional tape to use as a calling card for bookings. They made their first try in early February, reserving six hours of time in a small studio near Atlanta. For a bargain rate of $15 an hour, the basement space even included the services of producer/studio owner Joe Perry (not the Aerosmith guitarist). They banged out eight of their best songs ("Radio Free Europe," "Sitting Still," "Gardening at Night," "Mystery to Me," "(Don't Go Back to) Rockville," "Shaking Through," "Narrator," and a neo-surf-rock instrumental they titled "White Tornado") but the recording they emerged with sounded so flat, and the mix so dead, that they decided to trash it.

In search of a good but inexpensive studio to work in, Holt spoke to Peter Holsapple, a friend from North Carolina who was one of the founders of the indie power-pop band the dB's. Holsapple connected him with Mitch Easter, a Winston-Salem musician who had just built a recording studio in his parents' garage. Easter, who still played guitar in his own bands, wasn't certain how much energy he wanted to dedicate to recording other bands, but when R.E.M. came to play at the Pier nightclub in early April and dropped by Easter's house to spend an evening getting acquainted, he began to sense where his future lay. "I realized this is what I like doing . . . meeting rock people I like and playing records."[1]

The band returned about ten days later and set up in the Easter family's garage (which Easter dubbed Drive-In Studio) to take another stab at recording. This time they limited themselves to three songs: "Radio Free Europe," "Sitting Still," and "White Tornado." Easter was impressed with the year-old band from Athens, and not just by the quality of their songs and the professionalism they brought to the sessions but also with how distinctive their personalities were, and how easily they melded into a unit. "Peter was totally a central-casting record store guy," Easter says. "He knew everything that existed and could tell you what was on the B-side, in a really digs-it kind of way. Michael wanted to talk about these little pieces of copper he was melting glaze on—he really was an art student and was very creative."

Bill and Mike were obviously the most experienced musicians in the group; both halves of the rhythm section were conversant enough with other instruments to double on keyboard or vibes parts when needed. "Bill and Mike were more conventional musicians—they'd been in bands that played 'Whipping Post,'" the Allman Brothers' epic blues jam. But what really impressed Easter was how easily the conventional musicians worked with the less experienced, and quirky, bandmates in their midst. "When I listen to those records now, it's great how much oddness there is in Michael, and he was as confident of his place in the band as anyone. I remember all of them being really confident in a really jolly way. They didn't have a hierarchy in the band, and they had fantastic respect for each other, which is remarkable. They were also quite young, and a lot of young people aren't that nice. Their egos get in the way. But these guys were emotionally mature."[2]

When the recording was done, they dubbed the tracks onto a hundred or so cassettes, put them into cases they'd hand-decorated over the usual credits and contact information and the hopefully intriguing instruction DO NOT OPEN, and shotgunned them to club owners, bookers, and music writers in key cities around the nation. Meanwhile, word of the up-and-coming band had found its way to Jonny Hibbert, an Atlanta musician (lead singer of a band called the Incredible Throbs) who had recently traded the stage for law school. But Hibbert still had a hankering for the music business, and with an eye toward starting his own record company he had asked a friend who knew the Athens scene if there were any other bands that might follow the arc of the B-52's, from nowheresville to the upper reaches of the record charts. She told him about R.E.M., a band she said was really tearing it up, and at some point in the winter of 1981 Hibbert drove up to the university town to catch a show at Tyrone's. Impressed by what he saw, he came back to see them again early in the spring and introduced himself to the band after their set. They remembered the Incredible Throbs, Hibbert says, and were excited he'd come to see them. They were even more delighted to hear his offer to record and release a single for them. "They expressed a lot of admiration and enthusiasm," he says, "so it was on."[3]

The single, the first to be released on what Hibbert called Hib-Tone Records, would feature "Radio Free Europe" on the A-side and "Sitting Still" on the flip. Feeling like he had an ear for these things, Hibbert drove up to Winston-Salem, North Carolina, to enhance and remix "Radio Free Europe" for commercial release. The extent of his influence on the finished release depends on whose version of events resonates with you the most, but what was inarguable was that the deal they put together traded Hibbert's expenses and labor for ownership not just of the songs' master recordings but also their publishing rights. Bertis Downs didn't like this one bit: he knew where the real money in rock 'n' roll was. But Peter, Michael, Mike, and Bill were happy to make that trade. Hey, they'd already written a lot of songs, and they were writing more and better songs all the time. If they had to give these two up to get themselves to the next level of the music business, *to be a band that had a record out*, that was a sacrifice they were willing to make.

The Hib-Tone release of "Radio Free Europe" came out in late July.

14

Lots of Impressive First-Time Songs

At home in Athens, Peter practiced with obsessive focus. Hour after hour after hour. Guitar in his lap, the familiar weight across his thighs, the strings digging into his fingertips. "My brother [John] lived upstairs from him at 169 Barber Street, and I remember hearing Pete playing," Sam Seawright, who studied art at UGA, says. "He'd have a record and you could hear him pick the needle up and he'd play it over and over and over. Learning riffs and stuff off of records."[1] Teasing it out in slow motion at first, tracking down the notes on the fretboard. The shape of the chords, the way they slid together. First the left hand, the melody and the chords, and then the right hand, the rhythm of the strumming and picking. He'd stop, listen again, stop the record, and then play some more. Listen and play. Listen again, then play. Repeat. Repeat. Repeat.

"I'd hear him painstakingly learning riffs," says photographer Terry Allen, who lived in another one of the apartments in the house. "Playing the record, pausing it, trying to play it, putting the record back on, over and over and over again."[2]

When Peter talked about it in public, he made it all sound like an accident. He hadn't set out to be in a band; he just met a guy who was also into music, and then they met these other guys who were into playing music, and they all started playing together because there was nothing else to do. Another friend asked them to play at her party and one thing led to another and it was still just because they were friends who all liked music and were living in a boring town where you had to make your own entertainment.

"This is the first band I've been in," Peter told one reporter a few years later. "When the band started I knew about five chords and a Chuck Berry lick. I didn't even know bar chords."[3] This was, at best, only partially true. By 1980 Peter had been playing for nearly a decade, and if he hadn't made himself into a sizzle-fingered soloist in the Clapton-Page mode, it was because he had a whole other idea. The rock 'n' roll stage was swarmed with aspiring guitar heroes, all twisting their faces into pained rictuses of concentration as they squeezed epic runs out of their Strats and Les Pauls. Peter was much more interested in writing songs, particularly ones that emphasized texture and feel, and the interplay of a dynamic ensemble.

For Peter, being a part of a band was more compelling than being the star of one. He'd always been too stubborn an individual to join things—teams, clubs, any kind of student groups. But the joint identity that came with being in a band called to him. The threads of rebellion and connection, of joining with friends to take over the world, or at least a small part of it, had captivated him since he was a kid, his bedside table stacked high with the books and magazines that told the stories behind all the records that mattered to him. Hunter Davies's authorized biography of the Beatles; Robert Greenfield's *STP (Stones Touring Party)*, about the Rolling Stones' 1972 tour of America; *Nobody Here Gets Out Alive*, the biography of Jim Morrison. *Rolling Stone, Creem*, and the other music journals reported on all those acts and dozens, hundreds, of others.[4] All of the backstage stories and in-studio accounts, the road journals. How the bands came together, how they found their shared voice, working their way from the basement or someone's garage to neighborhood clubs, talent shows, and the barroom circuit. How they wrote songs, got recording contracts, and went into the studio to craft their first records. How they took their new sounds on the road, playing bars, showrooms, and theaters, and finally into the cavernous concrete palaces,

the arenas and stadiums where it all became triumphant, then surreal, then dangerous and, almost inevitably, deadly.

One article about Jefferson Starship made an impact. After the
revived '60s band had a surprise number three hit with the single
"Miracles" in 1975, and the song lifted their album *Red Octopus* to the
top of the charts, their drummer took note of the songwriting royalties his bandmates were collecting and demanded that the next album
include some of his tunes. The conflict added to the tension in the
already fraught band, which started shedding members soon after. As
Peter noted in his reading, that sort of disagreement happened again
and again with rock bands. And it seemed so ridiculous to put a band
together and do all the work it took to create a unique sound, build a
following, and score a hit, only to let such an obvious and predictable
argument blow it apart.

Not many young musicians thought that far ahead. But this was
the sort of thing that spun through Peter's mind while he listened to
his records and ran his fingers up and down the frets of his guitar. All
four of the guys in the band were writing songs, or coming up with
riffs and chord progressions that could be made into songs. So far
it'd been an easygoing process: the initial discovery of their collective voice had been so exciting, and the stakes of ownership so small,
they didn't have to establish who had written what. Which meant
they hadn't even started to consider how they'd divide songwriting
credits, and royalties, if they started making records. But then they
recorded a few songs, the deal with Jonny Hibbert came up, and
suddenly they *were* making records. One, at least, and they needed
to establish who had written it. Then Bertis Downs, who was still
shaking his head over the band's agreeing to give Hibbert the publishing rights to "Radio Free Europe" and "Sitting Still" in exchange
for putting out the record, suggested they get ahead of the game
by establishing their own publishing company and, while they were
at it, incorporating the band. The musicians thought it was absurd.
Did they really need to jump through so many hoops to protect the
little wads of cash they were collecting from Tyrone's or the 688 or
wherever else they played? But Downs was firm, and convincing. He
wasn't going to charge them anything; he just wanted to make sure
nobody else was in a position to screw them over.

Meanwhile, Peter had another idea: to keep themselves from fighting and breaking up the way so many other bands had, they should agree now to divide all the credit and money for their work in equal shares. All original songs produced by R.E.M. would be credited to Berry-Buck-Mills-Stipe, no matter who was responsible for how much of an individual song's creation. All of the band's proceeds should also be divided equally, but into fifths, with Jefferson Holt receiving 20 percent for his contributions. The four musicians voted; all agreed. R.E.M. would be a confederation of equals: all for one, one for all.

A couple of months after his meeting with Don Braxley at Paragon in Macon, Bill called Ian Copeland in New York, where he was launching Frontier Booking International (FBI), his own booking agency. They caught up for a bit, and Bill got to what seemed to be the point of his call. The Police, the British trio managed by Copeland's brother Miles and booked by Ian, were coming to Atlanta's Fox Theatre in December. Could Bill get on the pass list for the show, and bring his buddy Mike Mills, too? Of course; not a problem. Oh, and had Ian heard that he and Mike were playing in a band in Athens now? Bill gave him the whole rundown: how they'd started at a party or two, moved into Athens bars, then Atlanta, and then played up in North Carolina and a couple of nights in Nashville. And they were doing well, too . . . especially in Athens, where they actually played to packed houses. And they even had a manager now. Copeland had always liked Bill; beneath that mighty dark brow and laconic sense of humor thumped the heart of a go-getter. Even as a teenage office boy, Bill had kept his eyes open and gotten the details right. He wasn't a bullshitter: if he said his band was tearing it up down there, Copeland didn't doubt it. With the Police's itinerary in front of him, he had an idea. Original openers XTC couldn't make the tour, so now they didn't have an opener for Atlanta. Why didn't Bill's band take the slot? Bill's initial surprise—Really? Seriously?—gave way to certainty. He didn't have to run it by the others. Of course they'd do it.[5]

It was a huge break. And yet R.E.M.'s first theater show, in front of a sold-out crowd of four thousand at the Fox Theatre, was a mixed bag. Accustomed to the confines of a nightclub, Michael didn't know how, or if, to address whoever was watching from the back, or off in the balconies, somewhere in the blackness above them. But as Copeland noted, the songs had a propulsive energy that drew the crowd in and kept them engaged throughout the set. Michael had good instincts as a performer, and even if he infuriated the promoter by inviting the crowd to join the band onstage for their final song, Copeland's congratulations afterward were heartfelt. Bill kept the agent apprised of the band's progress during the first months of 1981, and when Gang of Four needed an opening act for a half dozen East Coast dates in the late spring, including two showcase shows at the Ritz in New York City, the agent invited R.E.M. to join the tour.

All through the winter and spring, the band gained momentum. They were still playing the loop they'd established in the college towns of Georgia and North Carolina, with occasional jaunts to Tennessee, but the bookings were coming at an ever-increasing pace, usually at a clip of about three or four a week. The three-song sampler cassettes had gone out earlier in the spring, with their DO NOT OPEN instruction on the box, targeting club owners, college radio programmers, and some journalists. Most of the results were hard to quantify, but the entire project paid off just before they got to New York, in the form of a brief note in the music column of *Village Voice* critic Robert Christgau, who recommended their upcoming appearance at the Ritz by mentioning the young Georgia band had been "sending out a tape with lots of impressive first time songs on it."[6]

Ian Copeland saw the column—the musicians made sure he didn't miss it—and it primed him for an opening set that got his heart thumping. The band he saw at the Ritz, performing in more intimate surroundings with an additional six months of experience and a set full of newer, better songs, solidified his confidence in Bill and his band. The foursome still had rough edges, but they played with a strength and confidence that made it sound raw and thrilling. After the set he came back to the dressing room and made his offer. FBI didn't ordinarily work with bands that didn't have record company deals, but Copeland could sense that it was just a matter of time for R.E.M., and besides, they were already good enough for him to sign now. The four musicians were thrilled.

Holt was already thinking of the next step. Ian's brother Miles was fast establishing his independent label I.R.S. Records, whose roster included a litany of leading indie and punk bands, including the Go-Go's, the Damned, the Stranglers, the Cramps, and John Cale. Could he help them get set up with Miles? Ian couldn't make any promises.

Just a few weeks later, the single of "Radio Free Europe," with "Sitting Still" on its B-side, was officially released by Hib-Tone Records. Hibbert pressed a few thousand, many of which he sent as promotional copies to radio programmers, and especially to the college stations that had the youth and the progressive ears to give a listen to a band nobody had heard of from a town nobody had heard of on a label nobody had heard of. But they were college kids too, playing music that would resonate with their generational cohort.

Hibbert was heading into his final year in law school, working two jobs to keep himself afloat. As he recalls, he passed his late nights and early mornings doing publicity for the record, taking advantage of the low overnight rates to dial the studio lines of the college stations he knew had received copies of R.E.M.'s premiere single. "I'd get 'em on the phone and ask if they'd heard the new R.E.M. record," Hibbert says. "I'd say, 'I know it's in the stack, go dig it up. All I'm asking is that you play it for yourself, and if you like it put it on the air. I'll call you back in ten or fifteen minutes." He'd keep an eye on his watch, then call back as promised. "And they'd say, 'Oh, man, it's on the air and I'm getting phone calls!' And it'd be like 2:30 or 3 a.m. on college campuses all over the country."

As they would learn a few months later, "Radio Free Europe" wasn't just getting noticed on college campuses. In Minneapolis, Peter Jesperson, who managed the Oar Folkjokeopus record store, on Lyndale Avenue, picked it up the moment R.E.M.'s disc had its turn among all the new indie singles he was auditioning in the store. "I remember two or three of us listening to the Hib-Tone record and we lit up instantly. That snappy drumbeat, and the chiming guitar, and the fact that you couldn't figure out what the fuck he was singing made it all the more intriguing. And we went bananas." Jesperson ordered a dozen copies and was both chagrined and intrigued to see them all bought up by his staffers. He had another twenty-five shipped in and, with the single on heavy rotation on the store's sound system, sold them all in a day and a half. With a large clientele of outsider types who came in specifically to find records they would never hear on the radio, Jespersen's store was, he recalls, part clubhouse and part radio station. "People would come in and say, 'What's good and new?' and you'd put the needle on the R.E.M. single and it was like, *boing,* sold."[7]

Robert Palmer of *The New York Times* had the same reaction. When the newspaper of record printed his selections of the year's best releases on December 30, the daily's chief pop critic's list included the latest albums by X, the Rolling Stones, David Byrne, and Rickie Lee Jones, along with singles by Prince, Yoko Ono, Chic, and Grandmaster Flash. And the tenth best single of the year, Palmer decreed, was the one he listed as "Sitting Still"/"Radio Free Europe," by R.E.M.

15

Wolves Out the Door

The beast slips through the darkness, light on its paws, muscles taut but pliant. His ears twitch, his nose sifts the loam and the leaf, seeking, always seeking. The wolf in the night, wild with appetite and wily in his hunt. He knows what he's after, just as he knows what's after him.

Suspicion yourself, suspicion yourself, don't get caught.

The words are oblique, the action just beyond the edge of the frame. What isn't said comes through clearly in the whirling guitar and the skittering heartbeat of the drums, in the thrumming bass and the sinister edge in the voice. *Wilder, lower wolves*, he sings from deep in his chest. *Wolves out the door.*

Or maybe it's *wolves* at *the door.* The confusion is both minor and, in a way, crucial to the narrative. The elusiveness. The not knowing. "Wolves, Lower," a new song that emerged in the midst of a long haul of dates in the fall of 1981, and in the immediate wake of a short run through New York, describes the fangs of desire through the perspective of both the predator and the predated. Maybe they're one and the same.

On May 9, 1981, R.E.M. drove to Princeton, New Jersey, to play Princeton University's annual Beaux Arts Ball, a seemingly traditional college social that took a turn for the bizarre thanks to the year's theme, Lust in Space. As Peter recalled, the affair was a large-scale preppie bacchanal, thronged by drunken Ivy Leaguers dressed as intergalactic sex creatures, complete with extraterrestrial dildos hand-fashioned from aluminum foil. The booking had come through an art student named David Healey, who had first seen the band while visiting his girlfriend in Chapel Hill, North Carolina. Like Jefferson Holt and Bertis Downs, Healey was inspired not just to meet and befriend the band but also to do whatever he could to help them. He got them the Beaux Arts gig, then made sure they had someplace to stay when they were in town.

It was a big weekend for Healey, an art major whose thesis project was about to open as an exhibit at a university gallery. His musician friends not only were happy to see the show, they also agreed to provide music at the party. When they came to New York a little later, Healey had his parents put the band up in the family's home in Greenwich, Connecticut. Talking to Holt about the band's recording prospects, Healey had an idea: he could get some money together and help them start their own record company. They already had a single out, so they could take the next step: record four or six of their best new songs and release an EP. Healey would co-own the company with the band, and because he was done with school and could go anywhere, he'd move down to Athens to be close enough to really be a part of it. They all liked the sound of that, so Healey borrowed $2,000 from his dad, convinced some friends to pony up a few grand more, then packed up his stuff and drove to Georgia. The new company, they all agreed, would be called Dasht Hopes.

Given the momentum created by the "Radio Free Europe" single and a handful of newer, arguably even stronger songs, Holt and Healey decided the time had come for R.E.M. to go back into the recording studio. The band drove to Winston-Salem at the start of October and spent a weekend working with Easter in his Drive-In Studio, emerging with finished or close-to-finished recordings of "Gardening at Night," "Ages of You," and a new take on the instrumental "White Tornado," along with the newer songs "1,000,000," "Stumble," "Shaking Through," and, most intriguingly, "Carnival of Sorts

(Boxcars)," a dark fantasia describing a circus traveling by train, the animals, carnies, and performing freaks bound by a secret stigma, the train wheels spinning into reaping wheels. *Don't get caught*, Michael warns, again. The sessions, Peter told the magazine *Trouser Press* in 1983, were heavily experimental, with extensive use of overdubs and looped, often backward sounds.[1] "We were looking for a claustrophobic effect, like you're struggling into a world where you don't know what's going on and you have to figure it out by using clues," he said to the same magazine a year later. "It was a learning experience."[2]

The band took a brief break in the middle of the month, then headed back to New York to play a few dates, including a lackluster set delivered to a scattering of under-enthusiastic observers at Zappa's, a grungy rock club in the Marine Park section of outer Brooklyn. But a free show at Tribeca's Mudd Club a few nights later went much better. Kurt Munkacsi saw the band and was struck immediately by what he heard. "I thought they were fantastic," he says. "They were very well formed, completely together, and they had a distinct sound."

Munkacsi, who worked regularly with the modern classical composer Philip Glass, had also produced sessions for the Waitresses (including their breakthrough single "I Know What Boys Like") and the North Carolina–bred alt-pop band the dB's. He ventured out to see the band from Athens at the behest of his friend Jim Fouratt, a club booker who was also hoping to launch a music production company. Munkacsi, who had particularly close contacts at RCA Records, was friendly with Fouratt and quite happy to get involved with his recording schemes, particularly with a band as intriguing as the foursome from Georgia. "They really knew what they were doing. From a craft point of view, their songs were really well constructed. With other bands you didn't know where the songs started and stopped, but these guys were a tight unit, with a real defined sound."[3] Munkacsi recommended the band to his colleagues at RCA, and they agreed to fund a studio audition. Fouratt contacted Holt, who set aside a couple of days during the band's next visit to New York at the end of January.

———

The band's intentions for RCA were unclear. They were already working on the EP they planned to release themselves and had their long-term sights set most intently on Miles Copeland's I.R.S. Records, whose catalog of punkish and new wave bands felt like much better company for R.E.M. No matter: they were excited to meet Munkacsi in person when he came to see their performance at Maxwell's, in Hoboken, on January 30. And when they went to RCA's studios on East Twenty-Fourth Street the next morning, the musicians were eager to work in a real professional studio and to see how RCA's executives would respond to their music. The four musicians and their manager arrived on time and cheerfully set up their gear in Studio C, the largest of the company's rooms, according to Munkacsi's instructions.

Getting to work, the band was exceptionally prepared and easy to deal with, Munkacsi recalls. The goal of the session was to capture the band's sound as it existed, rather than expand on it with an intricate weave of overdubs and orchestration. The four musicians were upbeat and engaged in the process and were quite respectful of the producer and the other staff engaged in the session. "Sometimes you get a hostility from bands, but they were very friendly," Munkacsi says. "They knew what they wanted, and when it was right or wrong."[4] They ran through seven songs, including the new tunes they'd been recording with Mitch Easter in North Carolina, all of which they'd been performing in clubs and were quite comfortable playing. They captured all the basic tracks on the first day, then spent the next day overdubbing Michael's vocals and a few piano parts by Mike. One of Munkacsi's most vivid memories of the sessions is his exchange with Michael about the best way to record his singing. "Michael wanted to make sure you couldn't understand the lyrics," he says. Munkacsi, who had produced Philip Glass operas with lyrics that were largely made up of numbers, was not fazed. "It was part of the sound, what they wanted."[5]

When it was over, Munkacsi took the band and their manager out to dinner at a comfortable Japanese restaurant and was tickled by how thrilled they were to be treated to a meal by the munificence of a large record company. He was also struck by the evident affection they had for one another. "When you hear about bands, you hear about arguments and people throwing things, having fights. But they were respectful of each other; everything was discussed, no infighting. And nobody threw a tantrum."

Munkacsi delivered the tapes to RCA's executives, who gave the music a quick listen and came back a day or two later with an offer. But RCA was a big company, and not especially eager to make a long-term commitment to an untried band from a small college town nobody had ever heard of. So the company's offer was about as limited as it could be: they'd put out a four-song EP, see how it did, and then, maybe, make a more substantive offer. It was something, just not nearly enough.

In Atlanta, R.E.M. had piqued Mark Williams's interest the first time they came to perform at the 688 Club. The college DJ at Georgia State University, moonlighting as the club's disc jockey, bonded with Michael Stipe after soundcheck one afternoon when he spun an obscure British industrial noise record, one of the offbeat things he played to set the mood before they opened the doors for the evening. "He came up to me and said, 'Wow, Throbbing Gristle!' We had the same taste in music."[6] He and the singer were pals after that, and Peter was even easier to talk to, flipping through the records in his booth, asking about his work at the college station and the bands coming through the club. They were all the same age, more or less, all listening to the same records, following the same bands.

Williams also got to know Holt and Downs when they came to the club for shows and tracked the Athens band's swift ascent from unknown opener to reliable headliner. When Jonny Hibbert brought a copy of "Radio Free Europe" to the Georgia State radio station offices, Williams made a point of playing it on the air. The phones usually started blinking when it came on—listeners wanting to know who that was, where they could find it. He was only twenty, a college kid with a backpack full of books and classwork that needed doing. But Williams wanted to do something for his friends in the band. And he could.

Williams had come to the attention of the publicists at A&M Records and scored another job as a campus representative for the label. His favorite releases always came from I.R.S. Records, whose music A&M distributed, and he'd connected with the company's vice president Jay Boberg, a busy but approachable twenty-three-year-old who had been an A&M college rep at UCLA just a couple of years earlier. When Williams got a copy of R.E.M.'s three-song demo tape in 1981, he forwarded it to Boberg. "Something's happening here," he wrote in his note. Boberg listened and was intrigued, but, as he recalls, nobody else at the company shared his enthusiasm. "They weren't willing to hear what seemed so obvious to me, because it wasn't punk," he says. "I'd play it and people would go, '*Whuuuuut?*' But there were melodies and hooks all over it, and it was so original, and I loved it."[7]

It was a new kind of post-punk, alternative music that straddled obscurity and directness, dissent and delicacy, unapologetic and unashamed pure pop. Boberg knew he was hearing something special, but he also had a lot going on, and it was hard to find a moment to push forward on a band nobody else at the office cared about. But Boberg was I.R.S.'s founding vice president, and because founder and president Miles Copeland couldn't afford to pay him much, he had a stake in the company. And, along with that, authority to pursue nearly anyone who interested him.

Early in 1982, Boberg got in touch with Jefferson Holt and asked him to send the band's itinerary for the next month or two. Boberg's girlfriend was in graduate school at Tulane University, and when he saw that the band had a date in New Orleans in mid-March, he scheduled a trip. Holt had also sent over a tape of the new songs they'd been working on with Mitch Easter, and it only deepened the young executive's enthusiasm. When he walked into the Beat Exchange, a small, grungy club, on the evening of March 12, Boberg was nearly certain he was going to try to sign R.E.M.

For the band it started as a dud of an evening. The club was cramped and smelled like a dumpster, which might have been why it was so deserted on a Friday night. Boberg remembers an audience of maybe half a dozen people, plus a hazy-eyed soundman who seemed to be nodding off during the set. No matter: once the band started playing, he was transfixed. "I was familiar with the songs already. But onstage they had this energy, this interplay. Michael was in his own world, but Mike and Pete had this chemistry. And Michael was so interesting to watch. Sometimes he'd sing with his back to the audience, which sounds like the wrong thing to do, but it created this sense of mystery and, in a weird way, a greater connection with the audience. Michael created intimacy through mystery, and this kind of coyish sort of thing."[8]

After the set Boberg went to the dressing room and introduced himself. *Hi, I'm Jay from I.R.S.* Michael, perched on a countertop, his body folded into itself like origami, cringed. They were afraid he'd be there; it was such a sucky night . . . Boberg waved him off. He knew the mix was shitty, but he'd loved what he'd heard anyway. Did they want to meet for lunch and talk more the next day? The musicians glanced at one another, brows cocked. Yes, of course they did. They met at an oyster loaf restaurant the next day and Boberg set to charming them, asking how they saw their future, what they wanted to do with their music, what kind of records they wanted to make. They'd already been hoping to sign with I.R.S., but Boberg gave them the sales talk anyway, about how the company really was about the music, and how they'd be able to make the records they wanted to make and do things exactly as they wanted to. "We basically agreed they'd sign."[9]

Boberg's enthusiasm, and a deal built on a commitment for several albums, instantly blew RCA's more tentative offer out of contention. It also spelled a quick end to their relationship with Jonny Hibbert and his Hib-Tone Records. And then there was David Healey and Dasht Hopes.

From the first time he heard it, at a show in North Carolina that fall, "Wolves, Lower" spun David Healey's head around. This was a few weeks after the October sessions in North Carolina and the new song struck him immediately: *You guys gotta record that! Sure*, they replied. *Pony up the dough and we'll do it.* Healey, eager to add another solid track to the first EP they'd been planning to issue on their Dasht Hopes label, found the money, and in late January 1982, on their way to the New York visit that included the RCA audition, they stopped in Winston-Salem for another two days of work at Drive-In Studio.

They finished an early, fast version of "Wolves" and "Carnival of Sorts (Boxcars)" and took a first stab at "Catapult" before continuing north for the studio sessions and dates around New York City, plus others in Washington, D.C., and Boston. They were racking up the miles in their van, and after one show the thing ground to a halt. In search of the $200 it would take to get back on the road, they called Healey to hit him up for the dough. But Healey was tapped out, or that's how Peter recalled it to the writer Rodger Lyle Brown. "We got back home and fired him."[10]

Dasht Hopes indeed. But Healey had problems beyond his unwillingness to part with the money they needed for the van. A talented artist with a charismatic personality, he was also prone to fits of darkness that he fended off, and perhaps made worse, with alcohol and other drugs. But while his musician friends entertained many of the same appetites, they had a level of discipline and an emotional foundation Healey lacked. "David had incredible magnetism, but also a big self-destruct button," says his brother Bill, a psychiatrist.[11] The relationship was strained before the other record companies entered their lives, and once they appeared, Healey was not just superfluous but troublesome. The broken van symbolized a relationship that had already stopped working.

Presumably, the band repaid Healey for his investment. But they were going to have to work a much more intricate deal to settle accounts with Jonny Hibbert, the former musician who had founded Hib-Tone Records to issue their first single. They hadn't liked the mix of "Radio Free Europe" he had come up with (though they subsequently used it on a compilation released in 1988), and Hibbert says Jefferson Holt did everything he could to alienate the musicians from him, complaining bitterly, and inaccurately, Hibbert says, that he wasn't promoting the record. His exclusive right to the recordings, he recalls, was only six months. But he owned the metal masters and, most significantly, the publishing rights to "Radio Free Europe" and its B-side, "Sitting Still," outright. As the band's legal adviser, Bertis Downs had cautioned them against selling off their publishing, and made no secret of his dismay when they agreed to give Hibbert the rights to their first two songs. And now that they were going to be recording for I.R.S., an indie big enough to launch million-selling records, they were determined to get the songs back. Downs approached Hibbert offering to buy back all their rights for $1,000 per song, but Hibbert wanted to negotiate a better deal. As much as $10,000, according to Peter,[12] who said Hibbert threatened to sell the rights to another song publisher who had offered him that much for the songs.

This was not a price R.E.M. was willing to pay. And Hibbert, who was working his way through law school as a stagehand at Atlanta's Omni Coliseum, says he began to realize how displeased they were when he was wheeling amplifiers through a tunnel after a concert and was approached by Andy Slater. A recent Emory University graduate who had known Peter during his college days, Slater was just starting a career that would take him from contributing stories to *Rolling Stone* to becoming, in 2001, president of Capitol Records, and the two men already knew each other. "I said, 'Hey, Andy!'" Hibbert recalls. "And he waved me over and gets this mobster voice, really serious, and said, 'I hear the boys are making you an offer for all of the stuff.' I'm quoting him word for word. What he said was 'Give them what they want or else your name will be mud.'"[13]

The threat, however veiled it might have been, wasn't necessary. Hibbert needed cash a lot more than he wanted to hold out for a bigger payoff. What he wound up with, he says, was a little more than their original $2,000 offer. "I promised Bertis I wouldn't go into this part. But my back was up against the wall. I had debts out of the original deal, and my stress knob was already at eleven. I just didn't have what it takes to tell them to go to hell. Look, I'm really proud of the guys I knew. The fresh, eager, focused, and urgent band. I loved that urgency. But I would really not be representing myself fairly if I were to say that the treatment, or lack thereof, of me by the band didn't carry a little bit of pain."[14]

Wolves out the door . . . Down there they're rounding a posse to ride.

16

Chronic Town, Poster Torn

Jay Boberg came back from New Orleans certain that R.E.M. was going to be the next act signed to I.R.S. Records. Technically he needed Miles Copeland's sign-off to make it so, but he already knew that his boss would back him, particularly given his brother Ian Copeland's enthusiasm and the fact that Ian had already signed the foursome to his FBI booking agency. Everyone else at the company, Boberg recalls, greeted the band with something closer to a collective shrug. They'd hand the tape back to Boberg and kind of nod. There wasn't anything *wrong* with it; it wasn't like this band was *hurting* anyone. But that was the problem. The punk scene, the whole post-hippie, outside-the-mainstream zeitgeist of the early '80s, *wanted* music to hurt. Or at least be troublesome to somebody.

"People didn't get it at first," Boberg says. "They weren't a punk band. It's nothing like listening to the Sex Pistols or the Cramps. There's full-on melodies and hooks everywhere, words you don't understand you can still sing along to."[1] Boberg had been listening to the songs for months, not quite connecting with them at first but always intrigued enough to put the tape back in the machine, hit play, and hear the whirling guitar, the leaping bass and loping drums, the odd vocabulary and shadowy inflections of the singer. The thing they made was both elusive and magnetic. He didn't get it, certainly not at first, but the intelligence of it kept drawing him back. That and all those melodies. Now he'd seen what the band could do onstage, even with a crappy mix and a small, ambivalent crowd, he was convinced.

I.R.S. didn't have the money to give out significant advances, but as Holt and Downs made clear during their talks, R.E.M. was happy to take a small per-album guarantee if they could control how their records sounded and looked. Presentation was particularly important to Michael, given his grounding in visual art. But they were all determined to keep a tight hand on their music—which songs they'd record, how those recordings would be produced, mixed, and mastered. That, Boberg says, was the standing agreement the label had with all its artists. "We were very into [giving artists] creative control. We believed we signed artists who had a vision, and we were there to maximize it, not change it," he says.[2]

The artist-centric record company model had been perfected in the rock era by Warner Bros. Records in the late 1960s, led by company chairman Mo Ostin, who along with fellow executive Joe Smith anticipated the generational shift from clean-cut pop idols like Frankie Avalon to shaggy countercultural oracles such as Jimi Hendrix and the Grateful Dead. Allowing the artists near-complete authority over their music not only respected their artistry but was also a canny commercial strategy, given the artists' superior grasp on what would appeal to their audience: a youthful, rambunctious throng just growing into adulthood, with adult-size spending power. It was paradoxical, to say the least. Respecting the anti-commercial whims of the artists and using the power of the record company's corporate financing to promote the artists' revolutionary ideals led to enormous sales and astounding profits for the corporation. A decade later, Miles Copeland's I.R.S. Records adapted the strategy for the next generation of music fans, replacing Hendrix and the Dead with Gary Numan and the Buzzcocks. They had pop acts too, such as the all-women Go-Go's, but even their sunny, radio-friendly singles came with an alternative spin, given their ability to make vintage pop tropes sound so fresh and cool: the musical equivalent of thrift store shopping. For R.E.M., a young band whose outsider vision was in no way opposed to appealing to a large-scale audience, it was a perfect fit.

Downs called in an experienced music industry attorney to help work through the finer points of the deal, then the entire band went to New York for a formal signing ceremony at I.R.S.'s East Coast offices in May. They dropped by Mitch Easter's studio in Winston-Salem in early June to make some small adjustments to "Wolves, Lower" and "Gardening at Night," then played shows around their usual Southeast haunts for the next two months before relocating to Los Angeles for a month. It was a busy few weeks for the band, Boberg recalls, full of photo sessions, a video shoot, and interviews with music writers. It also gave them a chance to connect with the staff of their new record company. "We spent a ton of time together," Boberg says. "I think we went to see a lot of other bands, and I know I went to record stores with Peter. And they got to meet the rest of the staff, which was about five people then."[3]

The video they shot was for "Wolves, Lower." The I.R.S. publicity staff set up the shoot for August 31, after the soundcheck for their set opening for the Minneapolis new wave band the Suburbs at the Club Lingerie, in Hollywood. If they were bemused by the task of performing for the camera, video outtakes from the shoot also reveal a giggling excitement at being the focus of so much industrial showbiz machination. Directed to sit together near their instruments, they come scampering like puppies, flopping together and then breaking spontaneously into the "Hey, hey, we're the Monkees" from the TV show theme song. Just a year into MTV's existence, the form was still in its infancy, and the clip, a basic performance video shot on the stage, hews closely to the accepted format, the band miming to the recorded track, with occasional cuts to Michael leaping in slow motion.

The "Wolves, Lower" video, the last lip-synching performance Michael would submit to for nearly a decade, didn't get much of an airing on MTV or anywhere else, but the band's opening set that night earned a rave in the *Los Angeles Times*, whose critic described the quartet as "disheveled choir boys" who kept the audience dancing even as they tried to figure out what to make of them. Were they more like the Byrds or the Psychedelic Furs? Herman's Hermits or U2? The comparisons didn't matter, he concluded. "The clean Rickenbacker guitar sound and the pretty vocal harmonies were compelling and strong . . . Playing with crisp dynamic force, R.E.M. delivered a power-pop set that was clean and light, but never lightweight."[4]

To get a foothold on the West Coast, the band steered their van around California, opening shows for the Suburbs, Romeo Void, the Untouchables, and, for a single show in Portland, Oregon, Gang of Four. Most went well enough, but the group was more concerned with the release of *Chronic Town* on August 24, 1982.

The accolades won by "Radio Free Europe" a year earlier had been encouraging, but the momentary enthusiasm of a couple of critics didn't guarantee anything, other than a more painful landing if the fuller vision on the EP didn't get the same kind of attention. Certainly Jay Boberg would see to it that I.R.S.'s publicity and promotions staffs would do everything they could. But all the band could do for their record was what they always did: get back in the van, drive to the next show, unload and set up the gear, play as well as they could, pack up their stuff, get back in the van, and do it all over again. They finished their California dates in mid-September, then played their way back across the Southwest, veered north to pick up shows in Nebraska, Missouri, Minnesota, and Illinois, then headed east to Ohio, Pennsylvania, New Jersey, New York, and Rhode Island before heading south and arriving back in Georgia in mid-October.

As the band moved eastward, *Chronic Town* landed in radio stations and on journalists' desks. It was an instant smash on the college airwaves, staying in the *College Media Journal* (*CMJ*)'s top five for three solid months. It sold briskly for a debut EP, moving more than twenty thousand copies in the first couple of months, and close to fifty thousand by the end of the year. The reviews were, if anything, more generous than the notices received by "Radio Free Europe." Though it received faint praise in Robert Christgau's *Village Voice* column ("For R.E.M. . . . hooks and a certain rough emotionality are part of the form, signifying only themselves, and that's not why I like rock 'n' roll"),[5] the UK's influential *New Musical Express* liked it just fine, calling *Chronic Town* "five songs that spring to life full of immediacy and action and healthy impatience. Songs that won't be denied."[6] *Creem* also came in impressed, describing the band's sound as something like a throwback to the music of the 1960s, but only in its imagination and inventiveness: "We have come to identify innocence with pop as if it springs from an eternal fountain of youth, but R.E.M. deflates that preconception by taking the full, gleeful sound of pop into the secret recesses of the mind."[7] *Musician* said there was only one thing wrong with the record: "You end up wishing for a larger dose."[8]

Peter's old Emory University classmate Andy Slater managed to land a short feature on the band in *Rolling Stone*, which mostly consisted of Michael and Peter explaining how different their band was from the B-52's, Pylon, and all the other acts from Athens. "Basically, we're just four pretty vague people," Peter said, explaining the obscurities in the *Chronic Town* songs. "We're definitely not writing in one specific tradition."[9] Or maybe they were just moving too quickly to come into focus. With or without Christgau's approval, *Chronic Town* was named the number two EP of 1982 in *The Village Voice*'s year-end critics' poll and ranked number forty-one in *CMJ*'s year-end chart. They were already on their way, boxcars rattling down the track, picking up speed.

17

Murmuring

Everywhere they went in 1982 and 1983, R.E.M. played their new material, most often turning in sets that were dominated by songs their audiences wouldn't have heard before. The crowds, drawn heavily if not entirely from the ranks of the students on the campuses they were either on or within a few blocks of, absorbed it happily, delighted to be hearing the new music just as the musicians were discovering it for themselves. To go to an R.E.M. show, or any show by one of the emerging art bands from Athens or any of the other alternative music scenes developing around the country, was a statement of purpose, or at least of membership. You were part of something new, something outside the ordinary, something that had nothing to do with conservative, mainstream society, politics, or, especially, the boomer-defined rock 'n' roll that had dominated the radio dial and the sales charts for more than a decade. When the normies went to a concert they flocked to a sports arena to see celebrities perform stock versions of well-worn hits. These other music shows were where the weird people could gather, the ones who didn't fit into the accepted categories of Reaganauts or retro-hippies. The freaks and the fags, the kids with sideways haircuts and oblique sexual interests. All of them pulled together by the off-kilter sound they heard, coming together to recognize one another and become a community.

And R.E.M. was part of it, too. After the shows, all four musicians made a point of quickly toweling off the sweat and throwing back a beer before going back out to meet the people who had stuck around to greet them. They'd shake hands, talk about the songs they'd played or other bands they knew or liked. And if someone invited them to a party, as often happened, they usually went. Of course they did: they were strangers in town, they didn't have anywhere else to go. Also, they were almost certainly hungry. They were still living on next to nothing from day to day, and chances were there'd be food, always a draw for fast-moving, underpaid musicians.

And their fans felt like their friends, even if they'd just met. They were all the same age, more or less, and all interested in the same kinds of books and politics and music. The house parties they went to on the road felt almost exactly like the ones they went to back home in Athens. Jason Ringenberg, whose band Jason & the Scorchers often shared bills with R.E.M., had plenty of opportunities to see his fellow musicians both on- and offstage, and was always impressed by how conscientiously they treated the people they met. "They had a philosophy as a band, that when they went to parties they represented R.E.M. and they needed to honor that," he says. "They were as crazy and wild as anyone, but they did it with a sense of class. They never got stupid drunk or stupid high; they were always kind of in control of themselves. And they were kind to people. That impressed me a lot."[1]

Riding high from the better-than-expected sales and critical reception for *Chronic Town*, the members of R.E.M. were both cheered and dismayed when I.R.S. Records vice president Jay Boberg came to them with a big idea. His enthusiasm was delightful, but his inspiration, to pair the young band with an up-and-coming new wave producer named Stephen Hague, was worrisome. Hague was a keyboard player whose productions for Jules and the Polar Bears and for Gleaming Spires, a splinter group featuring members of Sparks, burbled and sizzled with synthesizers. Not that there was anything unartful or wrong with that, per se, but everything about Hague's ways, means, and sonic palette ran against the grain of R.E.M.'s guitar-bass-and-drums sound. They were, to put it mildly, leery.

Boberg, by contrast, was thinking synergy: an unexpected combination that just might be crazy enough to work. Give it a chance, he said. They could do a test session with one song and see how it came out. "I don't think he wants to push you into synths," he said, reassuringly. How bad could it be? Forty years later, Boberg answers his own question: "It was a fucking disaster."[2]

The song they chose for the session was "Catapult." Premiered just after the start of 1982, the song was a crowd favorite that they had played at nearly every show that year. The song's hurtling pace and soaring one-word chorus contrasts a tender vision of children at a sleepover, cuddled together in front of a glowing screen as the hour grows late (*It's nine o'clock, don't try to turn it off*) with something unseen drawing closer. The children are anxious, determined not to be overlooked. *Did we miss anything? Did we miss anything?* Michael repeats, chanting over the thumping drums and clanging guitar. But that catapult may hurl you somewhere you weren't expecting or desiring.

Sometimes talented, well-meaning people have different aesthetics and different ways of going about their work. The test session for "Catapult" was held in an Atlanta studio in December 1982. It started badly when Hague directed Bill to keep his time straight by drumming to a computerized click track. R.E.M. was neither accustomed to nor aspiring to this level of mechanistic perfection for "Catapult," nor any other song in their catalog. The musicians had developed parts, and a musical rapport, on the tune many months before they launched into their first studio take. But Hague kept hearing something amiss. He interrupted the band again and again, pointing out flaws in their rhythm, unappealing textures in Peter's guitar, bits where the bass notes created bad harmonics with the vocal melody. It went on like that for hours, Hague inserting himself into the spontaneous chemistry that existed between the four of them.

And even after they nailed down what struck him as a suitable performance, Hague took the tapes with him back to Boston and did the unthinkable, overdubbing jingly keyboards and shiny synth lines into the choruses, adding echo to Stipe's vocals, and basically dragging the quirky rock band from Athens into line with the sort of new wavy pop you could already hear coming out of the radio. Which might have been the savvy commercial move for a largely unheard-of band coming out of some rural Georgia backwater, but R.E.M. was having none of it, and once he heard Hague's mix, neither was Boberg. "I was dead wrong," he says.[3] "I'm learning. I make mistakes. And that really taught me that [R.E.M.'s] artistic impulses about what they should and shouldn't do were dead-on."[*]

The recording sessions for R.E.M.'s first full album came in short bursts. Two days here, three days there, through February, bracketed by shows back in Athens and in various college towns in North Carolina. When they were in Athens, resting up between the days of performing or recording in the cheap student-caliber apartments they still called home, they got together every day at 5 p.m. If they weren't working out a new song, they'd rehearse for the next show, or work through songs that hadn't sounded right at the last one. The work was focused and painstaking, each musical passage set right through deliberate, focused effort. They weren't marathon sessions, usually no more than ninety minutes at a stretch, but they were consistent and disciplined and almost always began on time, no matter what else was going on. The commitment to the band, and to the music they were capable of making together, took precedence over everything else.

Given the authority to choose their producer, the musicians went back to Mitch Easter, though they opted to move the setting from his parents' garage to Reflection Sound Studios, a professional outfit located in Charlotte, North Carolina. To help run the larger console, Easter tapped his friend Don Dixon to coproduce, and the pair's comfort with each other, and the band's comfort with them, helped nurture the songs' purposefully mismatched parts.

[*] Which isn't to say that there's anything wrong with Stephen Hague or the music he makes. Hague went on to produce or contribute to cool records by artists as diverse as Public Image Ltd, Robbie Robertson, and Tom Jones. He just wasn't attuned to R.E.M. circa 1983.

_____

Your luck a two-headed cow.

"Pilgrimage" paces, frets, scolds, and cries out. It examines the legacy of the South, the promise and the poison, and speaks its name. *Pilgrimage.* The tours offered by the women of Mississippi's Natchez Garden Club, of the remnants of the antebellum South. The plantations, the mansions, the glories and fortunes built on the backs of the enslaved. Some of the older homes around Athens, the grander ones, still had slave quarters in the back of their property. You could see the remnants of human bondage around you. How it was woven into the fabric of daily life. How it warped the hearts and minds of everyone it touched. The garden club ladies speak of religion. They speak of glory. They avert their eyes from the brutality. *Rest assured this will not last,* Michael proclaims icily. But the yearning for the past goes on, and so the music picks up again, ringing and true, the three voices linked into a round of melody, harmony, and countermelody, as if that might bring the twisted empire crashing down for good this time.

Take a turn, take our fortune.

One after another, the new songs dove into the deepest end of existence—the biggest quandaries, the most hideous injustices, the most disturbing images. Murder. Cruelty. Corruption. Innocence torn asunder. "Talk About the Passion" invokes the death of Christ in an elliptical portrait of hunger and society's casual acceptance of suffering. "Laughing" draws in the tale of Laocoön, who attempted to warn the soldiers of Troy about the warriors hiding within the Trojan Horse, only to be killed, along with his two sons, by serpents sent by the gods. Even "We Walk," whose cheery music skips along in a seemingly lighthearted gambol, comes with an eerie undertow as Michael's climb up the stairs of one of Athens's creaky old apartment buildings pauses to recall the painting of French revolutionary Jean-Paul Marat as he was discovered after being assassinated in the bath. The darkness comes in glimpses, a word here, a phrase there, not quite hidden between the buoyant rhythm, the tuneful chime of Peter's guitar and the cheering harmonies of Mike and Bill.

As a lyricist and a singer, Michael hides in plain sight. He takes shelter between the instruments, careful to keep his vocals mixed alongside, not above, the guitar, bass, and drums. He atomizes his thoughts, breaking sentences into fragments, sticking them into apparently random order. He is, almost defiantly, at odds with himself, commanding the spotlight and then turning away. He grabs the microphone, tests its power, and then swallows his words. "9-9" begins in a hail of rock 'n' roll glory, a pulsing bass, speedy drums, whirling guitar, a recitation that climaxes with a prayer: *Now I lay me down to sleep, I pray the Lord my soul to keep* . . . except he's muttering it all so far beneath the music that you can barely hear him speak, let alone decipher what he's saying. The music hurtles and snarls, drums cracking, guitar stuttering and snapping, while Michael shouts about pointers, twisting tongues, conversation fear. The song collapses, and a beat later "Shaking Through" kicks in, its layered acoustic guitars and piano as lilting and welcoming as a folk-song sing-along: *Could it be that one small voice / Doesn't count in the room?* The song echoes, if not quite expands upon, "Sitting Still," the "Radio Free Europe" B-side that was re-recorded for the album, with its recurring assurances—*I can hear you*—and the concluding question, *Can you hear me?* People can hear everything, but are they truly listening to anything?

They called the album *Murmur.* In search of a cover image that captured the dark southern comedy of Flannery O'Connor's fiction, the group settled on a photograph made by their friend Sandi Phipps of a wintry field grown over with kudzu, the profligate weed whose tendrils spread so rapidly as to all but grow before your eyes. Phipps found the field near Athens, which was also where she discovered the railroad trestle decorating the back cover. Phipps made the portraits of the four band members, too, capturing them individually, bundled against a chill that has taken any traces of warmth from their expressions. Mike scowls at the lens. Peter, in a leather overcoat, white shirt, and tie, presents only a profile. Bill, a bolo tie peeking past his overcoat, looks puzzled and a little sad. Michael, behind bookish spectacles and wrapped in a poet's scarf, purses his kewpie lips and peers moodily at the floor.

Released on April 12, 1983, *Murmur* was an instant smash on college radio. It didn't rate much airplay on mainstream radio, and the exceedingly elliptical video they made for a freshly re-recorded "Radio Free Europe," most of which followed the band members meandering through Howard Finster's sculpture garden, guaranteed MTV would never air it at a time when anyone beyond a tiny segment of its audience would see it. Even so, the album rose to number thirty-six on the *Billboard* chart, selling around 150,000 copies by the end of the year.[4] The single of the new "Radio Free Europe" only made it to number seventy-eight on *Billboard*'s Hot 100; a disappointment for the I.R.S. staffers accustomed to seeing the catchier songs by the Go-Go's pull their albums into the top ten. But the reviews were, if anything, even better than they had been for *Chronic Town*.

In *Rolling Stone*, Steve Pond gave the album four stars. "An original sound placed in the service of songs that matter," he wrote. "It reveals a depth and cohesiveness to R.E.M. that [*Chronic Town*] could only suggest."[5] Writing in *The Village Voice*, Robert Christgau traded the faint praise he gave to the band's debut EP with something closer to an all-out rave: "They aren't a pop band or even an art-pop band—they're an art band, nothing less or more, and a damn smart one."[6] In England, the *New Musical Express*'s Richard Grabel also uncorked high praise: "Their overall mood is mystical, revelatory, gentle and open," he wrote. "R.E.M. have a claim to being one of the most evocative pop practitioners around."[7]

18

R.E.M. Submits

The opening of *Rock on TV*, a local cable program seen in Chicago, describes the state of pop music circa the summer of 1983 in quick cuts and teaser narration, through the eyes of people who aren't entirely unhip. Flash cuts of some unrecognizable band onstage, then the Tubes, then one of the guys from Devo, then Paul McCartney sporting one of his less elegant '80s hairstyles. Now here's a glimpse at the crowd at the vast Us Festival, a split second of Kiss, then the Residents, that San Francisco band that wore big eyeball costumes. The singer from Spandau Ballet, then the witty Bay Area rocker Greg Kihn makes a funny face into the camera, and that leads into the previews of tonight's feature stories. First, we hear, it's the razor-sharp sounds of the new Canadian hitmaker Bryan Adams, glimpsed in the video for "Cuts Like a Knife," in which he and his band rock out at the bottom of a swimming pool. Next, the announcer promises, David Bowie falls in love! Or at least he smooches with the woman in the latest cinematic video from his smash *Let's Dance* album. And finally, here are newcomers R.E.M., who, it's said, leave it up to our imagination.

A few features play out, including the piece with Adams, who sits backstage with a towel draped around his neck, a confident smile tugging at his lips as he lays out what it takes to make it in the rock 'n' roll business. "You gotta want it," he declares. "If you don't want it, then, *psssshhhht*, don't bother, man. Ya gotta do it 'cause you love it."

Adams is saying something about legitimacy in rock 'n' roll, about the importance of work and desire, even for bands that are willing to occasionally simulate performances at the bottoms of swimming pools. When it's their turn, the members of R.E.M. work just as hard to establish something about themselves. It begins with Peter being interviewed on camera, saying that the name R.E.M. doesn't mean what most people think it means, but that doesn't bother them. " 'Rhinoceroses, elephants, and mooses' is okay with us, too," he says. This is funny, and also plays against type, since so much about the band's public identity is so very serious.

"Wolves, Lower" plays again. Those spinning guitar notes, the restless bass and skittery drums, the elliptical words and that deep, nearly sinister voice. The show's cohost, Norm Winters, starts his narration. "Ever wake up from a vivid dream to find that the details have vanished and only the feeling remains? R.E.M. re-creates that feeling with music so effortlessly primal it seems to spin straight from the subconscious. You've heard of dance music? Well, this is dream music. Tunes that make you quiver and shudder."

That's pretty smart, actually, and no wonder. Winters is also a disc jockey and the program director for Chicago's WXRT-FM, one of the most influential progressive radio stations in the country. He's got an ear for interesting, left-of-center music, and a canny sense of what it takes to sell it to a broad listenership. He plays a snippet of the "Wolves, Lower" video, the band miming their performance, including the cool part where Michael spins and jumps in slo-mo as Winters recounts the popular beef about R.E.M. being purposefully obscure, with lyrics and even a name geared specifically to mystify. But then comes a fuller version of Peter's line about rhinoceroses, elephants, and mooses, and Michael and Bill admitting that they take fans' incorrect guesses of what the lyrics are and sing those instead. "Sometimes their words are better than ours," Michael says.

The scene changes to the band's hotel room, where the musicians are tending to their laundry, including an I.R.S. Records T-shirt on which the camera lingers. "As you can see, R.E.M. are real down-to-earth guys," Winters continues. "Their current road tour is no rock-star chauffeured-limousine affair; they pack their own bags and wash their own socks." This narrative thread plays over carefully staged shots of the band in repose, kicking back on the bed, flipping channels on the hotel room TV, as Winters celebrates the band's rejection of all the glitzy rock 'n' roll trappings. Particularly the traditional videos, he says, "that sell music with clichéd images of breaking glass and gorgeous girls."

Mike steps up to declare that rock 'n' roll should focus on "honest emotions. Whatever your feelings are, played through your music." This sets up a peek at the new video for "Radio Free Europe," which trades the aforementioned beautiful women and breaking glass for the southern folk artist Howard Finster and some deeply inscrutable action sequences involving the band members' acquisition of a portentous-seeming box from an eerie, looming Jefferson Holt and the presentation of said box to Finster, who opens it to find a doll that tumbles end-over-end down an angled board. The I.R.S. Records team edited in a few glimpses of the band onstage, but that didn't keep the whole thing from landing somewhere miles away from anything resembling an MTV playlist. Which might have been the point of the entire project.

By the spring of 1983 the band's touring operation, which had launched three years earlier with all the musicians and gear crammed into Bill's old family station wagon, had expanded along with their professional prospects. The lightly battered 1975 Dodge B300 van they bought in 1981 was decommissioned, traded for a more spacious beige Dodge, customized with four captain's chairs in the back and a separate compartment for the band's instruments and stage amplifiers. Now traveling with their own sound mixer, lighting operator, and guitar tech, they rented a second van for the crew, which Bill sometimes rode in so he could pal around with his high school friend Gevin Lindsay, a guitarist who had signed on to help care for Peter's instruments.

The year's intensive road work began at the end of March, two weeks before the release of *Murmur*, when they launched a month of opening for the English Beat, focusing mostly on college dates in the Southeast and then the upper Midwest and the Northeast. That left them in New York at the end of April, just after the release of

Murmur, from which point they set out on their own, playing clubs on their way down through Virginia and North Carolina and back to Georgia, then back out to venues all across the nation as the new record found its way into stores, magazine review columns, and a few radio playlists.

Peter Jesperson, the Minneapolis record store manager who also cofounded the indie label Twin/Tone Records and both produced and managed the Replacements, its most popular act, had become friends with his band's compatriots from Athens, and when they asked him to serve as a fill-in road manager that spring, he signed on eagerly. The powerful but notoriously chaotic Replacements were gaining momentum, and giving Jesperson a working sabbatical within the smooth-running R.E.M. operation struck everyone in the Minnesota rockers' camp as a good move. Immediately, Jesperson was impressed by how professional the Georgia musicians were. "For one thing, they didn't light my shoes on fire when I was sleeping," he says.[1] On the road with the Replacements, Jesperson not only had to do all the driving and navigating, he also had to make regular stops to buy new atlases, since the band members thought it was funny to tear out the maps leading to their next destination. In R.E.M.'s van, both Jefferson Holt and Bill liked to help with the driving, and any one of them could be called on to take up the map and point the way to the next show. And there was always a next show.

From the Ritz in New York to St. Paul, Minnesota, to open a festival-style show for the Suburbs, with the Replacements, the Phones, and Mitch Easter's band Let's Active filling the daylong bill. Then came club shows in Milwaukee, Madison, and Chicago, with Let's Active and the dB's opening. Bloomington, Lincoln, Kansas City, then an opening slot for the English Beat and Bow Wow Wow at the Red Rocks Amphitheatre, outside Denver. Then came an ill-advised show at the Sheppard Air Force Base, in Wichita Falls, Texas, where the heavy-metal-loving airmen responded to the collegiate band's elliptical art rock with a hail of empty cups and cries of *Die, faggot!* They pulled out some of their old covers, "Route 66" and "Secret Agent Man," etc., in an attempt to appease the crowd, but it didn't work, and knowing the base MPs were there to keep the soldiers from physically attacking them, Peter and Michael couldn't resist boogying up against each other, rubbing asses and making kissy-faces that caused the drunk, hyper-macho throng to roar with rage. "In the end they booed so loud we came back and did an encore," Peter told *Musician* in 1984.[2]

Onward. Dallas, Austin, Lubbock, then the long haul to San Diego and up the coast to Los Angeles, Sacramento, San Francisco, then south again for a solid week of one-nighters starting at the Showcase Theatre at the Six Flags Magic Mountain amusement park, in Valencia, near Los Angeles. Costa Mesa, seventy-five miles down the coast, came the next night. Then they doubled back to central Los Angeles the night after that. They jumped back into the van after that show to drive 350 miles north to Santa Cruz for the next performance. Then came three more nights in a row: Berkeley, Palo Alto, and San Francisco. It went on like that, week after week, month after month. Some nights they drew three hundred people, other nights it'd be closer to thirty. Occasionally they slept in cheap motels. More often they found a friendly local to let them crash on a sofa or a living room floor, or else slept in their seats in the van as they motored to the next town, the next club, the next show. "I don't think I touched a bed in two months sometimes," Peter told journalist Tony Fletcher. "We'd play, go to a party, drink, steal food from the fridge and then at around four in the morning, we'd go, 'OK, time to go on to the next town.' We'd drive into the next town, and arrive there at noon, park behind the club and sleep until five."[3] They'd rouse themselves in time for the soundcheck, maybe wander off to find something for dinner, then get back to the club to prepare for the show.

Murmur sold steadily, if unspectacularly, through the summer, and the mounting critical buzz, amplified by the machinations of I.R.S. Records' publicity crew, elevated R.E.M. into the sights of magazine and newspaper editors and bookers for TV news shows. After all those years of reading about other musicians, Peter knew how to use the media to build a band's image. To expand upon their music and frame themselves not just as artists but as rock 'n' roll missionaries, opponents of the prevailing culture.

Speaking to a reporter from the ABC affiliate in Los Angeles in 1983, he girded the band's anti-professional credentials. "None of us are really experienced musicians," he said. "I never played guitar, never played in another band. So we learned to play as a four-person unit."[4] This is, at best, only partially accurate. But the deeper point, a staunch opposition to the sleek commercial rock 'n' roll that dominated the mainstream, came through even more clearly in an appearance Peter and Mike made on an afternoon television show aimed at Atlanta high schoolers. "The rock 'n' roll business has more or less been changed into a series of gestures and conventions you have to do in order to have a hit, and by and large that's garbage,"[5] Peter told the kids. Speaking to another reporter from Georgia after a club show in Scotia, New York, Peter laughed off the thought that his band had a reputation they had to live up to. "We live *down* to it if possible," he retorted. "We don't feel like we have to live up to that whole rock star image of going onstage and, ya know, like U2, being dramatic or melodramatic or whatever. We get up and play and mess around and sometimes we're bad and sometimes we're good, and it should be fun for us before anything else. We certainly don't want to become too professional. Most bands die because of their professionalism."[6]

Early in the summer, Ian Copeland, who was booking them through his agency, FBI, in New York, called Jefferson Holt with an offer. The Police, who had ascended to new heights with their album *Synchronicity* and its chain of hit singles, including the number one "Every Breath You Take," were mounting an enormous tour of the United States that summer, playing the biggest venues possible in every city. In August they had dates set up at New York's Shea Stadium, which the Beatles had played at the height of Beatlemania in 1965, and the even bigger JFK Stadium, in Philadelphia. They needed an opening act for those shows, and also for a few relatively smaller engagements in basketball arenas, so the engagement would amount to seven shows spread over ten days, during which R.E.M. could play for something like a quarter million people, the vast majority of whom would be hearing them for the first time. A huge opportunity for any band, let alone one that was still performing in clubs they didn't always fill. The only problem was that they didn't want to do it.

A couple of years earlier, they'd been thrilled to open for Gang of Four, and they did weeks on end with the English Beat, mostly in the same sorts of clubs and small halls they had eventually worked their way to headlining. But the prospect of opening for enormous crowds, particularly in arena-size venues, left them cold. What was the point of playing to a big crowd if none of the people wanted to hear you in the first place? They liked being close to their audience, to see them eye to eye and present themselves as people, not untouchable stars you would need binoculars to see. So they had turned down an offer to tour with Squeeze, and they had turned down a proposal to tour with U2. The offer from the Police, however, was a different matter. Everyone at the record company, particularly Jay Boberg, wanted them to get the exposure of playing for the Police's audience. Holt noted how much money was at stake—$10,000 a show for the stadiums, which was exactly five times what they were accustomed to getting for club shows. They'd get a little less for the arenas, but still significantly more than what they usually earned for a night's work. So. What to do. They thought it over.

Or maybe they didn't have to do that much thinking. "It was astounding to them," recalls the temporary road manager Peter Jesperson. "They were so excited."[7] Not that they talked about it in public. In fact, Peter Buck made a point of saying the opposite. "It was boring," he scoffed to the *Los Angeles Times* a year later. "As close to having a day job as I've come in rock 'n' roll."[8]

True enough, the band's twenty-minute set at Shea Stadium came in the midst of a rainstorm, at the bottom of a bill that also included Joan Jett and the Blackhearts. But they nonetheless rose to the occasion and gained a respectful, even enthusiastic, hearing, according to Jesperson. Ian Copeland agreed, telling British writer Johnny Black that he was astonished to realize that the kids he'd befriended when one of them was a teenage office boy at Paragon Booking in Macon were playing Shea Stadium and getting across to such a mammoth crowd. "When they played 'Radio Free Europe,' the whole crowd went fucking berserk," he said. "That was the moment I finally realized, 'Shit! This isn't just my buddies out there. This band is going to make me rich! And I'm going to make them rich!'"[9]

19

A Collective Fist

This is how it happens. You set out with your friends on a road trip. Climb into the car, crank up the tunes, stop-start your way through the lights to the highway, and then hit the on-ramp and off you go. Trees and clouds, trucks and cars, crack the window and feel the warm southern wind in your hair. You're young and on the move, you're going somewhere, anything could happen.

At the start of 1983 it seemed like a flood tide had gushed into town, sending all of Athens's bands, the clubs, the artists, the scenesters and random passersby, bobbing gaily on its current. In January they drifted into the slick pages of *People* magazine, of all places. That bit of absurdity began a few months earlier when the magazine's editors, from the heights of the Time-Life Building in midtown Manhattan, sat down to ponder the current state of rock 'n' roll. In search of a happening scene, they turned their ears south and noticed the racket coming from the B-52's' hometown. Suddenly it seemed like half the bands playing in New York were skinny college kids from that little town nobody had even heard of last year. Pylon, R.E.M., Love Tractor, Oh-OK, Art in the Dark, the Squalls, the Side Effects . . . all of them rumbling up I-95 like a Confederate army of quirky new wavers. So the assigning wires were composed, bureaus notified, correspondents and photographers dispatched.

Two reporters showed up in town, notebooks unfurled, to hear all about the bands and the clubs, the spirit of art and fun and how little anyone cared to have hits or money or anything like that. "No one has an eye on vast success," Jimmy Ellison, late of the Side Effects and now of Group 3, was quoted as saying. A little recognition was never a bad thing, though, so when the photographer called for musicians to gather at the Revolutionary War monument for Elijah Clarke, right there in the middle of Broad Street, near campus, more than three dozen showed up, many toting instruments, as requested. They posed yearbook style, sitting, squatting, and standing in rows.

To look at them now is to see a lot of nice young people exhibiting good manners. They are neatly if casually dressed, in jeans, shirt-sleeves, and sweatshirts. Many wield guitars, basses, an accordion, a clarinet, a banjo, something that might be a didgeridoo. They are young, serious, quizzical, maybe a touch smirky. Did anyone notice, or care, that they were, to a person, all white? Some faces are famil-iar, but the ones you'd recognize immediately are missing—off on tour, thousands of miles from Athens already. There's no caption information and now the image has gone a bit blurry. You might not even see the guy in the third row, a little to the right, in the black silk top hat. Look closely and you'll also notice the slight tilt of his head, and how long and graceful his fingers are. And also that his entire face is shielded by a cartoonish wolf mask. What was that song again? *Here's a house to put wolves out the door* . . . Perched at the center of everything and also hidden from view. Jeremy Ayers, as he lived and breathed.

The same week the *People* issue came out, in mid-January, R.E.M. played a pair of their increasingly rare hometown shows at the I&I Club, in downtown Athens. The place was packed with friends, neighbors, folks the farther-and-farther-flung musicians hadn't seen in months. A few songs in, Michael took a moment to read through some announcements—coming shows from friends' bands, includ-ing Boat Of, which featured his friend Carol Levy. And speaking of Carol, it was her birthday, and she was right there dancing in front of the stage, so how about wishing her a happy birthday! She and

Michael had met, along with so many of the others, in art classes, but she had also lived in Reed Hall alongside Mike, Bill, Kathleen O'Brien, and all the rest.

Levy was relatively petite, but she cast a long shadow around Athens. Her photographs drew attention, and so did her strikingly androgynous style, and the music she made in her avant-garde trio. Levy had a natural way of making connections, of putting people together, of following her star no matter where it led or what anyone might have thought or said about it. She had shortish dark hair and full lips, and dark eyes that flashed with intelligence, wit, and, when she smiled, the best kind of mischief. Michael led the crowd in a chorus of "Happy Birthday," and the voices rang out. Levy laughed and waved back across the footlights.

They met somewhere, probably an art department party or event, and were drawn together. Michael and Jeremy. Ayers was a dozen years older, but gentle, prankish, and very alive to the moment, every moment. He was thin, sandy-haired, and strikingly beautiful. "He was a spectacular-looking person . . . very ethereal, and he always had a poetic sense about him," says Jim Herbert, the painter/filmmaker/art professor.[1] Ayers didn't take classes at the university, but his dad was a well-known religion professor, and he started hanging out around the art department as a teenager in the late 1960s. In the early 1970s Ayers moved to New York, visited Andy Warhol's Factory headquarters, and caught the eye of the artist, who saw the striking young Georgian as Silva Thin, a superstar creation whose face was alabaster smooth and white, his lips ruby red, his brow darkened and arching, his eyes soft but affectless. Ayers orbited through Warhol's gay art celebrity galaxy until disaster struck: a pool party he attended was attacked by vicious malefactors armed with baseball bats. Physically and emotionally battered, Ayers returned to Athens and gentler climes.

He was sweet and soft-spoken, a fount of art and music whose greatest medium was other people. Befriending them, inspiring them, connecting them to their future partners in art, music, and life. In late 1976 he invited Ricky and Cindy Wilson, Keith Strickland, Fred Schneider, and Kate Pierson to make some music, helped them set up, and then put his coat on to leave. No, he explained, he wasn't in the band . . . *They* were the band. That was the B-52's. Ayers wrote the lyrics to "52 Girls," on the band's first album, and contributed ideas and inspiration to an array of other Athens artists and musicians.

Michael grew close to Ayers and soon began to evolve. The singer's clothes grew more spacious, and he took to wearing them in layers. His hair got longer and often fell over his face, a curtain behind which he'd withdraw when he felt nervous. He'd always wrestled with shyness, but there were layers of meaning in his diffidence. After experiencing how magnetic Ayers's stillness could be, Michael learned to say fewer words and to limit his movements, particularly onstage. To be the absent center while standing in full view. The front man nobody could touch or stop looking at. Born with a sexual orientation that did not conform to the lines drawn by a homophobic society, Michael discovered that taking shelter behind his hair allowed him to exist in the spotlight without disclosing or disguising his essential self. It also allowed him to make an aesthetic virtue out of necessity. His mystery was evocative and, at the same time, blank—a space where the listener could project her own story.

Jeremy Ayers eventually formed a band to join. Limbo District was an avant-garde outfit. They wore antique clothes and made a clattering racket that sent casual observers rushing for the door. But, like Ayers, the other musicians were spellbindingly beautiful, and in 1983 they starred in and provided the soundtrack for one of Jim Herbert's art films, a ten-minute collage of photos and stop-start action he called *Carnival*. The band members, in various states of Victorian dress and undress, disport next to a pond. In some shots they are made up like clowns. A horse appears, is mounted, then vanishes. The music clanks and spins, the vocal is gibberish, or in another language, and tuneless. Colors fade out, then in. The men are shirtless, muscular abdomens rippling. A woman wades into the water, first in a diaphanous sheet, then nude. Someone hoists an accordion, pulls at its bellows. A keyboard appears, a flute. Naked bodies, whirling music, rattles, bangs, and a thumping bass. *Hey heeee, yah, yah, yah:* that might be the lyrics at one point.

On April 12, R.E.M. opened for the English Beat at the University of Western Ontario, in London, Ontario, and on April 13 the tour moved to upstate New York and the University of Rochester. A different city and a new venue every night. More faces, more music, more parties, beer, bowls of potato chips, pretzels, pills, and back into the van. Chilly dawns, spaced-out days, the van's reek of gasoline, fast-food containers and dirty socks. Crowds, lights, music, and cheers, then back into the van, the familiar fetid waft, and dozing again to the hum of the wheels, the flashing lines on the highway, the next city, the next venue, the next crowd. The glow coming from the far side of the horizon, pulling them onward and onward and onward.

Now everything was happening, and not just for R.E.M. On April 14 the band was on the highway in western New York, heading to Buffalo to join the English Beat at Buffalo State College. Down in Athens, Carol Levy, Mig Little, Rodger Lyle Brown, David Helmey, and Larry Marcus jumped into Little's Toyota Corolla to drive to Atlanta for the Southeast premiere of *Smithereens*, the first film directed by Susan Seidelman. Her second effort, *Desperately Seeking Susan*, would be a smash hit in 1985, catapulting both Rosanna Arquette and Madonna to global stardom. *Smithereens* was a similar story, about a bourgeois New Jersey woman drawn to the punk demimonde in New York. The punk band the Feelies provided the soundtrack, and Richard Hell, the former bassist for the Voidoids, plays a musician named Eric. Hell was slated to appear at the showing and answer questions when it was over. Richard Hell! In the flesh! It was a glorious night, and when the film and Richard Hell talk were over, the Athens kids stopped for coffee, then piled back into the car in the highest spirits, gunning it up the dark highway on the way home to Athens.

———

This is how it happens. You're on the road with your friends, music is playing. Maybe it's a new record, maybe it's an old favorite. Maybe it's something your friends made. So many Athens bands were making records in 1983. Love Tractor was about to release its second album, Pylon had a new one, R.E.M. got all that buzz with their EP and now their first full-length album was just out. Larry Marcus's band Little Tigers had a single out, and there were others coming soon. Little's band, the Squalls, were putting things together. Maybe they were listening to one of those records in the car, maybe it was cranked up, maybe they were singing along.

The woman driving the car behind them was thirsty. She had a water bottle, but it was on the back seat, or maybe on the floor, and she couldn't reach it. Not at first, so she reached back farther, really stretching out, not knowing that she was putting more pressure on the gas pedal, speeding closer to the car ahead of her. She was focused on her hand, on the elusive water bottle, on reaching just an inch farther so she could corral the thing and, finally, cool her tongue. What happened next happened in an instant. The thirsty woman's car jolted forward, colliding with the rear of the car full of Athens kids. This sent it spinning, then flipping, over and over and over, at least five times. What was it like inside their car? A dream about a Ferris wheel, lights flashing in the darkness, then a nightmare. *Secret stigma, reaping wheel, don't get caught, don't get caught.*

The lights, the music, the cheering, the road, more lights, more noise, horrible noise, then silence. The lights, the sirens, the crying, the moaning. The silence.

This was how it happened.

Carol Levy.

Larry Marcus.

Five months later, R.E.M. got back from their summer tour, including the supersize shows with the Police. Now it was September. They had a couple of weeks of rest, then got back into action in Athens with a show in the abandoned Stitchcraft Inc. factory, a cavernous building just across Oconee Street from the site of their first-ever show just forty-two months earlier. Splayed between their past and future, they opened with a jokey take of Sonny & Cher's "I Got You Babe," and salted the originals with a generous handful of rock 'n' roll covers, including a few they'd first performed in the church that night in April 1980: "Secret Agent Man," "Route 66," "Wild Thing." Michael led the crowd in "Happy Birthday" for a few friends who had September birthdays. It was an upbeat show, the band as happy and excited to see their friends in the crowd as the hometown crowd was to see them. They also debuted a few new songs, including one that opened the second set, a slow, sad tune with mournful if typically elliptical words.

When the party lulls, if we fall by the side.

Michael's voice hanging in the air, Mike's harmony dancing around him, Bill's drums ticking like a clock, Peter's guitar chiming gently, quizzically.

I still like you, can you remember?

This was how it sounded. Heartbroken, confused, loving. Mostly heartbroken.

Will you be remembered? Will she be remembered?

One night that October the telephone rang in Melanie Herrold's mom's house in Collinsville, Illinois. Michael's bestie from high school, his fellow singer and partner in weirdness, in *Rocky Horror*, in rock 'n' roll daydreaming. They hadn't spoken in more than a year, maybe two years, but Melanie was home and recognized his voice immediately.

I'm gonna be on David Letterman!

"I was like, '*What?! You fucker!*'"

He told her everything then, about his band, about the club shows, the van, the records, the insane experience of playing Shea, all of it. She tuned in the next night, Herrold and her mom in their little suburban living room, and there he was. Hair long and hanging in his eyes, face lowered, standing almost motionless at the microphone as he belted out "Radio Free Europe," the other musicians bopping and moving around him. When Letterman stepped over to chat, Michael vanished from view, stepping back to sit on the drum riser. The host chatted with the guitarist and the bassist, then set up the band's second song. Michael returned to the microphone, the musicians kicked in, and he was singing again.

Herrold's mom was beside herself: *I can't believe it! That boy baby-sat your nephew!* Herrold was still chasing the dream too, singing in bands in St. Louis, in Los Angeles, then again in St. Louis. Nothing had taken, but she wasn't done yet. Mike Stipe, meanwhile, was singing for millions of people on national TV.

"I thought, *He's done it! That bastard's done it!*"[2]

Mike's voice, coming to her through the speaker of her mom's TV. Amazing.

I'm sorry . . . I'm sorry . . .

He didn't need to apologize to her. She was happy for him.

Tom Smith felt differently.

He was another art student–and–musician, one of Carol Levy's bandmates in Boat Of. The band had broken up in the wake of her death, and though Michael had been close to the entire group, Smith saw what he was doing with R.E.M. and felt disgusted. He couldn't abide the commerciality, couldn't even tolerate Pylon making a record for Danny Beard's little DB Records label. "He was incensed that we had sold out," drummer Curtis Crowe recalls. "We'd made a record, and so that was a sellout. But we didn't get anything for that record, and I was like, *Huh, I thought there'd be more money in selling out!*"[3] Pylon could have made more money. They could have opened for U2 in 1981 and played to thousands of people in big clubs and theaters all across America. Or they could have toured more heavily on their own, doing it like R.E.M. had done, working night after night to build a fan base in city after city after city. They could have gone on television, they could have pursued a major-label deal, or even a deal with a major indie like I.R.S. Records. They could have gone to the meetings, been taken to the dinners, shaken the hands, laughed at the jokes, and done what it takes to get there. They could have, they could have, they could have. Instead they took stock of themselves in mid-1983, of the work they'd done, the reviews they'd received, what lay ahead, and decided, *Oh, screw it.* Remember what Michael Lachowski and Randy Bewley said when they started? That this band wasn't really a band as much as an art project about a band? Now it was time for the project to end. They set a final show for the Mad Hatter on December 1, had a great night, put down their instruments, and that was that.

But Tom Smith was far more enraged at R.E.M., and particularly at Michael, his fellow art student and supposed friend to Carol Levy. Michael had been an honorary member of Boat Of and performed with them on several occasions. But the release of *Murmur,* and R.E.M.'s ceaseless pursuit of even greater success, drove Smith berserk. He printed up a T-shirt, maybe more than one, and sported it around town. The thing seethed with Smith's rage. A COLLECTIVE FIST, it snarled, UP M. STIPE'S ASS.

Jimmy Ellison, Vanessa Briscoe's ex-husband and once the bassist with the Side Effects, now playing with Group 3, wasn't feeling right. He went to the doctor, got checked out. They performed more tests, the doctors pointed to a shadow on his MRI. The diagnosis was bleak: a brain tumor. *Secret stigma, reaping wheel, don't get caught.* The headlights spinning, the machine out of control, spinning in his direction. A few months later Ellison was dead.

This is how it happens. At the end of the year the amassed critics for *Rolling Stone* reconsidered Steve Pond's four-star review of *Murmur* and cranked the volume even higher. Measuring the merits of all the albums released in 1983, which included pop culture epics no less monumental than Michael Jackson's gajillion-selling *Thriller* and U2's acclaimed *War* and the Police's multi-platinum apotheosis *Synchronicity,* they bestowed their Album of the Year title to . . . *Murmur.* R.E.M. also took honors for Best New Artist and, again beating out U2 and the Police, Band of the Year.

Secret stigma, reaping wheel.

PART III

This One Goes Out

20

Here We Are

The songs are all in motion. Whirling guitar notes, restless drums, the bass untethered, bouncing all over the scale. The lead vocal here, the supporting vocal there, a third voice somewhere in between, all singing different words, in their own rhythm, telling their own stories but still somehow in perfect, unexpected harmony.

Another Greenville, another Magic Mart . . .

Highways, rivers, climbing and falling, drifting and churning, currents flowing, the world swept up in a flood tide. It's all velocity, distance, and isolation.

These rivers of suggestion are driving me away . . .

The fall of 1983 came at them at top speed. After the Letterman show, in early October, it never stopped. More shows in the Northeast, then on to California, then England, the Netherlands, and France. They got a week off, then back into the van to Charlotte to spend nine days recording songs for their next full-length album with Mitch Easter and Don Dixon. A couple of weeks off for the holidays, then back to Charlotte in January 1984 for another ten days in the studio.

Vacation in Athens is calling me . . . Heaven is yours where I live.

They got a few weeks in Athens to sleep and reconnect with friends, family, and whatever romantic partners they might still have, though it also featured a lot of musical side projects and guest appearances on other people's shows. In early March they played a couple of hometown club dates at the Mad Hatter, then hit a few college-centric one-offs, a spring break appearance at the bandshell in Daytona Beach, Florida, then a couple of gigs with the Minneapolis punk trio Hüsker Dü in Boston. Back in Athens a few days later, they spent a day with UGA art professor/painter/filmmaker Jim Herbert shooting video to accompany some of the new songs. With the new album set to be released around the world in early April, they flew to London for two days of interviews and then a month of shows in Europe and the UK.

It's what I want, hurry and buy . . .

Writer Anthony DeCurtis was working on a PhD in literature at Emory University when he got his first assignment from *Rolling Stone* in 1980, reporting on a homecoming (of sorts) concert the B-52's gave in Atlanta. The magazine assigned a piece about Pylon next, then sent him back to Athens a few months after that to report on the town's music scene. Michael Lachowski served as his guide for that 1981 trip, showing him the clubs and directing him to the most interesting artists in town. Lachowski also took him to see R.E.M. And though the Pylon bassist made his skepticism about the band clear, calling them a *pop band*, the writer was floored by what he saw at Tyrone's O.C.

He became friendly with the band members, and when they went to North Carolina to work on their second album in early 1984, Peter invited DeCurtis to come and hang out. What he saw, DeCurtis says, was like a dream about what recording sessions should be. The new songs were as eccentric as the ones on *Chronic Town* and *Murmur*, only catchier and more propulsive than before. The sound in the studio was punchier too, from the crisp tone of Peter's guitar to the slap of the drums and the pulse of the bass tones. And if Michael's lyrics were still elliptical, his singing was more pronounced. "It was like the kids had taken over the candy store," DeCurtis says. "They were doing exactly what they wanted to do with Mitch and Don, and it was so exciting, so inspiring. And it was like *Fuck, this is how it should always be! Smart people doing exactly what they want!*"[1]

They'd had to be strategic to steer clear of the creative input from I.R.S.'s executives, making certain Jay Boberg didn't visit the studio until the record was all but finished, then counting on Jefferson Holt and their producers to insulate the band from Boberg's urging to give the company at least one song that sounded like a hit. Ultimately they could do whatever they wanted. And what they wanted to do was make an album full of crunchy, melodic songs, many of which were designed to subvert every expectation a casual listener might have for their, or anyone's, modern rock songs.

"Harborcoat," the opening track, was titled after an imaginary garment or, more likely, a made-up term for protection. Who's being protected, and why, can only be inferred from a chain of references to statues of Vladimir Lenin, banned books, and feigned belief. That all of this comes in a hummable melody strung across an upbeat, danceable instrumental track makes it all the more difficult to parse. The verses of "7 Chinese Brothers" play out across a tuneful if pensive guitar figure, before blossoming into a ringing chorus that should herald something a lot more glorious, were the lyric not a cryptic description of romantic perfidy crowned by a reference to a Chinese children's parable about greed. "So. Central Rain (I'm Sorry)," the urgent, fretful song that was still nameless when they debuted it on *Late Night with David Letterman*, is far more straightforward, a tale of broken communication from a distant lover who finds himself plagued by foul weather and a guilty conscience.

Two of the songs dated back to the band's earliest days. "Pretty Persuasion" is a group composition from late 1980, a blazer that opens with an electrifying twelve-string guitar riff, hanging two vocal lines (Michael's melody and a higher harmony by Mike) across another romantic triangle with a bisexual twist: *He's got pretty persuasion / She's got pretty persuasion*. The other oldie, "(Don't Go Back to) Rockville," was the solo Mike Mills composition that went all the way back to June 1980. The Athens-set triptych concludes with "Camera," which memorializes Carol Levy in spare instrumentation, a mournful, hanging melody, and disconnected memories of friendship and grief.

Apart from the plainspoken narrative Mike wrote for "Rockville," the most direct songs on the album describe the surreality of the band's real life as working musicians. "Letter Never Sent" and "Little America" are hard-rocking dispatches from the road, while "Second Guessing" takes a not terribly veiled swipe at record company executives and other critics who feel obliged to comment, critique, or otherwise revise the band's work, ending with a full-throated chorus of *Here we are, here we are*, a celebration with a defiant subtext: take us or leave us.

They agreed to make a traditional music performance video for "So. Central Rain (I'm Sorry)," with a couple of significant differences: the instrumentalists would mime their parts while standing behind translucent scrims so they would register as shadows, and Michael, who drew a hard line around pretending to sing on television, would record a new vocal as the cameras rolled. They shot it in Reflection Sound Studios during the week of recording in January, with director Howard Libov keeping Michael in tight focus as he sang, eyes shut, his chestnut curls haloed from the backlit scrims. The lighting gave him an angelic look while simultaneously hiding and revealing his bandmates, a visual representation of how R.E.M. was both pursuing and dodging its growing success.

The governing duality in the band is also symbolized on the cover of *Reckoning*, as they titled their second album, by a two-headed snake. The viper, sketched by Michael and then colored and enhanced by Howard Finster, twists through a dark field filled with the artist's childlike drawings of faces, houses, and fantastical animals. Homespun and strange, the cover illustration ran counter to the glossy images on nearly every other new album on the shelves. The band found a variety of other ways to subvert expectations, starting with the spine of the LP, which repurposed the old-fashioned FILE UNDER indicator (meant for record store clerks who might not know if an album was pop, folk, jazz, or whatever) into FILE UNDER WATER, a reference to the number of songs with lyrics mentioning rivers, oceans, and so on. The album's label dispensed with "side one" and "side two" labels, substituting a prankish LEFT SIDE/RIGHT SIDE designation.

The going got even stranger on Jim Herbert's music video. With no interest in making anything like a traditional MTV clip, Herbert took the band to a sculpture garden built by the Georgia artist Bill Miller and filmed the musicians wandering around the assortment of wind-powered whirligigs. Captured in the fading light of a March afternoon, the band's images freeze, jump forward, double back, and come in and out of focus through a visual process that allowed Herbert to isolate and manipulate individual frames of film. None of the action was edited to correspond to the music, and because Herbert was accustomed to making films of about twenty minutes, the video covered all the songs on the new album's opening side. It was titled according to its puckish label designation, *Left of Reckoning*. And though the film was financed by I.R.S. and packaged as an R.E.M. music video, it's actually a Jim Herbert art project in which the musicians happen to appear. At a moment when mainstream music videos had the gloss and bounce of big-budget Hollywood movies, it was, to put it lightly, a striking departure.

All of it, the catchy, bright-spirited songs paired with dark, oblique lyrics; the *see me/don't look at me* videos; the subversion of the mainstream pop album's customary look, feel, and most prosaic details (file under . . . water?) expressed something essential about R.E.M., the performative ambivalence that was crucial to their project, and to their connection to their core followers. It was the same thing Michael had been saying in public since he made himself the focus of the TV news camera at the *Rocky Horror* show in St. Louis in 1978. A declaration of deviation. A public abandonment of normative principles. Dress up in full, extravagant drag, gaze right into the lens, and shrug it off. *We're all quite normal, really.*

Here we are, and this is fine. This is more than fine. And if you can hear this and see this, and you understand what we're saying, you're one of us.

It was like a bat signal coming through the clouds. *If you don't belong, you belong here.* Even as the band ascended, they knew where they could find their people. When they came to town, the members of R.E.M. still beelined to the campuses, still booked interviews on the college radio stations, still spun their favorite records on the air and then hung around afterward to talk to the staff and anyone else who showed up. About bands, about books, about the best place to get hummus and organic juice near campus, or where they'd find some pitchers of beer and a jukebox loaded with cool records. And if you were with them now, you could be with them later, too. Everyone they met could get on the list for the show and knew where the party would be when it was over. For the fans who couldn't get to the show, the invitation had already been etched in the vinyl. In the songs that didn't work like any other songs you'd heard. In the records that came packaged in weird Howard Finster paintings. In the music videos that said music videos are dumb, and fuck music videos.

Released on April 9, 1984, *Reckoning* climbed to number twenty-seven on the *Billboard* album chart and sold at a steady clip for the next few months. More significantly, it shot to the top of the *CMJ* campus airplay charts and dominated the college airwaves for the rest of the year. So while commercial radio and MTV clattered, whirred, and flashed with Michael Jackson, Bruce Springsteen, Prince, Madonna, Dire Straits, and all the other megastars of the supersize mid-1980s, on the left side of the dial, where the low-power stations spoke a spikier, deeper language, the air buzzed *R.E.M., R.E.M., R.E.M.*

And R.E.M. buzzed back at them. When they were presented with *CMJ*'s Album of the Year award at the New Music Awards in 1983, they missed the ceremony but sent a video of the four of them singing the theme to the Monkees' TV show, with new lyrics to mark the occasion. Peter strums an acoustic guitar to start it, Mike and Bill look into the lens from behind him, and Michael sits to his left, a hand held over his face until Peter counts four and they all start to sing in unison: *Hey hey, we're acceptin' the award you're givin' today / Thank you, everybody there at* CMJ. *Hey, hey!* When they won the same award and also Group of the Year in 1984, they sent another video acceptance, only this time it was an elaborately staged silent movie costarring Jefferson Holt, attorney Bertis Downs, and staffers Liz Hammond and Sandra-Lee Phipps, who receive the news at R.E.M.'s office, respond ecstatically via old-fashioned dialogue cards reading *Oh My God!, Shazzam!,* and so on. *Let's Go Tell The Combo!* they cry, then ride bikes across Athens to the band's rehearsal space, a garage in which the four musicians stand around a microphone like a bar-bershop quartet, snapping their fingers and singing what the next title card transcribes as *Shoop Doo Doo Wah Ooby-Dooby*. When the office team delivers the news, each band member mugs his shock and delight, the entire gang stages an ecstatic dance, and the scene fades as awkwardly and cheerfully as any no-budget dormitory gag film would. Just a bunch of college kids having fun while the rest of the world wasn't looking. Yet.

21

My Soul Doth Magnify the Lord

Nine songs in, *Reckoning* takes a sharp right turn. The rhythm slows to midtempo and the electric guitar is subbed out for an acoustic strum as a honky-tonk-style piano rolls to center stage. When the words come, Michael sketches the scene with a distinct, and distinctly sad, southern accent. A friend in the bus station, packed up and leaving for some other, less agreeable town. She's not leaving the singer in the heat of quarrel or for any reason beyond the calendar and circumstance: work, family, something that feels unavoidable to her, if not him. All he knows is that she's leaving, he's going to be lonely, and as far as he's concerned she's making a terrible mistake. The one-line chorus, which repeats over a simple three-chord pattern, boils all of his feelings down to a simple declarative statement: *Don't go back to Rockville.*

"(Don't Go Back to) Rockville" is an outlier on *Reckoning*, and not just because it dates back to the spring of 1980, just a few weeks after the party at the church. It's also a solo composition, written entirely by Mike Mills. He wrote it at the end of the spring term, but it took four months for the song to make it into the band's set list, and nearly four years for them to put it on an album. The song, like its author, took a little time to grow on people.

Bill Berry hated Mike Mills at first sight. This became one of their favorite stories: how they had been ninth graders in junior high in Macon when they first saw each other, looking from opposite ends of a yawning cultural divide, because Bill, as he recalled later, was an aspiring troublemaker. Fourteen and sarcastic and seething with teenage contempt for school and teachers and all the shit they tell you, man. Bill and his thuggish little buddies wore jeans and T-shirts and slumped in the back row of class, muttering.

Mike Mills, on the other hand, was perched in the front, upright in his seat and dressed smartly in a button-up shirt and pressed trousers. He kept his sandy brown hair combed, even when it flowed over his collar, as per the style of the mid-1970s. He paid attention to his teachers and was unfailingly polite. *Yes sir, no ma'am*, in that reedy voice of his, the slightest hint of a drawl pulling at his vowels. He was thin as a beanpole and fair-skinned and looked to be about twelve, his cheeks smooth and untroubled by acne. Everything came easily to him, it seemed. Mike made the school honor society during his first year at Northeast High School and was named an alternate in the statewide Governor's Honors Program held each summer at Wesleyan College. It was just the start of the academic awards that came his way, and Bill, who figured it was smarter not to give a shit about school, could only watch and scoff. Mike might have pretended he didn't notice, but he didn't like Bill either. "I thought he was an asshole."[1]

Michael Edward Mills was born on December 17, 1958, near the military base where his father, Franklin, was stationed with the U.S. Marines in Orange County, California. A helicopter pilot, Frank mustered out of the military in 1960 and moved back to his hometown of Atlanta, where he worked as a salesman for an insurance company. Another boy, Mitchell, joined the family in 1962. Frank switched to heavy equipment sales, and when he took a new position in Macon in the late 1960s the family relocated to the smaller city eighty miles to the southeast. Frank was a good salesman and became successful enough to open his own heavy equipment sales company, also getting into the road-grading business for a while, but his heart resided elsewhere.[2]

A natural singer graced with a rich and powerful voice, Frank was a classically trained tenor who sang with the Naval Aviation Choir during his days in the Marines, and in an elite vocal quartet drawn from the larger group that performed at Miss America and Miss Universe beauty pageants and, on one stunning occasion, to an audience of millions on the nationally broadcast *Ed Sullivan Show*.[3] Married in 1956 to the former Adora Wood, Frank built a life with a woman whose musical ability and training rivaled his. A trained singer herself, Adora taught classical guitar and recorder, played the piano, and sang in various choirs alongside her husband and on her own.

Frank Mills had a big voice and a body to match, broad shoulders and a prominent chest, and his personality was just as large. He had red hair and freckles, chain-smoked cigarettes and sipped cocktails when he was with his friends, and laughed heartily when something amused him, which was often. Living in Atlanta during the 1960s, Frank sang with the Atlanta Choral Guild, and when a job took him to Macon at the end of the decade, he and Adora joined the First Presbyterian Church and connected with its choral director, Susan McDuffie, who soon made Frank her principal tenor.[4]

McDuffie and her husband, Bill, had kids near Mike's and Mitch's ages, and the families grew close. Bobby McDuffie, who was Mike's contemporary, was entranced by his friend's father. Already a budding violinist who would soon leave home to attend a high school conservatory in New York, the younger McDuffie spent hours listening to Frank Mills's voice. "He was a powerful musical force when I was twelve or thirteen," Robert McDuffie says today. "I'd listen to my cassettes over and over again—his performance of Saint-Saëns's 'Christmas Oratorio,' 'My Soul Doth Magnify the Lord,' also Handel's 'Messiah' and Brahms's 'German Requiem.' He belted, but beautifully. He phrased things so naturally in his solos. He was very powerful, very passionate, and so appealing."[5]

Given smart, supportive parents, Mike excelled in grade school and drank in the music his parents played on the radio and the family hi-fi. He studied piano and music theory during grade school and also took up the guitar, teaching himself with some guidance from Adora. He shared his parents' enthusiasm for choral singing and performed alongside Bobby McDuffie in their church's youth and handbell choirs. For a long time he was content to listen to his parents' music, pushing his toys across the floor to the sound of symphonies, operatic arias, and other classical works, along with a few lighter albums Frank liked, particularly the vocal jazz-pop of the Four Freshmen. But when Adora noticed her older son paying attention to pop music not long after the family moved to Macon, in 1970, she bought him a special gift: three recent hit singles. "Come Together," the swampy leadoff track from the Beatles' *Abbey Road* album, Harry Nilsson's cover of Fred Neil's bittersweet "Everybody's Talkin'," known as the theme song to the movie *Midnight Cowboy*, and Vanity Fare's sunny hit "Hitchin' a Ride." It was a quick overview of the modern pop scene, and it piqued the boy's interest. Mike started exploring the pop radio dial, and when he got himself to a record store, he came home with a broader variety, everything from Seals & Crofts' easy listening to the harder pop of Three Dog Night to the latest by the reigning hard rock behemoths Led Zeppelin.

By the time he got to high school, Mike's consciousness was saturated with music—listening to it, talking about it, playing it. He played sousaphone in the high school marching band, then combined his mastery of the bass clef with his knowledge of the guitar in order to take up the electric bass. Mike practiced in the basement for hours at a time, his amplifier cranked loud enough to send cans and plates rattling off their shelves in the pantry upstairs. Neither the volume nor Mike's deepening interest in rock 'n' roll music disturbed his parents. Their musical preferences might have run more toward classical and the pop music of their own youth, but they loved that both of their boys—Mitchell studied trombone, piano, and guitar—were so deeply engaged with their own music. And when Mike invited friends over to play in the family's basement and the beat made the windows rattle in their frames, Frank and Adora would just shake their heads and smile. At least they knew where the boys were. And weren't they getting pretty good?

Mike had no problem keeping up his grades. His near-perfect

SAT scores the fall of his senior year won him a place in the National Honor Society. He was the co-valedictorian of the senior class of 1976 and managed to look only somewhat queasy when posing with his cohonoree as they held up an appropriately thick book for the photograph in the Northeast High yearbook, the *Valhalla*. Mike's white-collar future seemed set: he had the essentials for a career in business, in law, maybe as a teacher or even a college professor. But he didn't want any of that. Which he made clear in the senior portrait that appears in the same yearbook. In which he poses next to the real focus of his time, attention, and fascination: his Fender Jazz electric bass.

22

Shadowfax

Mike shared Bill's same sinking feeling when he hefted his bass into that basement jam session and saw that heavy-browed kid glowering from behind the drums. "Bill showed up and I was like, *Oh no, no, no, I can't do it!*" Mike recalled to Debi Atkinson in 1984.[1] The drummer had moved to a different high school by then, but that brow was hard to forget, and the contemptuous glare that came from beneath it was even more memorable. "He was kind of rowdy, obnoxious, and mean," Mike said.[2] They were in his family's house; he could have ordered his junior high antagonist out the door. But Mike's nature was too gentle for that, so he took a breath, tuned up his bass, and waited for the music to start. When the others were ready, the drummer slapped his sticks together, hit the downbeat, and the bassist jumped in. In an instant they locked in together.

One song after another, the common repertoire for Macon rockers in those days—southern boogie classics, mostly, with some favorites by the Rolling Stones and others. They all knew their parts, and the guitar player who had brought them together, David Wilson, could play the leads with a quick-fingered assurance that kept them all on their toes. Mike kept his eyes on Bill, and they notched in together so easily he started to relax. The looks between them lost their chill, moved through neutral to a kind of warmth . . . a nod, then a smile or two. When the jamming ended, Bill looked over his cymbals and caught the bassist's eye. "Look, this is ridiculous," he said. It was as close to an apology as an adolescent boy could get, and Mike was quick to take the olive branch. "We ended up getting on really well," Mike told Atkinson. "We both grew up."[3]

And that was that, a largely unspoken end to their largely unspoken feud. "We've been best friends ever since," Bill said later.[4]

The jam session went so well, they decided to form a band. The leader was the lead guitar player, a long-haired sixteen-year-old named David Wilson, who was so proficient with a slide that he could play Duane Allman's parts with ease. The lead singer and rhythm guitarist was Alan Ingley, whose clean-cut look and squared-away persona set him apart from the others. "He wasn't like us," Wilson says. "He was real serious about baseball. An athlete who happened to play guitar and had a beautiful voice. He wasn't trying to be a rebel like us." The band moved their gear into the Mills family's basement and started practicing, building a repertoire of songs that leaned into the jam-heavy rock that dominated the airwaves and turntables throughout the South in the mid-1970s. The influence was particularly strong in Macon, which served as the headquarters for Capricorn Records, the independent company that put out records by the Allman Brothers Band, the Marshall Tucker Band, Wet Willie, and a legion of other southern rockers. The Allmans had moved to Macon when they signed with Capricorn in the late 1960s, and the band's commercial success, along with their unrivaled place as the best and most beloved of the southern boogie bands, made them a defining presence among music fans in the city.

Capricorn Records, its owner Phil Walden, and particularly the Allmans were so present in town they seemed to be everywhere, listening for music and getting involved with anyone who was making it. One afternoon in the early 1970s, Ingley was playing guitar with a bassist friend on the friend's family's back porch when a man with a beard and long hair stepped through the bushes and asked if they wanted to jam. He was Joseph Campbell, better known among Allmans aficionados as the band's roadie, Red Dog. They passed a

pleasant afternoon together, and later he took the boys to the recon-
ditioned mill the Allmans used as their headquarters. There he
showed them one of Duane Allman's old guitars and dug into the
band's gear box for cords, effects boxes, and other equipment. "Just
take it. They ain't never gonna miss this stuff," he said with a wave
of his hand.

A few years later Wilson befriended the Allmans' road manager,
Twiggs Lyndon, who came to the Mills house to hear the boys' band
and stuck around to play with them. He came back another night
accompanied by Jaimoe, the Allmans' drummer. "That was fun, god-
dammit, man," Wilson says. "It meant nothing to our future, but
it was an amazing experience. Jaimoe was a real nice guy, real nice
and humble. All these people were regular people, just older and
successful."

Wilson and the band worked out a repertoire of cover songs, jam-
friendly Allmans tunes including "Statesboro Blues" and "One Way
Out," plus a few Marshall Tucker Band songs and popular rock radio
hits such as Brownsville Station's "Smokin' in the Boys Room" and
Steppenwolf's "Born to Be Wild." Ingley made a signature piece out
of Chicago's ballad "Colour My World." They called the band Shadowfax, after the magical horse in J. R. R. Tolkien's *Lord of the Rings*,
and started playing parties for their friends and then for kids from
other schools. Shadowfax soon became a solid cover band, particularly for a bunch of high schoolers, and Ingley still marvels at how
accomplished his teenage bandmates were. "David was one of the
most pure musical souls I've ever met; he could play slide just like
Duane Allman. And Bill was the best drummer I've ever played with.
He didn't take himself seriously and could do anything."[5]

As the band's reputation grew, Shadowfax got professional bookings from adults: entertaining at kid-centric businesses at the nearby
mall, weekend events at the skating rink, a video game arcade, and
more. One local attorney paid them a few hundred dollars, plus all
the beer they could drink, to play a party at his lake house. The affair
was for members of some kind of civic organization for young leaders, but it turned into a bacchanal, with heavy drinking and a green
marijuana haze. "We just wanted to play, but we had a blast," recalls

Ingley, who got so swept up in the moment that on the drive home the otherwise clean-living young man took a turn with the band's communal joint. "They were so shocked, the car nearly stopped on the highway when I did that," Ingley recalls.[6]

Shadowfax had a good run, but as the band members approached the end of high school, they had to think about their futures. Either that or make a point of not thinking about them, which is what Mike and Bill resolved to do. Wilson was also content to stick with music for the foreseeable future, but Ingley, so often the odd man out in the band, had more traditional plans.

When the end came it was sudden, and jarring. Someone in the band scheduled a show for the coming weekend without consulting Ingley. Ordinarily, this wouldn't have been a problem: they were teenagers, they didn't have many other places to be on a Saturday. But Ingley was scheduled to visit a college out of town. He had an appointment for an interview with the admissions department and it wasn't something he could skip. No matter, his bandmates were furious. "It felt like instant hatred," Ingley says. "It breaks my heart, but I don't think I talked to those guys after that." The abrupt freeze-out from his bandmates turned Ingley against music, at least for a while. "I got rid of my guitars, everything."[7] Ingley ultimately went to the University of Georgia and graduated in the spring of 1980, just a few weeks after his former bandmates played their first show at St. Mary's Church.

The remaining members of Shadowfax recruited another guitarist, who didn't work very well, so they evolved into a three-piece called the Back Door Band. They stuck to Allmans-style jams and blues songs and started experimenting with originals, and they booked a few shows, but by summer's end they had lost steam, and in the fall of 1976 they drifted to a halt.

No longer in high school and not ready to think about college, Mike and Bill rented an apartment in Macon and went looking for jobs. Bill landed a cool one, working as an office boy and chauffeur for Paragon Booking, the concert booking agency associated with

Capricorn Records. Mike took a position at the Sears department store. They were done with playing music, they figured. "We quit and sold our instruments," Mike said later.[8] It might not have been literally true, but they certainly didn't need them anymore. Not for a little while, anyway.

23

So You Want to Be a Rock 'n' Roll Star

L os Angeles, June 19, 1984, the Palace nightclub in Hollywood. The place is packed with highly excited, highly coiffed club kids. Teased blond hair and Ray-Bans, sculpted brows and frosted lips. Trimmed mustaches and Vuarnet shades, unbuttoned shirts and a flash of glistening chest. Also cameras, swooping this way and that, capturing the dancers' jubilant fist pumps and gyrations, closing in and zooming out. Everyone in motion, everything moving in time to the music, and to the musicians, who are also moving and also looking excited, and entirely themselves. Michael Stipe, golden curls falling over the shoulders of his denim jacket, leans into the microphone stand, dancing it this way and that, while Peter Buck struts and leaps with his black-and-white Rickenbacker and Bill Berry, dense hair long and heavy with sweat, hammers and writhes behind his drums, occasionally looking up to sing into the microphone hanging over his head. Mike Mills is going full tilt too, his slight torso wrapped in a stylized Elvis T-shirt, his hands working a new Rickenbacker bass, leaping one way, then dashing the other before stumbling back to his microphone to pitch in a harmony.

This shiny setting, with all the stylish L.A. club kids exerting themselves toward delirium, or some camera-friendly approximation of it, feels a long way from the 40 Watt club in Athens. But they're taping an episode of Showtime's *Rock of the 80's*, a monthly concert series that focuses on up-and-coming acts, generally ones that programmers would describe as new wave. This evening's show includes the artful soul singer Nona Hendryx, then in the midst of a modern makeover, and is headlined by the surging Britpop band Simple Minds.

The middle portion begins with Jason & the Scorchers ripping through a brief set of flashy cowpunk. As the last notes of "Great Balls of Fire" hang in the air, the revolving stage spins, R.E.M. comes into view, and the pretty young crowd seems to erupt. It feels like an odd fit, playing their weirdly constructed, impossible-to-parse songs to this room full of camera-ready club kids. But somehow . . . maybe it's the cameras, maybe it's the booze you can see them quaffing, maybe it's actually the music . . . it works. The band kicks into a lightning-paced "Sitting Still," which segues into "Radio Free Europe." The opening chords of "Little America" ring out, the band clicks into an even higher gear, and when the camera finds Mike he's bouncing down the stairs to where a small knot of girls exult. He takes a seat on a lower step and keeps thrumming along, not missing a note, even when the camera comes in close. He thrusts a playful tongue into its lens.

If R.E.M. had learned how to dazzle audiences of all sizes in all kinds of settings with their live shows, their records were casting just as powerful a spell on critics in mainstream and underground publications, on both sides of the Atlantic. And *Reckoning* more than lived up to their expectations. Chris Connelly's review in *Rolling Stone* inventoried some of his least favorite aspects of the band's sound—the occasionally gnomic lyrics, what struck him as an underwhelming drum presence, and the album's occasional digressions into studio jams and chatter—but still gave the album four stars, concluding that "these guys seem to know exactly where they're going, and following them should be fun."[1] *The Washington Post*'s Joe Sasfy proclaimed that "there isn't an American band more worth following."[2] Writing for *Musician*, Anthony DeCurtis could only shake his head in wonder. "How much better can they possibly get?"[3] Over in England, the *New Musical Express*'s Mat Snow played the record and heard the cathedral chime of the American Dream: "the journey west to the

Promised Land with nothing but a shimmering horizon ahead and a blazing, deep blue sky above."[4]

Stellar reviews aside, the I.R.S. Records publicity team still encountered resistance from mainstream radio and media outlets that steered clear of anything that seemed too obscure for their audience. "You're competing with a lot of people that are willing to make artistic compromises R.E.M. was not willing to make to achieve a certain commercial acceptance," Jay Boberg told the *Los Angeles Times* that July. "We're looking at it as an educational process. We just have to go to greater lengths to inform them of the things going on in their backyard with this band."[5] But in the midst of Ronald Reagan's Morning in America campaign for reelection and the festival of nationalism the Summer Olympics in Los Angeles had become, the band members did everything they could to hone their insurgent reputation. "We see ourselves as the quintessential outsiders," Peter said in the same *Los Angeles Times* article. "Hell, our album was number 27 on the charts and MTV dropped [our video] from rotation because it wasn't naked girls or smoke bombs."[6] Ironically, this anti-mainstream stance earned the band the attention of the über-mainstream *Entertainment Tonight*, whose correspondent Scott Osborne noted that R.E.M. were "music rebels [who] don't buy into the homogenized sound they feel is prevalent today."[7]

For some observers, the band's anti-commercial/critics' darlings positioning seemed to wear thin. A reporter on Citytv's *The NewMusic* program in Toronto, after challenging Mike to justify having lyrics that are "mumbly to the point of incoherence," proposed that having "masses of accolades shoveled on top" of the band could become a problem. The bassist, looking collegiate in his English Beat T-shirt, horn-rimmed glasses, and bowl-cut hair, shrugged it off. "We know better. There are plenty of people in America and elsewhere that are just as talented as we are." The reporter, thoroughly defanged, chuckled and moved on. What about all the comparisons to classic rock bands like the Byrds, Jefferson Airplane, and Hot Tuna? (Where he came up with Jefferson Airplane, let alone Hot Tuna, is anyone's guess.) Again Mike shrugged it off as politely as possible. "I think we just have a similar sensibility," he said. "If we'd been around in the '60s we would've sounded like them. If they had just come along now and we'd been in the '60s, it would've been the other way around."[8]

If it seemed like a presumptuous way to answer the question, it was, at least, based on something other than baseless supposition. In early June, just a few days before the taping of the *Rock of the 80's* show, R.E.M. had performed a special concert in Passaic, New Jersey, for MTV's *Rock Influences* series, sharing the stage with 1960s folk-rock heroes Richie Havens, Levon Helm, Rick Danko and Richard Manuel of the Band, John Sebastian of the Lovin' Spoonful, and Roger McGuinn of the Byrds. The folkies started the evening by playing mini sets, setting up an hourlong performance by R.E.M., who opened with a stately version of the Velvet Underground's "Pale Blue Eyes," then jumped into a set dominated by songs that were either on the new album or too new to have been recorded. Dressed with casual collegiate flair—Mike and Peter in button-up shirts and Michael in an olive T-shirt worn over pleated wool trousers while Bill sported a sweatshirt with stylishly ragged torn-off sleeves—the band, which had grown accustomed to performing in clubs and theaters seating more than a thousand people, moved easily with the music, looking entirely comfortable working the three-thousand-seat hall.

When the main part of their show was over, the band encored with Sebastian on the Spoonful's 1960s hit "Do You Believe in Magic" and with McGuinn, who brought his own Rickenbacker to lead his inheritors in the Byrds' 1967 hit "So You Want to Be a Rock 'n' Roll Star." It was a powerful moment. The band had the tune down cold. Michael threw in some harmonies, though he hadn't quite mastered all the words. All of the younger musicians seemed to be having a ball, but McGuinn, who had had his first hit two decades earlier, glanced around the stage meaningfully as he sang about the verities of the popular musician's life: the emphasis on clothes and sex appeal, the fast-talking managers and music industrialists, the rapacious fans, the record company that is in the business, ultimately, of selling pieces of plastic. You get rich, maybe even relatively quickly, but at what cost?

The price you paid for your riches and fame, was it all a strange game? You're a little insane.

It sounded like a welcome. And a warning.

Don't forget what you are, you're a rock 'n' roll star.

The Passaic show was the last booking R.E.M. traveled to in a van. They flew to Los Angeles after that and were picked up in a Golden Eagle touring bus, specially outfitted with reclining seats, a bathroom, café tables, a sound system, and bunks for those long overnight drives. The crew got their own bus, and the gear went into a truck. They spent a few days in L.A. doing interviews and taping TV shows, then on June 16 got back on the road, performing that night in Fresno, California, then heading up the coast on the first leg of a tour that would have them crisscrossing the continent, playing clubs and, increasingly, auditoriums until mid-October.

At some point along the way, Bill was having a few beers in his hotel room with Gevin Lindsay, an old friend and guitarist from Macon who had set aside his own music for a while to serve as R.E.M.'s guitar tech. Looking out the window, the drummer noticed the tour buses waiting in the parking lot and let it all wash over him. Buses! Trucks! All that gear, all those people to ferry it from one venue to the next, all of them filled with fans who would listen and cheer them down the road to the next place and then the place after that. "He got kind of emotional there for a moment," Lindsay recalls. He and his three friends just wanted to be in a band and play rock 'n' roll for their friends, and somehow that had led to all this. "I could see the revelation on his face. He was just astonished for a moment."[9]

Not that he had a lot of time to sit and reflect. They had about a week off after the end of the U.S. tour before it was time to fly off to play a Halloween show in Honolulu, en route to a week of concerts in Japan, then a month hopscotching through the UK, Ireland, and Norway. They weren't quite rock stars—they could walk down nearly any street without being recognized. But four years of work, the touring, songwriting, rehearsing, and recording, the interviews, autograph sessions in record stores, visits to college radio stations, in-studio visits to commercial radio stations, meet-and-greets with industry insiders, post-concert hangouts with fans, beers hoisted, and nights in the van, had started to show results. Bigger halls with crowds in the low thousands, better stage equipment, the buses that made their endless travels at least a little more comfortable. They weren't getting rich yet, but the weekly road salaries allowed for real meals in real restaurants, assuming they had the time to go out, find a decent place, and sit down to eat. They got most of the holiday season off but regrouped in time to play a homecoming/New Year's Eve show at the 4,600-seat Atlanta Civic Center. That was as close as they could get to Athens, which no longer had a venue big enough to satisfy the demand for tickets.

Gravity Pulling Me Around

river 8" and "Old Man Kensey" debuted at the Passaic show in mid-1984 and were followed that summer and fall by a variety of other new songs: "Good Advices," "Wendell Gee," "Auctioneer (Another Engine)," and a few more. The new songs, written largely in hotel rooms, worked out at soundchecks, and first performed in cities hundreds and thousands of miles away from Athens, evoked home in a distinct way none of their earlier work had done. There was a clarity to the writing, a sense of place and character that seemed to have grown more vivid from afar. Both Peter and Michael were fans of the writer Flannery O'Connor, whose tales of the Deep South bristled with prophets, murderers, priests, hermaphrodites, the disabled, disfigured, and deranged. The new songs were written in her thrall, grounding them in a crooked vision of home that was both dark and affectionate, spiritually hobbled yet radiant with love. _He sees what you can't see_, went one of the new songs. _Can't you see that?_

The planning for 1985 started in the fall of 1984, when R.E.M. was working through the final leg of the year's American tour and then taking flight to Japan and England. They were all out of their bodies then, their shared momentum carrying them farther and higher than they'd ever dared to dream. Eager to develop new facets of their sound, they decided to make a break from the production team of Mitch Easter and Don Dixon and find a new partner to help them explore. Peter, with his intricate knowledge of rock history, suggested they try to connect with Joe Boyd, an American expat who had spent the past twenty years in London producing ambitious records for everyone from Pink Floyd, back in the band's earliest, Syd Barrett– led days, to the brilliant, doomed singer-songwriter Nick Drake and the folk-rock duo Richard and Linda Thompson, among many others. At first it seemed like Boyd wouldn't be able to help: he was in the middle of a record for the Canadian art-rock singer-songwriter Mary Margaret O'Hara. But in mid-February, when that project ended earlier than expected, he rang up Jefferson Holt, and a few days later he arrived in Athens to help R.E.M. record some demos and see how it felt to work together. The band cranked through thirteen of their new songs in a day, and it felt so good they signed up Boyd on the spot. He'd need to do the recording in London, as he was running his own record label at the time and needed to be close to his office. That didn't bother them at all. In fact, they were delighted. "They said, *Cool! London! Fine!*" Boyd recalls.[1]

The band got to London in the third week of February, just a few days after the demo session in Athens. They moved into a multifloored town house Holt found for them in the elegant Mayfair district, near Hyde Park. It was a beautiful neighborhood, the streets chockablock with restaurants, pubs, and all the swank shops and bustle of central London. The only problem was that Livingston Studios was in the Wood Green section of North London, eight miles away. Boyd had tried to convince the band to stay closer to where they'd be recording; he had even secured them reservations at a nearby hotel. But the American musicians were set on Mayfair.

They should have listened. London doesn't have the kind of car-friendly streets American cities do, and the drive to the studio in the morning, navigating the crowded, twisty streets, could take an hour or more. The trip home in the evening wasn't a lot faster, and between that and the gruesome winter weather, moods sank and tensions rose. They'd been riding in the same cars, sleeping in the same rooms, breathing the same air, thinking the same thoughts for five years, nearly without interruption. Now they were doing it in a strange city in the least pleasant time of year, in an unfamiliar studio with a new producer who didn't know how they'd always done things, who kept opening doors, snapping on lights, asking ticklish questions—*Would a click track help keep the rhythm straight? Shouldn't the vocals be louder?*—that poked at the band's soft spots and forced them to reconsider decisions they'd made years before. The days dragged. The nights were endless. British food was pasty, and last call at the pubs went out before 11 p.m. The TV had only two channels, and neither of them showed sports they cared about or could even follow. None of it was fun anymore.

How long could they tolerate this? Even if they got through the next few weeks and made it home in time for the start of spring, which is the best time to be in the South, they'd have approximately six days to enjoy it before they were set to take off on another concert tour. Then they'd head up to the frigid Northeast, where April still meant snow, ice, and skeletal trees. They'd been going and going and going, nearly nonstop, since the party in the church. And what the fuck was it getting them?

They had some beers one night and groused to Jefferson Holt, who peered back at them through his glasses and nodded. Yes, yes, he totally got it. Yes, what they said made sense. Yes, they could completely revamp how they did things. They could cut back touring by half or more, spend a lot more time at home, and make the band more like a part-time job. Of course, they'd have to reduce their expectations accordingly. *Reckoning* hadn't gotten a lot of radio play, but their constant touring had pushed sales to about 250,000 copies. If they toured significantly less, they'd sell maybe 100,000 copies of the next record, so that'd be less money coming in. And they'd make significantly less from performing, too, so maybe they could go back to college, get other jobs, or figure out how to live on next to nothing? That or they could continue the work they'd been doing over the past five years and leverage the great new record they were making into becoming an even bigger, more artistically powerful and profitable band. The musicians listened, nodded, looked at one another. *Hmm. Well. Huh. If you put it* that *way* . . .

———

For Michael the gloom had little to do with the weather or the commute. He usually came to the studio a few hours after the other guys anyway, and spent his solitary time visiting the city's museums, galleries, and other cultural hubs. He learned to get around on London's Underground, and made his way to work on the Piccadilly Line, which deposited him just a block or two away from Livingston's front door in something like half the time it took to drive, with only short walks to and from the stations. R.E.M. was still hardly known in England, and it was easy for him to stay below the radar, especially since he had lopped off his chestnut curls, razoring the remnant to stubble, which he dyed a chemical shade of blond. Anonymity was a relief. But he knew it was only a matter of time before they'd be back in the United States, back onstage, and he'd have to face it all again.

All those eyes looking at him, all the lights and noise, the same dizzy feeling night after night after night. He'd be onstage singing, the band blasting away behind him, the crowd at his feet and everything he ever wanted right there for the taking, and think, *What am I doing here?* He knew that Peter, Mike, and Bill made a terrific band, and they wrote great songs, too. They'd come up with chord progressions, verses, and choruses and play them for him, and all he had to do was string together some words, figure out a melody to hold it all together, and then dance around and look cool while he sang. It seemed like an idiot's game. He'd bought himself some good clothes, had grown out his hair until it fell over his shoulders like a golden waterfall, and as long as he made eyes at the spotlight and played hard to get, everyone swooned. And what were they cheering, exactly? And what did it have to do with him? Cutting off his hair was one way to find out. The other guys had their own ideas about the band; they didn't care what he thought, and why should they? Back in Athens, talking to his friend Chris Slay, a poet he'd met at school who had a similar look and passion for art and music, Michael grumbled that they could change places and nobody would be the wiser. "You could stand up there and it wouldn't make any difference!"[2]

Or maybe he was feeling something else, the emotional riptide created by such a powerful, unrelenting wave of energy. The rootlessness that went along with touring and the stimulants they all used to keep going, to keep their light burning bright enough to fill every room they entered. It sapped him in a way he didn't even notice at first. That's what the beer and the pills had been for, to fill in the gaps and give him a leg up. But then he'd wake up in a tangle, a piercing throb behind his eyes, and all the doubts would return.

It wasn't just the glare of the spotlight, or the pie-eyed adoration of fans who had no idea who he was or what he was saying in the songs they said they loved so much. That was all hard enough, but Michael had even more trouble in mind. The part of himself he never hid, but never really talked about either. It wasn't anyone's business, for one thing, just the basic function of his mind and body, the animation of his spirit. He was drawn to women but also to men, and he bonded emotionally and physically with both. His sexuality never troubled him. He didn't lie about it, was often frank in his pursuit of partners of both genders. But he also didn't speak of it in public. First because it wasn't anyone's business, especially in a society so governed by phobia and hostility. Then came the poison tide of the AIDS epidemic, which not only made tenderness a potential vector of death but also provided another reason for people, and his own government, to despise him, to talk about sending everyone like him into concentration camps, in the name of not just common decency but public safety. And what if he had it? Michael hadn't gone in for a test yet, partly because he was so well known, but also . . . mostly . . . because he was terrified to know what the result might be. So he kept moving, kept himself at a distance, kept finding other things he could control or change. Other ways to express his terror and his yearning in words that wouldn't reveal too much of his heart.[3]

Where were they, where had they come from, where did they want to go? Part of the decision to move away from the Easter/Dixon production team stemmed from a thought, maybe an abstract suspicion, that they might want to clarify the sound of their records. To make them an easier fit for radio, without going full synth-pop Top 40. If the band felt ambivalent about the change, Joe Boyd made it easier on them. He was sweet and sympathetic and knew how to work with artists, how to turn murky feelings and half-thought ideas into sound. He quickly figured out how the band's internal disjunction—the clash between Michael and Peter's arty, intellectual approach and the R&B party-band grounding of Mike and Bill—magnified all their strengths into a unified attack that was adventurous, tight, and tremendously powerful. Boyd also encouraged the musicians to clarify their sound. To push Michael's vocals a little higher, create more separation for Peter's guitar parts and more depth for the bass and drums. He also got them to enhance some of the songs with outside musicians, adding a string section to "Feeling Gravitys Pull" and an exuberant horn section to "Can't Get There from Here."

Work in the studio went relatively smoothly. The songs were sounding good. And yet the bad mood persisted, the rubbed-raw feeling that came from too much proximity under too many high-pressure situations for too long. How long could they keep it up? And where would it leave them?

Michael's crisis continued to unfold. He had always been a quirky eater, prone to strict regimens such as the macrobiotic diet he'd subsisted on for most of the '80s, which allowed only grains, vegetables, and legumes and forbade meat and dairy products. But the British restaurants, with their emphasis on virtually everything he couldn't, or wouldn't, eat, bent his palate in increasingly odd directions. For a long time he lived on some kind of all-potato diet that ravaged his digestive system and made his face look puffy and distorted. He continued to find new ways to make his hair look odd, clipping it in a monk's tonsure for a time, then coloring it yellow with mustard and other household products.

Still, Michael's intellectual curiosity thrived. He was shy around Boyd until it turned out that the producer not only knew of but had actually met Brion Gysin, the midcentury artist who had worked with poets William S. Burroughs and Allen Ginsberg on cut-ups, a kind of poetry composed by writing down sentences, cutting them into fragments, tossing them into the air, and then gathering the random shards into verse. "From that point on I was cool," Boyd recalls. "And when I saw his lyrics I said to myself, *Aha, I get it!* They're quite like cut-ups."[4]

Michael's words were also full of energy, and increasingly clear-eyed and direct in their portrayal of his thoughts and feelings. As the record came together, so did Michael's sense of himself. "I found a sense of purpose," he told National Public Radio many years later. Depression, like the chilling blankets of fog that cloak London during the winter, can clear as abruptly and inexplicably as it descends. One moment you're trapped, lost within yourself, with no idea where you are, where you're headed, or how to find your way home, then the dark goes gray, turns wispy white, then sunlight gold. It took some time for it to happen to Michael. But he kept himself going, one foot in front of the other, through that dismal winter and sleepless spring and into the summer, which was when he felt the light warming his shoulders. "Suddenly I just felt elevated, free of the concerns and fears I'd had. It got as dark as I could possibly get . . . Then I came out of it, and it felt transformative."[5]

The opening guitar figure sounds cattywampus. Loud and dissonant, the first notes of "Feeling Gravitys Pull" tumble into the speakers like a beam of light warping through outer space. Michael's voice calls through the noise. He's asleep and reading, he sings to himself, setting the scene for the vision he describes as the rhythm section kicks in, joining the guitar in a gut-rippling groove, the thudding drums and rumbling bass, the caterwaul guitar. *Peel back the mountains, peel back the sky*, Michael sings, pulling the listener into his dream. *Stomp gravity into the floor.* It's the artist's statement, a governing rationale for himself and for his band. He evokes the surrealist artist Man Ray, signaling that we're entering a place where laws don't hold, where time and space bend to the imagination, where dreams prevail. A cello, viola, and violin rise, low and warm, and the artist ascends with them. He controls the light; gravity bends to his touch. The song builds, crests, falls back, builds again. Go back to the start of the second verse and this might be the pivot point for the song, the album, the year, an entire life:

> *Somewhere near the end it said,*
> *"You can't do this." I said, "I can, too."*

They called the album *Fables of the Reconstruction*, or alternately *Reconstruction of the Fables*, or possibly *Fables of the Reconstruction of the Fables*. Whatever: the use of "Reconstruction" set the album not just in the American South but in the ruins of the Confederacy, where history and fantasy weave together. "Driver 8" launches at full throttle, a drawn-out guitar line spinning like the wheels of the train its narrator pilots. The thing thunders across the terrain as its exhausted driver catalogs the landscape flashing by. Farms, fields, stone walls, tree houses, power lines, churches, the rural South blurring at a mile a minute. Home is distant, but closer by the second. "Can't Get There from Here," the lightest of the songs, bops along the back roads, kicking up dust with its R&B horns as it zips here and there, waves to the locals, ignores their instructions—*You can't get there from here*—and keeps on going: *I've been there, I know the way.*

Throughout, the sound shines a bit brighter than the Easter/Dixon–produced albums; Boyd leaves space between the instruments and allows their individual textures to stand in higher relief. Mike's and Bill's backing vocals swell into gorgeous harmony in the choruses of "Green Grow the Rushes" and "Maps and Legends," and Michael's solo voice climbs into a sweet falsetto at the end of the lovelorn "Kohoutek."

But the heart of the album is in the songs that serve as portraiture: character studies set to music. The spirit of Howard Finster flits through most of the record, and "Maps and Legends" is dedicated to him by name. The song moves purposefully, waves of guitars and backing vocals pushing the minor chord pattern into something more thoughtful than brooding. The singer describes an artist, clearly Finster, whose eyes don't perceive the same world on view to the rest of us. It's easy to dismiss him as a fool, but, the song cautions, just because a truth is broadly accepted doesn't make it right. *Maybe these maps and legends have been misunderstood.* One of Finster's friends inspired "Old Man Kensey," the tale of a fantasist whose career plans are rarely hampered by experience. "Life and How to Live It" describes the worldview of a real Athens eccentric/schizophrenic who turned his house into a fully stocked duplex so he could live on either side depending on his mood. "Wendell Gee" concludes the album on an elegiac note. A banjo twangs, the strings and backing vocals weaving together as Michael describes the final moments of its title character, a certain kind of old-fashioned southerner, "reared to give respect," who lives on his own, communing with nature until another dream—the album begins and ends with them—signals his death. *So whistle as the wind blows*, Michael sings, his voice gone wistful. *Whistle as the wind blows, with me.*

25

A Magic Kingdom, Open-Armed

They came home in April to a nation with a supersized sense of itself. Ronald Reagan, reelected in an enormous landslide the previous November, now rode astride a Cold War nationalism that had made the United States even noisier than usual. American forces, operating in view and in secret, were at work all across the planet, toppling governments in Central America, warehousing nuclear weapons in Europe, and propping up oil-rich tyrants in the Middle East. And the nation's movies had become just as bellicose. Rambo and Rocky, Indiana Jones and Axel Foley. Speeding cars, gunfire, cavernous mansions, and mountains of cash. The music was just as noisy: Michael Jackson and Madonna, Prince and Bruce Springsteen all looming over the globe like star-spangled behemoths, beaming the American fantasia to the masses of seven continents. They were all video stars too, dancing and feeling and sort of performing their songs for the cameras, often in elaborately plotted mini movies that had the same velocity as the movies that unspooled in the multiplexes. You could go to the theater, the arena, or a stadium, or simply sit in your living room, TV remote in hand, and feel the booming in your sternum, your hair blown back by the sheer holy fuck of it all.

Or you could snap on the radio and spin the dial to the left, where the college stations jostled for bandwidth with the public radio outlets, jazz devotees, and classical holdouts. Where the music could get murky and the between-song patter convoluted. Down here, anticipation for R.E.M.'s next record was electric. The challenge for the band was to beam a signal that would also register at a higher frequency.

The promotional campaign for the record began during the third week of April 1985, just a few weeks after the band returned from London, with a three-week swing through college auditoriums and sports arenas; they called it the Preconstruction Tour. This was their home turf, where they had come from and still felt most comfortable. Lori Blumenthal, who first got to know the band as a college intern working for I.R.S. Records' distributor, A&M Records, in the early 1980s, had scored a job with R.E.M.'s label by the time *Fables of the Reconstruction* came out, and she was impressed by how much energy and time the band, who were, as she recalls, "pretty much rock stars" by 1985, put into college radio stations. On tour they were always eager to drop in on campus stations, do whatever interviews were desired, and stick around to chat afterward. "They had a passion for college radio, because they helped [the band] come up, and they were passionate about the bands who got played alongside them," she says. "And they were important to college radio, because [the band and the medium] had grown together and lifted each other up."[1]

But the growing buzz around the band made it feel a little like a farewell, a series of graduation ceremonies. MTV sent a reporter to Rutgers University, in New Brunswick, New Jersey, where they were appearing that night, to see how the band's most committed fans, college students, were feeling about all the new attention R.E.M. was receiving. The guy spinning "Carnival of Sorts" at the school's radio station seemed delighted. "We played them because we like them," he said. "If they're becoming popular, it couldn't please us more." After the show, another fan broke down the music's appeal: "They talk about dreams. They talk about things inside us that we don't always think about."

Interviewed before the show that same day, Peter and Mike also talked about their connection with college students. Peter: "It's one of three things: they have more leisure time, more money, or they take more drugs. I haven't decided which one." The host, sensing the sound bite forming in front of him, asked if they'd worked out the answer yet, leading Peter and Mike to shoot back, reflexively and in unison: "More leisure time!"[2]

Production on a video for "Can't Get There from Here," the first single to be pulled off the album, took up a week in late May, most of the work being done by Michael, who codirected with his University of Georgia friend Rick Aguar. They came up with a silly art school twist on the usual MTV formula: a compilation of rural roadside food-stand signs (boiled peanuts, etc.), *A Hard Day's Night*-style sequences of Michael and Jefferson Holt leaping streams, rolling over hay bales, and sitting in a puddle coated in red Georgia mud, and footage of the band dancing and riding in old cars to a drive-in theater where they seem to watch a film and hurl popcorn at one another. And more: a globe, held aloft, then tossed across a stream. Wild animals on the hoof and wing. Backlit figures dancing, wielding hammers, playing horns. Occasional lines of lyrics in subtitles. Holt peering fishily at the camera over a pair of aviator shades. Cars in motion, movie projectors spinning. It was the most elaborate video they'd ever attempted, a confused and confusing explosion of seemingly everything Michael and Aguar could think of.

MTV opted not to put the clip in heavy rotation, but it aired on occasion, and the world's most powerful vehicle for popular music found other ways to feature the rising young band, most often in news reports about their whereabouts, some larger-than-usual college shows, and the release of the new album. "It seems to have more of a feeling of place about it," Peter told the cable channel's cameras in a sit-down interview with Mike that spring. "It feels like it was made in a specific place, down in the South, whereas our other records could have been from almost anywhere, really." This, of course, came with a built-in punch line, because where was *Fables* recorded? Peter and Mike answered, and cracked up, once again, in unison: "London!"

———

Making such an American album in the heart of England carried a certain poetic justice for Peter. From the moment reporters, or anyone, would listen, he had been grousing about British acts, and the way so much music made in England, Europe, and elsewhere had crowded American music out of the marketplace. "American bands don't get signed, American bands don't get promoted, American bands don't get played on the radio," he told the British magazine *Sounds* in the spring of 1984.[3] A few months later he expanded on his plaint for *Record* magazine back home. "There's deeply heartfelt music being made by American bands that most people in this country are ignoring," he wrote. "I'm moved by music made by real people for real reasons."[4] Peter had a distinctly non-mainstream kind of music in mind—he name-checked Hüsker Dü, the Replacements, and Mission of Burma, among others—but he and his band were on the leading edge of a wave that was just gathering force.

Peter's ears were tuned to the fringes, as usual, but that upsurge in American consciousness would soon elevate them all. You could see it building momentum on MTV in 1984 as Springsteen's *Born in the U.S.A.* album lobbed "Dancing in the Dark," the first of its handful of smash singles/videos, all constructed around distinctly American sounds and ideas. John Cougar Mellencamp's *Scarecrow* and Tom Petty's *Southern Accents* did the same thing in 1985, when former Creedence Clearwater Revival leader John Fogerty's long-delayed comeback album, *Centerfield*, arrived and promptly climbed to the top of the album charts. Rising alternative bands including Lone Justice and Los Lobos drew on distinct regional forms of Americana, and when MTV turned its attention to the upswell in domestic pop music for the Fourth of July with its 1985 All-American Rock N' Roll Weekend, R.E.M. was prominently featured. And though none of the mainstream acts could be mistaken for a musical wing of the Reagan administration—Springsteen was particularly explicit about being the face of an American character that opposed the president's form of patriotism—R.E.M. presented a distinctly alternative cultural grounding that resonated with a younger, increasingly restless audience. One whose patience with the prevailing culture of the 1980s was wearing thin. And whose size and tastes would soon become transformative.

The wave of publicity, on top of the band's years of effort, paid off. In most cities, demand for tickets had pushed R.E.M. into theaters and amphitheaters with capacities of three to five thousand or higher. The Arlene Schnitzer Concert Hall, in Portland, Oregon; the Paramount, in Seattle. The Cullen Performance Hall, in Houston; the UIC Pavilion, in Chicago. Minnesota's St. Paul Civic Center; the Leroy Theatre, in Pawtucket, Rhode Island. The Greek Theatres of Berkeley and Los Angeles, and Radio City Music Hall, in New York City. They didn't always fill the halls, and there were a few cities where ticket sales lagged noticeably, but that just meant they had more work to do, more shows to play, more interviews to conduct. And if there were a lot of things the members of R.E.M. weren't willing to do to sell records, they were definitely up for making themselves available to newspaper writers, TV cameras, and anyone else with access to readers, listeners, or viewers.

Along with the multiple appearances on MTV News, band members spoke to, were photographed by, and/or appeared on video on dozens of occasions, including an endless array of local newspapers, both dailies and weeklies, magazines of every size, readership, and geographic scope, radio stations up and down the dial, and television programs on national network and cable systems, local broadcast and cable, and, what the hell, cable access channels, too. In Los Angeles, Mike spent a couple of hours talking about his band and introducing videos by other artists ("This is 'Perfect Kiss,' by New Order!") on the local cable music station KWHY-22.

At the start of the summer tour, in early July, Mike and Peter promoted the night's show at Portland's Schnitzer Hall, appearing on ABC affiliate KATU's afternoon chat show *Two at Four,* where they sat around a coffee table fielding questions from the amiable host, Jeff Gianola ("First of all, how do you describe the name R.E.M., what does that stand for?"), and young audience members. Among them was Marshall from Portland, who noted that their singer, Michael Stipe, "has been termed pretty vague." He went on: "Do you guys have any messages you're trying to get across? Because the imagery in your lyrics is, um, pretty vague." Peter nodded thoughtfully. "The songs are pretty personal; sometimes they are a bit oblique," he said. "But I think one gets the meaning, and the heart to the songs, when you listen to them."[5]

More cities, more shows, more interviews. Some interviewers were more formal, meeting a deadline and working from notes someone else had typed up. They tended to be older. The younger ones, the ones who not only knew what they were talking about but *felt* it, leaned in closer, hoping to make an impact. In Vancouver, Michael sat with a young reporter who had some sharp questions to ask and tough observations to make. What did Michael think about the pro-American feeling that had been coming out in so much music? "Well, that has two sides to it," the singer said. "One of them is kind of Reaganistic, jingoistic, patriotic America that is pretty much a facade. The other one is this mythological America that doesn't really ever exist. Or doesn't seem to exist. We're probably dealing a lot with the latter." The guy nodded and moved on. He'd been listening to *Murmur* recently, and this time it struck him as naive. Actually, what he said was "incredibly naive." Michael took that in and nodded. "Yeah, that's the word that pops into my head, too."

The singer was wearing a Skoal chewing tobacco hat pulled low over his eyes, and glasses. He looked at the interviewer and blinked, girded for the next one. "Is the sound of R.E.M. bucolic art rock?" Uh-oh. Now Michael frowned. He didn't care for that at all. "Well, that's a dumb term," he shot back. The guy was taken aback, you could see him wince, but he also stood his ground. "Well, I don't know. There's a certain pastoral thing about the music, but it comes from people of a university background, in a university town." Michael smiled but shook his head, still bristling: "Well, what does that have to do with *art rock*? To me art rock is like Genesis and Procol Harum. What do you mean by *art rock*?"

In retrospect, it's easy to see that what happened here was a disagreement, a misunderstanding, about semantics and the definition of *art rock*. But in the moment it was just awkward. For the interviewer, at least. The guy stammered, explained that he wasn't talking about *prehistoric* art rock . . . said something about folk art and a naive sensibility, you know, Howard Finster? The sound of the familiar name made Michael relax a little, and the interview tacked back to a more companionable territory. Michael didn't like doing interviews. All that talking and explaining got on his nerves.

Even in the spring before *Fables* came out, a new narrative about R.E.M. started to develop. Taking note of the larger crowds at their shows and the increasing buzz around the stubbornly indie band from Athens, now reporters wanted to know: Would success spoil R.E.M.? The story reached *Entertainment Tonight* over the summer, and in August the nationally syndicated show sent a crew and reporter to Washington, D.C.'s Constitution Hall, where they shot the band in concert and pondered the group's ascent. "There's even a fan club!" the narrator marveled. Michael, sitting on the tour bus with his hat turned backward and several days' growth of beard on his face, conceded that nightclubs had an intimacy, a certain atmosphere, that bigger halls didn't have. Then he thought more and cracked himself up. "But they also have carpets that smell terrible, and I don't miss that at all."[6]

A tension emerged. What did the growth of the band's audience mean for its original, core supporters—the fans they'd greeted, and often talked and partied with, as friends? A large part of the band's appeal to their first fans had been how different they were. And what would all these thousands of new fans make of the songs that drew inspiration from literature and outsider culture, that painted unsettling scenes and asked uncomfortable questions, usually in a secret language of symbols and phrases that even the most committed listeners could only guess at? More casual fans would be mystified, assuming they even tried to figure out what was going on.

On yet another interview in front of another camera, Michael and Peter addressed the same question from slightly different perspectives. Michael fretted about the risk of approaching a larger audience, what might be expected, what they might have to sacrifice. In fact, he said, he'd prefer that the I.R.S. publicists limit outreach to the audience the band already had. "Because we're not really willing to change." But Hüsker Dü was on a major label, and so were the

Replacements, so maybe . . . Peter broke in, helpfully: "The main-stream changed, but we're still just us." And did they still consider themselves underground? Michael responded instantly: "I do."[7]

You could see them debating the issue for themselves, among themselves, in real time. Peter, who spent more time talking in front of cameras than any of his bandmates, talked about the importance of maintaining an adversarial relationship with the media. Or at least with the music industry—radio, the record companies, all of that. "We're on the outside looking in," he proclaimed. "We have to work in our own way . . . If we sell a million records, I'll still feel on the outside." From there they talked about what might come next. Sitting under the lights with the cameras trained on his face and the microphones pointed in his direction, Peter felt expansive. "I want to do blues stuff. I want to be a great band. I want to be on the Johnny Carson show."

> MICHAEL: "We don't want to do Pepsi commercials."
> PETER: "I was offered a Pepsi commercial, and that was one thing I decided not to do. I'm not a Pepsi commercial actor. There are some things I don't want to be. I don't want to be a Republican."
> MICHAEL: "We don't want to go on Dick Clark."
> PETER: "I dunno, I might want to do that. I mean, we went on *Solid Gold*. It could be fun!"

Released in the United States on June 11, *Fables of the Reconstruction* was an instant chart topper on the college radio airplay list. It stayed at or near the top of the *CMJ* chart for much of the rest of the year, becoming the most popular album in the chart's history. The record peaked at number twenty-eight on the *Billboard* chart, a notch lower than what *Reckoning* had achieved a year earlier, but sales remained strong for months, lifting *Fables* close to 300,000 in sales during its initial run. A healthy jump over the previous album, which in turn had sold far more than *Murmur*. The sour mood that hung over the recording sessions clouded the band's sense of what they had achieved with the album, but once again, reviews were almost uniformly positive, and once again the *CMJ* voters awarded R.E.M. with its Album of the Year honors, and were this time thanked by the band members in person. Mike did most of the talking behind the podium, thanking Holt, Downs, and everyone at the Athens office and, it seemed, nearly everyone he could think of. Except the album's producer, Joe Boyd. Watching back in London, Boyd had a realization. "Well, I won't do the next album, then."[8] He was right.

26

What If We Give It Away?

A quick flashback. It's April 5, 1984, the fourth anniversary of
Kathleen O'Brien's birthday party, and three members of
R.E.M. are sitting in the grass next to beat-up old St. Mary's
on Oconee Street, being interviewed by Debi Atkinson, from Athens's Observer TV. Atkinson, who once lived in the same group
house as the band's singer, is perched on a red blanket with Michael
Stipe, Peter Buck, and Mike Mills, marking the four years the band
has been together: where they've been, where they are, where they're
going. It's an easygoing, celebratory exchange, with plenty of inside
jokes.

"I have a question for Peter," Michael says near the start. "What
really happened on this very spot four years ago on this very day?"
The guitarist laughs. "That shall remain a secret," he proclaims.
"Some things are better left unknown." Michael, poker-faced, points
toward the street. "Pan to the van." There's no van parked there now,
but there was one in 1980, and apparently Peter spent a little time
inside of it before their first show, possibly not on his own.

Peter's more eager to talk about his distaste for the "wonderful rumors" that are circulating about R.E.M.'s members. "Like
Michael's disappeared or is raising monkeys in the Tibetan hills,
that we're all millionaires now, or that one of us has a terrible drug
habit and is about to be hospitalized . . . none of which are true."
But the guitarist seems delighted to be the subject of such feverish

contemplation. As Peter knows, it means that they've worked their way into people's imaginations. This doesn't seem like an accident. Both Peter and Michael have affected the otherworldly look of modern troubadours, the guitarist shaggy-haired, with sunglasses, a worn denim jacket, and a silk scarf around his neck. The singer's chestnut curls fall over his own denimed shoulders, his bangs blowing across his clear-framed, tinted glasses. But the problem with dressing to be noticed is that once people see you, they want to come up and say hi. "People should realize that it's the last thing you want to talk about when you're having dinner out, or if you're at Walter's [Bar-B-Q] or at a movie," says Michael, who hears himself complaining and turns to address the camera with a smile. "That's my big gripe! For today!"

But increased popularity offers as many opportunities as it does problems. Talking about the prospects of the long-form, abstract music video being made by Jim Herbert seeing airtime on MTV, Peter acknowledges that it's unlikely. "If we sell two million records, they'll play anything we put out. Not that we're planning to sell two million records." Do they want to hit the top, Atkinson asks, or are they happy on the plateau they've already reached? Michael: "It's a pretty good plateau."[1]

What's compelling is that this talk of reaching for the top is more than a fantasy. Just four years after that first party, R.E.M.'s blend of artistry, ambition, and luck, and their willingness to earn starvation wages while spending weeks, months, and years on the road while subsisting on fast food, beer, and pharmaceuticals and sleeping on people's floors, has put them in this position.

"We're really happy selling 200,000 records at a time," Peter says. "[But] you're always kind of ambitious. You always think, well, gosh, you wish that one more person had bought the record, and then everyone you see who hadn't bought it, you kind of wish they owned it. And I definitely wouldn't mind the money. But I certainly don't want to be famous. I don't know if the trappings that come with selling x millions of albums is anything we'd want."[2]

Or maybe they would. Of course they would. After all, being that successful—being a damn *rock star*, with all the money, fame, and power that come with the gig—gives you license to do nearly anything you want to do. Go anywhere, meet anyone, say exactly what's on your mind. To live as far beyond the bounds of society as you care to. And, most important, to make the art you feel like making.

At the end of 1985 they still faced the same questions, from an even higher perch in the pop culture galaxy. Where would they go next, what kinds of songs would they write, and how should they record them? Who did they want to appeal to, and why? Were they an art band like Pylon, an arty party band like the B-52's, or arena-scale rock heroes like U2? More than strategic, the questions felt existential. Vexed both by the external gloom of wintertime London and the internal murk that came from five years of uninterrupted grinding down the rock 'n' roll road, they had nearly come apart.

It wasn't surprising that Michael had taken it the hardest that year. Standing at the front of the stage, projecting fire and tumult through his chest every night, with all those eyes locked on him, made him all too aware of how unsettled he was about what he was doing. From where he was standing, it wasn't just the band; it was *him*. Was he an artist or a rock 'n' roll star? A celebrity or a social-critic-slash-commentator-slash-activist? And why did he want to be any of those things? Then they finished the *Fables* record and started playing again, and at first he looked like he wished he could be anywhere else. At the start of the summer tour, Michael stood stiffly behind the microphone stand, wrapped in a shapeless overcoat, tightly shorn head cradled in a broad-brimmed hat and eyes shielded by impermeable round sunglasses. But they played their way through the summer and into the fall, greeted again and again by cheerful, enthusiastic fans, virtually every hall crackling with energy, the eyes radiant with fascination and warmth, and by the time they got to the *Rockpalast* live music program in Germany in October, he had emerged from his shell. The hat was gone, and his hair, while still obviously dyed, was now a glossy platinum. The shapeless overcoat had vanished too, replaced by a stylish blazer and T-shirt, in which he cut a fine figure as he danced with the songs, moving easily in the spotlight.

This time they took the winter off, spending the first months of 1986 at home in Athens, enjoying the fruits of the year they'd spent touring theaters, selling far more tickets than ever before. Each musician received a significant check for his share of the tour profits, and an even greater sum in performance and publishing royalties from the sales of their record. The total amount wouldn't have been enough to make a real rock star blink, but for a quartet of young musicians who had never had the cash to move out of the sort of group houses and apartments frequented by college students, it was enough to transform the texture of their lives.

Peter was the first to buy a house, an older but not ill-kept yellow clapboard home with a big front porch and enough room out back for the swimming pool he had installed, and the others eventually followed suit, setting down real roots in the Athens soil. They all found extracurricular musical activities to keep themselves busy, Peter performing with his new side group, Full Time Men, and Bill and Mike playing sets of covers with Bill's old friend and former R.E.M. guitar tech Gevin Lindsay in the Corn Cobwebs. Peter also made a practice of hopping onstage with virtually any band or artist who asked him to come up and jam and signed up to spend one day a week back at his old job, working the counter at Wuxtry Records, taking his pay in records. The guitarist grew his hair until it hung down thick and dark, almost like Joey Ramone, the dense shag of a bone-deep rock 'n' roller. To emphasize his creature-of-the-night vibe, he took to wearing pajamas and a bathrobe throughout the daylight hours, walking around town like he'd just padded out of bed, though it was maybe four o'clock in the afternoon. Also he'd be carting around a tallboy can of Budweiser, because he was a rock star and had made enough money for the arms of the clock to no longer restrain him.

Mike lived the dream life of a different kind of teenager. He got a house on a quiet residential street off Prince Avenue and invited his friend Tony Eubanks to move in with him. Eubanks, who had come to the university to pursue a graduate course in accounting while having as much fun as possible, was an elite Ultimate Frisbee player and sports obsessive who earned his living tutoring high school kids in mathematics. Eubanks could talk politics and baseball, two of Mike's passions, and he had a way with women and knew how to party, two more of Mike's most avid interests. And if the musician wanted to go to Atlanta to see the Braves or get in a round of golf somewhere, or a softball game somewhere else, Tony was almost always up for it, so they traveled as a pair, these grown-up boys about town who were approachable and friendly and ready to have a good time.

Bill bought a house just a few blocks away and settled in with his girlfriend, Mari, whom he'd met and fallen for at a show in 1984. The couple, who would get married in 1986, oversaw the renovation of their home while Bill spent his free time pursuing various musical interests, playing in his cover band with Mike and Gevin Lindsay and writing and recording songs for his own amusement. One of these, "My Bible Is My Latest TV Guide," a satirical country song, would eventually be released under the pseudonym 13111, which, if you look at it carefully, spells "Bill." The drummer played most of the instruments and sang over the banjo and pedal steel with a country crooner's twang. *Drinkin' beers and flippin' stations / It's my strongest inclination.*

Michael bought his own house just around the corner from Mike's, spent his free time traveling to sing with Anton Fier's band the Golden Palominos, and assumed the role of Athens arts community leader by consulting for the producers of the documentary *Athens, Ga.: Inside/Out,* steering the filmmakers to capture the work and lives of friends and heroes, including the poets Chris Slay and John Seawright, artist/filmmaker/art professor Jim Herbert, and the folk artist Howard Finster. Michael also got his bandmates to agree to play for the filmmakers' cameras, gathering on the stage of the tumbledown Lucy Cobb Chapel to play the Everly Brothers' "All I Have to Do Is Dream" and an acoustic take on a haunting new ballad called "Swan Swan H."

The musicians also met regularly to work on new material, crafting a small handful of songs that built on the growing melodicism they'd displayed on *Fables'* "Wendell Gee" and "Green Grow the Rushes," while Michael's lyrics took on a new political awareness that resonated both as humanity and idealism. *Let's put our heads together and start a new country up,* he sang in one song. *Trust in your calling, make sure your calling's true*, he sang in another. The songs were a little trickier than they first seemed. Michael's skepticism of fame and idolatry made his narrators less than entirely reliable. They didn't come up with a full album's worth of new stuff, but a quick sift of the better tunes from the band's early days, including some that went as far back as mid-1980, yielded two or three bar-tested rockers that added punch and a boyish wit to balance the more serious new ones. Together they made for a compelling blend, with songs that described the darkness, songs that called out for hope, songs that shrugged it all off and headed for the dance floor, and songs that somehow did it all in three-plus minutes of electric, fast-moving rock 'n' roll. Was it the best thing they'd ever done? Maybe so. Was it as good as anything else you could hear on the radio? They certainly thought so. Was it even better than that? That was for other people to judge. But first they needed to make a record that was too powerful for mainstream radio to ignore.

Now the stakes were rising. They'd worked so hard for so long. Put so much of themselves into their music, into making their band the best it could be, into writing songs that felt vital and alive and maybe even important. Of course they wanted people to hear them. And not just a few people. Peter had made that clear that day outside the church during the interview with Debi Atkinson. "I mean, I like our records enough that I think people should own them. So I guess that means [I] do want people to buy eight million copies."[3] They'd taken a significant step in that direction with *Fables*, and it didn't feel like they were compromising anything. So why not keep going?

Surely there had to be a way to both enhance the power of the new songs and reach out to new fans without sacrificing the band's uniqueness. A way to draw the attention of mainstream listeners without shrinking themselves into the lowest common denominator. And it wasn't as though everything on the radio was awful; when word came that the producer of John Cougar Mellencamp's records was interested in working with them, the band was standoffish at first, then intrigued. Of course they knew the rootsy Indiana rocker's songs; his singles "Jack & Diane," "Pink Houses," and "Lonely Ol' Night" were part of a chain of hits he'd sent into the top ten in the past few years. The songs weren't anything like what they were doing, but their sound was both powerful and distinctive. A weave of traditional instruments and modern rock instruments that resonated with a huge audience without copping to the sonic tropes that defined so much of the 1980s pop mainstream.

His producer, Don Gehman, had also made records with Stephen Stills and the Stills-Young Band in the mid-1970s, and all had the same clean, timeless sound the members of R.E.M. hoped to hear on their next album. Gehman wasn't an R.E.M. fan; in fact, he was a little skeptical of their brand of murky artiness. But he agreed to see the band perform near the end of the Reconstruction Tour, then meet with them in Athens and help them work on some songs at a local studio. The producer spent a few days with R.E.M., recording demos that, to the ears of the band members, had a power and clarity that suited their ambitions for their next record. Gehman signed on to do the album, and R.E.M. prepared to get to work.

They went to Indiana to work at Mellencamp's Belmont Mall recording studio, a new facility he'd recently had built not far from Bloomington. Gehman arranged for R.E.M., Jefferson Holt, and their assistants to stay in some condominiums Mellencamp owned at the Eagle Pointe golf course, next to Lake Monroe, about ten minutes from Bloomington and twenty minutes from the studio. The remote location was a hit with the band, who liked being able to focus on their work without distractions.

Bloomington was a college town, the home of Indiana University, and its array of bars, restaurants, and shops catered to the musicians' tastes and interests. The lakeside/golf-centric condominiums were perfect for Bill and Mike, who brought their golf clubs and rented a boat so they could start their days with a round on the links or an hour or two of fishing. Peter would hoist a pole from time to time, and the whole band, plus Gehman, engineer Ross Hogarth, and band assistant Curtis Goodman, tended to stick together after the sessions when they went into Bloomington to eat dinner and hit the bars near campus. Delighted to have the members of the nation's most popular college band in their town, the IU students greeted the musicians as something between heroes and old friends. "Those guys were stars to the college kids," Hogarth recalls. "But they were also one of them, so we all had a great time." The engineer was even more impressed by the closeness of the musicians. "Those guys were really connected; they were really friends. They dug each other and hung out."[4]

Much of the instrumental work in the studio went smoothly, and quickly. Seasoned by their years on the road, the three instrumentalists laid down the basic tracks easily, sometimes with Michael singing a scratch vocal along with them. Then they'd work to enhance the songs, overdubbing additional guitars, keyboards, and other effects. This process began with all three of the musicians, but Mike took the lead, and eventually it came down to the bassist/multi-instrumentalist working with Gehman and Hogarth to add new layers and textures to the songs. Realizing how conversant Mike was with other instruments and how inventive he could be, Gehman brought in a pump organ for him to fiddle with, and then a set of water glasses the bassist and Hogarth filled with different levels of water so they'd hum different notes when they ran their fingers across their rims, playing the set like a harmonium.

"I realized early on that this guy was the secret weapon," the engineer says. "Anything that was orchestrated in some interesting way would be him. He'd be coming up with countermelodies, cool organ parts. Then he'd talk to Don about his counter-vocals and harmonies. That impressed me, because in a lot of bands the bass player is done when the bass parts are done. The drummer and bassist just take off, they're off in town. But Mike and Bill were there every day, and the band always worked as a unit. Bill would come up with stuff and cheerlead whatever was going on, and Mike would be scheming different parts."[5]

For Gehman, the band's gradual way of building their records, letting the songs evolve during the recording process, at first grated against his impulse toward productivity and efficiency. He was used to working at a pace of about a song a day, building a basic track with everything but a few overdubs and perhaps a finished vocal by the time they closed up shop at the end of the evening. But R.E.M. was accustomed to a more fluid process, sometimes rewriting the songs when they were half recorded. "It was hard," Gehman says, "because producers are supposed to be under budget and on time, and I.R.S.

wanted hits. But their process seemed aimless. [Eventually] I learned the beauty of it: once I realized everyone was really talented, I realized that if I didn't relax and let it flow, it'd never come to fruition."[6]

The most difficult part for the producer was trying to convince Michael to put more effort into polishing his lyrics, and then sing clearly enough to be understood by even casual listeners. "I was definitely pushing Michael to make more narrative sense," Gehman says. "I can remember laying on the couch in the studio saying, 'What are you trying to say here? I'm frustrated.' I definitely didn't want to make another moody, abstract record. I wanted [the lyrics] to be concise and punchy, and have the listener feel like they'd been through something. And he pushed back. He'd get angry: *What does it matter? I like these words, I like how this feels! I'm not gonna make a record that is some stupid pop thing!* That was a daily discussion, as I recall."[7]

They never fought, per se. "He was so genteel, there was never any screaming," Gehman says. "But it was as close as you could get to arguing with him." Instead they both found ways to adjust to the other's style. "He could see I would have his voice up loud and there'd be no doubt about what he was saying." Hogarth, the engineer, was a part of those conversations, too. "Telling Michael, look, these are amazing lyrics, let the people hear them! I mean, listen to those songs. 'Cuyahoga,' 'Fall on Me.' There's so much to those lyrics." Feeling more at ease in his role as the band's front man, and increasingly interested in investing his lyrics with political and social statements, Michael continued working. "And at the end of the day he'd come in with lyrics that would be amazing," Gehman says. "And his melodic sense and the sound of his voice would make things blossom. I relaxed, and he admitted later, maybe even during the process, that I was having an impact."[8]

The I.R.S. executives flew in to visit and have a listen. Boberg, who worked most closely with R.E.M., was delighted. "I felt like it was a major step," Boberg says. "The songs were great, the lyrics were clearer, there were a few songs that were constructed to maximize the melodic punch in a way that other songs . . . that I had suggested [earlier] songs could have been, were not. I was excited."[9]

Miles Copeland, on the other hand, still wasn't sure. "I played him the record," Gehman recalls, "and he said, 'Uhhhhnnn, maybe you've got something here.' But he was hoping for something more like Fleetwood Mac."[10]

They finished the album in May and headed back to Athens for their first summer apart since before they came together in 1980. All resumed their various side pursuits through the end of July, when they reconvened to rehearse and sit for round after round after round of interviews to promote the new album. In contrast to the heavily freighted title of their previous album, they titled this one *Lifes Rich Pageant*, after a throwaway line from the Pink Panther movie *A Shot in the Dark*, delivered by Peter Sellers just after Inspector Clouseau tumbles into a fountain and climbs back to his feet, dripping wet. "It's all part of life's rich pageant," he says philosophically. R.E.M. trimmed the apostrophe from "Life's," for Stipeian reasons that are impossible to parse, but the cheerful sense of resignation in the face of potential humiliation shone through.

27

Life's Rich Demand

September 10, 1986, the Grand Ole Opry in Nashville. The theater goes dark, the crowd roars, and onstage the show starts with a shout from Mike Mills, *One-two-three-four!*, triggering a sharp downbeat from Bill Berry. Then, *wham*, the whole band blasts into "These Days," the deceptively sardonic call to duty from the new album. It's the opener for every show this year, and no wonder: the song starts at full throttle and doesn't let up. *Now I'm not feeding off you, I will rearrange your scales*, Michael Stipe begins, and he belts every word like a preacher whose faith is as fervent as it is ambiguous. He's dressed all in black, lurching around the stage in a black stovepipe hat that seems lifted from a nineteenth-century medicine show. But the band rockets him forward, volume, clarity, and velocity that sound like stone-cold belief. Mike's supporting vocal shouts are so ardent, a call for happy throngs to absorb his joy as their own, that they feel like a stirring invocation.

Volume, clarity, and velocity. Rock 'n' roll at its most. Mike's fingers flying up and down his fretboard, his shoulders moving to the rhythm as he staggers backward, slides sideways, then snaps forward to sing, looking sharp but still comfortable in a pressed button-up shirt and vest. On the other side of the stage, Peter flings perfect runs and chords out of his black-and-white Rickenbacker, even as an invisible current sends him sprawling one way, then veering another, then launches him into the air, dropping him back to his feet to meet the downbeat of the next verse. Bill at the drums, a factory of rhythm. The sound is electric, and the charge they send out comes right back to them from the audience, which roars for the opening notes of "Sitting Still" and gives a solid cheer to "Hyena," also off the new album. A few more songs, with barely a pause between them, and then it's "I Believe," another anthemic rocker from the new album that catapults the crowd upward to cheer Michael's spiky declarations of belief and purpose. *I believe in coyotes and time as an abstract!* He yanks the microphone forward to face the audience, his band blazing behind him. Volume, clarity, velocity.

I believe my humor's wearing thin / And change is what I believe in.

Lifes Rich Pageant announces its squirrelly intentions with the first notes of the first song, a quick, snaky guitar riff that triggers the stomping, feedback-laced rocker "Begin the Begin." Singing in a taut but tuneful growl, Michael wields his impressionistic pen on his nation's conflicted present through the lens of its checkered history. Here's Myles Standish leading the slaughter of the natives; here's the brutalist authority of money, the moral compromises dictated by fear and convenience. Here also, the perpetual hope for renewal. *Let's begin again*, he declares, a bold assertion he undercuts in nearly his next breath: *I can't think clearly . . . I can't even rhyme, here in the begin.* This traces the tension at the heart of the record: the singer's impulse to lead coupled with his reflexive distrust of leaders, including himself.

The same contradiction appears in the uproarious "These Days," whose narrator alternates idealistic exhortations (*We are hope despite the times!*) with unsettling admissions about his motivations, and in "I Believe," with its calls to faith (*You're on your honor . . . trust in your calling*) ringing alongside inexplicable shout-outs to wild dogs and theoretical physics. "Just a Touch," one of the 1980 rebuilds, recalls Elvis Presley's death in a rollicking tumult of disconnected memories—shock, public mourning, and youthful incomprehension—ending it all with a drawn-out cry of *I'm so god . . . damned . . . youuuuunnnnnggggg . . .* his purposeful echo of Patti Smith.

The direct evocation of Smith, Michael's musical-poetic lodestar since his adolescence, opens another door, this one leading to the stark, unadorned emotionality that laces the album's more reflective songs. The midtempo "Cuyahoga" presents a clear-eyed portrait of the American settlers' toll on the land they claimed and the people they displaced, symbolized in a river running red, first with the blood of the natives, then with industrial waste. "The Flowers of Guatemala" opens on a delicate circle of arpeggiated chords, the guitar and bass joined by vibes and finger cymbals that evoke a child's music box. A dream, but for the discordant wail of feedback swelling just beneath the surface. Singing with airy wonder in his voice, Michael conjures a sweet vision: kind, colorful people on a street surrounded by flowers. But there's something off in this tableau. The flowers are amanita, which bloom at night. An eerie notion that draws a louder wail from the guitar, the sound of a darker truth that, like America's financial support of the government death squads leaving so many Guatemalan peasants in flower-covered graves, goes unspoken.

The same construct of plangent music, densely layered instrumentation, and dreamy, fretful lyrics joins with a soaring chorus in "Fall on Me." First performed in 1985 with a lyric about acid rain, the song was revised by Michael, who improved the melody and wrote new verses that switched the focus to government oppression, evoking Galileo's experiments with gravity. But if the Italian scientist's dark fate at the hands of his government comes through in the minor chords pivoting around the verses, the chorus tilts in a more hopeful progression, the chords ascending as the three vocalists pursue separate words and melodies. Michael's repeated *Don't fall on me* is contrasted by Mike's higher *What is it up in the air for?* and Bill's lower *It's gonna fall.* The power of the song, which the I.R.S. Records executives identified immediately as the album's best shot at a radio hit, comes less from the moody grandeur of the music, the comforting folk-rock chime of Peter's guitars, the warmth in Michael's voice, or the way Mike's and Bill's voices weave with his into such rich harmony than from the way all of those things come together into such perfect balance. As dark as its vision might be, the sound of "Fall on Me" is, ultimately, ecstatic.

Pageant has a few lighter songs, most notably the album-closing cover of "Superman," an obscure single from the '60s that Mike had been singing with his and Bill's side band the Corn Cobwebs, along with the galloping concert staple "Hyena" and the brief, all-but-instrumental Latin-esque "Underneath the Bunker," a musical gag that leavens the album's emotionally dense core considerably.

Released on July 28, 1986, *Lifes Rich Pageant* hit stores with a significantly harder impact than any of its predecessors. "Fall on Me" went out as a single a week or two later and soon gained a foothold on AOR playlists across the country. The song stalled in the mid-nineties on the *Billboard* Hot 100, but it became a favorite on rock radio, ultimately reaching the top five of *Billboard*'s Album Rock Tracks chart. The airplay juiced album sales, and by mid-October *Pageant* had climbed to number twenty-one on the *Billboard* album chart, half a dozen slots higher than *Reckoning*, selling more than 400,000 copies, on pace to reach 500,000 by the end of the year, at which point it would become R.E.M.'s first gold record. An exceptional achievement for any young band, and even more so for a bunch as stubbornly unconventional as this one was. For all the clarity of its production, *Pageant*'s songs were both offbeat and distinctive, the work of artists who were busily mining their own unique vision. Nevertheless, some people didn't care for it. In rock 'n' roll, certainly when you get to the leftward fringe, where music crackles like dissent, the first murmurs of something like mellifluousness can strike some ears as betrayal.

"This record is pretty much what you'd expect," began the review in *Spin* magazine, then at the apex of its run as the punky opposition to *Rolling Stone*'s aging hippie authority. "The big news is that R.E.M. used John Cougar Mellencamp's producer." The critic, Sue Cummings, was actually happy with the album's sharper sound, noting how the opening track "rocks right out, with a snare sound that pops like a firecracker, the rhythm guitar packs lead." But the clarity of Michael's vocals, and the glimmers of idealism in his lyrics, triggered her contempt. "What a strange burden it must be to be Michael Stipe these days," she wrote, "middle America's nouveau-hippy art school urchin turning up regularly at your doorstep to spend his nights on your couch, his days in your garden picking berries in futile attempts to manufacture natural hair dye." It's the *futile* that was engineered to sting, apparently in response to the part of "These Days" where Michael sings, *We are young despite the years . . . We are hope despite the times.* Cummings didn't seem to catch the eruptions of silliness in the song that continually deflate the narrator's proclamations, e.g., for heaven's sake, *I wish to eat each one of you.* Which would seem to indicate that something a little more complex than moist sloganeering was afoot. But Cummings was too busy mourning the lost obscurities of *Murmur* to notice.[1] And it wouldn't be the last time in their career that they'd hear that plaint.

Other critics had similarly critical, if more deeply considered, complaints. Tom Carson, writing in *The Village Voice*, located a disconnect between the political/social observations in Michael's lyrics and the persistent haziness in his writing. "The sounds of challenge, possibility and change all work as pleasant sensations, but nothing more," he wrote. What resulted, Carson continued, was "an uncritical preference for sentiment over thought . . . (if something can't be mythicized, it doesn't exist for them). This is the emotional syntax of Reaganism, pure and simple."[2]

The Pageantry Tour kicked off on September 5, 1986, at the 10,500-capacity Oak Mountain Amphitheatre, just outside Birmingham, Alabama, before heading back to the band's springtime residence in Bloomington, where they packed the Indiana University Auditorium with 3,200 cheering fans who had come to see R.E.M. as hometown favorites. Stories about the band fanned out across the mainstream media, landing them on the covers of magazines like *Spin, Creem,* Tower Records' in-house publication *Pulse,* and *Rock Bill.*

They spent the next three months playing medium to large auditoriums in most cities, performing to crowds typically ranging from 2,500 to 5,000, with a few 10,000-seat venues thrown in. In Nashville they played the 4,400-seat Grand Ole Opry, then they were booked into the 10,000-seat City Coliseum, in Austin, and the 4,950-capacity Mesa Amphitheatre, in Mesa, Arizona. They drew more than 6,000 to the Universal Amphitheatre, in Los Angeles, more than 9,000 to the UIC Pavilion, in Chicago, and then played back-to-back shows to the 5,600-capacity theater then called the Felt Forum, at New York's Madison Square Garden. In city after city, the crowds pressed so tightly against the stage that the shows had to be paused so Michael could urge the fans to back up or in some way tend to the injured. During the encore on the first night in New York, he stopped singing "Driver 8" to help lift a woman to the stage and escort her backstage for assistance. He returned to say it seemed she'd suffered a broken rib, then led the band through a dispirited cover of "Femme Fatale" and ended the show.

Security became more important. Not just out front, where the crowd would get so worked up they'd all but do one another in to get closer to the band, but onstage and offstage, too. Playing larger venues required the band to carry a larger sound system, a sizable lighting rig, multiple screens, and projection gear for the onstage light show that now accompanied the band's performances, so the road crew expanded to more than two dozen, plus management staff, personal assistants, instrument techs, trucks, buses, multiple professional drivers, and whatever friends the musicians asked to keep them company on their travels. Reporters, photographers, and camera crews cycled in and out too. Getting the gear in place, set up, plugged in, turned on, and made ready to do its job required dozens of workers and precise attention to detail. A litany of new rules and policies came into play, including a tiered system of backstage passes and access limitations, particularly for the musicians' dressing rooms and lounges. "It got more businesslike," says tour manager Geoff Trump. "That's because a tour is a business. And in that period you had to create boundaries where the artist had their space and their time, and the guys on the crew did their thing. But it begins to get a little more impersonal."[3]

The tour came to a climax just before Thanksgiving with three shows at Atlanta's Fox Theatre. Almost exactly six years had passed since they first performed at the theater, playing twenty wide-eyed minutes to warm up the crowd for the Police. Now the Police were a memory, broken into angry shards after their 1983 tour, and the band that had once opened for them had sold out the same theater for back-to-back-to-back shows.

28

Things We Never Thought Would Happen Have Happened

T
he *Athens, Ga.: Inside/Out* documentary opened in Athens a week after the end of R.E.M.'s 1986 tour, a few weeks before *Lifes Rich Pageant*'s sales officially crested 500,000, reaching the Recording Industry Association of America's threshold for gold status. The B-52's had sold more than a million copies of their first album and passed the mark for the gold record award with the next two albums, making them the most commercially successful Athens-bred musicians at that point. But the Bs had also relocated to New York when they signed their first record deal, in 1979, so while they appeared in the film reminiscing affectionately about their early days, they spoke as veterans of a time that had faded into memory. Now R.E.M. represented the apex of the Athens art/music scene. They were why MTV broadcast the film nationally on the night of its Athens premiere, and why I.R.S. Records released the accompanying soundtrack album, which launched local club bands the Squalls and Flat Duo Jets to the upper reaches of *CMJ*'s college radio charts.

Michael's and the band's authority radiates across the film. Director Tony Gayton and producer Bill Cody had found it difficult to connect with locals until R.E.M.'s singer met with them and volunteered his band's services, at which point all the doors in town swung open. Gayton hired University of Georgia art professor, local

artist, and R.E.M. video director Jim Herbert to be his cinematog-
rapher. Many of the people featured in the film, including Howard
Finster and the poets Chris Slay and John Seabrook, were friends
of the singer. Jeremy Ayers, Michael's onetime lover, leader of the
recently disbanded group Limbo District, and an influential figure in
Athens's bohemian circles for a decade, served as a consultant on the
project. Michael and Peter Buck both speak on camera—the guitarist shows the camera the Elvis-themed bathroom in his house, and
the singer sets up a song performed by Reverend John D. Ruth and
his wife and does a little dance for the camera ("This is how Pop-
eye exercises!")—and the four band members perform twice, taking
their acoustic instruments to the stage of the Lucy Cobb Chapel to
play "Swan Swan H," then, over a concluding montage of the film's
interviewees, a Michael-and-Mike duet of the Everly Brothers' "All
I Have to Do Is Dream."

The implication for the faces flashing over the sound of the
increasingly successful R.E.M. was obvious. At the end of the year
Michael would seem nearly stunned by how far he and his three bandmates had been carried by the dream they had dreamed for themselves. "Things we thought would never happen have happened,"
he would tell MTV that December for the channel's *Top 100 Videos
of 1987*. The interview segment would set up the clip for one of the
band's most recent songs, one that, unbelievably enough, took them
into the top ten of *Billboard*'s Hot 100 singles. "And I'd say we're at a
real crossroads right now, in a lot of different ways."[1]

The first step on R.E.M.'s road to the top ten took place at the end of
November 1986, when the members of R.E.M. gathered to record a
song for the soundtrack of *Love at Large*, a romantic comedy directed
by Alan Rudolph. Digging again into the sack of disused originals
from the band's first few months, they came up with "Romance,"
an ardent, upbeat rock song with snapping drums, an assertive bass
line, and one of Peter's simple but memorable guitar riffs. At first
they figured to have Don Gehman behind the controls, but the producer, who was busy with John Mellencamp's next album, begged
off. Instead, he suggested, they could work with Scott Litt, a thirty-

two-year-old engineer from the Power Station studios, in New York City, who was building a career as an independent producer. Litt didn't have a lot of solo production credits yet but had coproduced the hit single "Walking on Sunshine" for Katrina and the Waves, helmed a record for the dB's, and mixed an album for Mitch Easter's band Let's Active. With only one song to work on and the clock ticking, the band gave their okay, with one condition: they would have the authority, and credit, of coproducers. Litt didn't have a problem with that, so they met at Soundscape Studios, in Atlanta, on November 28, the day after Thanksgiving, and got to work on "Romance." It wasn't the song that would elevate them to the upper reaches of the Top 40, but the day after that they had the song in the can, a coproducer for their next album, and a new sense of possibility.

As they had done the previous year, R.E.M. took most of the winter off, the members largely devoting themselves to side projects. Peter, Mike, and Bill went to Los Angeles to back Warren Zevon on his *Sentimental Hygiene* album and did so much jamming on cover songs with the singer, tape rolling, that they wound up with enough material to construct a Zevon-Berry-Buck-Mills album under the moniker Hindu Love Gods. (The self-titled album would not be released until 1990.) Michael also traveled to Los Angeles to record, contributing backing vocals to an album by the band 10,000 Maniacs, with whose singer Natalie Merchant he had been spending quite a bit of time.

The band also got together to work on new songs, and in early February they spent a couple of days recording demos at John Keane Studios, in Athens, including a revised version of a tune Michael had performed a few times with the Golden Palominos, called "Finest Worksong." As performed by the Palominos, the song had a pensive, coiled sound, and a bridge with lyrics about a Judas stone and marching off to sea. In R.E.M.'s hands the song became thunderous: pounding drums, grinding guitar, and slapped bass notes behind a steely Michael vocal. The Judas-stone bridge, and anything beyond the barest essentials of rhythm and a monochromatic melody, had been excised, seemingly to draw focus to the urgency in the verses. *Take your instinct by the reins . . . What we want and what we need has been confused.* There was a message in there, and it had nothing to do with dreaming.

At the end of March the band met Scott Litt in Nashville and prepared to make a new album. They rented a big house to live in, the four musicians, their producer, and Jefferson Holt. When they weren't recording, Michael relaxed by working in the garden out back, while Bill, Mike, and Peter went out to see music or just grab dinner and have a few drinks. Young guys on the town with plenty of cash and a healthy appetite for fun. When Bill got into it with Sound Emporium engineer Gary Laney over who made the best guacamole, they bought a huge sack of avocados and other supplies, plus tortilla chips and a couple of cases of beer, and invited everyone in for a competitive guac-off. "It was all creative and fun," Litt says of the time they spent in Nashville. They'd start in the studio at about 11 a.m., work straight through until 8 p.m. or so, grab a bite, and either head home to rest or go back to the studio for another couple of hours. "When we weren't working, we were getting amped up to do more work."[2]

Michael also spent some of his free time exploring Nashville with his camera, taking black-and-white photographs that he developed and posted around the studio, along with architectural images of Works Progress Administration–era buildings and other similarly imposing structures. Something about monochromatic images, particularly ones that evoked the heroic ideal of the mid-twentieth century, resonated with his growing vision for the album. Getting deeper, he brought a video monitor into the control room and played *Olympia*, the German filmmaker Leni Riefenstahl's icily composed documentary of the 1936 Berlin Olympics, propaganda for Adolf Hitler's Nazi regime. They alternated this with footage from the 1954 Army-McCarthy Senate hearings, which ended Senator Joe McCarthy's anti-communist crusade and led to his censure by the U.S. Senate. "It's a very black-and-white record," Litt says. "It's a singer, a guitar player, a drummer, and a bass player. And nothing gets in the way of that. They're strong in their identity; their personalities are coming through."[3] But their personalities went beyond the simple voice-guitar-bass-and-drums instrumentation, and Litt helped the musicians incorporate keyboards, a dulcimer, a Fairlight synthesizer, and an array of found sounds, including crickets, the clatter of the manual typewriter Michael used to write lyrics, and snatches of dialogue from the McCarthy hearings.

The mood of the photographs and the videos seeped into the music, giving some songs the flickering light of an industrial furnace and others the clang and bang of a factory. Oppression looms, sometimes through governments, sometimes through more intimate arrangements. "The whole album is about fire," Michael told *Musician* magazine that fall. "About everything you think about fire as being cleansing, or something that destroys everything in its path."[4] One song seemed to burn a little brighter than the others. It was taut, tight, blazing from the slam-bam drum pickup that triggered the opening guitar riff, a jagged four-step run up the neck that repeats before Michael belts the first line: *This one goes out to the one I love / This one goes out to the one I've left behind.* And there it was, alive in the light of its paradoxes. Love and rejection. Dedication and abandonment. Power generated, power wielded, power abused.

"The One I Love." Titles deceive, words don't always mean what they seem to say. The song's two verses are abrupt—four short lines, including one line that repeats. The second verse reprises the first, the third does the same, except for one line that shifts to the past tense. And when the words run out, another repeats: *Fire!* Four letters stretching over three syllables: *Fiiiii-yuuuhhhhh-huhhhh.* Not much of a narrative when viewed on the page, but, coupled with Peter's seething guitar, it says it all, and then some. "We'd play that to people when they came in to hear what we were up to," Litt recalls. "And it sounded killer. You just knew." Litt knew, anyway. That this song, for all its rock 'n' roll snarl, could play alongside the hookiest pop songs on the Top 40. Whitney Houston, George Michael, Madonna, take your pick. Nothing on the air sounded more electric or more immediately memorable. "It was too much fun to listen to," Litt continues. "It was infectious. And everybody felt that way."[5]

Throughout the 1980s the MTV music video channel served as the locus of pop music and, to a great extent, Western popular culture. Drawn from some combination of the Beatles' 1964 movie *A Hard*

Day's Night, the Monkees' mid-1960s TV sitcom, teen dance shows like *American Bandstand,* and no small amount of musical theater, the most popular videos emphasized glamour over musical verisimilitude. Guitarists flailed at unplugged instruments atop towering desert mesas or, as with Bryan Adams, at the bottoms of drained swimming pools. Singers spilled their hearts from the bows of yachts cutting across Caribbean seas or while dancing amid choreographed street gangsters in a subway station. Sometimes they pretended to make music where music might actually be made—on a stage or in a recording studio—which seemed to give viewers a glimpse into the moment of creation. Wherever, the point of the form was to distill the essence of the song or the performers and translate it into visual shorthand for what made the music so exciting. That's what MTV's viewers wanted to see, time and again, and the channel's size and cultural ubiquity guaranteed that a popular video could sell a song, and an artist, with unprecedented speed and impact. But time and again R.E.M. refused to make videos MTV would consider adding to its playlist.

If anything, the band's videos seemed designed to show their contempt for MTV. Apart from the clip they made to accompany "Wolves, Lower," in 1982, the band, and particularly Michael, refused to be filmed lip-synching to their songs. They tried one compromise with "So. Central Rain (I'm Sorry)," pairing shots of Peter, Mike, and Bill feigning to the recorded track behind translucent screens while Michael stood in the open, performing a new vocal for the camera. But in every other video they made, the visuals accompanying R.E.M.'s music had little or nothing to do with the songs. When the band members appeared on camera, they were usually nowhere near their instruments. They toured sculpture gardens and chatted with old men in trucker hats. The hurtling train song "Driver 8" was set to footage of locomotives rounding a bend and pulling into a rural station, greeted by unglamorous men in work clothes. When the band incorporated stage performance footage, it was blurry and pointedly not synchronized with the rhythm of the song being heard. Even as R.E.M.'s songs gained punch and even as Michael stepped forward as a singer, the band continued to produce videos that all but insisted MTV's programmers avoid them. The clip Michael directed for "Fall on Me" consisted entirely of black-and-white footage of an Indiana quarry. Shown upside down. When Don Gehman, who produced *Lifes Rich Pageant* and had particularly high hopes for the song's prospects as a single, first saw the "Fall on Me" video, his reaction was succinct: "Oh, fuck."[6]

For Jay Boberg and the rest of the I.R.S. staff, the band's resistance to making accessible videos grew more frustrating as R.E.M. started to play larger halls and sell more records. "Fall on Me" cracked radio playlists across the country and became popular enough to spur occasional airings on MTV. But four minutes of upside-down quarry footage was a tough sell for the channel, no matter how catchy the song. "Can you imagine what would have happened with that record if we'd had an arty but watchable video with Michael singing in it and the band playing?" Boberg asks. The executive did his best to convince the singer, describing the way a hit video could raise the band's profile and break them overseas in countries they hadn't been able to play in yet. But Michael's artistic sensibility leaned toward the avant-garde, and he liked pairing his band's music with visuals that challenged the audience's expectations. Maybe because being in a band with a good shot at having a hit song that would land them on MTV's heavy rotation playlist challenged his own expectations. "I had those conversations with Michael. I knew it was Michael we had to convince. And we sat there and had very long and multiple conversations about what the impact would be if we could get a video. But we weren't successful. And part of what made him such an interesting figure was that he'd do that to himself."[7]

They called the new album *Document*, as shorthand, Michael said, for *documentary*. We use the term most often to describe filmed journalism, the weaving of fact, anecdote, and other documentation into a narrative. But as ever in the quicksilver consciousness of Michael Stipe and R.E.M., fact and meaning can shift from one moment to the next. The fire imagery weaving the songs together (the original vinyl edition had FILE UNDER FIRE written on its spine, an answer to *Reckoning*'s FILE UNDER WATER) lends a chaotic air to the piece: lovers detached, societies in flux, nations at odds, the planet on the brink.

Whether we're teetering toward destruction or renewal is unclear. As one song title puts it, "It's the End of the World as We Know It (and I Feel Fine)." It could go either way, it seems. For now the only thing to do is buckle up and try to hang on.

Released on August 31, 1987, the album kicked off a new era for R.E.M. in appropriately determined form with "Finest Work-song," the grinding martial stomp that worked both as an anthem to a worker revolt and a mission statement: *The time to rise has been engaged.* Most of the songs look beyond such personal matters. "Welcome to the Occupation" describes the toll of economic imperialism in South America (*Sugar cane and coffee cup / Copper, steel, and cattle . . . Fire on the hemisphere below*), while "Exhuming McCarthy" takes on hyper-patriotic scoundrels such as the titular senator, whose anti-communist investigations proclaimed fealty to the U.S. Constitution while shredding the rights the charter supposedly guaranteed.

"Disturbance at the Heron House" tells an *Animal Farm*–like parable about a failed rebellion against an oppressive government, and "The End of the World . . . ," which starts with four machine-gun-like drumrolls, rockets forward with staccato urgency, unspooling the whole riotous scene, earthquakes, wars, TV news, religion, patriotism, heroes, villains, and who knows which is which, all flashing by at the speed of a TV remote clicking around the television omniverse. *Offer me solutions, offer me alternatives, and I decline*, he cries near the end, but the world keeps right on spinning, hurtling into its uncertain future at breakneck speed. And yet the possibility of transcendence persists. The speed-waltzing "Fireplace" alludes to the ecstatic dancing of the Shaker communities in the eighteenth and nineteenth centuries, and "King of Birds" ruminates on existence to the exotic twang of a dulcimer.

Song to song to song the guitars sparkle, the bass pulses and thrums, while the drums lock into the groove even as they remain loose enough to swing. The textural embellishments, from Los Lobos saxophonist Steve Berlin's honking assertions to the dulcimer to the found sounds that pop in here and there, add even more dimension to the music. Michael's performances have also gained clarity and depth. Whatever self-consciousness he might have once felt about standing at the fore has vanished. His lyrics straddle the poetic and the sharply observed, and he takes full advantage of his strong, resonant voice, as fierce on "The One I Love" as he is sensitive on "King of Birds." It was as if the purposefully murky image of themselves that R.E.M. had been projecting for half a dozen years had finally snapped into focus.

Document's combination of pop hooks, rock grit, and thoughtful, arty elaborations hit, and hit hard, on every level. "The One I Love" took pop radio by storm, elevating R.E.M. all the way to the ninth slot on *Billboard*'s Hot 100. The album climbed nearly as high, just entering the top ten and selling a million copies in the space of four months, enough to earn platinum sales status. Both were helped along by the similarly focused video, whose director, Robert Longo, employed a visual vocabulary that combined the steamier side of southern gothic with doubled images of flowers and fireworks and quick, tight shots of Bill's sticks on his drums and Peter ripping at his guitar strings to underscore the impact of the song's opening seconds. This time MTV embraced the video, broadcasting it to its millions of viewers at least a dozen times a day, every day, for months on end.

Two months before *Document* was slated for release, I.R.S.'s national publicity director, Cary Baker, composed a letter to Jim Henke, the editor of *Rolling Stone*. The two-page missive got right to the point: R.E.M.'s fifth album was coming out at the end of the summer, and the label, along with the band, was pulling out all the stops to make sure this record would launch the band as a fully fledged mainstream act. And, he continued, "once the record is out, the tour is crossing America and the songs are on the radio, it may finally be time for a *Rolling Stone* cover story."

Every record company publicist on the planet wanted to get their acts onto the cover of the most prominent popular culture journal in the United States. But in the course of eight numbered paragraphs, Baker made an exceptionally strong case. Start with the fact that *Lifes Rich Pageant*, the band's most recent album, had earned the acclaimed band its first gold record and launched "Fall on Me" to the top of the album-oriented radio charts while also making a respectable impact on contemporary hit radio charts. Then consider how *Rolling Stone*'s readers had voted R.E.M. and *Pageant* into the top three of the Band of the Year and top four of the Album of the Year lists, while the magazine's writers voted it into the number six slot of their year-end poll. And while *RS* had chosen not to publish a feature about R.E.M. or anything beyond a review of *Lifes Rich Pageant* in 1986, the band had made the covers of nearly half a dozen of *Rolling Stone*'s competitors, including *Spin*.

The new album, he predicted, was "the most accessible and vexing work R.E.M. has ever recorded," and more than strong enough to fuel a popular breakthrough. And he had more: *Dead Letter Office*, the collection of B-sides and leftovers I.R.S. released in the spring of 1987, had climbed to number fifty-two on *Billboard*'s album chart despite having next to no publicity. Then there was R.E.M.'s star turn in the *Athens, Ga.: Inside/Out* documentary and the recently released collection of the band's distinctly inaccessible music videos, *R.E.M. Succumbs*, which was making a surprising amount of noise on *Billboard*'s videocassette chart.

Baker saved one of his most potent sales points for the letter's second page, and it had less to do with R.E.M.'s commercial hopes than it did with *Rolling Stone*'s. The growth of college radio, and the rest of campus media, had obviously made a big impact on the magazine's publisher. Sensing the existence of a large and largely untapped readership, the magazine had taken after the college audience with a vengeance, publishing special college issues and devoting significant chunks of regular issues to collegiate concerns. So Baker played his ace: "R.E.M. is the #1 college act of all time."[8]

Baker's letter made the desired impact. Five months later, the cover of *Rolling Stone*'s December 3, 1987, issue was dominated by four serious, half-shadowed faces gazing out from under the magazine's red title, and alongside the large white cover line describing who, and what, they were:

R.E.M.
AMERICA'S BEST ROCK 'N' ROLL BAND

29

Conquest

It makes sense that it's Mike Mills doing the talking. Michael Stipe sits right behind him, face alight as he shakes his bandmate's hand. The singer's hair is long again, the curls backlit, while the big, not quite sheepish grin on his face seems to light him from the front. It's an up-and-coming young man's smile, just a little bit prankish as he shakes and shakes and shakes Mike's hand (the bassist eventually turns to him and says "That's enough" as he reclaims his paw), at which point Michael starts waving to the camera, waving and waving and smiling and waving, and he's being silly, but also happy to be where he is, and proud to be here, too.

"Hello, Warner Bros.," Mike says. "Welcome to New Orleans, the sun and sin capital of the world!"

They are not in New Orleans; this is a videotaped introduction made in the summer when they were working on their new album in Woodstock, New York—where, Mike makes sure to point out, they're working hard on R.E.M.'s new album. "Which we're thrilled to be putting out with all of you." They did two takes of this intro; in one Michael is waving; in the other he's just sitting there, beaming, and they've been edited so it blinks back and forth, lending a whole other layer of ironic distance to the spiel, though Mike is in no way being backhanded, or even tongue-in-cheek, when he holds up a quarter-inch instrument cable that is still looped to the brand-identifying cardboard packaging, which Mike points at with a drumstick, thwacking the name for emphasis because, he says, this is what they're looking for with this new record: conquest. So much so that Michael says the name with him in perfect synchrony, nodding for emphasis: "*Conquest.*"

It's all new songs, Mike continues. "And it's great stuff. And I hope you like it as much as we do, and, uhhh, I hope it's big. Big, big, *big.*"[1]

There's that way people describe how things change: slowly, and then all at once. It's a cliché, but only because it's so often true, or at least it describes the way people perceive change. Anyway, it's also how R.E.M., after spending half a dozen years with the not-small-but-also-not-big independent label I.R.S. Records, came to sign a multi-million-dollar deal with a major label.

At first, signing a contract with a major-label record company was such a remote prospect it was easy to dismiss. It was already amazing that anyone would come to see them play, let alone pay for the privilege, let alone want to hear the songs they made up, let alone pay them to record a couple of their tunes and release them on vinyl. That was so crazy at first that it was impossible to imagine it going much further. "We're serious about what we do," Peter told the University of Georgia's *Red & Black* newspaper in May 1981. "But we're doing it for fun. This really isn't a big career for us. Whatever happens, happens. That's the big thing. We're doing this because we enjoy it."[2] And wasn't that the point of the whole enterprise? It still sounded that way three years later when *The Red & Black* profiled the guitarist on the eve of *Reckoning*'s release in 1984, a year after the full-length *Murmur* had won so much acclaim and then, how could this be, sales in the low six figures. "As long as you can keep on playing, that's privilege enough," he said. "Everyone would like more money, but I'm not sure I'd want to sell a million records. A million records might make it one of those situations that might not be fun."[3]

Which wasn't to say they didn't have their eyes on what the future might hold for them. They just wanted to be realistic about their hopes and not bite off more than they might want to swallow, as

Peter acknowledged to a reporter from *Musician* in 1983. "We're kind of unassumingly ambitious, in that we never do anything expecting any kind of feedback," he said. "We just do things to please ourselves—we write to please ourselves, record to please ourselves, do the cover, hand in the record and then we think, 'Hmmm, I wonder how this is going to do?' And we still wonder—we still talk about how many records we want to sell. 'Okay, no more than this many, because more than that and it starts getting kinda bullshit.' "[4]

And as far as Peter was concerned, he told *Trouser Press* magazine, R.E.M. had already gone as far as they would ever need to go. "To me, 'making it' means being able to play and make records, having people appreciate your music, and enjoying what you're doing. Right now, we've made it. If we went on like this forever, I'd be happy."[5] And that was in 1983, just as *Murmur* was coming out.

The I.R.S. contract they signed in early 1982 called for one EP and five full-length albums, and though they at first resisted making the sort of records that would pop on Top 40 radio, and refused to make watchable videos at the height of MTV's power, and would rarely tour as the opener for bigger bands whose audiences would have been likely to fall hard for their tuneful indie sound, each of R.E.M.'s albums sold significantly more copies than the one before it. Once *Lifes Rich Pageant* went gold, Jay Boberg and the rest of the I.R.S. executives knew their years of work and dedication to the band were going to pay off, almost certainly in a profound way. When the band started work on *Document*, the final album in their contract, Boberg and his team campaigned hard to get their fast-rising act signed to another contract.

Actually, the I.R.S. executives, including company president Miles Copeland, had been trying to extend R.E.M.'s contract for at least a couple of years, offering to give the band a richer deal immediately if they agreed to extend their contract for another few albums. But the band, following the counsel of manager Jefferson Holt and attorney Bertis Downs, didn't take the bait. They'd stick with the deal they had and trust that their album-to-album sales would continue to move in the right direction. In the United States, anyway. Because as far as they could see, I.R.S. was doing a terrible job selling the band overseas. And this, for the members of R.E.M., was a problem.

In 1985 they had taken two swings through Europe and the UK and were consistently underwhelmed not just by the sizes of the audiences they faced but also by the amount of promotion that I.R.S.'s overseas distributor, CBS International, had done to draw attention to their records and shows. Again and again, Peter complained, he'd wander the streets of the cities they were about to perform in across England and Europe and not find any evidence that R.E.M. existed or that they were about to perform in town. "I'd go into stores in, like, Germany and not find our records, or else they'd be filed under miscellaneous 'R' or whatever," Peter said in 2017.[6] Bill noticed the same thing: "It was a little disheartening to go over there and you go to Germany and there aren't posters *at all*. You play to like two hundred people and there are a lot of American GIs stationed over there."[7] And for R.E.M., even in 1985, that wasn't good enough. No matter what they said about it in public.

In 1986 Mike shrugged off the suggestion that his band might want to become bigger stars. "It's not our design to be really big. It's not a goal," he said. "We just make as good a record as we can and hope that it satisfies us first and then satisfies our audience. A small increase over the last one is enough for us. If a record breaks any bigger than that, that's fine. There are a lot of bad things that come with a huge, successful album." He listed a few of them. Being called a sellout was one. Having to perform in sports arenas was another. "I mean, a lot of people are going to scream if [*Lifes Rich Pageant*] is a big success. But we didn't do anything different than we usually do." You can't please all of the people, especially the ones who'd had to stomach all the acclaim R.E.M. had received in the preceding half dozen years. "I think that people get sick to death of hearing how good we are. All the acclaim we've gotten from critics has just really turned a lot of people off. They look for the first thing they can find that reeks of sell-out."[8]

They kept working, and working, and working some more. Track their progress from 1983 to 1984, 1985, 1986, and then 1987. They're like an army on the march. Bigger halls. Bigger crowds. Bigger reactions. Bigger numbers tracking the units they were shifting. And even bigger talk: about making a hit single, about selling a million records, about touring basketball arenas. Big, getting bigger, nothing to stop them from being even bigger than that. All the while they would shake their heads, roll their eyes, and say things like . . .

"Everything that's big is bad."[9]

That was Michael talking to MTV in 1986. So was that why he wasn't interested in making a single that would get played on the radio and maybe even become a hit? Michael shrugged. "I don't think radio deserves me. Yet."[10] A year later, after R.E.M. had launched a single and an album into the top ten and were well on their way to selling a million copies of *Document*, Michael still shrugged it all off. "I don't like big things," he said to MTV's *Year in Rock* wrap-up at the end of 1987.[11]

And yet that was the year the band's self-composed narrative began to shift, when annoyance over the prospect of becoming successful started to get edged out by annoyance over people who assumed they weren't successful. That they were little more than an overhyped cult band. "I don't know any cult bands that sell four or five hundred thousand copies of a record," Mike told the Toronto *Globe and Mail* just as *Document* was coming out, in August 1987. "It's just a case of a tag sticking, which I don't mind, except that's the excuse radio programmers use not to play our records. They say 'they're a cult band and you can't understand any of the words.' Well, that's a bunch of crap."[12]

For Mike, success only made it all better and better. And better. Achievement had always come naturally to him, which was part of why Bill Berry had loathed him so thoroughly when he first encountered Mike in school. But once he got to know him, Bill realized that the teenage bassist, for all his natural abilities, wore his talents with a casual élan that made him good company and a wonderful coconspirator. Mike didn't need to brag or condescend to others to shore up his sense of himself. He knew who he was, and that he was capable of things that not everyone else could do. But that didn't mean he had to lord it over you. Mike was comfortable enough inside his skin to be kind and to live with his decisions and even enjoy himself, no matter how absurd his circumstances became.

R.E.M.'s growing success may have triggered an existential crisis in Michael; it might have spurred Peter to make like a rock 'n' roll wastrel, walking the midday streets of Athens in his pj's and robe, sipping Budweiser like some kind of bastard scion of Keith Richards and Brian Wilson; it might have irritated Bill's skin and made him so expert at locating, and then vanishing through, back doors that his nickname within the band became "I Go Now." But Mike never doubted what they were doing, and never worried about how it was changing him. Maybe because the life he had come to be living was only a slightly different version of the one his father had once dreamed for himself.

That was the crucial thing: that Frank Mills had never stopped singing, and never stopped wanting to sing for others. Even after his glory years with the U.S. Army chorales and then the Atlanta Singers, he always made certain he had an outlet for his music. Most often with the church choir, but he also had a friend who played piano and they'd team up to play standards at retirement homes, veterans' centers, or anywhere that people liked hearing the good old songs. He didn't mind the attention, of course, Frank had a big personality and loved to see the glow of his talent reflected in other people's eyes. And when his older son centered his life on music, his father couldn't have been more delighted. Both the Mills parents, Frank and Adora, would come to the shows and know all the songs, singing along as they watched their son working his bass and pitching in his harmonies. After the show, Frank would be backstage buttonholing his son's friends, hoisting a cocktail and reveling in the moment. "I think he loved everything about it," says Mike's close friend Tony Eubanks. "He was proud of his son and his son's band, not only for their success but how they carried themselves."[13]

―――――――

Julie Panebianco met R.E.M. in 1983 when she was still at Boston University, writing occasionally for *Boston Rock* magazine and for the city's *Phoenix* alternative newspaper. Entranced by "Radio Free Europe," *Chronic Town*, and then *Murmur*, she arranged to interview the band when they got to Boston, and they all hit it off. The musicians invited her to come with them to their show in Providence, Rhode Island, so Panebianco jumped into the van, beginning a friendship that continued after she graduated and scored a marketing job for Warner Bros. Records, focusing on the label's growing list of alternative music acts. Panebianco worked out of the company's New York offices but made occasional visits to the central headquarters in Burbank, California. And that's where she was in May 1987, just when her friends in R.E.M. were in a nearby studio putting some finishing touches on the *Document* tracks. Panebianco stopped over to say hi and hang out.

She was taking in the action when Jay Boberg noticed the visitor, figured out who she was, and made straight for Jefferson Holt. The two spoke urgently for a minute, Panebianco recalls. Holt nodded and whispered something to Peter Buck, who sighed and shrugged. Then Holt went up to Panebianco and, as gently as possible, told her it'd be a good idea if she left. He didn't explain why she had to go, but when Peter took her out for drinks later, he told her the whole story: R.E.M.'s deal with I.R.S. was about to end, and the last thing Boberg wanted was to have employees of competing record labels hanging around recording sessions his company was paying for. Up to that point it hadn't even occurred to Panebianco that she might have any role in signing artists to Warner Bros., or any label. But, still burned by the scene in the studio and jazzed on margaritas, she went home and wrote a memo to her boss, telling him how R.E.M. was up for grabs and that I.R.S. was nervous.

Two weeks later she was strolling into her New York office when the receptionist flagged her down: company president Lenny Waronker, her boss's boss, was looking for her. She had barely met him, and they'd never had a substantive conversation, but that clearly didn't matter to Waronker. "He didn't ask how I knew them; he just knew I knew them really well," she says. "And he said the company was absolutely interested in landing them." Waronker left her with one standing instruction: "If they ever invite you to go anywhere with them, you go."[14]

Set loose with a company credit card and carte blanche to go anywhere and do anything that would shore up her friendship with the members of R.E.M., Panebianco became a consistent and generous presence, going to multiple shows on their 1987 tour, taking the musicians out to dinner, picking up their tab wherever they were drinking, and occasionally introducing them to friends who, as it turned out, were also Warner Bros. Records executives. When they played Radio City Music Hall that fall, Panebianco came to the show with Karin Berg, the A&R executive who specialized in Warner's slate of alternative artists. "Michael was so excited, because she'd signed Television and Hüsker Dü," she says.

When the tour got to the final stand of shows in Atlanta a month later, Waronker arranged to go with Panebianco. The Warner president was knocked out by what he saw, and when she introduced them all after the show, the band members were happy to meet him, too. Waronker, as they knew, had started his career as a record producer and had helped make dozens of landmark records, including longtime Peter favorites such as Van Dyke Parks's *Song Cycle*, Randy Newman's *Good Old Boys*, and Gordon Lightfoot's "Sundown" single.

At the beginning of 1988 the band, along with Holt and Downs, started scheduling meetings with executives from an array of record companies including I.R.S., Warner Bros., Arista, Columbia, and several others. When the industry gathered in New York for the Grammy Awards at the start of March, the band and its representatives came to the city for a week of meetings. Warner Bros. had a head start thanks to Panebianco, who served as a conduit between the band and her bosses. "Peter would be telling me what they wanted, and I'd tell Karin and Lenny," she says.[15] Warner Bros. Records chairman Mo Ostin, Waronker's boss, was in New York for the Grammys, and the company's two top executives came to Panebianco's small, crowded office to talk strategy before their first official sit-down with R.E.M. When the band arrived, the executives seemed to forget that they were there to talk business, instead leading a freewheeling bull session about music and the records they all admired.

For Peter, who had been following Warner's artists since he was a teenager, it confirmed a long-standing sense he had that the label was uniquely committed to its artists, and to music that ventured past the mainstream tried and true. Now they were all learning that the company's leaders were simpatico, unlike the executives they'd met who were quick to badmouth the other companies or tried to sell themselves in ways that made the musicians wonder what they were thinking. "Clive Davis [the former head of Columbia Records, then with Arista] showed us a little film about himself and then was like: Any questions?" Peter recalled in 2017. "And we were like . . . *What the fuck?*"[16]

They still entertained offers from other labels, but the talks with Warner became more serious when the band flew to Los Angeles and had a longer, more focused meeting with Ostin and Waronker in their Burbank headquarters. Peter was further impressed by the company when he stepped out of Waronker's office, got promptly lost on his way to the men's room, and poked his head into an open office door to ask directions. "These five hipster-like kids were sitting around an office listening to music and they told me where the bathroom was, and one of them said, 'Hey, why don't you sign with Warners, we love your band.' And I was like, 'Okay!' So whoever she was . . . that helped a little."[17]

As the talks with Warner Bros. picked up steam, Jay Boberg and Miles Copeland tried to figure out how to hang on to the act they had spent most of the '80s building into platinum sellers. The thought of R.E.M. slipping from their grasp led to intense stress and a nauseating sense of incipient heartbreak all over the company. "Listen, that relationship was so cherished, and so important to us, and so authentic," Boberg says. "We had all grown up together, and we were peers. We were never going to outbid Warner Bros., and we were never going to outmaneuver them with our offices around the world. What we could offer them was to achieve the same result but in a manner in which they would have their process and their decisions fully respected and supported." But as Boberg and his colleagues were learning, Warner Bros., with their old friend Panebianco on board, could give them a version of that, too. "Julie really was the critical link," Boberg says. "If they hadn't felt comfortable about [the Warner staff], they wouldn't have been comfortable leaving."[18]

Warner Bros. had a lot of money to offer. But money, according to Peter, was never the decisive factor for the band. Ostin and Waronker were among the most admired executives in the industry, not just for their company's financial success but also for the quality of their records—Warner and its subsidiaries either were or had been home to groundbreaking artists including Neil Young, Van Dyke Parks, Van Morrison, Joni Mitchell, and Prince, as well as R.E.M. contemporaries/friends like the Replacements, Hüsker Dü, and Los Lobos—and their willingness to stick with artists for years, even decades, if they liked the music they made. Everything they said about being committed to their artists' creative freedom was confirmed by the Warner artists R.E.M.'s members spoke with. And the company also had one of the largest and most powerful distribution systems on the planet. Unlike I.R.S., which depended on CBS International to sell its records overseas, the Warner executives controlled virtually every aspect of their company's record production, packaging, national and international distribution, and promotion in-house. All that, plus a five-album deal reported to be worth somewhere between $8 and $10 million, sealed the deal. In April the news became public: R.E.M. was now signed to Warner Bros. Records.

In retrospect, maybe that's exactly where they'd been heading the entire time. Love Tractor bassist Armistead Wellford never forgot the twinkle of the Telecaster stud he saw in Peter's earlobe as he crawled through Kathleen O'Brien's closet on April 5, 1980. *That guy's a rock star!*, he'd thought. Kit Swartz, whose band the Side Effects also made their debut that night, sensed the difference too. "They were a breed apart," he says. "They had a mission, and they just approached it so much differently. They had an agenda. Me, I was just doing it for fun."[19] Pylon drummer Curtis Crowe, looking down from the perch his band had already achieved by the spring of 1980, saw it from the start, too. "We were tourists visiting the rock star world. But R.E.M. said, 'We are *going* to be rock stars.' And they thought and worked diligently, block by block, till they got to where they got."[20]

PART IV

The Monster

30

Hi, Hi, Hi, Hi

They'd gotten into the habit of using an album's opening song as a kind of overture, and a commentary on where the band found themselves as they dove into the new record. "Feeling Gravitys Pull" (*Fables of the Reconstruction*) described a band determined to stretch creatively, "Begin the Begin" (*Lifes Rich Pageant*) signaled the blossoming of a political consciousness, and "Finest Worksong," opening *Document*, sounded like a declaration of unity and professional intent. But the kickoff to their first major-label album required an explanation of sorts.

Had the 1980s' most successful indie/art band sold out? Had they sacrificed their edge for fame and fortune? The song launches at full blast, snare cracking on every beat, guitar and bass wham-whamming across a couple of chords, before a razored curl of a guitar riff introduces the singer, who also hit the ground at full speed. *Hello, I saw you, I know you, I knew you* . . . Dude is blurting out everything he can think of without pause, without heed, without a clue. *Should we talk about the weather? / Should we talk about the government?* By the second verse he's taking it all back—they've never met, he has no idea what he was talking about, he's not even sure who *he* is. But the come-ons continue, as transparent and ridiculous as the song's title. Which is the joke, and the point, for a self-described outsider band kicking off its first major-label album. They want to introduce themselves, hopefully to a whole new galaxy of record buyers and potential fans.

But of course they do; they're stepping onto the big stage now, making their bid for pop stardom. It's all been said and done before, but here it is one more time: "Pop Song 89."

Hi, hi, hi, hi, Michael chants as the intro's careening open riff repeats over and over.

Hi, hi, hi, hi.

Hi, hi, hi, hi.

The new five-album contract with Warner Bros. Records provided the band with more up-front money than they'd ever seen. It's always hard to separate the actual money a recording artist will receive from a major label from the theoretical kind that might come if they hit certain sales targets and finish paying off whatever expenses the company dumps onto their side of the ledger, but still. Signing with Warner Bros. elevated R.E.M. into a new orbit, and as they started work on their next album in the spring of 1988 they could feel the difference immediately. After spending a few days making demos of new songs in Athens, the band moved operations to Memphis in May, setting up shop in Ardent Studios, where their 1970s power-pop heroes Big Star had once recorded. The renowned, if star-crossed, band's drummer, Jody Stephens, managed the studios now, which made the connection to the past feel real. The Warner Bros. money meant that every band member could rent his own condominium in midtown, though Peter and Michael decided to share a place. They could eat in any restaurant and drink in any bar for as long as they wanted to without worrying about blowing through their per diem.

More importantly, the Warner Bros. deal provided more than enough income to keep themselves afloat for the year, so they could afford to take a break from touring, focus entirely on writing and recording, and let the new music dictate the pace of the sessions. With the eyes and ears of Warner Bros. on them, and many millions of dollars riding on the outcome, they got to work. "There was definitely pressure to follow *Document*," producer Scott Litt says. "But we had a ball there. It was just a little different . . . a different environment. And the record came out more soulful; there were definitely more instruments involved."[1] That was the money talking again, in the new instruments Peter and Mike brought in, in the time they spent experimenting with texture, in the side musicians they hired to add strings, pedal steel, and more, and the array of found sounds—crickets, music boxes, more—they invested time in locating, recording, and mixing into the tracks.

"They were excited to be working at a higher level," recalls engineer Jay Healy. They weren't profligate spenders, at least not in the jewels-and-furs-and-sports-cars way. But the influx of cash had clearly changed their outlook. "I think that's where the title *Green* came from, in part," Healy says. "These were people who were buying houses; they weren't concerned about spending money. It was a different lifestyle they were able to lead."[2]

Another song, another journey into the sonic beyond. "Get Up" comes storming out of the gate, drums pounding beneath a criss-crossing chord pattern traced by Mike's wordless vocals on the way to a chugging verse. Here Michael's perky vocal admonishes the sleepyheads around him (particularly Mike, according to legend[3]) to untangle themselves from their bedclothes and face the day. Particularly when there's work to be done and your bandmates are waiting, was the unstated message, but before long the song is stopped in its tracks, courtesy of Bill, who contradicts every word Michael has uttered. Because even as the singer was penning his up-and-at-'em lyric, the drummer had a dream about a room full of clocks, or clock sounds, ticking and chiming a gloriously psychedelic sound that came with him into the daylight, and then into the studio, where he and producer Scott Litt hatched a plan to re-create it for the microphones with a dozen wind-up music boxes, all chickering and chiming at once.

After six weeks in Memphis and Ardent Studios, they took a three-week break, then reconvened in upstate New York, in the rural hills of Woodstock, where they continued working on the new songs. Warner Bros. president Lenny Waronker had heard some of the developing tracks and had a couple of minor notes, but they were on a roll, all working harmoniously, all eager to expand their palette of sounds, feelings, and ideas. Peter had recently bought himself a mandolin, and the instrument's fluid chime became a central part of a few of the tracks. Mike brought in an accordion, and when he set his bass down to play it, or to sit at the piano, Bill would take up the bass, and they would either overdub the drums later or come up with other forms of percussion. The new instruments pushed the music in new directions, particularly for Peter, whose self-taught, trial-and-error style of learning allowed him to fall into chord changes and modulations that he wouldn't find on the well-worn fretboard of his guitar. The songs they wrote on their customary guitar, bass, and drums started on more familiar ground, then meandered in unexpected directions, due to either eccentric structural ideas or the melodies and lyrics Michael draped over the top.

When the instrumentalists presented him with a jaunty set of circular changes that reminded him of bubblegum pop from the 1960s, Michael responded with a lyric he figured was just as dumb, only his idea of dim-wittedness turned out to be quirky and strange and sort of hilarious. *Your feet are going to be on the ground,* he wrote. *Your head is there to move you around.* Peter used a wah-wah pedal to give his solo a wonky late '60s psychedelic sound, and Mike added a circuslike organ that completed the kandy-kolored silliness of it all. "Stand" was born.

A new sense of possibility was blossoming, and not just for the band. The Reagan administration was entering its final months, and the Democrats' presidential candidate, Michael Dukakis, then the governor of Massachusetts, was a bookish technocrat who came off like the mirror opposite of the gung-ho Hollywood cowboy who had occupied the White House for almost the entire decade. Dukakis's opponent, George H. W. Bush, the sitting vice president, seemed like a weak candidate: too geeky to emerge from Reagan's shadow, but not nearly as smart as Dukakis. It's always a risk to take up a candidate or a cause: the moment you stand for a cause or a candidate, you risk being let down. But after eight years of feeling alienated from the American political system, Michael was ready to believe in something. "There's a lot of store-bought cynicism traveling around

America these days," he said. "It was time for an album full of songs that weren't particularly happy but had an element of hope. Music that's more uplifting and less cynical."[4]

The optimism came less in the text of the songs, which avoided explicit mention of politics or ideals of any sort, than in their open-heartedness. In the way their meanderings beyond traditional pop instrumentation and song structure challenged listeners' sensibilities without being punishingly discordant or maddeningly oblique. There's a vulnerability in the music, in the hopeful peal of the mandolin and the melancholy hum of a cello, but also in the spoken regrets of an authoritarian leader, or perhaps lover, and even in the lunatic appeals of the man bursting through the door to say all the wrong things. Memories and dreamscapes, apologies and sweet melodic filigree. Increasingly, Michael's lyrical perspective came from within. He sang about his childhood, he sang about beauty, he sang about his fears and the feelings of love that could sweep over him like a tidal wave. *I stayed up late to hear your voice*, he sang in one song. *I'm not supposed to be like this*, he sang in another. *You are here with me*, he sang. *You have been here and you are everything.*

He also sang about his father and the wartime haze that had hung over him when he returned from Vietnam more than fifteen years earlier. The band gave Michael a grinding pattern set to a martial beat, and he matched it with a lyric he called "Orange Crush," a soldier's impressionistic portrayal of the thrill of battle. The finished track began with a torrent of machine-gun-like snare hits, establishing a groove that played out between Peter's guitar notes, hanging like tracer fire while the vocalists trade lines, Mike and Bill calling cadence against Michael's swaggering lead, shouting out his own courage, righteousness, and infallibility. *I've got my spine, I've got my Orange Crush*, he sings, invoking soda pop and Agent Orange, the deadly defoliant America sprayed across Vietnam, in one go.

When the song breaks down halfway in, it heads straight into the war zone, helicopters buzzing overhead, a platoon drilling, and Michael, through a megaphone but only just audible above the cacophony, speaking in the voice of what sounds like a helicopter pilot, circling and circling, seeing everything, not even needing to look because he had it all wired. *I knew it all*, he proclaims. *I knew every back road and every truck stop*. He could be speaking with the voice of a Vietnam recon pilot, like his father, or as a road-crazed traveler speeding through the wee hours. Or he could be talking for both of them, the son of the recon pilot psyching himself up for his most daring incursion yet: R.E.M.'s assault on the sports arenas of the United States, Europe, and beyond.

31

Are You Ready to Rock 'n' Roll?

Another April 5, another show. Nine years had passed since Kathleen O'Brien's birthday party in the crumbling church on Oconee Street, and other than the four young men making the music, nearly everything had changed. They were in Detroit, seven hundred miles to the north of Athens. They were also performing for more than ten thousand people, all of them on their feet from the moment the lights went out, according to Gary Graff's review in the *Detroit Free Press* the next morning.[1] Behind the musicians, the projection screen, which had panned across a scabby landscape while the band sprinted to their places on the stage, shifted to a black screen with tall white letters spelling out HELLO. Which worked on two levels, since it's also the first word in the first song they were about to perform. But a lot of what was about to happen would take place on two levels—as ironic commentary on the tropes and tactics of arena rock, and also as spellbinding arena rock.

They opened with "Pop Song 89," the leadoff track for their new album, *Green*, a crunchy, power-chording portrait of a man, or a band, trying too hard to make a good impression. He's up for anything—talking about the rain, talking about politics, whatever—and the letters on the screen projected it into the back row: WEATHER for a moment, then GOVERNMENT, flashing back and forth to underscore the ludicrousness of it all. And yet that made less of an impact than Michael Stipe. Because the singer's transformation from reluctant front man to rock 'n' roll demigod was complete. When the band came out at the start of the show, he marched straight to the lip of center stage and faced down the arena. Standing tall in a boxy white two-piece suit, spotlights glinting off dark Ray-Ban Wayfarer shades, hair shaved tight on the sides, a long, ratty ponytail hanging most of the way down his back, he stood there for a long moment, looking utterly impermeable. And also a little absurd, something about that boxy-jacket-and-Ray-Ban combo edged him a tiny bit toward Max Headroom, right up until the band started playing. At which point he erupted. Legs working, shoulders moving, his body electrified by the rhythm. Then he was singing, his authority, assisted by a top-drawer sound system, rippling your diaphragm. All that, and then there was the music at full blast, the lights and the noise, the throngs and the cheers, the trucks and the buses, the vast machinery it takes to put on a show this big. Wrapping his arms around it, kissing it on the lips, and then shoving it away and dancing out of reach.

R.E.M.'s new era began with the release of *Green* on November 8, 1988. In the next few weeks the album was greeted with good, if not spectacular, sales, and positive if not overwhelmingly terrific reviews. The matter of the band's artistic integrity in the wake of the Warner Bros. deal still loomed, although the critics couldn't agree on whether the band had responded to its big break by becoming too commercial or not commercial enough. Arguing for the former was the *San Francisco Examiner*'s Barry Walters, who began his review (headline: "Simplistic *Green* May Leave R.E.M. Fans Seeing Red") by declaring allegiance to the shadowy depths of *Murmur* (their "first and finest album"), then asserted that the quartet, the "Beatles of college radio," was so intimidated by *Murmur*-loving critics and so determined to prove it was something more than a Byrdsian jangle band that the musicians had made a crucial error, opting for slickness and commerciality. "These criticisms have provoked the band to leave behind what has given it its identity."[2]

Unless they hadn't, which was what troubled the *Baltimore Sun*'s J. D. Considine. "For in its haste to avoid the obvious, R.E.M. has amplified its eccentricities, as if the band were somehow ashamed of

Michael Stipe as a grade schooler.

Bill Berry in 1968.

Peter Buck as a fourth grader in 1966.

Mike Mills in his 1975 high school yearbook.

As a high schooler Michael, wearing his kimono shirt and Melanie Herrold's silver lamé pants in her bedroom, dresses the part of the 1970s rock star.

Michael with his first band, Bad Habits. Drummer Jim
Warchol drinks a beer, guitarist Joe Haynes bites his
fingernails, bassist Buddy Weber puffs on a cigarette
while Michael explores the deeper cavities of his nose.

Stipe and Buck bear down at one of the band's first shows at Tyrone's, 1980.

In the winter of 1980 Michael Stipe was best known around the University of Georgia campus as an art student.

R.E.M. on the road in 1981: Merlyn's Club, Madison, Wisconsin.

Backstage at Merlyn's, November 1981.

Mike Mills, Michael Stipe, Peter Buck, and Bill Berry, 1982

Taking a break from producing the Athens band Dreams So
Real in 1985, Peter Buck catches up on his reading.

Jefferson Holt and Bill Berry, with Mike Mills just behind them, toast the new Warner Bros. Records contract at Bertis Downs's house in Athens, Georgia, 1988.

The four members of R.E.M. celebrate together.

By 1989 Michael embraced his role as the band's front man.

Even the hectic 1989 world tour allowed Bill, with Mike in the background and his bandmates just out of the shot, time for sightseeing by kayak.

After the "Losing My Religion" video cleaned up at MTV's 1991 Video Music Awards, Bill Berry, Michael Stipe, and Mike Mills showed off Michael's many message T-shirts.

Michael at the top of the heap on R.E.M.'s enormous 1995 tour.

Once the most collegiate-looking band member, Mike Mills got ready for the 1995 tour by buying a rack of spangled suits to wear onstage.

When he wasn't playing his guitar for tens of thousands of cheering fans, Peter did his best to help feed and care for his twin daughters, Zoe and Zelda.

Mike on the '95 tour with Seattle musician Scott McCaughey, who would play a significant role throughout the second half of R.E.M.'s career.

After his 1995 aneuryism, and the brain surgery that repaired it, Bill took to wearing a cap onstage.

After devoting his life to R.E.M. for nearly twenty years, Bill reveled in the quiet of his farm and the thrum of his tractor.

Relaunched as a trio following Berry's 1997 departure, R.E.M. poses for the European press in 1998.

Michael stares down the doubters at R.E.M.'s triumphant appearance at England's Glastonbury Festival in 1999.

Michael and Peter share a moment onstage during R.E.M.'s 2003 European tour.

With Bill Berry on drums and Pearl Jam's Eddie Vedder joining in, R.E.M. plays at the band's 2007 induction into the Rock & Roll Hall of Fame.

its own accessibility."[3] Steve Morse, writing in the *Boston Globe*, also worried that the album wasn't accessible enough: "There's a general absence of Top 40 material."[4] Meanwhile, Robert Christgau, in one of the short, sharp reviews he packaged into his regular Consumer Guide column for *The Village Voice*, went big in both directions, celebrating the "bite of their realest rock [and] the shameless beauty their cult once lived for," then denouncing the "heavy tempos and dubious poetry" of "The Wrong Child" and the other songs he didn't like.[5]

More casual listeners heard something that stood apart from everything else that had been coming out of their radios. The album's first single, the marauding rocker "Orange Crush," was a mainstream rock radio smash, reaching number one on *Billboard*'s Album Rock Tracks chart. The album sold fairly well for the first month or two, but when Warner Bros. opened the new year with a single release of the jaunty "Stand," the pop-friendly song that had inspired Michael to compose the silliest lyric he could imagine, the skies opened. Boosted by a sweet, playful video that made great visual hay out of how silly this song by the oh-so-serious indie rock heroes truly was, "Stand" vaulted up the pop charts at an even faster pace than "The One I Love" had, climbing all the way to number six on *Billboard*'s Hot 100 and pulling *Green* into the top ten of the album list. The album hit the platinum sales mark easily and kept right on going, passing the two-million mark by the end of 1989.

Planning for that 1989 tour started in mid-1988 and picked up steam in the autumn. In the wake of two top-ten singles, a million-copy-selling album, and a new album on track to sell even better than that, and with one of the world's most powerful record companies now putting its muscle behind them, prospects for the coming year were well beyond anything the band had previously encountered. Projected audiences in every city ran to ten thousand and beyond, which put R.E.M. into exactly the sort of basketball arenas they had once sworn off playing. Peter had always been the most vocal about his hatred of playing arenas or anywhere larger than a theater, but after *Document*'s success put them into a few sports venues, including Philadelphia's eighteen-thousand-seat Spectrum, his position evolved. "We're successful enough that we pretty much have to play the large places," he told the Indianapolis music writer Marc Allan in 1989. He rarely enjoyed seeing other bands play arena shows, he admitted. "But I've seen Prince in big places, and Springsteen in big places, and I like those shows. There's a way to do it without selling yourself short or selling the audience short. There's a way around it. I consider that we're ourselves, we're just in a bigger place."[6]

R.E.M.'s touring apparatus had grown steadily since they first piled into Bill's parents' old station wagon to make that first trip to North Carolina. Now it had become something like a traveling circus. They needed semis to lug the gear and multiple buses to transport the band and crew from city to city, and arrangements for the flights and other forms of transportation required to get all of it, and them, to Japan, Australia, England, and the various European countries in which R.E.M. was booked to perform.

Dozens of rock bands could fill arenas in the late 1980s, and with so much money in play, an entire industry had grown to accommodate the oversize shows' many requirements. Now that R.E.M. had joined the arena-size ranks, they expanded their staff to meet their new circumstances. Geoff Trump, who had served as tour manager for the previous few tours, moved over to tour accounting to make room for David Russell, an experienced hand who had managed national and global tours for the likes of Tina Turner, Bon Jovi, and Pink Floyd.

The band tapped more than two dozen full-time employees, roadies, instrument techs, sound techs, lighting techs, personal assistants, drivers, and others to come with them. That workforce was matched in each city by a crew provided by the local promoter, which was obligated to meet the traveling crew before the show with half a dozen riggers, four truck loaders, six stagehands, a licensed electrician, one forklift driver with forklift, ten stagehands, and two runners with vehicles, along with security guards on all the doors. Four deck hands, a house-lights operator, and an electrician were needed to work during the shows, and the load-out at the end of the night was to be staffed by eight truck loaders, the six riggers, two forklift drivers with forklifts, and even more workers if the stage was farther than twenty-five feet from the stage doors. They also needed caterers to feed and water the band and the workers. Altogether it ran like a small, temporary city, and generated nearly as much revenue. The potential ticket revenue for one night at the Meadowlands Arena, outside New York City—which did not include sales of T-shirts, sweatshirts, concert programs, or albums, the majority of which went to the artist—was more than $325,000. A sellout at the Alpine Valley outdoor amphitheater, outside Milwaukee, could amount to nearly $675,000.

Rehearsals for the tour launched in Athens just after the start of the new year. They hired Peter Holsapple, the singer/songwriter/guitarist from the dB's, to serve as a utility musician onstage, playing second guitar and keyboards and adding to the backing vocals. In addition to preparing the music, they worked to coordinate it with the visual effects—films, written messages, and more—Michael helped develop for the large projection screens that would loom behind the band during the shows. They'd featured projected backdrops on previous tours, but now that they would be performing for larger crowds, a sizable percentage of whom would be too far from the stage to make out the expressions on their faces, the projections became a more significant part of the show. Particularly when it came to establishing the layers of their intentions as full-on arena rockers.

The entire production moved to a larger Atlanta rehearsal hall after a couple of weeks, and after a couple of days of work with the full ensemble, the entire group boarded a plane for Japan and the start of what would be a nearly yearlong world tour. They started with two shows in Tokyo's Sound Colosseum MZA, then moved to New Zealand for three performances before settling into Australia for eight shows over two weeks.

This is how the shows would go: thousands of people in the arena, the band blasting away, one slam-bam song after another. "Pop Song 89" to start things off on a sardonic yet ass-kicking note, then the one-two punch of "Exhuming McCarthy" and "Welcome to the Occupation" to give the show some political/social gravitas. Serious rock 'n' roll. Then there'd be a break, that moment when Michael, or another band member, was supposed to greet the crowd in that way rock stars always greet the crowd. To have ever seen a rock concert was to know exactly how that was going to go. *Hello, Cleveland!*, etc., etc. So instead of actually saying the words, they put them up on the screen:

HELLO (your city here)
GREETINGS (your city name here)
WE ARE THE BAND R.E.M.
IT'S GREAT TO BE BACK IN (your city here)
ARE YOU READY TO ROCK 'N' ROLL?
GREAT.

When Michael did talk to the crowd, he'd set up the next song by pointing at some random person in the crowd and insisting that the next one had been written *just for you*, or making some other obviously lame but stage-tested proclamation. And the screen, meanwhile, had its own rap going:

WHAT A GIANT PLACE THIS IS
LET'S TRY TO HEAR A PIN DROP
SHHHHH
GREAT
OKAY
ARE YOU READY?
(crowd noise)

Then they'd launch into song, playing with more power, precision, and depth—Holsapple really added another dimension to the sound—than ever before, and there was nothing the least bit ironic about that.

David Russell ran the tour like a military operation, with the roadies all garbed in black, carrying walkie-talkies on their belts like sidearms, every functionary moving in precise accordance with the instructions of the central command. All backstage doors were monitored by security staff, who gave or forbade access to the various levels, halls, and chambers according to the shape, size, and color of the proffered tour credential. True insiders wore a laminated tour pass on a chain around their neck; visitors had silk stick-ons good for that night only, and usually for a limited section of the backstage area. Russell also produced a daily tour bulletin, mimeographed and distributed among the tour personnel and always posted on the walls and doors backstage, to remind everyone what day it was and where they were, with a map of the venue and a sheet of "Mr. Load-In's Fun Facts" compiling technical details about the venue (the locations of power outlets, door dimensions, wattage and location of house lights, etc.) as well as the name and contact information for the night's promoter, the local stage manager, the union shop steward, and so on.

Russell also noted the name of the artist opening the show and the precise timing of their set, which usually began a few ticks less than an hour after the venue's doors opened and ended precisely forty minutes later. Not forty-one minutes later, and definitely not forty-one and a half minutes later, as the members of Pylon learned when they finished the first of the fifteen shows they opened on the tour. "We rehearsed and rehearsed to get a performance that was that tight," singer Vanessa Briscoe Hay recalls. "They've got a guy in a headset talking to another guy in a headset, and they count down, ten, nine, eight . . . and then you're up there. We were kind of congratulating ourselves a little when we came off the first time, but then the stage manager said we'd gone ninety seconds over. He was very nice about it, but we thought, *Uh-oh, we gotta cut something.*" As they learned, the crew needed a precise number of minutes to switch the instruments between acts, and if the openers ran even a few seconds late, the whole event got off-kilter. "It's all about professionalism," Briscoe Hay says.

Pylon's 1988 reunion, five years after they had disbanded, was due entirely to R.E.M. Specifically to Bill's offhanded comment to *Rolling Stone*, when told that the magazine planned to bill R.E.M. as the best band in America, that his band still took a backseat to Pylon.

The foursome had missed performing together, and when sales of their albums leaped after the publication of the interview, they began fielding offers to play shows. Then they dusted off their instruments and started rehearsing. They played a few shows around their old haunts in late 1988 and the first half of 1989, and when R.E.M. asked if they'd like to come with them for a couple of weeks on their big tour, they signed on. Knowing how unpleasant opening for a big-ger band can be, R.E.M.'s members tried to make it easier for the friends they brought with them, which included two Atlanta bands—Drivin N Cryin and the up-and-coming folk duo Indigo Girls—the Boston neo-punk band Throwing Muses, and the new band fronted by former Soft Boy Robyn Hitchcock, among others, paying them all a decent $2,500 a night, giving them enough time to play a full set, and instructing their crew to treat them with the same respect they gave the headliners.

Having Pylon with them felt particularly satisfying, since they had taken so much inspiration from their Athens neighbors and prede-cessors, and when Bill saw some fans waving signs with the opening band's name on it, the drummer waded into the crowd and invited them backstage. When the fans, in turn, invited the Pylon members back to their apartment for a party after the show, Bill and Mike went along too. "We ended up at someone's apartment with a kitchenette, dancing around to records," Briscoe Hay recalls.

Show after show after show after show. The tour divided into five legs, starting in Japan in January, swinging through the antipodes in the first half of February, then spending March and April barnstorm-ing the eastern and southern United States. The company headed to Europe in May, visiting fourteen countries before returning home in early July. They got a summer break through Labor Day week-end, then launched into another city-to-city-to-city crawl through the United States, hitting some regions they hadn't visited the first time around. But they were less popular than the projections had indicated—the failure of post-"Stand" singles "Pop Song 89" and "Get Up" to make an impact on radio or record stores cut into *Green*'s and the band's momentum, particularly in secondary markets—and by the middle of the fall they found themselves playing to venues that were, at best, half-filled.

After nearly a decade of serving in a working rock band, the members of R.E.M. had developed rituals and habits to ease their way through the days, weeks, and months of work. At first they had fueled their travels with amphetamines and heroic quantities of beer. They relied on the generosity of bartenders and fans to keep them lubricated and, particularly in the early days, fed with something more than subsistence rations. But success had given them more and better options. Like all entertainers working the bigger halls, they could require concert promoters to supply enough food and beverages to keep the band and their crew satisfied before, during, and after their labors.

The rider on their standard performance contract listed their needs in detail. Along with the assorted cereals, bagels, cream cheese, eggs, bacon, and sausage that greeted the crew in the morning and the pots of fresh coffee, sodas, juices, tea, and spring water that would quench their thirst during the days; the sandwich makings, cold vegetables, and cookies for lunch, and the hot and cold meat-based and vegetarian meals they'd need to serve twenty-five people; and the various waters, sodas, sliced lemons, cough drops, fruit baskets (no grapes!), gourmet cheeses, and other snacks the band members wanted in their dressing rooms, they also required several cases of beer, eight bottles of high-quality wine (to be selected by the production manager), and two liters of Absolut vodka. Often the promoter would add other treats as gifts, champagne or other kinds of liquor, or, on occasion, other, more powdery substances that could make a night feel extra fun and special.

Cocaine and other drugs laced the music industry in the 1980s, and though nobody in R.E.M. was a serious drug abuser, most of them weren't opposed to a convivial snort, particularly as the months passed and the road twisted into the distance. Vodka drinks, gin and tonics, and glasses of red wine rivaled beer in the dressing rooms, and though they all had their share, Bill more than kept up his end. The drummer's love for performing and his excitement about the band's mounting success had been worn down by a growing distaste for travel and the interviews, photo sessions, and meet-and-greets with promoters and local media figures that consumed so much of their time on the road. Long an enthusiastic drinker, Bill knew how much ease he could pour out of the bottles on the liquor table, but as the inside jokes on David Russell's daily tour bulletins made clear, the alcoholic tide left chaos in its wake. The drummer had a habit of losing his tour credentials and leaving other personal items in his dressing room. And in one of the bulletin's recurring gags, describing the various members as animals in a bestiary, Bill is designated by the Latin *Drummerus hungoverus* and noted for "frequenting back lounges and after-hours watering holes til sunrise."

The *Green* tour made one last swing through the Southwest in the fall before returning to the Southeast for two final weeks of shows, often visiting the university towns of North Carolina, Tennessee, Virginia, and Georgia they had first played during the earliest forays in 1980 and 1981. The tour made its final bow in Bill and Mike's hometown of Macon on November 11, performing a not quite sold-out show at the city's Coliseum sports arena. It was a particularly sweet night for the Macon boys, who had grown up seeing their heroes playing in the same venue. R.E.M.'s rhythm section stopped by the mayor's office before the show, where they were presented with a ceremonial key to the city. The band played one last show at the Fox Theatre, in Atlanta, a fundraiser for a local environmental group, then packed up their gear and went their separate ways, with a long decade behind them and no particular plans for the 1990s.

32

The Fever

Home in Athens during a short break between tour legs earlier that year, at the start of May 1989, Bill Berry went to his garden to unwind. He and his wife, Mari, were renovating a vintage house they'd bought in the city's historic Cobbham district, and the place came with grounds that had become overgrown. Always happy to do physical work outside, Bill spent an afternoon cutting back a wisteria bush. It was sweaty work, whacking away at the voluminous growth and then wrestling the cut tendrils into mounds that could be collected and taken away. The drummer was worn out at the end of the day, but the soft spring air and the tang of fresh greenery had restored him, and when he left for Europe a few days later his eyes were noticeably brighter than they'd been when he arrived. This would change.

Picking up their work again in Germany, on May 8 the band performed "Stand" on a TV show, then went to Düsseldorf to start the next stretch of concerts. The ease Bill had found in his garden dissolved into a headache somewhere in Düsseldorf, and his whole body hurt by the start of the May 9 show. But he powered through, then went to his room to try to sleep off whatever was ailing him. It didn't work. By the time Jefferson Holt went to check on him in the morning, the drummer's fever had spiked above 103 and he was seeing things that weren't actually in the room. Holt summoned a doctor, who promptly had Bill transported to a hospital. The next night's show in Munich was canceled, and when the drummer's fever continued to burn, the next two shows fell off the schedule too.

Nothing worked. It started to get scary, particularly when Bill broke out in a rash that covered his chest and face in red spots. The German doctors were mystified, but when Michael called home to fret to his parents, his dad figured it out immediately. A high fever and a blotchy rash? That sounded like Rocky Mountain spotted fever, an infection carried by ticks, which, while common in the United States and the wisteria bushes of Athens, Georgia, were unheard of in Europe. This explained the doctors' confusion. The band flew a specialist to Germany, and when Lieutenant Colonel Stipe's diagnosis proved correct, the doctors pumped the drummer full of doxycycline. The antibiotics knocked his fever back in a matter of hours, and though he was still visibly spotted a week later, Bill was determined to get back onstage in time for the Pinkpop Festival in the Netherlands on May 15.

"That was so important to him, because he hated to disappoint people," then-wife Mari says.[1] It was what kept Bill on the road, at the interview sessions, and in front of the cameras, even when he would rather have been anywhere else. "When they went onstage and played, he loved it," Bill's brother Don says. "But that's only a small percentage of the time. You have all this other stuff to do, and as you become more famous you have less control over your life. You're living by a schedule and timetable and soundchecks and being on the bus at the right time. I think that was what got him to thinking about giving it up."[2]

But how could he give up the only job he'd ever wanted to do?

Born in Duluth, Minnesota, on July 31, 1958, William Thomas Berry was the fifth and last child born to Donald Berry, an accountant for the Lippmann Engineering Works, and Jane, who ran the household and cared for the three sons and two daughters they'd started having soon after Donald returned from his World War II service. The four eldest, James, Jane, Don, and Katheryn, came between 1947 and 1952, Bill making his belated arrival six years later. Donald was

promoted to plant manager in 1960 and the family moved to Wau-
watosa, a suburb of Milwaukee. In 1967 a career shift sent the Berrys
to Sandusky, Ohio, where they stayed until another transfer moved
Donald and his family to Macon, Georgia, in 1972. The older kids
had moved away by then, leaving their youngest sibling to spend his
adolescence as an only child. He was fourteen years old, but the older
kids' interests, and record collections, had made a mark on him.

Both parents had tilted toward music, if only for fun. Donald
liked to entertain the kids by singing silly songs he'd learned in the
Army, and Jane played piano, although her repertoire was limited to
a few pieces she'd learned while taking lessons as a girl. The older
kids took up instruments in school, but none pursued them with the
drive Bill showed for the drums when he first picked up the sticks as
a fourth grader in 1967. He'd also developed a serious enthusiasm for
the pop music he heard coming from his older siblings' radios and
the family stereo. The Beatles were everyone's favorites, and Don
came home with albums by late '60s heroes ranging from Jimi Hendrix to Jefferson Airplane, the Rolling Stones, the MC5, and Frank
Zappa. Bill loved the Beatles the most, and when he found a ukulele
around the house, he fiddled with it until he could approximate the
chords in the songs and play along.

It all began with an announcement from the principal of his grade
school: any student who wanted to join the school band should come
to the lunchroom right now. Bill was in fourth grade, maybe ten years
old. He'd never thought about taking up a band instrument, but if it
was going to get him out of class, he was definitely interested. With a
roomful of instruments in front of him, Bill reached for the first one
that caught his eye.

"I thought, I've got to play something, why not the drums?" he
recalled.[3] He learned the rudiments of rhythm at school, then got his
parents to rent him a kit so he could play rock 'n' roll. The more he
learned, the more he wanted to know, and he'd spend hours in the
garage, pounding away. Music got under his skin. A catchy melody
would stick in his mind and follow him around all day. He developed

a deep connection to the Stax artists coming out of Memphis, and all the great rhythm-and-blues songs of the era. Anything with a good rhythm could get him going.

Relocated to Macon at the start of ninth grade, Bill felt drawn to the outsiders, the tough-talking guys who sat in the back row of class and snuck out to the parking lot to smoke cigarettes at lunch. He'd ride around with them on the weekends, guzzling beer and passing joints in the back of someone's car. Later he liked to talk about himself as one of the bad kids, sarcastic, two-fisted, and always ready for trouble. His heavy brows and hooded eyes helped give him a sinister appearance, and Bill could turn his glare on another kid who aroused his ire, like that geeky Mike Mills. But it was almost entirely an act. "He smoked weed with the rest of us, but Bill was never a bad kind of guy," Gevin Lindsay says. "He was friendly and nice."[4]

He enjoyed a warm relationship with his dad, playing golf with him at the country club and spending long afternoons together in a fishing boat, poles in hand, lines trailing across the surface of a lake. And if Bill's grades left something to be desired, he was obviously smart and had a good work ethic, mowing lawns so he could buy more and better drums and then, when he was old enough to drive, a beat-up old Volkswagen Bug. The thing had a broken starter, and he had to park it on hills so he could get a rolling start and pop the clutch, but he could fit his drums inside. Once he started jamming with other guys, it was good to be able to get around.

Soon music, and playing in a band, became the primary driver of Bill's life. The jam session in the Mills family basement that cemented his new friendship with Mike; the connection to David Wilson and Alan Ingley, the other two members of Shadowfax; the hours of rehearsals, of listening to records, the talking about what they heard and what they wanted to play. His parents could only shake their heads. "Oh we had fits, you know, about the noise and the kids that were coming around," Bill's mother, Jane, told the *Macon Telegraph and News* in 1984. "We just thought it was a passing thing, and he'd go on to something else after a while. But it was the only thing that held his interest."[5]

And not just as a boyish fantasy. Macon's music scene was incredibly rich and, thanks to the locally based Capricorn Records label and its star act the Allman Brothers Band, a lot of the action was taking place just around the corner. They'd met and hung out with some of their crowd and could talk to them about how a professional band went about its business. It was exciting and spoke to both sides of Bill's character: the music-besotted kid who wanted to rock out all night long and the practical kid who sometimes begged off rehearsals so he could tend to his lawn mowing clients.

When he decided to take time off after high school, Bill hustled his way into his job at the offices of Paragon Booking and came away a few months later with a working knowledge of the concert industry. When he first got to the University of Georgia, he figured he'd pursue his interest by going to law school and learning entertainment law. But when the band, against all odds, started to gain momentum, he not only quit school but also insisted that the two other students in R.E.M. do the same. Mike didn't hesitate, but Michael, who truly enjoyed his art studies, had to think about it a little longer. Bill made it clear that the band's future depended on what he decided: if the singer couldn't commit himself entirely to the band, Bill wasn't going to stick around. "Once Bill gets an idea in his head, he's going to go for it. He's not going to waste his time," Mari says. "He's like, 'This is what I want, and this is what we need to do.' He's very determined."[6]

In the weeks after the 1989 tour ended, Bill felt shattered. His summertime bout with Rocky Mountain fever had been terrifying; the days of feverish hallucinations cast a shadow across his memory like a near-death experience. He'd hated being responsible for the canceled shows and had left the hospital for the Netherlands against his doctors' strong recommendation, risking his recovery by coming back as quickly as he did. Then the underwhelming crowds they'd drawn in the autumn made him wonder what the point of it all had been.

The drinking he'd done had made it even more toxic. The beers and pills in the early years had been one thing, but now there were those bottles of Absolut greeting them everywhere they went. And everywhere they went, he'd been eager to crack them open, to pour himself one drink to get going, another to keep it moving, to top that one off when it ran low, and to pour another to come down from the show at the end of the evening. *Drummerus hungoverus* was funny when they were all a gang on the road, but when he was home it was a misery.

What was he doing with his life? After nearly a decade with R.E.M., almost all of it spent away from home, either bouncing from town to town on one of their endless tours or off in a recording studio spending ten to sixteen hours a day trying to make music that felt at least a little bit original, he'd washed up at home with a wife he loved but hadn't really gotten a chance to know.

The start of the new year, and the new decade it brought in with it, gave Bill a sense of resolve. He stopped drinking. Maybe not forever, he thought, but certainly for the foreseeable future. Almost immediately he felt unburdened. "Things started coming into focus," he said. "I'd been married since 1986 but it wasn't really a marriage until I got off the road and realized that I have other attributes apart from being a reasonably OK drummer with a very good group. I started respecting myself more and things just took care of themselves."[7]

Another thing he could take care of was how he and R.E.M. were going to spend their time in the next year or two. As far as he was concerned, they'd done quite enough touring. They were done, he said, "beating our heads against the wall."[8] Instead, they needed to focus on the artistry that mattered the most: writing songs and making records. They'd just have to find a new way to promote them. And if taking a break from touring meant settling for smaller sales, that was fine.

33

A Breath, This Song

A s 1990 dawned, the four members of R.E.M. had achieved something like rock 'n' roll grace. Almost exactly ten years after they had first gathered to play some rock 'n' roll songs at St. Mary's Church, they were, by every definition, rock stars. *Green* had sold more than two million copies, more than twice what *Document* had sold. Their music played on radio stations all over the world. Their videos could be seen on MTV, now available all across the globe, multiple times a day. They weren't the biggest stars in the music galaxy; "Pop Song 89," released as the follow-up to the smash "Stand" single, had stalled at number eighty-nine (numerical irony noted) on *Billboard's* singles chart, while "Get Up," released a few months later, didn't even sell enough copies to chart. But it didn't matter. Even with the underwhelming audiences during the final swing through the United States, their year of touring arenas had been enormously successful, clearing millions of dollars in profits. Now all four of them could go anywhere, do anything, and spend their time working on, or not working on, anything that captured their interest. What they did, less than a week into the new decade, was get together to write new songs.

They had set up their instruments, amplifiers, and other gear in a comfortable rehearsal space on the second floor of a building on Clayton Street in downtown Athens. It was a perfect clubhouse for four young men who liked nothing more than listening to, thinking about, writing, and playing music. It had always been one of their greatest strengths as a unit, that they'd always been industrious, always felt most comfortable hewing to a consistent regimen. So once they got going on January 6, 1990, they fell into something like a traditional work schedule: getting together five days a week in Clayton Street, taking turns playing the riffs and chord progressions they'd come up with, working together to weave them into verses and choruses until they started to feel like songs. When they had a handful of new tunes, they'd head to John Keane's recording studio to turn the latest constructions into demos. It was easygoing and fun, with no set schedule and no deadline, no need to worry about their income or what the folks at the record company thought. It was, in short, a dream. If you could have gone back to January 1980 and asked young Bill, Peter, Mike, and Michael what they'd like to be doing with their days in ten years . . . well, here it was.

This utopian breeze didn't just blow through the windows of R.E.M.'s workroom. All around the world, an unexpected series of developments had given the first days of the 1990s a more hopeful outlook than any time since the early 1960s, when the newly inaugurated president, John F. Kennedy, called his moment the New Frontier. The optimism was, as usual, fleeting. In the spring of 1989, an extended student protest in China's Tiananmen Square spurred a vast pro-democracy movement that was ultimately put down by the communist government, but not before it inspired similar action from oppressed people all around the world, and some of these rebellions proved far more successful.

The crumbling authority of the Soviet Union's government led to a protest in East Germany that climaxed with the breaching, and then destruction, of the wall that had divided the people of West Germany from their neighbors in the Soviet-controlled eastern half of the country. In Czechoslovakia, the absurdist playwright, anticommunist dissident, and occasional political prisoner turned pro-democracy leader Václav Havel was named president of the nation by the Federal Assembly. Three months later in South Africa, where the racist apartheid government was on its last legs, the anti-racism activ-

ist Nelson Mandela was released from twenty-six years of imprison-
ment. Within a few years he'd be the president of the nation that
once jailed him.

In the United States the currents were shifting, too. After a
decade of Republican rule in the White House, the solidly Democratic Congress was unified in its resistance to the executive branch.
And though President George H. W. Bush was still popular with voters, public support for environmentalism, the fight against AIDS, gay
rights, and racial justice in South Africa was surging. This was due in
part to Rock the Vote, a political advocacy campaign created to raise
the political awareness and participation of young voters. Sensing
the current of interest among its viewers, MTV began to invest more
resources into its news operation, ramping up political coverage as
the 1992 election approached.

And as political issues moved to the center of youth culture,
R.E.M.'s political advocacy was manifested in the information tables
for Greenpeace, the Nature Conservancy, and the Environmental
Defense Fund that accompanied them on all the stops on the 1989
tour. Songs like "Fall on Me," "The Flowers of Guatemala," and
"Welcome to the Occupation" made the members of R.E.M. seem
like oracles of a sort. For a younger generation of music fans, whose
tastes were informed by what they saw and heard on MTV, R.E.M.'s
political awareness was nearly as crucial as the sound of their music
or the fuck-off in their rock 'n' roll swagger.

A new year, a new decade, new ideas, new sounds. A decade of playing electric guitar virtually every day, climaxing with a year of playing it on arena stages every night, had worn down Peter's interest in
his primary instrument. Now when he got an itch to play, his hands
reached for his mandolin, maybe an acoustic guitar. Anything with a
different sound, a different set of melodic possibilities. Mike felt the
same way about the bass, and even the guitar, heading to the piano
or the electronic keyboard when he felt something brewing. Bill did
most of his writing on the guitar or piano, hearing songs that drew
their rhythmic punch from the grain of the strums or lighter percussion, such as congas or shakers. Piecing the music together, the three

instrumentalists sensed themselves moving toward a more orna-
mented, even baroque sound. Songs that were melodic and lush, textured with strings, horns, and keyboard sounds. The acoustic songs,
particularly the ones Peter started on his mandolin, had a keening,
poignant feel. Mike's keyboards layered and twined with the guitars
on the brighter songs, and the darker ones combined acoustic, electric, and pedal steel guitars, percussion, and feedback into a midnight
garden of sound, blossoms shimmering in the blue light of the moon.

Often new songs would begin with the three instrumentalists,
playing their latest riffs and feels, helping one another expand them,
match them with other pieces, merge them into something like
songs. Often Peter or Mike would present a set of changes, maybe
even a complete tune, for the others to respond to and possibly
revise. Bill had his own passages and song models too, and he served
as the band's editor, helping to keep the project focused and moving
forward, not overly defined by any member's individual habitual ten-
dencies. He was the earthy one, grounded and goal-oriented.

Sometimes Michael would be with them, listening in, describing
what he liked, where he thought a song could go. When the others played he'd sing along, looking for the right melody to follow
the chords, experimenting with syllables, words, phrases, trying to
match the feel of the music with what he was thinking and feeling.
One of the darker songs, a slow-burning piece with layered guitars
and organ, connected with something simmering in Michael's consciousness, and when he started singing along, the words seemed
to flow through him. *It's crazy what you could have had*, he repeated.
The music circled around him, guitar tone hanging, dissolving into
feedback. An electronic howl of anger, guilt, anguish. *I need this*, he
declared over the looping chords, the buzz and growl. *I need it, I need
this.* It was about a broken love affair, Michael said later. "It's a love
song, but certainly from the uglier side."[1] It wasn't done yet, but it
was working.

Creating their new music that winter, the band members were off
on their own, untethered from previous expectations as they charted
their course for the next horizon. One song they debuted during

the 1989 tour set the tone for the project. Starting with a simple but funky bass-and-drums pattern that expanded with a tense fingerpicked guitar, the instruments on "Belong" heralded a recitation from Michael, describing a strange but powerful scene. Standing in the light of a window, a woman watches some unidentified creatures escaping from bondage. *Her world collapsed early Sunday morning*, Michael intoned. There were barricades holding the creatures, he said, but now the unnamed creatures had breached the walls and were on the move. He could have been setting the stage for a horror movie. Wild animals in the streets. A lone woman cradling her child at the window. The weight of those first three words: *Her world collapsed.* But something else was going on. The guitar rang, the bass throbbed, voices rose and filled the sky with peals of harmony. The woman at the window wasn't frightened by the rampaging creatures; she was thrilled. *To breathe at the thought of such freedom.* What she tells her child, who is almost certainly too small to understand, is in the name of the song: "Belong." To a movement, to a moment, to a community, to the love of another. *A breath, this song, how long? . . . Belong.* The music swelled again, the voices rose, the heart filled with hope.

Michael went into the new project intending to write about anything but politics, but "Belong," with its *Animal Farm*–style metaphor, served as a sequel to "Disturbance at the Heron House." Only now the revolution had succeeded. As in East Berlin, as in Czechoslovakia, as in South Africa, the barriers fell. And while the stakes for a pop band are minuscule in comparison, R.E.M.'s self-directed liberation helped express the new sense of possibility rising all across the globe.

34

Near Wild Heaven

As winter turned to spring, the music continued to flow. Riffs and chord progressions, verses, bridges, choruses. They'd make demos with placeholder names: "Kerouac #4," "Speed Metal," "Radio Song," "Night Swim," "Country Feedback." They'd dub tapes for Michael—sometimes he'd be with them, sometimes not—and he'd cart them home to listen on his own, taking in the sounds and textures, waiting to feel something. See if words appeared.

That was just a dream . . .

If a piece evoked a memory, a flicker of feeling, some kind of visual image, he'd play it again, start to vocalize, look for the melody that went with it.

This could be the saddest dusk I've ever seen, turn to a miracle . . .

A melody and words, phrases, feelings.

The world is collapsing around our ears . . .

One track they gave him, an upbeat, multipart thing containing a few bars in waltz time, a driving minor-key verse, and a quick pivot to a sunny chorus, was built around a jangly riff that was so cheerful it struck Michael as the most frivolous thing he'd ever heard. Like "Stand," only goofier.

Shiny happy people holding hands . . .

More songwriting and individual side projects filled the spring—Michael making appearances with 10,000 Maniacs and Indigo Girls, Peter touring and recording with Kevn Kinney, Michael and Peter teaming up to play at various rallies and shows for Earth Day in Washington, D.C. In July the band congregated at John Keane's Athens studio for a few weeks of demo recording. In September they moved back to the Bearsville Sound Studios, in the rural hills of Woodstock, New York, where they'd tracked so much of *Green* two years earlier, with Scott Litt behind the board and Peter Holsapple adding guitar and keyboards.

If the songs they wrote for the early albums evoked the sonic equivalent of shadows and fog, the new music seemed to sparkle. Even the mysterious creatures of "Belong" wanted to gambol in the sun. Litt, as locked on to the band's signal as anyone, cast the light from obscure angles; the strings of the mandolins and acoustic guitars were so close and clear they shivered against your ear. The electric guitars came wrapped in violins, bathed in organ, or, often, both. Michael's vocals were as central as they'd been on *Green*, and even more textured with emotion. Simmering with frustration on "Country Feedback." Awed and yearning on "Half a World Away." Edgy and rambunctious on "Radio Song." Everything was fair game, nothing was off-limits. They brought in New York rapper KRS-One to add bite to "Radio Song," layered John Keane's pedal steel into "Texarkana," included a harpsichord on "Half a World Away," and washed swells of Beach Boys–like harmony everywhere.

The sessions shifted back to Georgia in October, with more work in Athens and then two days of string overdubs in Atlanta. This was where the more elaborate, baroque sound took full dimension. And that one song, the driving minor-key piece built on a fretful mandolin riff Peter had fallen into when he was learning the instrument, had been fitted with a particularly strong arrangement. Peter's dark-eyed music had struck a deep chord in Michael, stirring the voice of a desperate lover, one who can already sense his coming dismissal. He called the song "Losing My Religion," invoking an obscure southern expression for freaking out. Pinned between devotion and desperation, his narrator observes his beloved with obsessive focus, proclaims his love, apologizes for speaking. The mandolin peals, the acoustic guitars circle, the drums and bass march forward as Michael keens and worries, corrects himself, and finally throws his hands in the air. *That was just a dream*, he concludes. *Just a dream*. The basic track was powerful, but when invested with the cool, resolute authority of an orchestra, the thing went airborne. Warner Bros. staffer and longtime friend Julie Panebianco was in the studio in Atlanta that day, hearing "Losing My Religion" for the first time as the string section did its work. "And it was like, *Holy shit!*" she recalls. "When the orchestra finished, we were all in the hallway jumping up and down and screaming because we didn't want to act like that in front of the classical musicians. You just knew it was going to explode."[1]

Everyone in the band, Litt, Holt, and Downs, and almost everyone who'd been in the studio with them was certain "Losing My Religion" was the killer track, the obvious choice for a first single. But Warner Bros. Records president Lenny Waronker wasn't sure. "I was scared of 'Losing My Religion,'" he says. "I thought, *What a great song, but it doesn't sound like a hit.*"[2] Unique among record company presidents, Waronker had spent most of his career producing records, ears-deep in the music-making process. He was accustomed to finding the balance between artistry and commerciality, and as he knew, successful pop songs of the early '90s, the ones that stood a chance of capturing the ear of radio programmers, almost always had a few things in common: sleek electronic instrumentation, economically composed verses, and distinctive, catchy choruses. "Losing My Religion," by contrast, was built around a folky mandolin. Its verses were long and meandering, and its chorus, such as it was, sounded exactly like the verse. Litt was friendly with Waronker and had been playing rough mixes of the new songs for him, and the label president felt drawn to the punchier "Radio Song," which had verses and choruses big enough to see from outer space. Why not launch the album with the song that stood the best chance of capturing the fickle ears of the radio audience? What Litt said in response made Waronker think again. "He said, 'They've got an audience they're talking to, and it's not necessarily something we can understand.' And he was right. So, fortunately, Scott saved my ass on that one."[3]

More sessions in the fall, climaxing with a few weeks at Paisley Park, Prince's headquarters in the suburbs outside of Minneapolis. They got the B-52's' Kate Pierson in to add vocals to the super-sunny "Shiny Happy People" and the edgy "Me in Honey." It was early December by then; they'd spent almost a full year on the new songs and were close to being finished. They were also close to certain that what they were working on marked a significant step for them. "It's the best thing we've ever done," Michael told the MTV reporter who tracked them down in Minnesota. As ever, Peter shrugged off anyone's attempt at hyperbole. "It's still us," he added. "If you don't like us you probably won't like this one either."[4] Peter wasn't always right about those things.

A new year began, and a new moment for R.E.M. Lenny Waronker could hear it in the rough mixes Litt had been playing him: all the new textures, the strange constructions, the collision of obscure concepts and sparkling, ear-catching execution. "They were using strings, mandolins, all those instruments. You could tell that they were moving, which is in my mind a great thing. When you're observing an artist starting to take chances. And they went all out. They knew exactly what they were doing."[5]

The band members felt the same way. Ken Fechtner, Peter's closest and most consistent friend since their days at Emory University, heard a new excitement in his schoolmate's voice in the early weeks of 1991. Michael, through typical layers of irony, declared it a watershed, and not just for the band. "It's destined to be pop legend," he said through a chuckle. "Pop history. You're looking at it. This is it."[6] Michael tried to clarify his braggadocio a few weeks later. "When I say this record is going to alter the course of pop history, I say it with my tongue pretty firmly in my cheek and a snicker on my lips." But then again . . . "I don't think anyone else is doing what we're doing right now, so it really is out of time, out of place. It's not fitting in with what's going on in music right now. And I like that."

It wasn't just sales talk. Song after song, the new work had the shimmer of gems. "Radio Song" echoes the Beach Boys' "Sloop John B" in its opening notes, then shifts abruptly into a rock/funk rampage, flips back to power pop, then to the heavier sound, as if some large hand was spinning the dial behind Michael's vocal. Which is, of course, declaiming on romantic, cultural, and sonic disconnection: *The world is collapsing*, he sings. He might be talking about current events, about a romance gone wrong, about anything, but right now he needs inspiration, information, some kind of comfort. The radio dial is full of sound, but none of it helps.

When Michael runs out of words, he steps aside and KRS-One, whose voice kicks off the song (*Hey, I can't find nothin' on the radio. Yo, turn to that station . . .*) and who has been observing throughout, amplifying some words and interjecting others, steps up to deliver the final verdict in the form of a brief, furious rhyme: all the radio gives us, to paraphrase Shakespeare, is what it's always offered, a nonstop barrage of sex and violence ultimately signifying nothing. "Radio Song" became the album opener, an extension of *Green*'s "Pop Song 89," simultaneously denouncing and elaborating on the same thing. This time the punch line would come when the album featuring "Radio Song" launched and made R.E.M. a dominant force across all of the most powerful radio formats. The irony was nearly perfect.

Terse, dark, and amelodic enough to feel like a spoken-word piece, "Low" appeared on the *Green* tour around the same time as "Belong." The music, all plucked strings, hollowed-out congas, and organ drone, gains intensity as it goes, but the narrator is too far gone to notice anything beyond the blear of his malaise. "Near Wild Heaven" approaches the same terrain from the opposite direction, setting its end-of-the-affair gloom amid sunny Beach Boys guitars, falsetto harmonies, and a chipper beat that isn't just near heaven as much as pure Shangri-la-la-la. In that light the bleakness doesn't stand a chance.

The recurring clash of melancholic lyrics and elaborately tooled music gives *Out of Time* the same dynamic tension created by Brian Wilson for the California boys' *Pet Sounds*. "Half a World Away" contrasts a persistent mandolin with a regal organ and harpsichord duet, all of it animating the ecstatic confessions of a loner redeemed by love. *The storm it came up strong,* he marvels. *It shook the trees and blew away our fear.* "Me in Honey" is all fiery self-pity from a spurned father-to-be, set against a driving, droning two-note acoustic guitar riff and a powerful Kate Pierson harmony. "Country Feedback," the seat for one of Michael's most witheringly emotional lyrics, is a blistering breakup song, made manifest in layers of acoustic and electric guitar, pedal steel, organ, shakers, and a vocal that shakes like a fist: *I was central, I had control, I lost my head / I need this, I need this.*

Contrast, paradox, contradiction, confusion—they come up again and again. And the most jagged unrest springs from the agreeably goofball lyric Michael affixed to that sugary guitar riff Peter crafted for the tune Michael dubbed "Shiny Happy People." As per its title, the song plays like an explosion in a candy factory, raining multicolored gumdrops across the land. The wolves, lower or otherwise, are nowhere in sight, nor is the reaping wheel that spun through those early R.E.M. songs. Instead it's all good-natured guitar jangle, a rich organ line, another elegant string section, and three-part harmony (Kate Pierson's strong, warm voice taking the high end) supporting Michael at his most companionable, leading a sing-along about how nice it is to feel *good*. The guitar whirls past, the snare cracks on the beat, hands clap, the singers seem to be *do-si-do*-ing around the room, all so shiny, oh so happy, their hot little palms pressed together as they urge us to join in the fun. *Put it in your heart, where tomorrow shines!*

The song became a top ten hit when it was released as a single and was, for a time, ubiquitous. Whether it was also a catastrophic lapse in R.E.M.'s artistic-slash-countercultural-slash-intellectual taste depends on the listener's judgment and, often, their conception of the band's true mission. Did they exist to improve pop music or to blow it to smithereens? Had they cracked the code of the dominant paradigm or simply surrendered to it? Think again about the creatures swarming the barricades in "Belong." Were they breaking free or were they heedlessly leading the way into a cruel and chilly sea? Or was it simply a very good (and extremely catchy) joke?

The band's surging confidence evidenced something else: an itch to climb even higher in the cultural sky, to hear their music playing even more loudly across the mainstream airwaves. It was a measure of their belief in the new songs, and, perhaps, the echoes of the ovations they'd heard during the *Green* tour. They'd worked so hard to make this music, to create songs that sounded like an expression of who they were, of what mattered to them, of what they believed about music, about society, about truth. Of course they wanted it to be heard. And, as ever, they'd need to make a video to go along with the leadoff single. No longer resistant to making the sort of piece that could break through the litany of ordinary clips, Michael figured there were plenty of ways to pursue the most popular, and powerful, outlet for pop music with an artist's sensibility.

He connected with Tarsem Singh, a young Indian-born director with an eye for visual art, and an offbeat sense of grandeur. Michael, who had been besotted with Sinéad O'Connor's luminously emotional video for her cover of Prince's "Nothing Compares 2 U," offered the director a performance he had refused to do for a decade: a lip-synched vocal. After spending a day or two in Athens with Michael and his bandmates, Tarsem (as he is known) came up with a colorful concept melding images drawn from a Gabriel García Márquez story about a fallen angel, the homoerotic interpretations of religious iconography by the French photographers/artists Pierre et Gilles, plus the visual palette of the Italian Renaissance painter Caravaggio, in order to capture the overwrought emotions of the song's narrator. The words that tumble out in a rush. The feelings that can't be spoken. All of that, along with a particularly electric performance from Michael, made for a video that was both artful and emotional, thought-provoking and cinematic.

The video and the single came out together during the third week of February 1991, and they were just getting traction when *Out of Time* followed them into the world in mid-March. Then it all took flight. The sound of the mandolin coming out of car windows, playing in the corner café, drifting on the breeze. And on television too, with Michael dancing across the screen, Michael standing with angel wings sprouting from his shoulders. Michael abruptly collapsing out of frame. Michael sitting where he fell, face half-shielded, gazing into the screen with eyes burning, imploring, singing. Michael's eyes locked on yours, coming through the screen. *That's me in the corner, that's me in the spotlight, losing my religion.* The single started fast, then picked up speed. Leapfrogging the charts into the top thirty, the top twenty, the top ten, then the top five. It peaked at number four and stayed on the charts for nearly half a year, long enough to sell more than a million copies.

When *Out of Time* came out on March 12, it went the same way, shooting skyward like no record R.E.M., or any alternative music act, had ever made, until it got all the way to the top of the *Billboard* chart. *The number one album in the United States of America.* And not just for one week: "Losing My Religion" pushed it up there once, then the album slipped back a few slots, drifting down slowly until "Shiny Happy People" hit, lofting the album skyward again, up and up until it was in *Billboard*'s top spot again. *Out of Time* sold more than three million copies in the United States during its first year, and more than twice that number across the rest of the world, and it's kept right on selling through today, now standing at just south of twenty million copies. It made the individual members of R.E.M. multimillionaires and also international celebrities. It turned their path, from college town heroes to the club circuit, from college radio to mainstream success, into a superhighway for the legion of outsider artists that followed them. It kicked open doors for the likes of Nirvana, Pearl Jam, and Soundgarden. It solidified the relationship between rock 'n' roll and political activism and might have even led to the defeat of one president of the United States and the election of another.

35

Shiny Happy

It was the "Shiny Happy People" video that made Jay Boberg angry. Not because he didn't like the tune or begrudged the success of the band he'd gone out on a limb to sign to I.R.S. in 1982 and helped build into a platinum-caliber act, only to see them depart for the land of major labels. "I did five albums and an EP with them, in a period that was far more difficult to sell records in," Boberg says. "And I couldn't get them to be in a fucking video playing their instruments, or have Michael do anything like singing in one."

Boberg may be overstating things—the entire band mimed their parts in "Wolves, Lower," albeit in slow motion, and everyone but Michael feigned to the recorded "So. Central Rain" track on that video—but not by much. Recall the blurry, herky-jerky Jim Herbert film for the first side of *Reckoning*, or the upside-down quarry footage Michael submitted as the video for "Fall on Me." "The videos they did for us were more like art pieces, and I deferred to the artistic sensibility. I mean, the video for 'It's the End of the World as We Know It' is a fucking kid on a skateboard. The band's not even in it. And can you imagine what that could have been if they *had* been in it? And then they do what they did for 'Shiny Happy People'?"[1]

And yeah, the video, much like the song itself, is beyond eager to please. Directed by Katherine Dieckmann on the stage of the Georgia Theatre, in Athens, the clip is candy-colored and soft-focus. Michael, dancing next to Kate Pierson, wears an orange cap, his cheeks powdered and rouged like a kewpie's. Mike, miming his part on a stand-up bass, spins his instrument like an old-time country player and laughs for joy. Bill, whose loathing of music videos, and especially performing in music videos, was without peer, not only dances while thumping a strap-on snare drum, and not only points his sticks at the camera, but flashes a big smile at the lens while he does it. *Twice*. The only band member who seems put out by the exercise is Peter, who fakes his guitar part on a mandolin and refuses to look into the camera, let alone smile at it. And yet, when the stage fills with shiny, happy ordinary folks all joining in with the choreographed "Shiny Happy People" dance, even he makes a game attempt to bop around with them. And all the while Michael, no longer averse to pretending to sing for the camera, emotes cheerily, lip-synching in seeming harmony with Pierson as they dance and smile at each other like some kind of new wave Sonny & Cher.

Boberg, with visions of "Fall on Me"'s upside-down quarry video still playing in his memory, shakes his head and sighs. "Give me a fucking break."[2]

Now there were new things they wouldn't do. Or at least one main thing, which was mounting a concert tour. This twist did not delight Lenny Waronker, who went into R.E.M.'s second album for Warner Bros. as aware of how *Green*'s post-"Stand" singles had flopped on radio as he was of how well "Stand" had done, and how the band's road work through 1989 had kept the album selling even when "Pop Song 89" and "Get Up" left radio programmers and listeners so cold. The label president went back to Julie Panebianco and implored her to convince the band to rethink the decision to stay off the stage, but she knew them too well to think that any amount of arm-twisting would change their minds. Waronker understood. He knew how artists worked. He also knew how contracts worked. Fortunately for him, R.E.M. had no intention of letting their new album slip between the media cracks.

They devoted all of March and April to an intensive publicity road show, spending almost an entire month sitting for interviews in Europe and the United Kingdom before heading back to North

America for an array of television, radio, and other media appearances held mostly, but not entirely, in the media capitals of the United States and Canada. When they did perform live music for the cameras or radio, they played acoustic versions of their songs, usually just "Losing My Religion" and "Shiny Happy People" on television, and a few other mostly new selections when they played on the radio. A few of the in-studio radio performances went longer, including several new songs and a few older selections, also played entirely on acoustic guitars, congas, and organ.

They also planned to make a few appearances before live audiences, but the two club shows they played at the Borderline club, in London, in mid-March were semi-secret, the band performing under the name Bingo Hand Job. The three stateside shows with live audiences were mostly intended for television viewers, the first an appearance of NBC's *Saturday Night Live* in New York, an episode of MTV's *Unplugged,* the popular series that featured big acts playing their songs in stripped-down arrangements, and an extended set on the live public radio show *Mountain Stage,* broadcast from the Capitol Plaza Theater, in Charleston, West Virginia. They included band friends Robyn Hitchcock and the British political folk singer Billy Bragg playing their own sets at the London and *Mountain Stage* shows.

Broadcast live on April 28, the *Mountain Stage* show featured the band performing eight songs—half from *Out of Time* ("Radio Song," "Half a World Away," "Belong," and "Losing My Religion"), three favorites from earlier albums ("World Leader Pretend," "Fall on Me," and "It's the End of the World as We Know It"), and one cover, the Troggs oldie "Love Is All Around," with Mike singing lead. The show's other guests (Bragg, Hitchcock, and a handful of others) joined for a cover of Jimmie Dale Gilmore's "Dallas," which took them to the end of the national broadcast of the show, though the executives at West Virginia Public Broadcasting made a spontaneous decision to keep the band on the air, preempting whatever was scheduled to come on the air next as they continued to play. R.E.M. performed five more songs for the local listeners, including a retake of "Radio Song," which they had apparently botched on the broadcast, along with "Disturbance at the Heron House," "Low," "Swan Swan H," "Pop Song 89," and finally "Get Up."

In West Virginia the event had a momentousness that resonated all the way to the seat of the state's government, where Governor William Caperton declared the date of their performance on *Mountain Stage* R.E.M. Day in West Virginia. His official reasoning had something to do with the band's support of the state's public radio station, but his actual motivation had more to do with the band's surging popularity, and the opportunity to associate himself, and the state, with a group of entertainers whose influence and power had come to extend far beyond the boundaries of popular music.

Out of Time officially cleared the bar for platinum status, selling its millionth copy on May 24, 1991. It took twenty-six more days for the next million copies to be sold, and it hit triple platinum on October 11, almost exactly seven months after the album arrived in record stores. Then came awards season: overseas, *Out of Time* and "Losing My Religion" and the band itself won a bushel of trophies, including a BRIT award, an NME Award, and two Q Awards in the UK, while picking up four GAFFA award nominations in Denmark. In the United States they earned a nomination for an American Music Award, won a Billboard Music Award, and were nominated for seven Grammys, including Album of the Year and Best Rock Performance; they ultimately took home three trophies, for Best Alternative Music Album and (for "Losing My Religion") Best Music Video, Short Form, and Best Pop Performance by a Duo or Group.

But the band's biggest night that year came at MTV's Video Music Awards in September 1991, where the "Losing My Religion" video was nominated for no fewer than nine awards. Bill, Mike, and Michael came to the ceremony, at the Universal Amphitheatre in Los Angeles, accompanied by Holt, Tarsem, and other colleagues and friends. The video-loathing Peter chose to stay away. Mike and Bill looked to be having a fine time, all the more so as the night wore on. Michael, who until recently had approached pretty much all interviews and other nonmusical duties with impatience bordering on visible contempt, seemed giddy, and not just because his band was being celebrated so richly. He'd come to the evening, to this entire moment, with his own agenda, and it was playing out exactly as he'd hoped it would.

It started even before the awards began. Sitting with chief MTV newsman Kurt Loder on the channel's special riser outside the venue, Michael and Mike talked gamely about how excited they were for the coming show. ("When we make a video, I guess we make it right," Michael said.) After Michael noted that he didn't even own a TV ("Maybe I'll buy one if we win all these awards"), Loder, as if the thought had just occurred to him, pointed to the red ribbon pinned to the lapel of his jacket, which both musicians also wore on their chests. "Do you know what the story is on these ribbons? I know they've been circulating." This was a curious question, if only because Loder had already pinned one on, and obviously knew what it signified. No matter. Michael shifted into an airy but focused response about the AIDS crisis and the hundreds of thousands of people who thought the government hadn't done enough to confront it. "So a lot of people in the entertainment industry are wearing these red ribbons, and I'm trying to ask other people to do the same thing to show compassion for the AIDS crisis and people with AIDS."

Then the awards show began. Arsenio Hall hosting, bony index finger pointing, flashing that knowing, foxy smile. Flashy, perfect performances from MC Hammer, Metallica, and Prince. Awards dispensed by Cher, Billy Idol, and Pee-wee Herman. Categories, nominees, awards. Music videos, the bastard creation of the Monkees, Fellini, Dick Clark, and spandex. The early 1990s, in all their shiny, happy glory. And over and over, it was R.E.M. and "Losing My Religion." Given nine nominations and nine potential shots of prime-time air, Michael came with a sack of T-shirts, each with a different word or slogan printed on the chest. Ultimately the video won six of the awards: for editing, direction, art direction, Breakthrough Video, group video, and Video of the Year. Each time they won, Michael would lead the way onstage, skipping to the podium, billboarding a different message across his chest. RAINFOREST. LOVE KNOWS NO COLOR. He usually came flanked by Mike and Bill, and sometimes Tarsem too, and they'd take turns thanking their managers, the office staff, the Warner Bros. Records team, all the people who'd helped get them there.

When they got to the climactic Video of the Year acceptance, Michael bounced up looking strangely bulky. This was because he was wearing multiple T-shirts layered on top of one another. At the podium he stripped them off, one after another. WEAR A CONDOM. CHOICE. ALTERNATIVE ENERGY NOW. THE RIGHT TO VOTE. HANDGUN CONTROL. Huge cheers greeting each reveal. At the post-show press conference he pulled two others out of the sack: NATIONAL HEALTH CARE. LOVE KNOWS NO GENDER. They were all going to sign each shirt, then donate them to charitable groups involved with the shirt's cause to sell as fundraisers. "Now we're going to go home and go to bed," he concluded with a small smile. "Separately."

Once again R.E.M. walked in the footsteps of the B-52's. A year before *Out of Time* sent the band to the upper reaches of the charts, the original Athens art-pop band had the biggest album of their career with *Cosmic Thing*, a quadruple-platinum seller that launched two singles into *Billboard*'s top three. The video for "Love Shack" nabbed the MTV Video Music Award for Best Group Video in 1990. The Bs had always been larger than life—the sky-high beehive hairdos on Cindy Wilson and Kate Pierson, the retro-futuristic stage wear and decor, Fred Schneider's sardonic braying about extraterrestrials and possessed sea life. The 1985 death of guitarist and band visionary Ricky Wilson (Cindy's brother) to AIDS had nearly collapsed the group, but their comeback underscored the seriousness beneath the surface of their party songs. Because they were a predominantly gay group, most of the members' physical existence had been politicized by forces so far beyond their control that the only rational response was to dress like superheroes and sing the weirdest songs they could imagine. When Michael came to the MTV awards dressed as nine different political billboards, he was up to the same thing.

He was also evoking Bob Dylan's watershed promotional film (a music video in the days before music videos) for "Subterranean Homesick Blues" and the indelible image of the singer gazing into the camera while flipping through an armload of signs bearing key words and phrases from the song's lyrics. What all three artists shared was a connection to New York's avant-garde art scene and a talent for merging the artistic with the political in a way that resonated with the cultural mainstream.

The two Athens bands, it's worth noting, traced their connections to the New York scene through the same person: Jeremy Ayers. It began with his connection to Andy Warhol in New York, then the homophobic attack that sent Ayers back to Athens, where he had met, nurtured, and then brought together the members of the B-52's. He then befriended, encouraged, and helped shape the public persona of Michael Stipe. All were essential building blocks in the development of both bands, of the Athens music scene, of the indie culture of the 1980s, and of all popular culture in the 1990s.

36

The Most Improbably Successful Group in Music Today

F or a time it was perfect. The band, the music, the moment, all of it whirring away in such easy synchrony. Sitting in John Keane's studio in late 1990, with *Out of Time* in its final stages and the publicity machine just sputtering to life, Bill could see it all coming together. Relaxed in a white sweatshirt, his eyes clear and sharp, hair silky and well cut, he sat between two guitars and spoke excitedly about how they were doing the best work of their career, that this was the best moment in R.E.M.'s history. "It's our tenth year," he said. "And I'll tell you what, I think we're on fire . . . I mean, we work hard. But the songs, the records, they're coming easier and easier. It's pretty scary. So hopefully this is just the half point for us. Maybe we'll be here in 2000. I hope so."

When it all started to pay off a few months later, Bill could only marvel. "We are definitely the most improbably successful group in music today," he said during the promotional tour in Europe that spring. "We sell more records than anyone else who gets as little airplay as we do. But we kind of did it the hard way. We built our following slowly and steadily, and those foundations tend to stick with you longer."[1]

Could it get even better than that? Yes, it could. At the start of 1992, with more than three million copies of *Out of Time* sold in

278 | THE NAME OF THIS BAND IS R.E.M.

the United States and even more overseas, with two smash singles, including one that sold more than a million copies, and a crop of awards that were only just starting to accrue, including nominations for seven Grammy Awards, due to be handed out at the end of February, R.E.M. was in a position to do anything they felt like doing. So they gathered themselves, their manager, their lawyer, and a few close friends and left town.

Left the country. Left the continent and the Northern Hemisphere, bound for the jungle of Paraguay. Joining with some friends from the Nature Conservancy, including the musicians' friend Jim Desmond, one of their earliest fans and now the environmental group's assistant general counsel. Desmond had helped midwife the invitation to have representatives of the group at every stop on R.E.M.'s 1989 concert tour. The band followed that with a hefty donation of their own, and when they had a chance to visit one of the conservancy's signature projects in South America, they were all eager to go.

The band, Holt, Downs, Desmond, and the others in their party flew out of Atlanta on January 23, 1992. After a day or two in Asunción, they all boarded a bus for the Mbaracayú region, more than six hours east of the capital city. They spent the next week in the wilderness, hiking between tribal villages, marveling at the lush wildflowers and other flora, following some tribesmen on a bow-and-arrow hunt, slapping mosquitoes, washing in rivers, pushing trucks out of the mud, and sleeping in tents. When the tribesmen in one village put on a banquet featuring the local delicacy, the musicians took their bowls and graciously tucked into the monkey stew.

After a week they emerged unshaven and grubby but recharged by the experience of being so far away from the modern world. Seeing the work the Nature Conservancy was doing, and the real difference it was making for the Aché people, was inspiring. Even if they were just rock stars, even if they passed their days doing the silliest things they'd ever heard of, and even if their music wouldn't last, at least they could still help other people achieve worthwhile goals. And if people were going to look at them and listen to what they had to say, they could talk about things that mattered to them. And do what they could to make those things matter to everyone else, too.

———

They'd always set about their work in a different way. To be aware of how the things they said or did would impact other people, and how that might reflect back on them. It went all the way back to when they were still riding around in a used van, building their following on a night-to-night, hand-to-hand basis. Pat Biddle, the Athens soundman who traveled with the band from time to time near the start of their career, remembers how the musicians always seemed to know the names of the people they'd met the last time they were in a city or club. "They always remembered the people who helped them before," he says. "And they always took care of their friends."[2]

The band made a point of keeping their offices and rehearsal space in Athens, and when they were successful enough to buy houses, offices, and other buildings, they kept their money in town. They tried to model what struck them as responsible behavior, outfitting their workspace with desks and carpets made from recycled materials. And as their footprint grew, so did their opinions about how Athens should look and how city business should be conducted. All the band members, along with Holt and Downs, thought the city's essence resided in the historic buildings and houses that still made up so much of its urban core. When developers sketched plans to steamroll older buildings, or entire blocks, to make room for more modern developments, the band and its representatives joined with the citizens and groups opposing the developers. The band's manager and lawyer became familiar faces at planning commission meetings, and Michael was a regular attendee of public meetings too. In 1990 the group, along with Holt and Downs, were prominent supporters of Gwen O'Looney in her campaign for the Athens/Clarke County chief elected officer, the equivalent of a regional mayor. O'Looney was an underdog in a race against a developer-supported candidate, but the band's public support and financial contributions evened the playing field, and O'Looney, along with a like-minded city council candidate they also supported, won the election.

The band's engagement with politics flowed in significant part from Holt. Raised in Burlington, North Carolina, a conservative rural area an hour from the more urban centers of Raleigh and Winston-

Salem, Jefferson was the son of Bertha Merrill Holt, known as B., who was one of the first women to attend the University of North Carolina School of Law and, after being appointed in 1975, the first woman to represent her district in the state legislature. Reelected to her seat eight times, B. spent nearly twenty years in office, introducing and passing laws that protected the rights of women and workers, and furthered an array of progressive causes in a state not known for being a bastion of liberal politics.

B. also raised her children to be public-spirited, and when her son became an unexpected success in show business, he took his mother's ideals along with him. As Holt helped Michael grow into the charismatic front man he became in the 1980s, the manager encouraged the singer to invest his work, and his image, with his own political beliefs. At first Michael was hesitant. "If you want to talk about politics or your love life or social problems or what it's like to live in 1983, then you should do it somewhere other than on stage," he told *Record* magazine in 1983."[3] He would come to change his mind.

By the time *Green* came out, in 1988, political awareness was central to R.E.M.'s group identity. The album's title was at least in part a nod to environmentalism, one of the band's core issues. It might have been a coincidence that the album was released on Election Day, but the band's grousing about the victory of George H. W. Bush and the increased emphasis on activism was very deliberate. And, as the 1992 election approached, surprisingly effective.

The irony was that the songs on *Out of Time* were so deliberately nonpolitical. If the record had a central theme, Michael said repeatedly, it was about relationships and love. "Belong," the closest any of the songs came to being a social/political message, was cloaked in so many layers of metaphor and surrealism you needed a pick and shovel to uncover the point of the story. It was much easier to understand why R.E.M., along with their more socially/politically active fellow recording artists, were starting to protest how their albums were being packaged.

In the early days of compact discs, when record stores started carrying the new format, the record companies packaged the small discs in long cardboard boxes so they would fit into store shelves designed for vinyl albums. But the long boxes, as they were called, served no purpose for customers, who tended to toss the packages the moment they opened them. The environmental impact of the boxes was only too obvious to the likes of R.E.M., and talk of an organized protest among artists had started to grow. Then a Warner executive named Jeff Gold came up with a brilliant compromise: they could use the back of the long box to promote one of the band's pet causes. What Gold proposed for *Out of Time* was a clip-and-send card to petition the U.S. Senate to make it easier for citizens to register to vote. The band saw the potential immediately, and they signed on happily. Again, they were in perfect synchrony with the times.

The organization behind the petition was Rock the Vote, a political nonprofit dreamed up by a Virgin Records executive named Jeff Ayeroff, whose primary motivation had been countering the work of the Parents Music Resource Center, a group founded to pressure record companies into censoring their artists. Ayeroff found an ally in MTV founder Tom Freston, who was looking for ways to add depth and gravitas to the channel's cultural coverage. Teaming with Rock the Vote, which was already defending the freedoms of popular, edge-pushing MTV acts like Madonna, was an easy call. At the same time "Losing My Religion" saturated MTV's playlist, the channel's regular reports on the brewing 1992 presidential campaign came under the Rock the Vote banner. For a time they included detailed coverage of the clip-and-send postcards on R.E.M.'s new album.

Then Michael started appearing in an ad for Rock the Vote promoting the National Voter Registration Act, which was nicknamed the Motor Voter bill because a central part of the federal legislation involved Department of Motor Vehicles offices, along with other government centers, giving newly licensed drivers a chance to register to vote. The bill passed Congress in mid-1992, only to be vetoed by President Bush in September. Bush's opponent, Governor Bill Clinton of Arkansas, promised to sign the bill if elected, and when Clinton's running mate, Al Gore, came to a rally in Athens, Michael introduced him to the cheering crowd. Gore, whose wife, Tipper, was one of the founders of the censorious Parents Music Resource Center, a fact that went unremarked upon that afternoon, shook the singer's hand with evident enthusiasm and thanked him and his band for their support. "And to paraphrase Michael, some people may not know it yet, but George Bush is out of time," the senator proclaimed.

Gore was right. And when he and Clinton defeated the incumbent president and vice president on November 3, they did it with the help of younger voters, whose participation jumped 6 percent from what it had been in the 1988 presidential election.

Near the end of their week away in Paraguay, Bill sat for an interview with a reporter affiliated with the Nature Conservancy to talk about how much the visit to the wilderness project had meant to him and his bandmates. "Well, we try to be environmentally conscious, and it's important to be more than just rock stars," he said. "Now that we've reached a certain level of success, we can take the time to do things that are important to us, like coming here."

He looked relaxed, sun-kissed. A little grungy around the edges, his face still marked by the bee sting he'd suffered a few days earlier. But being out in nature and being surrounded by his friends always felt like the right thing to do. When the reporter noted that R.E.M. had been together for more than a decade and, unlike other successful bands, actually seemed to enjoy one another's company, he smiled. "It's amazing," he said. "One of the reasons is that we didn't get together with the intention of becoming big stars. We were in school together and we met first as friends. We became a band because we wanted to have fun together. We had no inclination of becoming, you know, big world music stars." The reporter nodded, then observed that they certainly *were* big stars now. "Right, but we didn't get together to form a band to get big. It was a hobby for us, and we all liked each other and liked the same kind of music. And we had so much in common. Our political beliefs, our moral inclinations are very much the same." He shrugged. "A lot of bands get together purely to make money and get famous. We didn't intend for that to happen, it just did."[4]

It had grown slowly, over a dozen years. For a long time they'd done their best to keep it at a distance, to make their music their way, for the people who liked what they did enough to treat it, and them, with respect. But then things had changed. They had changed, to a degree. At least, their ability to write songs and turn them into records had changed. Their music had become sharper and taken on a depth that resonated with a lot of people who had never cared to listen before. That had been going on for a few years, going all the way back to when "The One I Love" first blared across the airwaves. But now, in the wake of "Losing My Religion" and *Out of Time*, even that level of success seemed positively quaint.

They thought they were leaving their famous selves behind when they got on the airplane to fly down to Paraguay. They'd never been to South America before; nobody had ever asked them to come down and visit, let alone play their music for people. But they had only just stepped off the airplane after the long flight down and were drifting through the throngs in the airport when it started to happen. The kids, teenagers and younger, looking over at them and pointing. Shouting at one another and then chasing them, jumping up and down and singing "Losing My Religion" in perfect English. Which was odd, because none of them could *speak* a word of English.

"That was a real holy shit moment," Jim Desmond recalls. "That song had broken through in a way even they didn't understand at first. They were just shaking their heads in wonder."[5]

37

These Are Days

By the time Michael stepped to the microphone on an unseasonably warm Washington, D.C., morning in January 1993, it was just another in a long line of astounding things that actually happened. Standing at a lectern on the steps of the Lincoln Memorial, the singer wore a stylish black blazer, a crisp white shirt buttoned to the neck, and a gray fedora perched on top of his neatly shorn head. He'd spoken at his share of protests before, but now the outsider spoke from the highest corridors of power, celebrating the inauguration of President-elect Bill Clinton by joining a round-robin of celebrities reading inspiring quotations from other distinguished Americans. Michael recited a few lines from Woody Guthrie's "This Land Is Your Land," then a bit of an essay on the global commons from the environmentalist Les Brown. The presentation was a part of several days of celebration that had been given the heartening name An American Reunion, climaxing with the new president's oath of office on the steps of the U.S. Capitol on January 20.

An array of inaugural balls took place across the city that night, among them MTV's Rock 'n' Roll Inaugural Ball, which included performances by Don Henley, 10,000 Maniacs, En Vogue, Boyz II Men, and Soul Asylum. R.E.M.'s shadow loomed over the televised portion of the ball, even if the full band did not make an appearance. Instead, Michael and Mike joined with U2's Adam Clayton and Larry Mullen Jr. for a one-off acoustic performance of the Irish band's recent hit "One," with Michael handling Bono's vocal part and Mike playing guitar. The crowd greeted the two bands' union with unreserved enthusiasm.

But the dreamiest collaboration of the show had come earlier, during 10,000 Maniacs' set. Well known to the members of R.E.M. from the alternative club circuit in the 1980s, the Maniacs had been a part of the band's orbit for nearly a decade. They'd toured together for a few spells during the mid-1980s, with the band from western New York state opening, and both had released breakthrough records in 1987. The bands' singers had the same ability to blend artistry and performance, and both balanced the same impulses toward shyness and flamboyance. And, as it turned out, they also had a natural rapport. Once they got to know each other in the mid-1980s, they became friends, and then something more than friends. They didn't always get a lot of time in the same place, but when the groups toured together, Natalie Merchant would ride on Michael's bus. Sometimes Michael would pop up on the other band's tours when R.E.M. wasn't working; he sang background vocals on the Maniacs' "A Campfire Song" and would step onstage to perform the song with the band. And now here they were again, on the same bill.

10,000 Maniacs appeared just after the president and first lady's appearance, starting the music portion of the broadcast with the sunlit anthem to the moment, "These Are Days." A cover of Lulu's "To Sir with Love" came next, seemingly a direct nod to the new president. But a second microphone had been set on the stage next to Merchant's, and after the first verse Michael strolled out, dapper in his dark jacket, white shirt, and fedora, and the crowd whooped its approval. He bowed to Merchant as she sang the chorus, then stepped up to sing the song's next verse while she smiled and danced along. They slow-danced together during the saxophone break, then wove their voices together for the final chorus. They beamed at each other during the ovation, then split the vocal on the band's last song, "Candy Everybody Wants." It's a catchy song, one of the Maniacs' best, and the singers danced together as they sang, harmonizing on the chorus and following it with a joyous version of the bump during the guitar solo. When it ended, they stepped up together for their ovation, greeting the cheers at center stage, hands clasped together, standing exactly where the new president and first lady of the United States had waved to the crowd twenty minutes earlier.

The stagecraft of Clinton's inaugural celebrations, the American Reunion, like the political campaign that had preceded it, evoked a utopian ideal of American society. Of the nation as a community: good people coming together to make something bigger and greater than what they could achieve on their own. At the Athens rally for Al Gore in the week before the election, the vice presidential candidate had pivoted from his R.E.M.-informed crack about George Bush being *out of time* by promising, with another nod to Michael and his band, that "Bill Clinton and Al Gore are gonna be *automatic for the people!*" Whoever had written Gore's remarks that day had done a clever job. In the space of a single sentence, the candidate had ripped the opponent and underscored his own campaign's core promise while also name-checking the popular local star's two most recent albums.

The latter record, *Automatic for the People*, was released at the start of October. It had come together in the same unhurried, unhassled manner as its predecessor, starting with casual writing sessions in the band's rehearsal space, then continuing with bursts of recording in studios located in cities the musicians knew they liked or wanted to explore. Throughout, the process was collegial, collaborative, and abundantly fruitful. Utopian, in a sense. Which made it easier to produce songs that addressed a sadness that had been growing around them, and within the restless soul of their singer. *It's these little things, they can pull you under,* he cautioned in one song. So many little things, and so many not-so-little things, too. Surrounded by gloom, disease, and death, there is only one thing to do: *Live your life filled with joy and wonder.* The music they made in 1992 overflowed with both.

The writing sessions at the Clayton Street rehearsal space started in early January 1992, almost exactly two years after the start of the *Out of Time* project. They were even more prolific this time, coming up with dozens of pieces they started to turn into demos at John Keane's studio in mid-February. As on the previous album, the musicians made a point of avoiding their traditional instruments, Peter wielding his mandolin, bouzouki, and other stringed exotica, while Mike worked with an organ and other keyboards and Bill handled the bass and acoustic guitar. If Peter wasn't using one of his new instruments, he had his guitar in an open tuning, the better to find odd chord structures and unexpected changes.

Their ability to collaborate, to pull different pieces into a unified whole or otherwise enhance one another's work, was at a level somewhere beyond purely conscious. Recording an acoustic guitar for one song, Peter noted how sensitive the microphone on his strings was and cracked that while he played he'd have to try not to breathe. Michael, already sketching a lyric about mortality, took note: Peter had just given him the perfect title for the song. When Bill, his left hand forming a C chord on a guitar, accidentally slid his fingers up two frets while reaching for something on the floor, the sound of the change, the C major sliding up to an augmented D* and then back down, rang in his ears. Peter had already found the chords for the chorus for a song; now Bill had just provided the chords for the verse, in the correct key, too.

The sessions moved to producer Daniel Lanois's New Orleans studio for the first half of March, then reconvened at the Bearsville studios, in New York, one of their favorite recording sites, for most of April. They took a week off, then decamped to Criteria Studios, in Miami, where Aretha Franklin, Derek & the Dominos, the Allman Brothers, and the Bee Gees had all made classic albums. The members of R.E.M. were less interested in the echoes of the other artists than in the unique sound they were finding for themselves. It was apparently still taking form when Warner A&R executive Karin Berg came down from New York to check in. She was not thrilled by what she heard, and when she called Lenny Waronker in Burbank with her report, she told the label president he should intervene in the R.E.M. project, pronto.

"She said, 'We might be in real trouble here,' and I said, 'You gotta be kidding me,'" Waronker says. No matter: he flew to Miami a few days later. "I went in with low expectations and they started

---

* Technically a D major sus 4 add 9, according to my professional guitar-playing source, aka my girlfriend's brother, who adds that this in no way describes the delicious texture created when the open strings vibrate against the fretted ones, constructing a chord from notes across two-plus octaves, all ringing together.

playing stuff. And what she heard must have been in a rough stage, because I was just unbelievably relieved." They played Waronker a few unfinished songs too, and one in particular caught his ear: the one with the C-to-D slide chord pattern on the verse. "I just remember hearing that and saying to the guys, 'You've gotta finish *that* one. The chorus is a killer.'"[1] Indeed, he'd just heard the demo for what would become "Man on the Moon."

Some of the songs were louder than the others; two were flat-out rockers. One of those was melodic and lighthearted, with a vocal call based on the chorus of "The Lion Sleeps Tonight," the Tokens' adaptation of Solomon Linda's South African folk-pop hit of the 1930s, "Mbube." They recast it as "The Sidewinder Sleeps Tonite." The other raged, all slashing guitar, hard-pulsing synth bass, and wailing harmonica, the backdrop for a political rant Michael called "Ignoreland."

Bill came in with what sounded like an old-fashioned soul ballad, arpeggiated chords played out with graceful precision, music for lovers embracing on a darkened floor. A love song for hard times: "Everybody Hurts." Mike had his own ballad, built on multiple organ sounds, a vocoder-type synthesizer that played the sound of his voice going *ahhhhhh*, natural backing vocals, and a slinky, echoing guitar, over which Michael oozed the words for "Star Me, Kitten."*

Most of the other songs rising to the surface shared an elegiac quality: music that touched you where you felt a little sad, or maybe nostalgic, maybe a little rueful, but also gently celebratory and, inescapably, loving. This is what Michael picked up on as he traced the melodies and sketched his lyrics. He thought of people he'd loved, and people he'd lost. There had been so much loss lately. A grandparent or two, sad but inevitable. And also friends, and some ex-lovers, cut down by AIDS. It was everywhere in the arts communities, and the government's refusal to confront the disease or even acknowledge its existence for most of the '80s was a large part of what pro-

---

* Whose wink-wink use of the word "Star" in the title (though the phrase in the lyric is clearly "fuck me, kitten") tips the hat to the Rolling Stones and the 1973 song they similarly titled "Star Star," when its chorus is in fact a recitation of the word "*starfucker*."

jected him into the political dialogue. It was, to be sure, a matter of life and death. And so were the songs on the new record. So much death. And so much life.

Back in Georgia at the end of May, they went to Atlanta to record string parts, working with the help of ex–Led Zeppelin bassist John Paul Jones, whom they'd hired to orchestrate a few songs. A week later they went to the Bad Animals studio in Seattle to finish the last few songs and make final mixes for the tracks bound for the album. Michael had finished composing and singing his lyrics for almost every song, with one exception: the one they still referred to as "C-D Slide," named for Bill's accidental but lovely chord pattern. Ordinarily the instrumentalists and producer Scott Litt didn't pressure Michael to write to a particular track; the singer just focused on the pieces that caught his ear and spurred his muse into action. Michael hadn't resisted this one—if he flat-out rejected a song, that was the end of it—but everyone liked this song a lot, and then Lenny Waronker's half-joking instruction to finish the song with the killer chorus had only intensified their urging that Michael at least try to give it a go. Litt dubbed a cassette of the track for Michael, who put it on his Walkman tape player and listened to it as he explored the streets of Seattle. It took a few days, but the words he came up with, which drew from childhood memory, from 1970s pop icons, and from the autumnal melancholy that flowed through so many of the songs, not only distilled the essence of the track's music but also encapsulated something of the album as a whole.

What connected the song, now titled "Man on the Moon," to the other songs, what connected the band members to one another, what connected the band to its rapidly growing legion of fans, was also what connected the American voters to Bill Clinton, or at least the *idea* of Bill Clinton circa 1992. A sense of tenderness, of empathy; of hearts pulsing in the same rhythm, feeling the same hopes and fears. Of recalling the world as you experienced it as a kid in the family rec room, through games and books, through the hazy blue window of the television. The characters came and went, but they all seemed to be on the same show. Moses and Elvis. Sir Isaac Newton and "Classy"

Freddie Blassie. Prophets and rock stars, physicists and wrestlers. All with their own kind of magic, their own transcendent logic.

And then there was Andy Kaufman, the absurdist comic whose odd, reality-warping put-ons spun them all together. His moment was brief, a flickering comet that appeared on the old *Saturday Night Live* in 1975, lip-synching cartoon themes, gibbering in a thick foreign accent, abruptly affecting an Elvis Presley impression so masterful the King himself bowed down before him, assuming multiple personae, some helpless, others brutally toxic, right until his death in 1984. Kaufman was only thirty-four at the time, and his passing was so unexpected that many people assumed it was just another one of his weird bits. *Andy, did you hear about this one?* Michael sang, as if posing the question to the comic himself. To everyone else: *If you believe there's nothing up his sleeve, then nothing is cool.* He could have been talking about Clinton, too.

Elliptical, nostalgic, lightly satirical, and loving, the lyric met the music as easily as the new music slipped into the breeze. The album was finished, the summer turned to autumn. The airwaves buzzed, new music tingled against the skin. The new R.E.M. album arrived in early October. If you expected a descent from the heights of *Out of Time*—a reasonable expectation—you were surprised. "Fairly wonderful," observed MTV's senior newsman, Kurt Loder, asserting it as a fact in the midst of a news report. No one argued. When the wind blows with the tide, when the planets spin a particular way, there can be no debate. Just observation, appreciation, a sense that this right here, this sound, this feeling, is the sound of now.

The album title also arrived fully formed and without debate. The expression came from Weaver D's, one of the band's favorite barbecue joints in Athens, whose owner, Dexter Weaver, responded to his customers' requests with the same snappily delivered affirmation. Ribs and dirty rice? *Automatic!* Pork chops and gravy? *Automatic!* The sign outside put the philosophy in grander terms, and this was where they had found their title: *Automatic for the People.*

Once again choosing to forgo a concert tour, they prepared for the album's early October release with another round of interviews, though nothing close to the globe-trotting two months they'd done to mark the release of *Out of Time*. This suited them for a variety of reasons, including the fact that they didn't expect the new album to sell anything like its immediate predecessor. Which had been, in Mike's words, an aberration in the band's career. "That was the one big seller of our lives," he told a reporter for Canada's MuchMusic cable channel. "This one's as good or better than that one, but I don't think it'll zap people like that one."[2] Certainly the production was more spare, with an emphasis on acoustic instruments and strings, and much less sonic sparkle. This was due in large part to the nature of the songs, which, as the Canadian reporter observed tartly, concerned themselves with the gloomiest of topics: "It seems to me that the whole first side is dealing with death!"[3]

Her interpretation of the half dozen titles on side one wasn't quite right, if only because one of the songs is an instrumental and another includes a retelling of a key plot point in Dr. Seuss's children's book *The Cat in the Hat*. Its concluding thought, exclaimed over a ringing rock 'n' roll climax: *We've got to moogie, moogie, move on this one!* But she might not have been responding to the songs themselves as much as to the fact that Michael, who had done so many interviews in 1991, had decided to beg off his press duties this time around. The other three didn't begrudge his reticence. He'd never enjoyed having his molecules examined beneath the media microscope, particularly when the reporters were so determined to reveal the parts of him that felt most private. Which was exactly what the Canadian reporter had in mind as she pondered the intentions of the missing singer and the meaning of his absence. "It seems like he's closing a chapter on his life somehow," she mused, getting at something.[4]

Finally she just asked the question.

"What about these persistent rumors that Michael's sick?"[5]

"Drive," the opening track. Here comes a man, brooding, solitary, mysterious. You've seen him before, but what do you really know about him? He may be sick. He may be superhuman. He has an unspeakable secret. He has endless promise. He's collapsed in a gutter. He's reclining in the back of a limousine. Is he dying? Will he live forever? It can't all be true, except for when you reach a certain level of fame, at which point reality and fantasy become one and the same. This is where *Automatic* begins, in the platinum backwash of *Out of Time*, which the narrator of "Drive" observes from behind tinted glass, scrutinizing his followers from his freon-cooled remove. He greets them, tosses in a quote from a glam-rock favorite out of the distant past. *Hey, kids, rock 'n' roll* (David Essex, "Rock On," a signal song when it hit the top ten in mid-1974).

But the music behind him is spare, mostly acoustic, and not quite in gear. The guitar strums, the bass hits a desultory note or two, eventually an accordion joins, then the drums. But only for a few beats before it all pauses. A beat, then it starts again, and gains momentum. An electric guitar slices the air, a string section rises, smooth and powerful, Doric columns revealing the edge of a grand edifice. There is a crowd and he addresses them directly, congratulating them for their wildness, their freedom, for rocking around the clock. Maybe they're even *crazy*. More than anything, they are in his thrall, though they have no idea who he is, really. *Maybe I ride, maybe you walk / Maybe I drive to get off . . . baby.* The strings ebb, the electric guitar fades, the music grows sparse, then vanishes, taillights slipping away in the night.

The woman on MuchMusic wasn't the only one. Rumors about Michael, his life, his habits, his romances, had followed the band around for years. More recently, as the band opted to stay off the road and the singer's once lustrous mane of hair was shorn and then glimpsed only beneath a hat, the whispering turned to his health. Didn't he seem skinnier than usual? And why had he stopped doing interviews? What was he hiding?

With no answers forthcoming from Michael, the curious turned to the music. Many of them heard the references to death, to the sick and the resigned, and figured the songs described a grim truth Michael wasn't strong enough, or healthy enough, to tell them face-to-face. What they tended to miss, in the twilight of the songs' settings, was how much life they contained.

Spinning and ardent, speaking in the voice of a faltering man, "Try Not to Breathe" welcomes death by celebrating the life that was lived. An acoustic guitar strums, a simple bass part shores up the bottom, an electric guitar line lights the room. Michael's narrator enters, assured and determined, announcing his intention to let his life, at long last, come to an end. *This decision is mine*, he declares. And his demise, no matter how jarring, is not a tragedy. Not even close. His life has been fulfilling, his experiences rich. *I have seen things that you will never see.*

"Sweetness Follows" begins at another graveside as squabbling adult children prepare to bury their parents. A cello huffs beneath an acoustic guitar, an organ sanctifies from above. Michael's narrator examines his shattered family, notes his siblings' distance and the toll of the years. An electric guitar set to feedback swoops in like a raven, its wings beating waves of dissonance through the air. But Michael rises over it, his voice warm and even. *It's these little things, they will pull you under*, he sings. There is darkness all around, but every moment can be magical, every breath holds the possibility of redemption. *Live your life filled with joy and wonder.*

The life force shimmers in the night, triggers the dawn, troubles the dirt piled next to the freshly cut grave. It is the joy and wonder, the pleasure and pain, the rock around the clock, the *moogie-moogie* in *The Cat in the Hat*. But that urge to the pleasures in life is also, in the age of AIDS, a source of rage, shame, and death. We want to assume that the narrator of "Try Not to Breathe" is on the far reaches of elderly. *These eyes are the eyes of the old*, he says. But by 1992 AIDS had reduced too many healthy young men to shriveled, shivering husks to make that a safe assumption. The fear of and hatred for gay people had sundered enough families to form another possible subtext for the disconnection beneath "Sweetness Follows."

And it is, without a doubt, the unspoken force behind "Monty Got a Raw Deal." Singing above a stern set of chords played on a bouzouki, propelled by tightly wound drums, Michael addresses the story of Montgomery Clift, the movie idol of the 1950s and '60s forced to live a series of lies out of fear that his sexual orientation would destroy his life. As Michael recounts, Clift seemed to have it all. He was beautiful and gifted, an acclaimed actor with his choice of roles. But, as the singer acknowledges, *nonsense has a welcome ring.* Clift was drawn to other men in a time of overpowering homophobia. A well-placed fear of exposure, and the self-loathing triggered by the hatred around him, pushed Clift toward self-destruction. Drugs and liquor, car accidents, a life shot through with chaos before his death, in 1966, when he was just forty-five years old. Speaking across the decades, Michael doesn't trouble Clift's ghost with sympathy; it's neither useful nor wanted. What he can offer, to the spirit of the actor and to himself, is understanding. A loving nod from a fellow traveler who not only comprehends his own life force but accepts it. Not as a curse, but a blessing. *Mischief knocked me in the knees / Said "Just let go. Just let go."*

The specifics, and deeper implications, reside between the lines. In "Nightswimming," it's beneath the surface of the pond Michael recalls splashing in as a teenager. The wistful portrait of youthful pleasure, fit to a gorgeous piano piece by Mike, describes one of those warm summer nights where reckless, carefree kids can frolic without fear, their physical abandon perceived as nothing but good, clean fun. In this life such ecstasies are short-lived. *September's coming soon*, he sings. Now time has passed. Something unspoken has gone wrong between the narrator and his midnight companion. *You, I thought I knew you.* A friendship sundered, an intimacy violated. *You, I thought you knew me.* But a photograph survives, a memory persists. As does generosity. We forget to do so many things in our lives. To call our moms. To wash the dog. To tell a friend we love them. To understand and forgive. *You I cannot judge.*

The same spirit fills "Everybody Hurts," the slow R&B groove Bill brought in, swung in a distinctly humanistic direction with Michael's lyrics, a love letter to every vulnerable person within the embrace of its sound. "Find the River" concludes the album on a similar note, the gentle groove drifting lazily downstream to some other, greater form of existence. *The river empties to the tide*, he concludes. *All of this is coming your way.* Whether this is the sound of resignation, another song of death (as per the MuchMusic host), or an expression of the most transcendent kind of hope is up to you.

38

Does Everyone Still Want to Do This?

I f the members of R.E.M. thought that releasing an album full of quiet, textured meditations on sorrow, death, and forgiveness would give them a break from the glare of mainstream success, they were wrong. *Automatic for the People* was an immediate and overwhelming smash, drawing even stronger reviews than *Out of Time*, maybe the best reviews in all of their ecstatically reviewed career. There was a five-star write-up in *Rolling Stone* ("musically irresistible"), raves in *Time* ("a so-called alternative band can keep its edge after conquering the musical mainstream") and *The New York Times* ("beautiful and moving"). The videos for "Drive," "Man on the Moon," and "Everybody Hurts" all rated saturation play on MTV, further establishing the band's image as the most effortlessly artful pop act in the popular culture mainstream. In commercial terms *Automatic* hit the marketplace like a late-period Beatles album, with advance orders in the millions, and that still wasn't enough to satisfy popular demand as the songs played across radio formats and the videos lit up the screens. In a time when someone's CD collection served as an index of their engagement with the world, possessing a copy of the latest R.E.M. album felt as basic as owning a stereo or subscribing to the daily newspaper.

Ultimately, *Automatic* sold just as well as *Out of Time* had done, moving more than ten million copies around the world in its first year, a number that has nearly doubled since then. By the spring of

1993, when the four musicians, along with their manager and lawyer, gathered for a strategy session at Warner Bros. Records' vacation house in Acapulco, they were in a position to do anything with
their lives and careers that they could imagine. When they finally got
down to business, Bill kicked off the discussion with typical directness: "Does everyone still want to *do* this?"[1] He wasn't certain that
he did, was the thing. And Bill wasn't the only member of the band
having doubts about R.E.M.'s future. Extraordinary success can be
affirming, but it is also less fun, and more destabilizing, than it might
seem. Something about the sheer tonnage of CDs, albums, and tapes
they'd sold since the turn of the '90s, combined with the mountain of
magazines and newspapers bearing their faces, words, and thoughts,
along with the endless waves of R.E.M.-focused sound and images
humming through the atmosphere, seemed to warp the air around
them. It wasn't just strangers looking at them differently; it was their
closest friends and family. And it was in the mirror, too: how exhaust-
ing the sight of your own stupid face could become, the dopey sound
of the things you say, the grating sound of the simple riffs you made
up blaring incessantly from the radio, the television, from the open
window of a car cruising down South Milledge Avenue on an otherwise peaceful Sunday morning.

For Bill, R.E.M.'s outsize good fortune was beyond absurd. So
many of his friends were musicians, and so many of them were so
good, and in bands that were just as good as or even better than
R.E.M. "They weren't getting famous like him, and that made him
feel guilty," then-wife Mari recalls. "It was one of the things, how
much that bothered him. It didn't seem fair. That's just him being
self-deprecating, but it really did bother him a lot."[2]

He wasn't the only band member navigating an existential malaise. Propelled by the crumbling of his marriage (to Athens club
owner Barrie Green, whom he'd wed in 1987) and his distaste for his
own celebrity, Peter tossed his guitar in the back of a car and headed
into Mexico, where he spent most of the winter on his own, crashing
in cheap roadside motels, reading books, drinking beer, and strumming for his own amusement, just like he'd done in the days before
bands, gigs, records, and all the rest. He grew a beard, put on some
weight, slipped off his persona, and retreated into himself.

The other guys fell into fame more easily. In 1992 Mike appeared on the *Live with Regis and Kathie Lee* daytime talk show, the epicenter of middle American housewife culture, astounding cohost Kathie Lee Gifford by showing up at the taping with his mom. "We don't expect rock stars to have mothers," she observed. Her older cohost, Regis Philbin, agreed with customary enthusiasm, barking, "He looks like such a normal guy!" The normal-guy rock star chatted about his band's years on the road, the unexpected success of *Out of Time*, then sang "(Don't Go Back to) Rockville," accompanying himself on acoustic guitar.[3] When he wasn't on daytime TV, Mike was happily taking up invitations to play in celebrity-rich charity golf tournaments and to attend professional sports events and the sorts of parties peopled by the famous, rich, beautiful, or some combination thereof. Beneath his perpetually collegiate, such-a-nice-young-man exterior thumped the heart of an unreconstructed party boy, and if he was beckoned somewhere that promised to provide fun, music, and women in quantity, the bassist was happy to come. "Believe me, my life is stranger than any rumor you could come up with," he snapped when that MuchMusic interviewer started digging for fun facts about Michael's health in the summer of 1992. "Why? Because I'm living it, that's why."[4]

Michael rode the tidal wave of acclaim into Los Angeles, where he fell in with a glitzy crowd of movie stars, directors, and other A-list types. His interest in film went deeper than the glamour of his new friends. He and the filmmaker Jim McKay had been directing and producing videos and short films through their C-Hundred Film Corp. for several years, and the pair were launching a production company to make feature-length scripted movies. Michael grew close to the actor River Phoenix and cultivated a circle of other famous friends whose lives and concerns had little to do with rock 'n' roll, let alone the close-knit art-rock gang from Athens. The writer Anthony DeCurtis, who had known the band since 1981, recalls walking into a party Michael threw in New York in the 1990s and seeing the adolescent actor Macaulay Culkin, then best known for his role in *Home Alone*. "I was like, *What the fuck is going on here?*" DeCurtis says. "My turn of phrase was that Michael was the only person who had to get famous to get starstruck. He seemed to miss the point that rock stars are cooler than everybody. *Let me introduce you to Macaulay Culkin?* Oh, shit."[5]

Another dismaying side effect of their extraordinary success came when Peter Holsapple, who played guitar and keyboards with them throughout the 1989 tour and beyond, fell out with the group. The conflict centered on "Low," one of the two *Out of Time* songs that debuted during that tour. According to Holsapple, the song emerged during a pre-show soundcheck. He was playing bass, Mike was on organ, Peter on guitar, Bill playing the congas, when they fell into the song's central chord pattern. The foursome played through the progression for a while, then found the variation that became the song's bridge. Once that was established, Michael wrote the words and the minimalist melody that fit the changes, and they all liked it enough to perform it onstage at the show in Syracuse, New York, on April 11.

They didn't play it again until the fall, but the song became a regular part of the encores, appearing near the end of every show during the climactic fall leg of the tour. The composition of the music in "Low" struck Holsapple as a four-way collaboration: the bass part traces all of the song's changes, which in his memory came as much from his exploration as from any of the others. Still, when the song appeared on *Out of Time*, the credit read, as it almost always did, "Berry-Buck-Mills-Stipe." This struck Holsapple as both inaccurate and, given the flood of royalties due to anyone with even a partial credit on what was almost guaranteed to be a million-selling album (it eventually turned into something much more than that), well beyond disappointing.

Holsapple's manager encouraged him to pose the question directly to his friends in the band. They'd spoken so often of their admiration for him and for the dB's. Peter in particular had declared himself thrilled to meet the North Carolina musician when they first crossed paths in 1981, and Holsapple, who had known Jefferson Holt before either of them met the band from Athens, had played a significant role in connecting them with Mitch Easter. The dB's broke up in 1988, just as R.E.M. was planning its 1989 tour and looking to add a utility musician to play guitar and keyboards and contribute to the band's onstage vocal blend. Holsapple proved such a good fit that they asked him to join them in the recording studio for the *Out of Time* sessions, playing acoustic and electric guitars and, on "Low," his usual bass part. After the album was released, Holsapple accompanied them in all of their promotional appearances, including on *Mountain Stage*, where Michael introduced him to the audience as "the fifth R.E.M." But when Holsapple bumped into Peter at the 40 Watt and asked about his missing credit on "Low," the other guitarist shrugged. That was just how they did things, he said. The one time they'd made an exception, adding Jeremy Ayers's name to the credits of "Old Man Kensey" when Michael insisted he had cowritten the lyric, the disruption of their four-way credit policy had caused so much unhappiness that they all swore to never do it again. So. That was that.

At this point Holsapple had a few choices. He could, as his lawyer suggested, file a lawsuit. He could let it go and keep working with them. Or he could resign his position with R.E.M. and go back to making his own music, which is what he ultimately did.

As the talks in Acapulco continued in the spring of 1993, the band and their advisers sketched how R.E.M.'s next two or three years would go, and what they would sound like. Bill had a few points that were, as far as he was concerned, nonnegotiable. If they made a new record, it would have to rock. He was a drummer, he was tired of being presented with songs that gave him no opportunity to really play his instrument. And once the new album was done, they would have to go back on the road again. After all, R.E.M. was a rock band. And what rock bands do is make music in front of live audiences. If they wanted to be a band that didn't perform its music for living, breathing people, that was something they'd have to do without him.

Nobody argued. Peter was ready to crank up the volume again too, and was also itching to tour, but he had his own conditions. He was already in his late thirties, and by the time they had an album recorded and released he'd be pushing forty. As much as he enjoyed being on the road, he didn't want to slide back into the boozy, hard-partying habits that had defined their offstage hours during their tours in the 1980s. To make sure they were focused on something productive, he wanted the band to use the time they spent sound-checking and hanging out in dressing rooms and hotel rooms to write another new album. They could even work the new material into the shows, record the tracks, and end the tour with a live album of all-new songs. Mike liked how all of that sounded, and even Michael, who had felt particularly depleted at the end of the 1989 tour, knew that the time was right for R.E.M. to mount another global attack. By the time they got rolling, they'd have three full albums of new material to perform and a vast new audience of fans who had never seen them play. Which made for another enticing fact: the next R.E.M. tour was guaranteed to be the biggest they had ever done. Probably the biggest they would ever do. By the time they left Acapulco, the plan was clear, the next three years of their lives mapped out.

Nothing came easy this time around. In late August they aired out two or three new tunes at the Clayton Street rehearsal space, while they were preparing to play their two songs ("Everybody Hurts" and "Drive") at MTV's 1993 Video Music Awards, then went their separate ways until mid-October. Then they gathered in New Orleans to sift their new music, figure out what worked, what could be cobbled together, and how it might sound when the whole band had its way with it. They sketched out the music for about twenty songs, and Michael had just started writing when some devastating news stopped him in his tracks: the actor River Phoenix had died.

He had passed abruptly, in a drug-related incident that was all the more shocking considering his longtime adherence to veganism. Phoenix was only twenty-three, ten years younger than Michael, but the actor played music—performing in the band Aleka's Attic—with the same passion Michael brought to the films and videos he produced and/or directed. They had traveled together, and Phoenix had been something of a muse for Michael's visual art; he took numerous photos of the actor on their trips across the country. Michael was devastated; he'd finished lyrics for two of the new songs, but the shock of the death hit him like a lightning bolt. Numbed by grief, he navigated his days in a blank-eyed haze. He barely had the focus to read a book, let alone think about writing lyrics. He wouldn't start trying for four months.

Pop music evolved quickly during the first half of the 1990s, as R.E.M. was dominating the sales charts and Bill Clinton was mounting his charge for the White House. When *Out of Time* hit number one on *Billboard*'s album chart in the spring of 1991, it was the first rock album to top the list in close to two years. But since then something had shifted. After nearly a decade of dominance, keyboard-based pop acts with an emphasis on sleek, synth-based sounds started to recede, along with the Bon Jovi/Def Leppard–style pop-metal bands that had crowded rock 'n' roll radio and MTV. In their place rose a crop of alternative acts and, with an incandescent roar, an entire school of hard-edged rock bands coming out of Seattle.

Until then it had seemed impossible that music that loud and unrelentingly raw could connect with a mainstream audience. In the months after *Out of Time*'s debut, Nirvana had broken through, scoring a smash single with "Smells Like Teen Spirit" in late 1991. The tsunami unleashed by the song's impact swept the band's first major-label album, *Nevermind*, to the top of *Billboard*'s list in January 1992. Pearl Jam followed with its debut album, *Ten*, which also topped the charts in 1992, and both Soundgarden and Alice in Chains launched a string of top-selling albums soon after that. Most of those bands cited R.E.M. as an influence, if only for their ability to build a mainstream audience without watering down their sound or their values. But grunge had an emotional intensity and a clamor that altered the musical landscape for nearly everyone making pop music, including R.E.M.

Already determined to create an album of songs drawn from the band's harder-rocking side, the instrumentalists in R.E.M. recorded demos that leaned hard on distorted guitar sounds, basic bass parts, and prominent drums. Peter strummed power chords, used a tremolo pedal to make it pulse, and ran the whole thing through buzz-saw distortion. A few songs reached back to the band's more elegant, melodic works, but the tunes that caught Michael's ear were the ragers, the hard, ornery ones that tapped into the darker corners of his imagination, the appetites and passions, where the claws came out, where tongues emerged and teeth bit down. The world as seen through the eyes of a media sensation, a subject, a target. *I'm not commodity*, he wrote. But that's exactly what he was, what they had all become. And as they worked to follow their previous ten-million-selling album, which had followed their previous ten-million-selling album, while girding themselves for the biggest concert tour of their career, it put them all on edge.

Sparks flew, and not just the creative kind. Michael had started traveling with an entourage, a clutch of friends he could chat and laugh with during slow moments. That was fine almost everywhere, but when he started bringing his friends into the studio and getting distracted by them when the band was working, it could get on his bandmates' nerves. And a fissure had been growing in the band's core, a two-against-two creative divide between Peter and Bill, both of whom preferred to record with a minimum of fuss, overdubs, and post-performance embellishments, and Mike and Michael, who thought it was important to have every note and nuance on their records sound as right as possible. They'd always managed to find a balance that worked for everyone, but now that they were all intent on making a loud and rowdy album, the rough-and-ready pair felt like they'd been handed a mandate. The whole point of rock 'n' roll, particularly in the age of grunge, was to cut through the bullshit—to scream and flail at your instruments until the phoniness around you crumbled into dust. Which didn't amount to an absolute rejection of mellifluousness. It just meant, to two members of R.E.M., that they didn't have to overinvest time in making sure each note fell in precisely the right space, with just the right intonation. The only problem was that the other two members didn't always agree with them, and some days the bickering overcame the music.

There were other interruptions. In the early spring of 1994, Mike got appendicitis, requiring surgery to remove the inflamed organ and then ten days to recover from the ordeal. A bad case of the flu sent Bill to bed for a week, and Michael had a small medical emergency when he suffered an abscessed tooth. The delays mounted. Peter, who had fallen in love with Stephanie Dorgan, co-owner of the Crocodile

Cafe nightclub, in Seattle, had moved to the Pacific Northwest to be near her, and getting together with his bandmates now required planning and travel. This also put him in the middle of Seattle's thriving music scene, where he soon got to know all the key figures, including Nirvana singer/songwriter/guitarist Kurt Cobain, who was so impressed with Peter that he and his wife, Courtney Love, leader of the band Hole, bought the house down the street from where Peter and Dorgan lived.* Peter befriended a legion of the Seattle musicians, becoming particularly tight with Scott McCaughey, whose band the Young Fresh Fellows had traveled the same alternative music circuit R.E.M. orbited for most of the 1980s. When McCaughey started the Minus 5, a conceptual band with a rotating cast of members to record and perform his songs, Peter joined in as often as he could.

Cobain, meanwhile, honed his friendship with Michael. He had been particularly impressed with *Automatic for the People* and spoke at length with his fellow front man about the new songs he was working on, and how he wanted the next Nirvana album to explore the same acoustic palette R.E.M. had used on their record. Gazing at his new friend, Michael could sense the emotional instability just beneath the surface. Cobain was a sensitive kid who came from a broken family in a tough blue-collar town. He'd learned to channel his anger and sadness into music and to dull his angst with drugs. Cobain had worked hard to win his band a following and to get a contract with Seattle's influential Sub Pop record label, but the sudden move to a major label, a leap to multi-platinum status, and the relentless media attention such mammoth success spurred took him by surprise. Beset by depression and self-medicating with heroin, Cobain felt his vision grow increasingly dark as 1993 turned to 1994. He turned to Michael for emotional support, and as he continued to spiral, the more experienced singer tried to buoy Cobain's spirits. When an apparent suicide attempt ended Nirvana's European tour in March, Michael tried to interest Cobain in making a soundtrack for a movie he was producing—they could work on it together, it'd be fun and creative and get him away from his usual grind for a while.

---

* Their block of Seattle's Madrona neighborhood, overlooking Lake Washington, was quite a place in the early 1990s: Peter Buck in one house, Cobain and Love a few doors away, and Howard Schultz, the CEO of the Starbucks coffee company, next to them.

Michael sent Cobain an airline ticket so he could join him in Athens, but Cobain went into a rehab facility to kick heroin, then checked himself out and disappeared. When they found him a few days later, he was in the garage of the house so near to Peter's, dead of a self-inflicted shotgun blast.

Michael might have been closest to Cobain, but the death had a devastating impact on all four members of R.E.M. Cobain's suicide note had focused on the dehumanizing toll of the music industry. He'd become convinced that he'd been taken in by a conspiracy to package real emotions and the art they inspired into commercially salable materials, and in his diminished circumstances the feeling had sapped his soul until there was nothing left. "I haven't felt the excitement of listening to as well as creating music along with reading and writing for too many years now," he wrote. "The worst crime I can think of would be to rip people off by faking it and pretending as if I'm having 100% fun."

Cobain had a psychiatric illness; his perception of his life, work, and artistic corruption were distorted by misfiring synapses and the opiates he took to alleviate his psychic pain. But the members of R.E.M. also knew how the bohemian impulse to form a band with your friends, make up some cool-sounding songs, and buzz down the highway to play them for other people could not only land you in the midst of corporate industry but make you that industry's product. It had been a jarring experience for all of them, and they'd had many advantages Cobain lacked. A four-way creative team, for one thing. A manager and lawyer committed primarily to their physical, artistic, and spiritual well-being. And they'd all had ten years to grow into their roles, and to grow up, before the big lights swung in their direction. Cobain didn't have any of that, and when he faltered, the people closest to him either didn't know how to help him or didn't care enough to try.

Another death, another jolt to the band's creative spirit. This time the result wasn't frustration or anger, but joint creativity. Mike picked up a guitar, turned it up until the music frayed into noise. A couple of dark chords made the verse, then a step up into a major three-chord progression that sounded less like a celebration than an appeal, a plea. The others joined in, Bill on percussion, Peter on simple two-finger organ. Michael wrote his lyrics to speak directly to their vanished friend, the wounded man who had not found the strength to continue his fight. *Heeeyyyy, let me in*, he sang over the chorus, the point where Peter's organ line turned skyward, then tumbled back down again. That had been Michael's message to Cobain, in the form of the offered soundtrack, in the airplane ticket his fellow musician had never taken up for the journey to Athens. *Let me in*, he sang. Let me help, you don't need to do it all yourself. But by then Cobain's ears were beyond hearing. The band played the new song together in the studio, the four of them joined together by the song, the sadness, the unified call to a friend they could no longer reach.

Soon after Cobain's death, Peter's girlfriend, Stephanie, gave birth to twins girls named Zoe and Zelda, and he went back to Seattle to be with his new family. A glorious distraction, but still. Bill had settled on a farm outside Athens and fell into the slow, placid rhythms of farming hay. Michael had his array of film projects and friends. Mike was living his version of the high life, growing his hair, trading his postcollegiate wardrobe of jeans and T-shirts for flashier threads. With Holt, Downs, and company back in the office plotting a year-long world tour, the need for a new album, one strong enough to keep R.E.M. at the apex of global pop culture, was piercing. And yet the group continued to struggle, and work on the new album floundered. At one session in Los Angeles, the arguing grew so jagged that the four musicians could only agree that they couldn't take it anymore: *Fuck this, fuck you, we're done*. Four cars zooming off in four separate directions. No, but wait. They held a meeting outside the studio to see if they could talk through the problem and started remembering the things they still agreed on. That they'd built this band together, that they loved the work they'd done, that they could each give up a little in order to get a lot more of what really mattered. The work, the music, this huge moment they were about to create.

They called the album *Monster*. The blurry image on the cover, a bear with glowing, angry eyes, animated the implacable force they were addressing. As with the lower wolves from *Chronic Town*, the provenance of the beast in the night, the relationship between the hunter and the hunted, is unclear. The music offers no clues. Fast, distorted, and almost unrelentingly loud, it comes out of the speakers like a battered muscle car, all chrome, rust, and manifold rumble. Peter, trading his chiming Rickenbacker for the throaty power of a Gibson Les Paul (as per Jimmy Page, Pete Townshend, and nearly every testosterone-fueled guitar hero of the '60s and '70s) and used stomp pedals to distort its sound.

The keyboard sounds came out of roller rinks and fairgrounds, the sound of cheese and cheap thrills, while the bass stayed simple and close to the ground, more felt than heard. Bill, who had been the most insistent on making a rock 'n' roll album, used his drums the way an assassin wields a high-powered rifle: precise, percussive, deadly. Michael's lyrics taunted and teased, accused and denied, flirted, fingered, and fucked. *I'm the real thing*, he boasts. *Anybody can get laid*, he declares. *I pushed the button and erased your master tape.* Strutting and smirking, sulking and complaining, he rises naked, cloaked only in the neon glare of glam rock.

"What's the Frequency, Kenneth?," a guitar-forward rocker composed by Mike, strung together a long series of chords that Peter played through heavy distortion and elicited one of Michael's most urgent yet tuneful melodies. The lyric, which took its name from the insane cries of the man who had assaulted CBS anchor Dan Rather in New York in 1986, became a metaphor for every inexplicable thing the media culture broadcasts across the endlessly glowing screen. *I'd studied your cartoons, radio, music, TV, movies, magazines*, the narrator declares. *I never understood the frequency.*

In "King of Comedy," the perspective shifts to the inside of the screen, where the man on the business end of the camera refuses his role as industrial product. *I'm not your king of comedy . . . I'm not commodity.* The fact that we're hearing this via a shiny disc made available for purchase by a vast multinational conglomerate implies otherwise, but everyone's got an angle in this sheeny, monstrous world. In "Star 69," named for the code you used to have to dial to call back whoever had just dialed your number, the singer lambastes a hapless conspirator who is only just learning that the jig is up. *I know all about the warehouse fire*, he gloats. *I know squirrellies didn't chew the wires.*

When the pace slows, the music turns lurid, guitar chords hanging like come-ons, keyboards ripe and throbbing, cymbals sizzling, Michael singing in a leering falsetto, hot breath in your ear, arm slung casually, if unbidden, over your shoulder. *What I want to feel, I want to feel it now*, he declares in the sultry R&B ballad "Strange Currencies." *Don't leave that stuff all over me*, he sings in the suggestively titled "Tongue." Another steam-fest begins: *You kiss on me, tug on me, rub on me.* Did he tell his mom not to listen to "Bang and Blame"? It takes us straight to bed and does not pan away at the crucial moment. *You let go on me.* Talking to a TV reporter about the new album, Michael cheerfully affixed his own parental warning. "It's a dick record." When his interviewer laughed awkwardly, he glanced at the camera with a devilish sparkle in his eyes. "Can I say *dick* on this?"

39

Enter the Monster

This was how R.E.M.'s biggest year began.

On January 5, 1995, at Los Angeles International Airport, which briefly took on a tinge of Beatlemania. The band of the moment caught in transit, fielding questions about their new concert tour, their first in half a dozen years. The musicians were charming, laconic, bemused if not surprised to find themselves the subject of so much fervent curiosity. A few things had changed since the days of the moptops. This was a private conference held solely for the benefit of MTV, which was airing it live around the world, underscoring how significant R.E.M. had become to the network and to the tens of millions of largely youthful viewers watching all around the world. In the United States the interview was broadcast live, like Apollo space launches used to be.

MTV had been promoting the exclusive interview all day, counting down the hours until the live broadcast, which began with the network's chief anchor, Kurt Loder, at his desk in New York unveiling the dates of the American leg of the band's world tour. The stateside shows wouldn't start for another four months, but tickets would go on sale within a few days. Meanwhile in Los Angeles, Loder's colleague Tabitha Soren sat in a temporary set in LAX's international terminal, facing three of R.E.M.'s four members, all lined up in tall chairs to talk about the new tour. But first she had to congratulate them, because *Monster,* which had been released the previous September, debuted at the top of the *Billboard* album chart, and gone on to sell close to ten million copies, had just been nominated for two Grammy Awards. As it turned out, they hadn't heard. The nominations were for Best Rock Album and something to do with design. The musicians looked at one another and shrugged. *Well, okay,* they said. *Great.* For a moment Soren seemed taken aback by the musicians' indifference. "I guess you've won them before," she mused, and Mike nodded. "We've lost them before, too."

Bound for the tour's opening concert, in Perth, Australia, the musicians were all dressed for comfort. Mike in a white sweatshirt and jeans, Bill in a corduroy jacket, black jeans, and a T-shirt, with a tall, muffin-shaped hat and, less explicably, a spoon tucked behind his ear. Michael also wore jeans and a T-shirt, with a black watch cap pulled over his head and a scruffy blond goatee bristling on his chin. Peter was running late because his flight from Seattle had been delayed. Or maybe, as a prankish Bill announced, he'd just been fired. "So all you young, aspiring guitarists, send your résumés in." Or maybe, as Michael proposed a few minutes later, it was the drummer who'd been made redundant. "We're programming all the drums, so Bill just goes out to dinner." At the time, this was intended to be ridiculous.

More questions, more jokey answers, more glimpses behind the scenes of the moment's biggest rock band. How did they keep themselves entertained during long flights? Mike said he planned to sleep and play games on his portable backgammon set. What was the weirdest thing they packed? Bill pointed to the utensil tucked behind his ear. He'd heard they don't have spoons in Australia, he said. Was it easier for Michael to perform with spotlights in his face now that he'd grown out of being so shy? Sure, he said. "My skin got better too, and that helped a little bit." What songs were they going to play? A rain of jokes followed on that one: Nothing from their new album, but they would play the entire Green Day album. Also a lot of covers of Molly Hatchet songs, Michael said, digging back into his memory of relatively obscure southern rock bands of the 1970s. "I loved Molly Hatchet in junior high!" Soren yelped. "Really? Well, I knew that," Michael said flirtatiously. "That's why I said it."

Eventually Soren posed a question directly to Bill. Now that they were about to set off on their biggest-ever tour, a high-flying, globe-trotting marathon across scores of cities, dozens of nations, and multiple continents, with hundreds of thousands of fans cheering them and millions of dollars at stake, what part of it all was he looking forward to the most? The drummer answered without hesitating.

"The end of it."[1]

It had all been leading up to this. That was certainly Bill's position when they were in Acapulco, talking about where they were in the wake of *Out of Time* and *Automatic for the People*, the album they should make next, and what should happen after that. And he'd been clear about what he wanted: a rock 'n' roll album they could play on the road. That's what they'd set out to do, and even if the recording of *Monster* had come close to splintering the group, they had emerged from the process feeling excited about the work, and as unified as they'd ever been. Nearly fifteen years into their career, the band's ascent had only grown steeper and faster. Now, in the wake of their two most successful records by far, and with another strong album on the verge of being released, and with their first concert tour since their stunning ascent to the summit of Mount Pop Culture guaranteed to be the biggest, most lucrative enterprise in their career, they were ready to pull out all the stops.

Early the previous August, the band had spent a couple of days shooting a video for "What's the Frequency, Kenneth?" They worked with director Peter Care, who had already made strong clips for "Drive" and especially "Man on the Moon." Both of those videos had animated the spirit of their respective songs in vivid ways, but with "Kenneth" the charge was different. This time the video didn't engage with the song's mass-media-mayhem message or with the frustration of its befuddled narrator. Instead it focused on R.E.M. itself—the evolved identities of the musicians, and their extraordinary power as live performers.

Michael's resistance to lip synching now a distant memory, the "Kenneth" video is, from start to finish, a mimed performance, shot in an empty warehouse in which the band's instruments, amplifiers, and other gear are set in a stage formation. As the opening chords play, the camera frames Michael as a body: feet, legs, midriff, and shoulders, that's it. We glimpse the bottom half of his face when he hitches up his pants, but as the first verse begins and the other musicians start to move amid flashes of clear white light strobing from offstage, we see them first in quick, surprising glances. Mike, last seen performing in a lightly spangled suit at MTV's 1993 Video Music Awards, has been reborn as a glittering electric cowboy. Shiny boots, blue flared suit spangled in rhinestone peacock feathers, his hair long, blond, and curly, his soft eyes hidden behind sinister dark shades. Peter's loose white shirt and black pants are relatively plain, but he's cut back his hair to reveal thick muttonchop sideburns. Bill keeps it simple behind the drums with a sleeveless white T-shirt, his muscles working, his sticks flashing in the strobes. The song speeds and spins, they're all moving with it, pushing the sound forward. When the current finally hits Michael, his body erupts as if he's brushed against a high-tension wire. Feet pumping, arms flailing, hands grabbing at the microphone on the stand in front of him, body moving but face centered in the frame. And in that moment, as his eyes find the lens and the strobe ignites the top of his freshly shaven head, we grasp for the first time that Michael Stipe, or at least the version Michael is willing to present to the world, is no longer who he used to be.

The next stage of the process began in early September, when the band, plus Holt, Downs, and a variety of assistants, family members, and friends, relocated to Luttrellstown Castle, a fifteenth-century keep on the outskirts of Dublin, Ireland, that had been repurposed into a luxe resort. R.E.M. rented the entire place, making it their center of operations for the international press blitz that would herald both the release of *Monster*, scheduled for the end of the month, and the launch of the 1995 world tour in January.

For days on end the musicians, usually working in two-man teams, trooped from room to room and to the various camera-friendly corners of the grounds to face the cameras and the microphones and the open notebooks and the eagerly smiling reporters and anchors and correspondents, answering the usual questions about how they'd made the new record, about what the songs really meant, about why they hadn't toured to support the last two records and why they had decided to mount such a big tour this time around. MTV was preparing an entire weekend of R.E.M.-centric programming pegged to the release of *Monster* and had sent a camera crew to shoot the band introducing and talking about their old videos. The musicians took turns introducing the older clips and, in case anyone watching didn't already know who they were, themselves. For Michael it was a chance to acknowledge the rumors that had swirled around him for the past few years. And to start a conversation he was finally ready to have. "This," he declared with a wicked smile, "is the very skinny, bald, sexually ambiguous Michael Stipe."

He never hid who he was. If you knew Michael as a person, you knew that he always had girlfriends and boyfriends and that he had pursued relationships with members of both genders with equal enthusiasm. He might have been more public about his relationship with Natalie Merchant than he was with Jeremy Ayers or the other men he had dated, but maybe that was because she was famous too, and when they were together, people noticed. But there were always men in his life. And where he came from, nobody cared. In Athens the art music scene of the late '70s and early '80s was as inextricable from the town's gay community as it was from UGA's art school. Four of the five original members of the B-52's were gay, as was Love Tractor's Mark Cline. The gay members of other bands were less well known or less public about their romantic lives, and however they chose to live was their business. The musicians and the people who followed them were interested in their music and art, not who the artists might like to smooch when the show was over.

R.E.M.'s success, and the growing intensity of the media's interest in its charismatic front man, put Michael in a different position. Particularly given the overwhelming masculinity that had always defined rock 'n' roll. Even if they preferred to think of themselves as musicians and songwriters first and foremost, all four members of R.E.M. were aware of the band's image, of how they looked and who they seemed to be when they were in the public eye. Peter was a particularly canny narrator of the band's history, continually exaggerating the accidental nature of their formation and rise, and understating the time and attention he gave to mastering his guitar before he joined with the others.

Still, while they'd talk at length about their music and their cultural opinions, all four band members were remarkably disciplined about keeping their private lives to themselves. To the extent that reporters asked Mike, Peter, and Bill about their families or romantic partners, or even the juicier details of the intra-band relationships and squabbles, the members of R.E.M. rarely volunteered much beyond an anodyne sentence or two. In their early years Michael would respond to questions about his family and childhood with wild, often wholly invented stories about his Cherokee grandmother or how he'd been a piano prodigy as a boy, only to have all traces of his talent slip away when he grew into puberty. But that was before the hit singles and platinum albums made R.E.M., and particularly Michael, into subjects of mass adoration and, inevitably, curiosity. And at the altitude R.E.M. had come to inhabit in the public consciousness, the questions, and the expectation that they would be answered, would not go away.

At first this infuriated him. Like most people, Michael preferred to keep the details of his private life to himself and a small group of trusted friends and family. In fact, he was so averse to answering personal questions during interviews, and so prone to shutting down reporters who asked them, the producers of a 1989 documentary for MTV UK strung a few of his chillier refusals into an extended supercut of Stipeian rejections and dismissals. "I never stated that in public," he snaps. "I really don't want to talk about my past," he huffs. "I really don't want to talk about it," "I choose not to talk about it," and on and on.

When whispers about his relationships with men merged with the ongoing toll of the AIDS crisis, and the AIDS-related deaths of gay celebrities including the pianist Liberace in 1987, Queen singer Freddie Mercury in 1991, and the actor Anthony Perkins in 1992 led to persistent rumors about the state of his health, Michael was at first repulsed. He'd spent several years in the mid-1980s terrified that he might have contracted the virus but, like a significant number of other potential victims, he'd been too leery of his test results becoming public information to risk getting tested. Instead he lived in fear, staying celibate for long periods, using his near-endless travels as an excuse for avoiding intimate relationships. He eventually did get tested, in 1987, and was relieved to learn he was HIV negative. When the rumors about his health gained currency in the wake of the dark-hued *Automatic for the People* (Why isn't the band touring? Why won't Michael do interviews? Why does he look even skinnier than usual? Why are all these songs about death?), Michael felt torn. He didn't want people to worry about him, but he also didn't want to further stigmatize AIDS patients by distancing himself from them.

Then there was the matter of his sexual orientation, which fell somewhere in the murky region between the poles of straight and gay. Michael knew enough about modern sexual politics to know how rigidly dogmatic members of both camps could be. Even when he began to consider speaking out, he couldn't imagine what an honest description of his orientation would achieve, other than infuriating almost everyone. Who wanted to hear from a guy who couldn't commit one way or the other? The tension found its way onto *Monster*, stated directly in the media commentary "King of Comedy," in which Michael follows a line about the commercial value of controversy with: *I'm straight, I'm queer, I'm bi.* Would anyone wonder what he meant by that? Would they say he was telling the truth? And what if they did? Michael already knew he was going to be giving interviews, countless interviews, to promote the new album and the tour. He wasn't going to go out of his way to talk about his sex life, but if anyone asked, which seemed like a good bet, he knew he'd have to answer. And when he did, he intended to tell the truth.

He did not hold back. The first time someone asked, he made it plain: he was bisexual. Asked for further clarification, he refused, while not denying anything: "I don't think it's anyone's business what I do with my dick unless you're sitting in my lap," he told MTV. "If I suck dick or I suck pussy or I alternate between them, it's kind of nobody's business." When the tour got to its launch in Australia a few months later, he elaborated just a little bit: "If I had to go on record, I'd say that sexually speaking I'm more ambivalent than anything else. Anything that moves, that's my motto." With this he gestured to the reporter, perched just a few feet away. "So just sit there and be very still."[2]

A chart topper around the world, *Monster* rated reviews that were a tick or two below the raves earned for *Automatic* but still almost uniformly upbeat. Writing in *Rolling Stone*, Robert Palmer was particularly struck by Michael's handling of how fame had altered his identity, though other critics felt that the sardonic characters he embodied in the songs kept listeners at a distance. Which was almost certainly the point, though also a bit jarring in the wake of *Automatic*'s songs, so many of which seemed to come from deep within the singer's actual experience of life. Of course, seeing his own spotlit form refracted through the media's funhouse mirror was also an integral part of Michael's real life. And as they prepared to take on the new experience of being superstars on a world tour, "throwing ourselves to the dogs," as the singer told one reporter that fall,[3] they were excited, anxious, girded for what they were taking on. The one thing they knew for sure was that this was their time.

"I think all of us kinda realized that we're probably never going to be in a position like this again," Michael told one reporter. "We'll probably never be as popular, and never able to do a world tour on this scale again. And I'm looking forward to it. I'm gonna have a ball."[4]

Looking ahead to the tour, and the prospect of filling the world's biggest arenas with music night after night without Peter Holsapple in the fold, they started auditioning side musicians to add depth and breadth to their sound. Peter's first choice for a utility player was Scott McCaughey, of Seattle's Young Fresh Fellows. They had played together frequently since Peter moved to the Pacific Northwest, and along with his musical versatility (McCaughey was also proficient on bass and keyboards and could flesh out the vocal blend too), Peter knew he had the right mix of brains, wit, and easygoing charm. McCaughey passed his audition easily enough, but the search for a second player, one who would play guitar exclusively, proved trickier. A couple of guys simply didn't fit; T-Bone Burnett came in for a day, but more out of curiosity than anything else—he was too busy to consider going on the road for a year with another band. An L.A. guitarist named Brian Baker looked like a good candidate, but then he got an offer to join the band Bad Religion as a full member. He knew another guitarist who was plenty good, and an R.E.M. superfan, too. Nathan December was at his day job a week or so later when he got a call. "This guy says his name is Jefferson Holt and he manages a band called R.E.M.," December remembers. Of course he knew exactly who Holt was. "And I was losing my fucking mind."

After spending part of a day meeting everyone on the set of the "What's the Frequency, Kenneth?" video, December got a call to bring his guitar to a rehearsal. Once they all tuned up, Peter asked him which song he'd like to play with them. December shot back without thinking: "Anything you've ever written." Recalling the moment now, he chuckles. "That was the right answer." They jammed for a day, then six weeks passed before the guitarist got another call. Could he come to Atlanta to do some more playing? There he found the band in a big rehearsal complex where their entire stage had been set up. He rehearsed with them for half a day, then was preparing to fly home the next morning when he got another call. Could he come back to play a little more? December delayed his flight, and when he got back to the rehearsal complex the next morning he found the entire band, along with Jefferson Holt and Bertis Downs, sitting together, smiling at him. "We just wanted to welcome you to the touring unit," he heard. "I said, 'Oh, okay, cool,'" December recalls. "But I was totally losing it." That was Sunday, November 6. Six days later, on November 12, December made his live debut with R.E.M. on *Saturday Night Live*, before an audience of millions.

The documentary *Rough Cut*, made by Valerie Faris and Jonathan Dayton, the same filmmakers who had directed the "Wolves, Lower" video a dozen years earlier, reveals something of the day-to-day lives of the members of R.E.M. in the late fall of 1994. It shows the musicians in Atlanta, spending hours honing their show, constructing lists of songs they might want to play, trying to remember how they go, flipping through published songbooks of their own records to make sure they're getting them right. When the instrumentalists don't need him, Michael huddles with the artist putting together the graphics that will be projected behind the band during the shows, and with the designer choosing photos for the program they'll sell at the venues. When he's not doing that, the singer is surrounded by publicists, assistants, and other functionaries, all bearing urgent requests for one thing or another.

He's also got the filmmakers to deal with, and does so cheerfully but firmly. "I want them to have enough to make a great piece, but I don't want them following me into the bathroom," he says amiably. Then he starts joking around. "No, I will not be filmed on an airplane. This documentary thing has gone too far." The attention seems to animate him; even when he's hassled, he appears to be having a fantastic time. In the back of a limousine he introduces himself to the driver, then uses the car phone to call the hotel for messages. His room is registered to Mr. Cup. When the '70s hit "Brandy (You're a Fine Girl)" comes on the radio, he sings along with gusto. He's in a dressing room, he's in another limousine, he's in an elevator wearing a backpack strapped tight over his shoulders, like a kid on his way to grade school. "I'm a little tired, to tell you the truth," he says to nobody and everybody. "I can't sleep."

In the *Saturday Night Live* studios, they rehearse for the cameras, tracked closely by an older man with a headset and a clipboard, who relays information from the control booth. Preparing to shoot jokey little promos for the show with the week's host, Sarah Jessica Parker, they go over the quips that have been written for them. When Peter sees dialogue with his name next to it, he draws the line: "I just don't feel like talking. I hate the sound of my voice." In the hallways, staffers surround them, asking for autographs, which the musicians provide happily enough. The actor and *SNL* veteran Bill Murray appears, and when he overhears Peter saying something about not having enough clothes to change between all the songs, he pulls him toward the show's wardrobe room. "They have all kinds of crazy stuff in there," he says, then asks a worker to find Peter a coat.

It is big and furry, and he ends up wearing it during the third of the three songs they play: "What's the Frequency, Kenneth?," "Bang and Blame," and "I Don't Sleep, I Dream."

There are interviews. Endlessly, interviews. In Atlanta it's magazine writers and daily journalists, and some are better prepared than others. One guy seems uniquely clueless: "It's loud, guitars . . ." He seems to be talking about *Monster*. "I don't know how different it is from your other stuff." The musicians nod and don't seem terribly put out. A woman with a camera crew and elaborately sculpted hair smiles broadly while Michael talks about how other R.E.M. records came from the heart and the mind, but this one's from the crotch. Noting the discomfort beneath the woman's hairdo, he starts in on this being a dick record—and, oh yeah, can he even say *dick* on camera? The woman laughs, but her smile flickers.

Now the entire band is being interviewed together, all four perched tightly on a sofa. The sculpted-hair lady asks if they ever think about breaking up, and Mike says no. "Not till journalists bring it up, anyway," which makes everyone laugh. Michael adds that even when the band members disagree about something, they're always on the same team, if not always on the same page. They like and admire one another a lot, but it's the differences between them that make R.E.M. what it is, he says. Michael looks around him and seems, for a moment, to become genuinely emotional. "If anyone on this couch were to leave, then—" Bill, a sly smile on his face, breaks in. "Then the other three would be more comfortable." Everybody laughs, but Michael still completes his original thought. "It would not be R.E.M. anymore."

40

Did Someone Put a Curse on Us?

The Perth Entertainment Centre, January 13, 1995. The first moments of the first night of the world tour. When the arena lights flicked off, a vast roar filled the blackness. Eight thousand Australians standing up and going *waaaaaaaahhhh!* The moment lingered and expanded on itself. So much at hand, so much at stake. Onstage, they could feel a solid wall of noise coming at them, the power humming in the amps. The musicians slipped into their places, instruments in hand, the electricity in their fingertips. This moment they'd first anticipated in the spring of 1993, that they'd hoped for and dreaded, that they'd dreamed of, that they'd argued about, that they'd been planning and preparing for, was right here, right now. Peter, his left hand holding the neck of his guitar, took a breath, then raked a pick over the strings, sending a loud buzzing chord into the air. Then another chord, tripping a blast of drums and a bolt of clear light revealing five musicians and Michael, shouting a single word into his microphone.

WHAT!

The drums and bass hit and then they all shot off together.

"What's the frequency, Kenneth?" is your Benzedrine, uh-huh / I was brain-dead, locked out, numb, not up to speed . . .

And there it all was. The present and the past, the signal and the noise, the insiders and the outsiders, the melody and the dissonance, all of it rolled into sound and beamed upward until it exploded, the fractured light of a mirror ball.

This was the part Bill lived for, the moment when the lights went out and the music took over. He'd started talking about going back on the road in 1992. "We miss touring," he told a reporter from Europe's Super Channel in October 1992.[1] That was in the wake of *Automatic*, when he realized he was tired of all the midtempo songs that had no need for a drummer pounding away. Bill had helped write a bunch of those songs, but still. Enough was enough: the band's performance chops had dulled, the time had come to rock. When he was interviewed by MTV as it was all coming together two years later, you could see a gleam in the drummer's eye. "It'd just kinda be fun to go out and be a kid again," he told one of the throng of interviewers witnessed by the cameras of *Rough Cut*. "I've got new drums and I get to hit 'em real hard. Pete's got a new amp and he gets to turn it up all the way. We get to be kids again."[2]

But there was performing, the part that made him feel like a kid, and then there was touring, which made him, at thirty-six years old, feel like an old man: exhausted, disoriented, aching for home. The irony was in how hard, and how long, Bill had worked to get himself and his band to this position. If anything, they'd overshot the goal: he'd wanted to make music that was popular enough to earn them a living, but they'd become so big that the demands of popularity were drowning out the music. And still the music kept calling to him. Particularly the kind they could only make playing live, in front of an audience. The energy, the sound, the heartbeat rhythm connecting him to his three bandmates and to the thousands of people breathing and shouting and moving along with them. "As much as I hated a lot of the parts of being on the road and away from home, I was ready to go," he said. "Five years off—it was time to do it."[3]

And not in some half-assed way, either. When Peter proposed making the 1995 tour a small-scale enterprise, a return to the clubs they'd played back in their earliest days, Bill put his foot down. "Fuck that. I'm not going backwards."[4] This was where the drummer seemed to be at odds with himself. Even as the new tour was coming together, he spoke of how he'd loved the club years the most, when they could play whatever they wanted, for as long as they wanted to, without worrying about the rules and regulations that had first landed on them when they stepped up into theaters. "Going onstage exactly at 9.20 and making sure you got off at 11.15 or you were going to be fined," he told Gerrie Lim, writing for *BigO* in the fall of 1994. "Those kinds of strictures made touring a lot less fun. And it was kind of ironic, because the more money we made the less power we had over what was going on."[5]

But like most, or maybe all, aspiring rockers, Bill and his bandmates had set out to become something more than rock musicians. They wanted to be rock *stars*. And what the rock stars of the 1990s did, along with selling millions of records and ascending to the upper altitudes of celebrity, was tour the world, playing the biggest arenas, stadiums, and festivals they could play. And as Bill gleefully told MTV, that's what R.E.M. was going to do, starting in Australia in mid-January. "Friday the thirteenth," he said, elevating his impressive brows. "That's for good luck."[6]

The touring party gathered in Perth at the end of the first week of January, set up the stage in the Perth Entertainment Centre, where the tour would open, and spent a few days in full rehearsals, working the final kinks out of the set, making certain the light and film cues were in line and girding for the coming rigors. When they finished work on January 12, the entire touring party was invited to the Cottesloe Civic Centre, a converted estate near the sea, to attend the wedding of Peter and Stephanie Dorgan. A reception followed, with music provided by tour openers Grant Lee Buffalo. Peter recruited the band, plus McCaughey and December, to serve as his groomsmen. Later, when a reporter mused about how he'd sacrificed a honeymoon with his bride by getting married the day before the start of a world tour, Peter chuckled. "I get to play guitar and travel all over the world," he said. "That sounds pretty much ideal to me."

They fiddled with the set list over the next few weeks, moving "Kenneth" into the encores, then putting it back at the start of the set, shifting one or another old favorite (say, "Begin the Begin" or "Disturbance at the Heron House") into the first suite of songs, then shuffling the deck again. Eventually they settled on opening with three and sometimes four straight *Monster* songs, the better to establish that they were a modern band working in the moment, not milking their past to connect with the audience. They had all grown and changed in visible ways. Mike, thirty-six years old and spangled from his ankles to his neck and out to his wrists, hair long and silken, had traded his approachable nerd look for full-on glam rock. Peter, thirty-eight and now a father of two, prowled his side of the stage like a field general, dressed in plain pants and a lightly ruffled tuxedo shirt, limiting his spins and jumps, his mind firmly on the music. Often he drifted back to lock in with Bill, who marshaled the beat with no-nonsense authority, dressed in plain trousers and a T-shirt.

But it was Michael, now thirty-five, who embodied the spirit of *Monster* and the tour. Radiant with a kind of ironic audacity, he'd take the stage in aluminum-framed sunglasses, a T-shirt, and jeans, a wool hat pulled low over his eyes, then greet the crowd with a tetchy *WHAT!*, as if summoned by an unwanted knock on his front door. Then Peter would kick things off with the opening of "Kenneth" or "I Don't Sleep, I Dream" or "I Took Your Name," any of which might start the show, and when the song took him, Michael moved like a snake on legs, bending forward and backward, dancing with the microphone stand, batting it around, lurching this way and that.

When he addressed the crowd, he teased and flirted in the same breath. "I went down to the beach the other day. Did anybody down there see me?" he said one night in Australia. When someone shouted back, he looked down carefully, then nodded. "Oh, hi, I remember you." He pointed to the music stand next to his mic stand. "You may have noticed that I've been reading the lyrics off of a sheet of paper." A shout. "*Why?* That's a stupid question." He laughed and then barked with mock authority. "Take off your clothes and lick the floor." A beat. "I was *kidding*!" Everything he said came through a crooked smile. "Well, that was a song," he'd announce. "Now we're going to play another song. After that we'll play another song, and then another one after that. And it's going to go on like that for a while."

They picked up speed and took to the air, the ground blurring with their velocity. January in Australia, one show in New Zealand, then off to Asia at the start of February. A pair of shows at the Budokan, in Tokyo, then one-show-and-go visits to Taiwan, Hong Kong, and Singapore before the entire enterprise made the long flight across the planet to Spain. They got a few days to rest before the European tour began in San Sebastián on February 15. That trip, more than twenty-four hours from hotel-room door to hotel-room door, inspired the writing of "Departure," a full-speed-ahead guitar blast that was the first of the newly written songs to make it into the show. The song's first line—*Just arrived Singapore, San Sebastián, Spain, twenty-six-hour trip*—was a literal description of the band's recent journey across the planet. *There's so much to tell you, so little time / I've come a long way since, uh, whatever . . .*

During the 1980s, touring had been R.E.M.'s way of being. They'd traveled all over the world, by car, van, bus, train, boat, and airplane, had performed in venues large, small, and midsize, had faced audiences that ignored them and audiences that sang along with every syllable. But they had never toured as international celebrities, and what soon became clear was that this made for what Peter called a "weirdly unpleasant" experience.[7] Previously, whenever they'd found crowds waiting outside a hotel, they'd assumed someone far more famous than they were was also staying there. This time around, the crowds were looking for them. "Your phones would be ringing at weird hours, people would camp in the hallways," Peter told the British journalist Tony Fletcher. "It was so fucked up and chaotic I quit drinking. I stopped drinking in February and didn't have another drink until the end of November. I was just like, this is too insane. I have to be sober for this whole thing to keep it together."[8]

Peter also had his new wife and their twin baby girls to keep him grounded. The other band members did their best to keep their inner circle insulated from the weirdness triggered by their fame, and from the more toxic habits and rituals of the rock 'n' roll road. They revised their standard performance contract to limit the backstage beverage options to soft drinks, beer, and wine, no more bottles of vodka, scotch, and gin, thanks very much, and to make sure the buffets had plenty of vegetables and other healthy options for band and crew alike. They brought a treadmill for Peter and Bill to exercise on, while Michael combined his exercise with sightseeing, pulling a hat down over his head so he could explore his whereabouts on foot without drawing attention. Bill and Bertis Downs brought their golf clubs, and if there was a course anywhere nearby, they'd take off together to get in nine holes before soundcheck. After the shows, the band members and their wives or romantic partners often got together in the hotel bar or in someone's room to unwind together with party games—charades or a board game, Pictionary and Trivial Pursuit usually. "It wasn't rock-star-like," Bill's ex-wife, Mari, recalls. "Not a lot of partying. It was family-like, very quiet. People got really obsessed with the games."[9]

The pressure continued to build. The crowds, the lights, the cameras. *Monster* had sold two million copies in the United States alone within two months, and it was still selling, pushed along by the single releases of "Bang and Blame" and "Crush with Eyeliner," both of which scaled the various *Billboard* charts on the strength of heavy airplay all across mainstream rock and alternative radio outlets. Sales and airplay were just as strong in Europe, and the media coverage fed excitement when the band came to perform, which fed the crowds and the mood of mayhem that seemed to blow up wherever they went.

Weird things started to happen. At the first of two shows in Rome's PalaEUR sports arena on February 22, the band was still in the opening verse of the set-opening "What's the Frequency, Kenneth?" when the entire place lost power. A loud *bang!* and then blackness, a brief echoing silence, and then a big cheer—was it part of the show? Well, no. The lights came back on after a minute or two, the sound system came back a moment later. Bill slapped his sticks together and they picked it up pretty much where they'd left off, rock 'n' roll business as usual. For fifty-five minutes anyway, until the end of the first verse of "Man on the Moon," when it happened again. *Bang!*, then blackness. When the lights blinked back on, Michael stood at the center of the stage, shaking his head at the crowd. "What the *fuck* is going on here?" he said, sounding truly puzzled. "Does this happen all the time? Did somebody put a curse on us or something? I didn't think so."

Then they got back to it, taking "Man on the Moon" from the top ("It's one of the highlights of the show," Michael explained), then into the main set's emotional climax (". . . Moon" into the slow boil of "Country Feedback" into the outburst of "Losing My Religion"). A few more songs would fill in the main set, and there'd be a brief pause before the encore began with the bloody, mournful "Let Me In," which gave way to the soothing "Everybody Hurts." After that would come a few show-ending rousers and the new single, "Bang and Blame," before they finished with a riotous rendition of the beloved-hit-that-wasn't-actually-a-hit, "It's the End of the World as We Know It." The last note would still be echoing around the darkened hall, competing with the crowd's cheers, when the first of the band's buses would roar away from the venue. Inside would sit the band's ambivalent drummer, ears still ringing, spirit keening to be somewhere, anywhere away from the noise, the crowds and tumult.

They had a day off before the show in Lausanne. A six-hour journey from Bologna after the February 27 show, then a long, quiet day in a Swiss hotel to catch up on sleep in a real bed, get up whenever, maybe take a walk and explore, visit a park, or do a little shopping and go out for a meal or two before the 2 p.m. call for soundcheck at the Patinoire de Malley arena for the March 1 show. Grant Lee Buffalo was opening on this part of the tour, so they went first, playing for five or ten minutes while the crew got their balances right in the amps and PA. Then R.E.M. and their two supporting musicians came moseying out, the instrumentalists first, jamming a song or two before they'd go over something in the set that had thrown them at the last show, or get going on something new. Six weeks into the tour, the workdays ran more or less like clockwork; everyone had their pre-show rituals, the anticipation building when the doors opened and the place thrummed with voices, feet, the happy buzz of concertgoers gearing up for their evening with the hottest band of the season.

WHAT!

Onstage in Lausanne. The explosion of light and sound, the cheers and applause coming at you like a wave, a physical thing strong enough to knock you off your feet. This was where Bill could hit his drums hard enough to keep the noise and chaos at bay, where his beat kept everything orderly, moving at his pace. After fifteen years together, and now nearly two months into the tour, the performances were built on a combination of physical energy, emotional projection, and muscle memory. Michael's job was a little different, channeling so much feeling into the words he sang, his focus divided between singing, moving, and monitoring the crowd while also listening to the band. Behind him, Bill focused almost exclusively on the music, keeping his beat straight and strong, adding harmonies when his parts came up.

Then they were off, into the opening suite of *Monster* songs, then a pair from *Out of Time*, "Me in Honey," "Half a World Away," usually with one or two from *Automatic*. It was always great to hear the ovation the songs from the previous few albums got when they started playing them; nobody complained about not hearing "Radio Free Europe" or "So. Central Rain" or any of the early ones they'd put away. "Man on the Moon" was always a highlight: the music had such a nice groove, and Michael had taken to emphasizing the whole Elvis aspect, he'd be all slinky hips and sexy Memphis drawl for the *Heeeey bay-buh* bit, and the crowd loved it every night. That was a real pleasure for everyone, and also the point in the show, on this late winter evening in Switzerland, when Bill felt something go wrong.

A piercing throb in his head. A lightning bolt of pain he could nearly see, and certainly felt, behind his eyes. He might have slowed down for a moment or two, his backing vocal might have dropped out, nobody remembers. Somehow he got to the end of the song. "Man on the Moon" almost always prefaced "Country Feedback," at which point Bill switched to bass, so Nathan December was used to seeing the drummer heading his way just after "Man on the Moon" ended. Usually they'd have a moment or two to check in, trade a joke or laugh about something that had gone sideways earlier in the show. But now something was different about Bill. He was pale, and faltering. Usually he'd sling the bass over his shoulder, but now he was swaying on his feet. "God, Natty, I don't feel so good," he said. His head was killing him, he needed to sit down for a second. Bill leaned on the bass amp, December recalls. Then he keeled over. "It was the scariest thing on the planet," December says. "We had no idea what was wrong."[10] Peter, seeing Bill go down, dropped his guitar and ran over, as did a roadie or two. Together they pulled Bill back to his feet. He was conscious, sort of standing, but then he fell into Peter's arms. Peter and December helped him offstage.

They got him to the dressing room and laid him down on a sofa. Bill was conscious and talking. He'd had migraine headaches; those could take him down for a day or two. But this wasn't that; this was pain like he'd never experienced before. A couple of EMTs came in, took his pulse, peered into his eyes, asked the first question you ask a rock musician who collapses onstage: *Was he on something?* No? Well, better to not take him to the hospital—they'll just assume he was overdosing.[11] He had to get out of the hall, though; there was no way he was going back onstage. The EMTs put him on a stretcher and wheeled him away, taking him back to the hotel. But the crowd was still out there, stomping and cheering, waiting for R.E.M. Would they call it quits or . . . ? No. Someone ran to find Joey Peters, the drummer for Grant Lee Buffalo, who was unwinding in his band's dressing room. Could he play Bill's parts? Yes? He grabbed some sticks, sprinted to the stage, the house lights went off, the show went on. The band cut the rest of the set down to the essentials, came off the stage blank-faced and anxious, and were relieved to hear that Bill was resting in his room. It was a bad migraine, but he *seemed* fine.

Bill wasn't fine. The pain radiated down to his shoulders. Mari massaged his neck, but then he was nauseated and threw up. He couldn't sleep—it hurt too much. Mari wondered if he had meningitis. At 6 a.m. she called for an EMT, who came to the room, heard about the neck pain and nausea, put it all together, and called the hospital: Bill had suffered a brain bleed and needed immediate help. They put him back on the gurney, got him down the stairs and back into the ambulance, now with lights and sirens, heading to the hospital, where some kind of fate awaited him.

It could have gone either way. Some people make it and some people don't. That's how it is in life, and also in rock 'n' roll. It's all about where you happen to be, what street you walk down, who you happen to meet when you turn the corner. Bill's family moved to Macon, got a house in the same neighborhood where Mike Mills lived. Bill and Mike found each other, discovered their mutual love for music, and when they got to Athens they both met Kathleen O'Brien, who just happened to know Peter, who happened to meet Michael at Wuxtry Records, and when they all turned up at the same party, they decided to try playing together. There was no plan, no strategy, just dumb luck that they clicked together so well. They set out to make music and have as much fun as possible, maybe even make some money, if that's how it worked out. And it did work out. Club shows, a record, a record deal, onwards and upwards, upwards and upwards and forever upwards, all the way to Lausanne, Switzerland, where the aneurysm in Bill Berry's brain erupted less than two miles from the hospital, whose staff included some of the world's best neurosurgeons. Including a doctor who had studied with a neurosurgeon whose recently perfected vascular clip had been developed to treat exactly the sort of burst blood vessel Bill had suffered.

"He's not going to survive."[12]

This is what Mari Berry heard when Bill was headed into surgery and she called home to her friend who worked as a nurse. The friend had seen this before. She was so sorry, so very sorry, but when the aneurysm bursts they're done for, and it was best for Mari to be prepared. But that's not what Mari had heard from the doctors who were caring for him, so she dismissed her friend's version and focused on the here and now, in this Swiss hospital, where they seemed so much more optimistic.

They opened his head, found three bleeds, and employed the vascular clips to seal them. Seemingly repaired, Bill was still in blinding pain, but they didn't want to give him morphine; he needed to be conscious so they could see how his body was responding. A day or two passed and he seemed to be recovering. They were about to send him back to the hotel when a final test, a walk down the hospital hallway, got scary. Bill's left side went limp; something was wrong. They wheeled him back into surgery, discovered that his clipped veins were collapsing, then employed another newly developed technique, moving balloons up his carotid artery to expand the vessels until they had healed. Bill was back in his room soon after that, conscious and talking. This time he really was on the mend. He went back to the hotel, and a few days later they moved him to a resort in Evian, where he stayed until he was strong enough to board a jet and fly home to Georgia. There, his bandmates, who flatly refused promoters' attempts to talk them into performing with a substitute drummer, waited anxiously for their fallen comrade's return.

Considering how close he came to death, the speed of Bill's recovery was astounding. Back in Georgia, it took just a couple of weeks for him to get back on the golf course. And even before that he was on the phone to Holt in the office. When could they get back on the road? Bill was ready. Or he would be in just a few weeks. He was already going at his drums, getting his groove back, raring to go. His doctors were fine with it, too. He was as good as new; even better.

They were off the road for exactly six weeks. They lost a couple dozen shows, mostly in Europe and the UK and then a handful of dates in Southern California. But the touring party re-congregated in Oakland for a few days of rehearsals during the first week of May, and on May 15, R.E.M.'s tour, now dubbed Aneurysm '95, launched its American run at the Shoreline Amphitheatre, just south of San Francisco in Mountain View. Bill, wearing a black baseball cap over his recently opened head, played with all the power and poise he'd had before his fateful visit to Switzerland. Michael made a point of asking after his health a couple of times during the show, prompting the drummer to fake convulsions once and then fall off his stool altogether. It was all in good fun, as was the new image they'd added to the montage that played behind the band during the set: an X-ray of Bill's head taken in the Swiss hospital, burst aneurysms and all.

And I feel fine.

PART V

The Name of This Band Is R.E.M. and This Is What We Do

41

How the West Was Won . . .

A fter fifteen years of relatively smooth travels, the road got bumpy. They rumbled across the United States through the end of June, climaxing with three sold-out shows at New York's Madison Square Garden, then returned to Europe for a run of big outdoor shows: festivals, stadiums, castles. Everywhere, the audiences thronged and cheered in numbers large enough to reroute traffic, affirming R.E.M.'s place at the apex of rock 'n' roll.

And yet something in the air had changed. Ten days into the European swing, another medical emergency hit. Struck by a high fever and abdominal pain, Mike required surgery to repair an intestinal adhesion, an aftereffect of the appendix surgery he'd had a year earlier. They lost nine shows to his recovery, got back at it in time for an enormous show at Ireland's Slane Castle on July 22, then barely made it through the next three weeks of shows before Michael, also laid low with abdominal pain, was diagnosed with a hernia—a result of bearing down to sing night after night. He pushed himself through the final European show, in Prague, before jetting back for surgery at Emory University Hospital, in Atlanta.

The personal dynamics within the band were shifting. Bill, though happy to be alive and relieved that the "little boo-boo" in his head,[1] as he called it, hadn't spelled the end of the band's yearlong tour, pulled a baseball cap over his brow and kept his eyes beneath the brim. He'd always been shyer than the other guys, but now Bill withdrew even further. "He didn't want to be around everybody, didn't want to socialize," his then-wife Mari recalls. "He didn't do much game playing or hanging out. He was tired; maybe his brain aneurysm was making him feel sicker than he thought."[2]

They were seeing less of Jefferson Holt, too. He'd once been the indispensable fifth member of the band, perpetually available to lend support and counsel for every significant event in their day, but much of his role had been given over to the musicians' individual posses of assistants, spouses/partners, and friends. And while Bertis Downs could usually be found in the management office at the day's venue when he wasn't on the links with Bill, Holt started to find more time for sightseeing or visiting museums or just doing his own thing. Still, the manager stepped up in a big way during Bill's crisis, staying at the drummer's side to the point of sleeping in his hospital room, until he was back on solid ground. Their luck held—everyone got better, the tour went on, the crowds continued to cheer.

Michael was mostly healed from his operation when work resumed in the United States in early September. The band dropped by MTV's Video Music Awards at Radio City Music Hall to collect the Video Vanguard Award, a career achievement kind of prize that Michael, in his acceptance speech, described as indicating that they'd been around for a long time and made a lot of videos "that don't suck."[3] Also invited to give a musical performance, the band chose to play "The Wake-Up Bomb," one of the brand-new songs they'd composed on the road, but had yet to record. Most artists would take advantage of the national/global platform by featuring a new single or anything that was commercially available. But with more than two more months of road work ahead of them, R.E.M. were already promoting themselves within an inch of their lives. Which was, in large part, what "The Wake-Up Bomb" was about. *I've had enough, I've seen enough, I've had it all, I'm giving up,* Michael sang as the band crunched and blasted behind him.

From New York to Miami, Florida, to Antioch, Tennessee, to Birmingham, Alabama, to Baton Rouge, Louisiana. Heading west for half a dozen shows in Texas, up to Missouri, Illinois, Indiana, and

Michigan, to upstate New York and on and on into October, then November. They continued working on new songs along the way, and as they settled into the fall leg of the tour, they were performing as many as four new songs during the set. Like "The Wake-Up Bomb," most were big, loud, and blurry, the products of musicians who had spent the year seeing the world through the window of a fast-moving tour bus. *Distance is my tendency*, Michael sings in "Binky the Doormat." In "Undertow" the road mania becomes a wall of water closing over the singer's head. *I'm drowning*, he repeats in the chorus, and Mike, tracing a higher melody, fills in the rest of the thought: *Breathing ourselves*. And while the singer of "The Wake-Up Bomb" struts and preens like a character off of *Monster*, he's stopped believing his own hype: *My head's on fire in high esteem*.

The last three shows were a homecoming stand in Atlanta, at the eighteen-thousand-capacity Omni Coliseum. A camera crew shot all three nights, capturing performances for what would become the *Road Movie* concert film, released the next year. The end of the tour, along with the hometown setting, prompted a little goofing around. The first night's encore included a cover of Suicide's "Ghost Rider," and the next night's encores worked in Blue Öyster Cult's "(Don't Fear) The Reaper." And though Michael made a point during the final show of saying how unsentimental he was about the end of the tour, the band still surprised the audience, and possibly themselves, by pulling out "Radio Free Europe." ("Let's do it!" Mike shouted just after they finished "Departure." "Yeah, fuck yeah, why not," Michael said.) It was a sluggish rendition, grungy and about half a beat too slow, but after such a long and unexpectedly jarring year, they seemed thrilled to be able to play it at all. The usual show closer, "End of the World," came next, but the night and the tour weren't over until they stomped through a thudding, sloppy version of the Troggs' "Wild Thing." Finally, the sweaty, exhausted band members took their final bows, waved, and left the stage. It was the last full show the four of them would ever play together.

They all went home to rest, but not for long. So many things were going on, all at once. In January 1996 the band got together at John

Keane's studio in Athens to start working on the songs they'd written and partially recorded during the *Monster* tour. They worked sporadically through February, then upped sticks to Seattle in early March, where they worked in the Bad Animals studio through mid-April. The initial plan to build the new album entirely from the soundcheck recordings went by the wayside when they started coming up with newer songs they liked even better.

Both the new and newer songs echoed the blur and blare of the road, of the relentless pace of a life lived in the spotlight, of the media that both served their interests and, in turn, served them up like so much fresh-sliced roast. For all the creative energy they had going, most of the songs had a flat, monochromatic feeling. As if they had been written while in a defensive crouch, absorbing one blow, girding for the next. The only thing harder than not getting what you want is getting even more than you'd hoped for. *I attain my dream, I lost myself,* Michael sang in "Leave," over distorted guitar growl, pounding drums, and a relentlessly shrieking siren. *I know it well, ugly and sweet.*

Everyone had their appetites, and Jefferson Holt was no exception. He was a courtly fellow well known for his kindness and progressive sensibility, but he was also a little eccentric, with a few eyebrow-raising habits. Even before R.E.M. came into his life, Holt reportedly kept a Polaroid camera behind the counter of the North Carolina record store where he worked and used it to snap photos of attractive women who came in to shop. He was also said to keep an illustrated history of erotica on the coffee table in his living room, and to doff all but his underpants when in his home, even when entertaining friends and other company.[4] None of those things are crimes, though it's hard to know how the women in the shop felt about being photographed. And none of these things were a secret from the members of R.E.M. when they invited Holt to join their touring group and then serve as their manager.

And if Holt was a sexual libertine, he was not the only passenger in their van who could have been described that way. They were healthy young men who spent a lot of time away from home, in a traveling rock band that made them the center of attention nearly everywhere they went. It was easy for all of them to meet new friends with similar enthusiasms. "They probably slept with all their fans in those days," says Karen Glauber, a college radio disc jockey who went on to work for I.R.S. Records. "I was talking to Bertis about it recently and I told him, 'You have no idea what sluts your boys were.' He was like, *'Really!'* He had no idea."[5]

We can only assume that everyone had a good time. That they were of age, and clear-minded enough to give their consent, and then walk away with happy memories and maybe even a friend they might see when their paths crossed again. R.E.M. and their associates were nice young men, it seems. Mostly. "Jefferson never did anything with me to make me lose my trust in him," says Ingrid Schorr, who knew them all from the start. "He never did anything to me, but I've seen him be pretty sleazy."[6] Apparently he wasn't the only one, as Michael told the newspaper *The Guardian* in 2020 when the reporter asked to whom he'd like to apologize. "Everyone I slept with before the age of twenty-seven, because I was a selfish, cold-ass bitch."[7]

"New Test Leper" was one of the new songs they worked on in Seattle, built around a fast-strummed acoustic guitar, an organ pad, and shaker percussion. The acoustic guitar and understated percussion put it squarely in the folkier end of R.E.M.'s catalog, as does its discussion of faith and how the words of Jesus can be distorted. But Michael's lyrics, voicing the thoughts of a man appearing on a television talk show, describe a scene from a celebrity's life. And not just that, but a celebrity mourning an appearance that went sideways when he attempted to refute his host's bullying religious views. The song aims for social commentary, a denunciation of the sort of small-minded evangelicals who use faith as a cudgel against the weak and the different. But this isn't about the persecuted or the downtrodden. It's the tale of a celebrity who finds himself on the wrong TV show, getting bullied by a bunch of dicks. Whether he knows it or not, his real problem seems to be his own hubris. *I thought I might help them understand*, he proclaims. Sadly, no one is interested. The other guests shout him down, the host cuts to commercial. Ridiculed and ignored, the benighted celebrity thinks again of the Bible and identifies with Jesus's lowliest friends. *Call me a leper.*

Look, everyone has problems. The angst of a celebrity is still angst; nobody likes to be insulted and humiliated, let alone on television. But it's hard to tell exactly what this glimpse into such a rarefied world is intended to achieve, other than to make us feel ooky about the recurring references to actual *lepers*, whose problems are so much more real and profound than those of a guy who has a bad day on the talk show circuit.

At one point during the recording, a few executives from Warner Bros. Records came up to Seattle to hear the new tracks. What they heard made their mouths water. The album was, by their estimation, packed with hit singles. This was excellent news for the Warner executives, and also for R.E.M., and not just because the top people at their record company were now that much more motivated to promote their next release. It was also the last album on the contract R.E.M. had signed in 1988. And given what was taking place within Warner Bros., it could not have been a more perfect time for R.E.M. to be heading into contract negotiations.

"Be Mine" was one of the songs that chimed with hit potential. Based on a delicious, elegantly modulating chord progression Mike came up with during an all-night bus ride, the tune begins quietly, just Mike's guitar (taken from the demo he recorded on the bus) and Michael's gentle protestations of love. At first his love language is childlike, evoking the Easter Bunny, a Christmas tree, then fairy tales about birds and the lion with the thorn in his paw. But as the music builds—drums, bass, another layer of guitar, and the wail of a synthesizer—he dines on lotus and peyote and his imagery becomes epic. Sacred fountains, temples, the Ganges River, a vast and stormy sea. *And if you make me your religion,* he sings at one point, *I'll give you all the room you need.* It looks daffy, maybe even a little sinister on the page. What kind of maniac offers himself as a deity? But the music is so lovely, and the layers of sound so overwhelming, it makes sense.

———

Playing music with other people is maybe a little like sex. You keep your clothes on, you stand a respectable distance apart, but there's a physicality and an intimacy to the act. A rhythm is established. A sound, a feel. The energy builds. The pace might quicken. Thoughts are intuited but rarely spoken. Sometimes you think you're doing one thing, but then someone does something else and it's even more perfect than what you intended. When it's done, you look at each other and smile, or sometimes laugh. *That was fucking amazing*, someone might say. Or maybe that's just what they're thinking.

One day in Seattle, Bill walked into the studio and found Mike playing a little piano figure. *Dee-dee-dee-DEET.* Over and over again. *Dee-dee-dee-DEET.* He went to his drums, found the rhythm, started playing a light but vaguely funky pattern. *Boom-boom-POP, bah-boom-boom-POP.* When Peter came in, he picked up a bass and started playing with them, a simple four-note part, tracing the root chord. It was a midtempo groove, a kind of Ennio Morricone vibe, something out of a modern *The Good, the Bad and the Ugly*. The whole thing came together very quickly. They played it through, recorded it, and built it up. Mike added a piano solo, chords, and notes tumbling here and there. He was thinking about Thelonious Monk when he played it, though he wasn't certain he knew what Monk sounded like. Michael listened, scratched out some lyrics about bad breaks, things falling apart, then a title: "How the West Was Won and Where It Got Us." It became the leadoff track. Later they all said it was their favorite song on the album.

Love is grand. Sex can be fun. As "Be Mine" implies, sex with someone you love can feel like religion. Two souls touching, intermingling, ascending briefly to heaven, then drifting down to earth cradled in each other's arms. But sex with someone you don't love can be empty and sad. And sex with someone you work for, particularly if you're not entirely sure you want to have sex with them, can be beyond dispiriting. That's when passion can evolve into something else entirely. A wielding of power. An expression of fear. Two people can fall into bed, even repeatedly, uttering words they either don't mean or wish they didn't have to say.

A woman at R.E.M.'s office in Athens said Jefferson Holt, her boss, had propositioned her. She didn't make an official complaint with the state's equal opportunity office or file a lawsuit, but she did complain to the band members, who declared themselves shocked and launched a monthslong investigation. Holt denied the charge, heatedly and repeatedly, but apparently there had been a relationship between the two. When the investigation was completed, his association with R.E.M. ended. In mid-June, Holt and the band announced a separation agreement that involved quite a bit of money and extremely strict restrictions on any of them ever uttering a word about what had happened between the band and its former manager.

What's more, the parties were also forbidden from saying anything critical about the other in public, or else they'd face hefty civil penalties. But someone leaked something to the *Los Angeles Times* in June, resulting in a story headlined, "R.E.M.'s Former Manager Denies Allegations of Sex Harassment." Hmm. Who could have done the leaking? And why? Asked for a comment, the band released this statement: "The reasons for this decision and terms of the termination are private and confidential, and no further discussion of these matters will be made by any of the parties." Holt said this: "I've become more interested in other things in life and wanted to spend more time pursuing those interests. I'm happier than I have been in a long time."[8]

It was not an amicable parting. From that point forward, no member of R.E.M. has uttered Holt's name in public, even when describing long-ago events in which he played a significant, even crucial, role. Recounting their past, they merely pretend the manager they treated, and listed on their albums, as a fifth band member never existed. When they dusted off "Little America" in live shows a decade after Holt's departure, Michael changed the concluding line, *Jefferson, I think we're lost* to *Washington, I think we're lost*. Revisionist history. A quarter-century after the rupture, the anger is still pal-pable. When his name comes up in conversation with anyone from R.E.M., their faces grow steely and their eyes narrow. Holt refers to them only as "the band that cannot be named," this in part because of the limitations imposed on all of them in the financial agreement.

The same limitations make it impossible to know for certain if sexual harassment, or even just sexualizing what was supposed to be a work environment, was entirely to blame for the rupture between R.E.M. and their manager. Assuming it played a significant role in what was a jarring disruption to the band's operations, it would stand as the most progressive act, creative or otherwise, R.E.M. ever made. In an era in which men, and not just the ones in the decadent, male-dominated world of rock 'n' roll, commonly treated the workplace as a sexual game farm in which employees served as quarry, such antics were tolerated, even encouraged. But the members of R.E.M., no matter their own indulgences, apparently drew a hard line around their office and the women who worked there.

42

. . . And Where It Got Us

While the band was putting the final touches on *New Adventures in Hi-Fi*, the delightful name they gave their new album, Bertis Downs prepared to negotiate a new contract with the executive team at Warner Bros. Records. All the chips were on R.E.M.'s side of the table, and not just because the band had sold so many more records than anyone had ever expected when they signed their first contract, in 1988. Due to a shift in management at the record company's corporate parent, Time Warner, Warner Bros.'s longtime chairman Mo Ostin and company president Lenny Waronker had both resigned in 1994, ending decades of stability at the record company. A series of ill-advised decisions at the corporate headquarters in New York kept the record company in chaos for nearly two years and threw its future in doubt. When Warner Bros.' reins were finally handed to Russ Thyret, a roundly admired holdover from the Ostin-Waronker days, his team identified R.E.M. as the most prominent link to the company's golden era. Keeping the band at the label became the company's top priority.

Downs, working under the catchall title of adviser and thus no longer serving as the band's attorney, hired an outside counsel to help work through the terms. They spoke to representatives of other companies too, including Mo Ostin and Lenny Waronker, who were now running DreamWorks Records, the musical arm of the entertainment complex cofounded by Steven Spielberg, David Geffen, and Jeffrey Katzenberg. Whether those were serious negotiations or merely ploys to turn up the heat on their current label is unclear.

The talks with Warner Bros. shifted into higher gear in mid-August. The principals set up in a hotel in Orange County, not far from where the annual sales convention of Warner-Elektra-Atlantic, the umbrella organization for Time Warner's many record companies, was taking place. The convention loomed over the Warner team and created a deadline. "Our goal was to reach an agreement and come back and tell the assembled sales reps at WEA that we had just re-signed them," says David Altschul, then the head of business affairs for Warner Bros. Records.[1] After two years of turmoil, the executives were desperate to bring some good news to their sales force, evidence that the company's future could still be as bright as its past. As the clock ticked, the numbers got larger. When they reached toward the astronomical, the mood at the R.E.M. end of the negotiating table brightened. Then the skies opened and the sun broke through.

In the midst of the convention's Saturday afternoon session, a special announcement was made. The members of R.E.M. had a message for everyone. Bertis Downs strolled onstage holding a piece of paper and began to read. They had all done so much good work together in the past few years, he recited. *Let's keep it going!* R.E.M. was staying with Warner Bros. The WEA salespeople jumped to their feet and cheered. Some were said to have wept for joy. The reactions of the members of R.E.M. went unrecorded, but a few tears might not have been surprising. The deal they had reached was the biggest in the history of the recording industry, worth an estimated $80 million. That top-line number might have been aspirational—a calculation based on potential royalties assuming the next few records netted the astronomical sales numbers the band had achieved on their previous five records. But the guaranteed payments for each album would still be immense, and the potential for sales in the multimillions still seemed overwhelming. No matter what happened, R.E.M., whose members had been floating in a flood tide of record royalties, publishing royalties, and tour proceeds for close to a decade already, would earn, by the most conservative estimates, a shit-ton of money.

The blowback started before the new record came out, before the details of the rather astonishing new contract they signed with Warner Bros. Records had been finalized. But after sixteen years together, throughout which they had cultivated a nearly unblemished reputation as the hippest, most artistically pure, and yet refreshingly nice guys in rock 'n' roll, perhaps a reckoning was overdue.

The *Los Angeles Times* published its anonymous leak-sourced story about the reasons for Holt's departure in late June, just as the British music magazine *Mojo* was gearing up to publish a cover story on the band. Though *Mojo* had been around for only a few years, the size of the magazine's readership—and its reputation for publishing thoughtful stories about art-forward acts—should have made the band happy to speak to its reporter. But the entire R.E.M. organization was being jolted by the Holt investigation just when the *Mojo* writer, Barney Hoskyns, came looking for interviews. When they sent him away, Hoskyns turned to other sources for information. His story, published on the magazine's cover with the headline "R.E.M.: The Final Act?," relied on anonymous quotes and a generous amount of speculation to posit, among other things, that the band might well break up soon.

It wasn't an entirely far-fetched proposition. As Hoskyns detailed, the rigors of the *Monster* tour had sent three-quarters of the band to the hospital. The four members had scattered across the country, only a few years after Mike said their proximity was crucial and that any one of them moving away from Athens would be "destructive." And then there was Holt's departure, which at least some of the nameless insiders considered terribly unfair, given that the band was about to enter into what would almost certainly be an enormous new recording contract. And hadn't they said they would play one final concert on December 31, 1999, and break up just as the second hand swept the world into the twenty-first century? Yes, they had. Jokingly, but still. Only three years earlier, Mike had more or less confirmed that they were contemplating packing it in: "R.E.M.

can't last forever . . . You get too old for that kind of thing."[2] Still, Hoskyns included a generous number of quotes from his insiders about how strong the new album was, along with his own assertion that the musicians "remain resolutely idealistic after all these years— still rooted in a punk-rock aesthetic that would forbid them turning into undignified breadheads."

What Hoskyns and his *Mojo* editors didn't know, or didn't care about, was how the article would be received by the band and its record company. Not very well, as it turned out. When *Mojo* editor Mat Snow heard from Warner publicist Barbara Charone, she was, in his words, "incandescent."[3] Confronting Snow with the full rage of Warner Bros. Records, she pulled all of the company's advertisements from the magazine and promised that no member of R.E.M. would ever again utter a word to a reporter from *Mojo*. Snow was mostly unperturbed by the threats. *Mojo* had not only a sizable readership, but one whose core of educated, prosperous thirty-to-forty-five-year-olds amounted to ground zero of the record company's target demographic. Warner Bros. couldn't spurn them for long without hurting the prospects of their other artists. But as Snow told the American music writer Jim DeRogatis, it was a sobering glimpse into a band that had become so big and powerful, it had come to "see press merely as an aspect of promotion as opposed to what you might call journalism."[4]

Meanwhile, DeRogatis, a Chicago-based writer, was working on his own story for *Request*, a music magazine published by the Musicland record store chain. He was in the thick of it that summer when news broke that R.E.M. was about to become the highest-paid recording act in the history of the music business. To DeRogatis, who had followed the band's career since they were skinny outsiders traveling in a beat-up van, this was jarring news indeed.

Ushered into R.E.M.'s company to write a feature pegged to the new album, DeRogatis joined a small clutch of reporters allowed to observe the band as they filmed the video for "Bittersweet Me," slated to be the second single on *New Adventures in Hi-Fi*. To start, he noted how predictable R.E.M.'s media routine had become. In earlier times they had invited writers to visit them in Athens, often taking them into their homes and to their favorite restaurants, to holiday parties, and more. But since ascending to major-label stardom, they had ritualized their media availabilities, allowing a small number of writers measured portions of access that would include scene-setting doses of "color" (e.g., watching them shoot a video), then one or more interviews during which one or more band members described their new record as the band's best ever. Allowed access only to Mike and Peter, both of whom were greeting reporters in one of those RV-like portable dressing rooms you see near movie sets, DeRogatis had plenty of questions for both of them. And he heard and reported far more than what they said, or intended to say.

The story, published in the fall issue of *Request*, was withering: a catalog of apostasies rendered against the church of alternative music and culture. It started on the set of the video, where DeRogatis noted that Michael was lip-synching his vocal ("something he vowed he'd never do"), then observed Mike having a hissy fit over having to share his trailer with Peter (they had separate rooms within the vehicle, but still). When the bassist submitted to an interview, he was extremely peevish, particularly when asked about the insiders who'd provided the blind quotes in the just-published *Mojo* story. (His directive to the band's loose-lipped intimates: "Mind your own fucking business.") From there DeRogatis described the astronomical terms of their latest major-label deal, then ripped the band for charging an average of $40 to $50 for tickets to concerts on the *Monster* tour, twice what younger alternative acts such as Pearl Jam and Green Day had charged their fans. And speaking of concerts, what ever happened to Peter's promise, back in the 1980s, that R.E.M. would never play halls with more than five thousand seats? "The band now regularly breaks promises it made early in its career," DeRogatis wrote.

Ouch.

Writing as an outsider with more contempt for than knowledge of the music industry, DeRogatis strayed toward the absurd, as when he asserted that the size of their new record contract would make the band hostage to their company's demands for market-friendly product. R.E.M. had never signed a contract that didn't grant them complete control over their music, and at this point they wielded more power than ever before. But he was right about his central point: they had come quite a distance from the anti-commercial indie band they had once proclaimed themselves as being.

But was that really such a bad thing?

The members of R.E.M. had always been smart about their decisions. Their instincts had also been good, both in the loftiness of their artistic ambitions and their commitment to the hardscrabble labor necessary to build an audience. And their music, like all great rock 'n' roll, was about something larger and grander than songs, albums, and shows. It was about being an outsider, about working against the grain of mainstream society, about being by, for, and often about the artists, the freaks, and the weirdos in the room. The secret to their success was their ability to locate the sweet spot where the band could be, in Peter's words, "the acceptable edge of the unacceptable stuff."[5]

Rather than soft-pedal their eccentricities, they made them a selling point. Which was daring on one level, and extremely conventional on another. For the simple reason that rock 'n' roll has always been about rebellion. It happens over and over again, each new wave of artists subverting whatever came before them. Elvis undid Sinatra; the Beatles supplanted Elvis; the Sex Pistols rode over the horizon to gun down the increasingly fat and happy hippie generation. What they all had in common, and what R.E.M. offered in their time, was an alternative to the assumptions and prejudices, the sheer terribleness, of the dominant culture. But what happens when the rebels get to be so successful they *become* the dominant culture? That's the inevitable reward for successful revolutionaries, and also when rock 'n' roll gets complicated.

Indeed, the vastness of R.E.M.'s success in the mid-1990s was breathtaking. In the United States alone, *Monster* shipped platinum on the day of its release, cleared double platinum a few weeks later, then triple platinum, then went quadruple platinum in early August 1995. The album sold millions of additional copies around the world, making it the fifth-straight R.E.M. album to sell in the multimillions and the third in a row with worldwide sales in the eight figures. The global *Monster* tour, which included 113 shows (a slightly reduced number due to the members' various illnesses), drew nearly three million attendees around the world, grossing an estimated $95 million in ticket sales alone. Adjusted for inflation, that's close to $200 million in 2023 dollars, and it doesn't include what they earned on sales of T-shirts, concert programs, and all the other associated merchandise. Then came the $80 million deal with Warner Bros. Records.

How did this happen? So many of the artistic goals and policies R.E.M. had set for themselves during their first decade, the buried vocals and unparsable lyrics on the early records, the rejected offers to tour with U2 and Squeeze, the refusal to lip-synch or to put in anything more than brief cameo appearances in their own video clips, might have slowed their commercial progress. But it had also been a crucial part of establishing their bona fides as cultural renegades. And yet, bringing about cultural revolution wasn't *all* they were after. As much as they'd set out to subvert the mainstream expectations of pop music, they also wanted their music to be heard. They worked hard to be a good band, and when that work began to pay off, they worked even harder and got even better. Better performers, better songwriters, better record makers, all of which helped them build an even bigger audience. Still, becoming a big deal didn't change their core values or their conception of themselves as people. When they looked in the mirror, they recognized the artists, freaks, and weirdos they'd always been. And what could be artier, freakier, and weirder than injecting their outsider ideas into the heart of the mainstream? Pylon was not the only Athens band that imagined its career as a kind of portable art installation. The difference was that each member of R.E.M. came into their band already dreaming rock-star dreams.

"You pick up an electric guitar when you're a kid, you want to be like your heroes," said Wayne Kramer, who cofounded the revolutionary proto-punk band the MC5 in 1963. Kramer was addressing a question about Bruce Springsteen, but he could have been talking about R.E.M. or Nirvana or dozens of other artists who have publicly agonized over the cost of fame. "You don't say, 'Well, I only want to be *this* big, not *that* big, because it's more manageable, and I'm a humble guy.'" The MC5 might have been radical leftists, Kramer continued, but they really and truly wanted it all. If they failed to achieve it, it wasn't because they were conscientious objectors. They simply failed to get across. "I never wanted to be just *kinda* big," he concluded. "That's *ridiculous*."[6]

That certainly was Bill's attitude when he dropped out of college to focus on R.E.M.'s career and then insisted that Mike and Michael do the same. It was still his attitude when he rejected Peter's idea that the band spend 1995 touring clubs instead of the mega-arenas they could, and did, fill most nights. "He said, *No, we're gonna do what we're supposed to do*," Bill's ex-wife, Mari, recalls. The drummer stuck to the plan and made sure his bandmates did the same, and look where it got them. And they'd gotten there with their artistry, their ideals, and their minds and bodies generally intact. Heading into the fall of 1996, with a few close scrapes and one personal/organizational catastrophe behind them, with another strong album on its way into the shops, and their financial security—and thus their artistic freedom—set for life, the four members of R.E.M. had everything they'd ever dreamed of, and too much more to mention.

43

I'm Outta Here

The lead single for *New Adventures in Hi-Fi* was "E-Bow the Letter," whose mystifying title was a cobbling together of the name of the electronic device Peter used to get the howling guitar tone on the song and the fact that Michael's lyrics were the text of a letter he'd been writing during the *Monster* tour. Midtempo and dark, the music had an engaging slinkiness, and Michael's epistolary lyrics describe the detached reality of a wanted man (*This fame thing, I don't get it / I wrap my hand in plastic to try to look through it*). Descending like a hawk, the voice of Patti Smith swoops over the chorus, drifts in for a few lines, then takes off again. "E-Bow" scraped into *Billboard*'s top fifty, but just barely, peaking at number forty-nine before it, too, flapped out of sight.

The soundcheck songs filled in most of the album with reverberations from the *Monster* year, glam bluster muffled by road-weariness. But the final track, "Electrolite," glimmered like a new dawn. Singing atop a cheery piano riff backed by a folky acoustic guitar, lightly spanked drums, and banjo, Michael describes the lights of Los Angeles as viewed from atop the Hollywood Hills. Surrounded by film stars and swelled with hope, he senses the end of one century and the start of the next one with something like contentment. A guiro hums, a fiddle joins the party. On the cusp of immense change, it's a moment of respite, a gathering of wits, a foot on the threshold. In the end, the music stops and Michael's voice hangs in the air. *I'm not scared*, he concludes. *I'm outta here.*

Released on September 9, 1996, *New Adventures* was greeted with the usual critical accolades and a fast leap to the highest reaches of the album charts. They had to settle for number two, however, and then a relatively speedy descent. For the first time in a decade, an R.E.M. album only just squeaked to platinum status. Overseas sales added up to another million copies, but after the multi-platinum performances of the previous three albums it was a notable come-down. And it wasn't just them, as Mike noted on Irish television in 1998. New albums by U2, the Smashing Pumpkins, and other pre-eminent rock bands had faltered in the past year or two. "We're in very strange place in the world of rock 'n' roll right now," he said. "If you don't have a hit single, the bulk of the people are not going to go out and buy this record." He spoke of computers, the internet, all the new media distracting people from the music that used to define their identities. "There's just so much competition for kids' attention and your money; the days of a ten-million-album-selling rock band could be over."

It was that light on the eastern horizon again, the dawn of a new century. "Rock 'n' roll as we knew it is gone."[1]

The last R.E.M. project of 1996 came in early November in Los Angeles, a three-day shoot for the video of "Electrolite," slated to be the third and final clip for the *New Adventures* album. As visualized by the director Peter Care, it combined shots of the band members and of people in the street. The ordinary Angelenos, young and old, black and white, male and female, animated various kinds of captivity, chained to street signs, lampposts, palm trees, and one another, drag-ging balls and chains around their ankles, while the band members express freedom. In the first band scenes, the musicians' images are upside down, a (perhaps unwelcome) reprise of the notorious quarry video Michael shot for "Fall on Me." The image rights itself after a minute or so as we see, but don't hear, the individual band members speaking enthusiastically to some unseen interlocutor. There is lip-synching and slapstick, light psychedelia. It starts to feel like a lost episode of the Monkees' TV show.

They're playing their instruments dressed in neon shades of satin. They're zooming across the desert in dune buggies. They set up in band formation in the parking lot of a truck stop, and on a street. As they play, they perform magical feats, tilting sideways until they're parallel to the ground, falling over and through the surface of the earth, popping up into the air. They all get their close-ups, their moments to shine. But given what was about to happen, it's hard not to focus on Bill. We'll never see him like this again.

So here he is. Smiling warmly and gesturing as he talks, soundlessly, to the other side of the camera. He whacks a set of congas, wearing a gold spangled top, orange satin pants, and a bright green feather boa. Now he's sitting in a chair in a yellow satin shirt going at a pair of bongos, his upper body moving fluidly with the rhythm of his playing. He looks young and handsome, a small smile on his lips, happily lost in his music. The dune buggy sequence is mostly fast cuts, but when the camera finds the drummer, it lingers for a moment until it catches his eye. He holds up a hand in greeting, then spins his wheel to the right and zooms off in another direction.

The clip's final moments have the musicians set up in the parking lot, and then in the street, digitally rendered into various uncanny positions. At one point Bill seems to grow into a giant, stooping farther and farther to play the drums shrinking beneath him. As the song moves into its final moments, everything goes berserk. Mike leaps into the air and hangs there, frozen. Peter shrinks into the ground and vanishes. In the final seconds Bill jets upward and hangs briefly in midair. When they made the video, this was just another moment in a cheerfully surreal clip, but in retrospect it's something else altogether. *I'm not scared,* Michael sings. *I'm outta here.* At which point R.E.M.'s drummer soars abruptly out of the picture.

The band took a few months off, then, in April 1997, went to Peter's house in Hawaii to work on songs for their next album. As always, Peter had a bunch of new material to share. He'd spent much of his time off in the studio he'd built in his house in Seattle, fiddling with synthesizers and other electronic doodads, coming up with atmospheric grooves that tilted toward electronica. Mike also had plenty of new tunes, and the two of them engaged in the usual push-me-pull-you, seeing what fit together, while Michael came in and out, listening, sketching melodies, thinking about words. Bill was there, too. Sort of.

He was sitting outside. He would pop in and listen but not say much of anything. He was walking on the beach. So, okay, he had a lot going on. His marriage to Mari was ending. A divorce could knock anyone sideways. Bill had also been particularly upset by the Jefferson Holt rupture. And now, in the wake of *New Adventures'* relative flop (if that's what you call an album that sells only two million copies), they had decided to end their run with Scott Litt and make their next album with a new producer. Bill was a big fan of stability, so maybe all that change was doing a number on his head. Anyone could have a bad week, right?

They all went back to their respective homes at the start of May. Peter set off on a tour called "The Magnificent Seven vs. the United States," a project he'd started with Scott McCaughey, the American Music Club's Mark Eitzel, and a few other musician friends. They barnstormed the country for a month, heading to a final performance on May 31 in Atlanta. The three other members of R.E.M. came to see the show and were expected to play a few songs together at the end. But by the time the encores rolled around, only Mike and Michael were still in the theater. Bill had slipped out a side door and was already on his way back to his farm.

Even in the earliest days, Bill had an eye on the exit. Late in 1980, the drummer started moonlighting with Love Tractor, the mostly instrumental band put together by art students Mark Cline, Armistead Wellford, and Mike Richmond. The band's first drummer was Kit Swartz, who left to devote himself more fully to his other band, the Side Effects. Bill loved Love Tractor's fluid instrumental style, so when they asked him to fill in at a show or two, he surprised the others by offering to join outright. He'd already dropped out of school to focus on music and could figure out a way to work them into the holes in R.E.M.'s schedule. He brought his drums to Love Tractor's rehearsal space and launched right in with them; he already knew their songs. When they played shows, he'd fall into a groove with bassist Armistead Wellford, those twin guitars spinning their curious textures on songs like "Hairy Beat" and "Chilly Damn Willy." When it was over he'd be laughing happily.

Soon Bill was overflowing with ideas and plans: they should play here, get some recording time there, really make a go of it. And that led to a question: "Are you guys ready to quit school and make this real?" Bill, it turned out, was ready to ditch R.E.M. and devote himself to Love Tractor. But he wasn't going to do that until the other guys went all in on the band, too. And as Cline recalls, that's where it ended. "I was so close to graduating, and Armistead was too," Cline says. "I knew I could be in school and do the band too. It was an art project for me. So I said, 'Naw, I gotta graduate first.' And he went to the R.E.M. guys to see if they'd drop out to focus on their band and they said yes."[2]

Bill recommitted himself to R.E.M. But, for a few moments at least, it was that close.

In most bands the drummer isn't quite so essential. Even the truly distinctive drummers, Charlie Watts in the Rolling Stones, Ringo Starr in the Beatles, Dave Grohl in Nirvana, don't touch the architecture of the music. They may elevate a song, but the writing, along with the conceptualizing of the band's sound, spirit, and identity, is the purview of the guitarist, the singer, the guys on the front line. This was not true in R.E.M. Bill not only was a composer of songs as central to the band's repertoire as "Driver 8," "Everybody Hurts," and "Man on the Moon" but also contributed key ideas to the arrangement of "Losing My Religion," among other songs. "His musicianship was super special," says Scott Litt. "I depended on him, and I know the guys did, too."[3] Particularly when it came to keeping songs tight and focused. "If anyone was going off into left field, Bill would be depended upon to say 'This is too much' or 'not enough,'" Litt continues.[4]

Nathan December, who joined the band for the 1995 tour and

worked with them on the songs that became *New Adventures*, says the other band members trusted their drummer's instincts. "He was the gut of the band. If a song passed Bill's litmus test, then it moved forward. And if he wasn't on board it got shitcanned. I saw that happen on the tour. And his instinct was real good. If he said a song didn't work, he was right." And, December continues, he was very clear about what made a song work: "Basically, it's gotta rock."[5]

The band returned to Athens at the start of October to work on studio demos of the songs for their new album. They had chosen Pat McCarthy, an Irish studio engineer who had worked on some *New Adventures* sessions and done some striking mixes for albums by Madonna and Patti Smith, to produce the new material. Peter came to town in the company of Scott McCaughey and Barrett Martin, a multi-instrumentalist who played the drums for the Seattle band the Screaming Trees. Peter had bought a drum machine for his home studio, and the demos he'd been making with the electronic gear made him think about new ways R.E.M. might approach drums and percussion. Which could also reignite Bill's interest by liberating him from the drum stool and allowing him to take up the guitar, keyboards, or any other instrument he felt like playing. Work at John Keane's studio started on October 3 and continued for a few days, with Peter, Mike, and Michael, supplemented by McCaughey and Martin. Obviously, someone was missing. "We kind of started thinking something weird was going on," McCaughey says. "But they weren't talking."[6]

What they weren't saying was that Bill had told the others that he'd had enough of being a pop star. He wasn't mad at anyone. He still loved playing music. But everything that went with it, the constant travel, the long hours in recording studios, having to perform in videos, and the many life-altering requirements of fame, had finally worn him out. After seventeen years of doing nothing but being in R.E.M., he didn't want to do it anymore. In fact, he *couldn't* do it anymore. He'd broken the news to Mike first, calling from his farm a few days before the sessions were supposed to begin. They'd talked a few times after that, but the bassist resisted telling the others until he was certain his old friend couldn't be swayed. Finally, the night before they were supposed to meet at Keane's studio, Mike called Peter and Michael and told them both, individually, to gird for trouble. *Bill's going to say something to you, and you won't want to hear it.* Neither of them guessed how sweeping, and final, his announcement would be.

First they wanted to make sure he wasn't depressed, and that he wasn't making an impulsive decision he'd regret later. Bill assured them he'd talked it through with several people, including a therapist, and he knew what he was doing. They tried bargaining with him: He didn't have to tour with them. They could do all their recording in Athens. He could play any instrument he wanted to play. No and no and no. Actually, Bill said the only thing that would convince him to stay was knowing that the band would dissolve if he departed. That had once been their promise to one another if any one of them decided to leave, but he was too big an R.E.M. fan to let that happen now. "I did not want to be the schmuck who broke up R.E.M.," he said later.[7] He'd stay with them under those circumstances, Bill said. "But I'll be miserable."

What could they say to that?

Some lingering questions were more difficult to pose. Mostly the ones about the effects of the aneurysm. Had something in Bill changed after the events of March 1, 1995? And if so, was it an emotional response to having a near-death experience? Or was it more neurological than that? Had the aneurysm and all that blood that soaked into his brain in the hours after his veins had burst done something to change his personality? One friend put it to me like this: "Before the aneurysm, Bill saw the world like an ordinary thirty-five-year-old man. But after that, he saw the world like a sixty-five-year-old." More cautious. More fearful. Something would come up that involved the band going to a different city and he'd shake his head. "Denver? Why do I want to go there? I didn't leave anything in *Denver.*"

But his ex-wife, Mari, says Bill's retirement talk began before Lausanne, before the *Monster* tour and even before *Monster* was recorded, when they first moved into the country and he settled into life on the farm. The peace, the quiet, the absence of crowds or anyone with urgent questions about this, that, and everything else. This was where he belonged, Bill said, not living the hectic, high-profile life of a damn rock star. So maybe it was time to call it a day. "I said, 'You're too young to retire. What are you going to do, ride around on your tractor all day?' "[8] He thought about it and agreed with her. Then he was back with the others, saying it was time to make a noisy rock album and get back on the road like a real rock band. If they didn't want to do that, he added, he'd quit the band. In retrospect, the paradoxes are clear, up to and including how he was, in effect, setting their course straight to Lausanne.

We should take a moment to discuss the eyebrow.

In terms of classical male beauty, Bill's unibrow, the dense bank of fur that stretches like an ancient land bridge from the far corner of one eye to the most distant corner of the other, is a problem. The sort of thing the other kids make sport of, that you would never see on a matinee idol, that an aspiring pop idol, or anyone concerned with looking like everyone else, would eliminate from his visage with extreme and rigorous prejudice. But for Bill and for R.E.M., it was an enormous asset. Because it was so very distinctive. And also a metaphor for who he was and who they were.

Which is to say, guys who were determined only to look like themselves and not care at all about how anyone else thought they should look. It became a trademark, a kind of logo. So much so that the only time the band put a recognizable portrait of a band member on an album cover during the first twenty-five years of their recording career was when they put Bill's face on 1986's *Lifes Rich Pageant*. Divided into two, the cover's bottom half shows a pair of buffalo. The top half is dominated by the top two-thirds of Bill's face, with that epic brow at the center of the image. It was their first album to sell enough copies to be certified gold.

They made the announcement at the end of the month. On October 31, all four band members sat together speaking to MTV News reporter Chris Connelly. Peter wore sunglasses. Michael's eyes looked red-rimmed, as if he'd just had a good cry. Mike looked steady, and Bill looked immensely relieved. Interviews were his least favorite thing, but this was the last one he'd ever have to do. Asked for his feelings, he was forthright. "I feel horrible," he said. "I wish it wasn't me. I wish one of these other guys would do this first." He talked about knowing what it took to make a record, the enthusiasm and inner mettle, and knowing he didn't have it anymore. That it wouldn't be fair to the other guys to be there giving anything less than his all. Asked if he had any words for R.E.M.'s fans, Bill looked into the camera.

"Thanks for giving me the greatest job a guy could ever have. I really mean that," he said, eyes glistening. "It's been a lot of fun right up until right now. And I'm sorry."[9]

44

Airportmen

A lot of things were unsettling about R.E.M.'s appearance at the massive two-day Tibetan Freedom Concert in Washington, D.C.'s RFK Stadium in mid-June 1998, and not all of them were the band's doing. But it was hard to get around what Michael chose to wear for his band's first concert appearance in nearly two and a half years. Which was also R.E.M.'s first-ever appearance without Bill Berry. It would have been stressful enough, given the large crowd (an estimated 66,000 people) and the wattage of the acts sharing the stage, including Radiohead, the Beastie Boys, the Fugees' Wyclef Jean, the Dave Matthews Band, and the Red Hot Chili Peppers.

To add to the pressure, the organizers had been forced to collapse the two-day concert into a single day when a bolt of lightning hit the stadium partway through the first day, sending at least one concert-goer to the hospital and forcing the cancellation of the rest of that day's sets. R.E.M., on tenterhooks, had to squeeze their performance into the next day's schedule. By the time they came out on Sunday afternoon, the tension was high on- and offstage. Musicians from the other bands, so many defining artists of the late 1990s, crowded the wings to see what the revamped R.E.M. would do. And here came Michael, dressed like . . . well, it was hard to say.

His shirt, a heavily patterned long-sleeved chemise in a kind of washed-out off-gray, was about three sizes too small, revealing the bottom half of his forearms and most of his gaunt midriff. Beneath that he sported an ankle-length sarong, also densely patterned, but in floral colors that neither reflected nor matched the color of his top. It looked uncomfortable, to say the least. And when the band launched into "Airportman," a heavily atmospheric electronic piece with no drums or apparent melody, the new-edition R.E.M. sounded about as magnetic as its singer's clothes made him look. The stadium audience sagged visibly. And though a quick pivot to "Losing My Religion" pulled the crowd to its feet a few minutes later, the rest of the band's eight-song set, consisting of three unfamiliar, largely electronic new songs, two tunes from the underloved *New Adventures in Hi-Fi*, and a set-closing "Man on the Moon," amounted to something less than an auspicious relaunch.

Work on the band's new album wasn't going nearly as well.

When they announced Bill's departure the previous October, Michael had described the challenge of a three-man R.E.M. like this: "I guess a three-legged dog is still a dog. It just has to learn how to run differently."[1] Looking on the bright side, it could be a rebirth. A way for a veteran band to reinvent itself into an entirely new phase of discovery and creativity.

The loss of their partner overwhelmed any thoughts of work that fall. When the band resumed their efforts in San Francisco in February 1998, they discovered that their three remaining legs no longer seemed to be connected to the same animal. Peter had added so much equipment to his home studio, including synthesizers, sequencers, and drum machines, he could bring in demos that sounded like finished recordings. Mike didn't know how to collaborate on those, or if Peter even wanted him to try. The bassist, meanwhile, no longer wanted to play the bass. He was much more interested in his own keyboards, while Michael, who had added minimalist keyboards and other instruments to the art-noise band Tanzplagen in the early 1980s, now felt pulled to the guitar, from which he could draw similarly rudimentary lines. So many things had changed, so many standard operating procedures peeled away, it felt as if they had evolved into a different creature altogether.

Whatever they were, they no longer seemed to speak the same language. Often they didn't speak at all. The work on the recordings went slowly, and painfully. They spent a lot of time at loggerheads, resolving some conflicts by working in two separate studios. After two months in San Francisco, they emerged with a handful of tracks that sounded less like traditional songs than banks of vaguely musical fog; sonically dense and yet amorphous, many with lyrics that were, to put it mildly, elliptical.

They also had a few tracks that sounded more like what the world, and they, had come to understand as R.E.M. songs. But a chill had leached into the studio air. Mike, never the most punctual person, took to showing up for sessions hours late, much to Peter's unhappiness. Already unmoored by Bill's departure, Michael sensed the growing disconnection between his remaining partners and felt his muse slip away. Words stopped coming, and stayed away for weeks, then months. As the sessions dragged on, Peter, whose hours in the studio meant taking time away from his wife and young daughters, grew even more resentful.

They left San Francisco in early April, resumed in Athens in mid-May, slammed through rehearsals for the Tibetan Freedom show in mid-June, then, with the album still unfinished and the intra-band relationships somewhere between distant and icy, felt themselves coming to the end of something. Realizing the situation was spiraling out of control, Bertis Downs petitioned the three band members to join him for a getaway in a remote lodge in Idaho, where they could talk, or perhaps shout, through their disagreements with no one but the trees and perhaps a passing moose to overhear. All three were skeptical that a resolution could be found. Peter was so unconvinced, he nearly didn't bother to go. But his wife, Stephanie, urged him to give it a shot, and after three days of talks that Michael described as "vomiting on one another," they found their way back to the band. R.E.M. finished recording and mixing the album during the second half of the summer, then prepared for a late October release. The album would be called *Up*.

Still raw from all the upheaval of the preceding year, the band opted not to mount the concert tour they had once assumed they'd use to promote the first album on their new contract with Warner. Instead they played a number of smaller but high-impact performances, starting the week before *Up*'s release with an acoustic set at Neil Young's annual Bridge School Benefit shows at the Shoreline Amphitheatre, in Mountain View, California. Playing with Scott McCaughey and drummer Joey Waronker, Lenny's son and a seasoned player fresh from engagements with Beck and Portland singer-songwriter Elliott Smith, as well as Ken Stringfellow, from the power-pop band the Posies, to fill out the sound, the band performed eight-song sets that opened with "Losing My Religion" and included two of the stronger, non-electronic tracks from *Up*, "Daysleeper" and the Beach Boys–like "At My Most Beautiful." In New York the next week, and then in a few media capitals in Europe, they made special TV appearances playing full-band sets of older favorites and a few new songs, including powerful new arrangements of the new album's "The Apologist" and "Walk Unafraid."

Back in New York by mid-November, they appeared on *Sesame Street*, joining the show's famous Muppets on a cheerful performance of "Shiny Happy People," revised for the occasion to "Furry Happy Monsters." When they made the original, candy-colored video for "Shiny Happy People" in 1991, Peter had appeared dour, not the least bit shiny, let alone happy. But now, as a forty-two-year-old father of four-year-old twin girls who were in the studio watching from just beyond the cameras,[2] he was all smiles, clearly delighted to strum a banjo along with the recorded track and dance with those silly, endlessly reassuring Muppets.

Reassurances. The title of the album provided one—upward and onward, despite everything—and the interviews given by all the current band members described a litany of others. As usual, they seemed to have agreed on the themes beforehand: that it had been a tough year, a hard album to make, a difficult transition following Bill Berry's departure. They had nearly broken up, maybe more than once, but had rediscovered themselves instead and emerged with, yes, that's right, the best album they'd ever made. "Who's to say that all the stress and strife and arguments and unspoken anger didn't make it a better record?" Peter said in the hourlong *This Way Up* documentary that the band produced to promote the album. "Because I think it's our best record." Old habits die hard, even for former R.E.M. members. When the VH1 video channel (MTV's second network, aimed toward older music fans) produced an R.E.M. episode of its *Behind the Music* documentary series, Bill sat for the camera and talked about the band's first record without him with a sweet, rueful smile. "When I heard it, I felt like a chump," he said. "I quit, and they make their best record."[3]

With fourteen songs adding up to more than sixty minutes of music, *Up* is long and, at times, elusive. "Airportman" opens the set, with its haze of looped synthetic and natural sounds. Michael sings in a low murmur, describing a man in an airport taking in the fluorescent light, the processed air, and the travelers standing passively on the moving floors. A guitar enters, feeding back on itself somewhere on the edge of the scene. *Labored breathing and sallow skin,* Michael breathes amid the whir and whoosh. *Great opportunity blinks, great opportunity blinks.*

For R.E.M. the opportunity was reinvention. Absent its drummer, who had also been the band member most focused on songcraft, they set themselves adrift on the sonic tides. "You're in the Air," "Sad Professor," and a few others are ambient and still, hazy and nearly arrhythmic, the work of what sounds like an entirely new band. Often they seem to be consciously avoiding themselves. "Hope" has the ringing chords and driving melody of a tuneful rocker, but tucked into the synthesizer icebox. "The Apologist" is dark and crafty, its verses building to a riveting chorus—*I'm sorry, so sorry, so sorry*—that, on a different album, could have been volcanic. Here, not so much. "Walk Unafraid" also tilts toward the anthemic, then goes the other way, crowding the chorus with synthesizers, auto-drum clicks, and atonal guitar howl.

A few songs edge back to familiar territory. "Lotus" is a new variation on the *Monster* sound, with the synthesizer lines strung through electric piano, a blazing guitar hook, and pounding drums courtesy of Joey Waronker. "Daysleeper" sounds closer to *Out of Time*, with an acoustic guitar foundation, pensive verses, and ascending, spiraling choruses. The delicate love song "At My Most Beautiful" tips its hat to the Beach Boys' *Pet Sounds*, with natural piano, organ, a huffing bass harmonica, cellos, stuttering drums, and dense backing harmonies. Still, the album's final song, "Falls to Climb," returns to the electronic realm with peals of synthetic sound. The song, and the album, ends in the most heroic terms. *Meeee*, Michael sings. *I am free.* Then he sings it again, *I am freeeee*, holding on to the key word for as long as he can, his voice rising, falling, and rising again. *Free.*

Unleashed on a large and eager American audience, *Up* shot instantly to number three on the *Billboard* chart, where it resided for a week, just long enough for their most fervent fans to give it a spin and tell their friends about what they heard. Then came another unexpected sound, the whistling of the album in free fall, hurtling out of the top ten, then off the chart after just sixteen weeks—six fewer than *New Adventures* had enjoyed and scarcely more than half of *Murmur*'s thirty weeks on the list. Granted, the band's first album had never climbed higher than number thirty-six in 1983, and *Up* still sold enough copies to win gold certification. But it was the first R.E.M. album in more than a dozen years to not sell enough copies to yield platinum. Part of the problem was that "Daysleeper," the single released two weeks before the album's appearance, barely cracked the top sixty of the Hot 100, and did only moderately better on the other charts (Alternative Airplay, Adult Top 40, Mainstream Rock, etc.) before it too sank without much of a trace.

Overseas, and particularly in England, where Britpop bands such as Blur, Suede, and Oasis still defined the airwaves, it was a completely different story. In the UK, *Up* jumped to number two on the album chart and stayed in the upper reaches for months, thanks to the strength of "Daysleeper," which rose as high as number six on the singles chart. *Up* ultimately sold more than 1.5 million copies in the UK and Europe, nearly three times what it sold in the United States.

Critical reaction on both sides of the Atlantic was almost entirely positive. Writing in *Rolling Stone*, Ann Powers gave the album a four-star review, while the influential UK music magazine *Q* also awarded four stars. David Stubbs, writing in the UK's *Uncut*, termed it an "unexpected return to peak form."[4] What made it so unexpected, apart from the loss of Bill Berry, was unclear. Perhaps it was the fact that R.E.M., in the wake of nearly two decades of experience, tens of millions of records sold, and untold scores of millions of dollars in profits, had no business making a record as experimental and vital as *Up*.

The songs on *Up*, and perhaps R.E.M. as an entity, didn't enchant American listeners in 1998 in quite the way the band and its records had during the first half of the decade. And maybe it had as much to do with larger cultural tides as anything else. In the United States the year's dominant albums were almost all by pop, soul, or hip-hop performers. The most successful rock albums, apart from a greatest hits collection by U2, were by the mainstream likes of Kid Rock and the Offspring. Guys with guitars, the classic rock formation, had ebbed. The sounds of urgency, avalanching drums, caterwauling guitars, and singers whose thoughts came in a snarl or scream had lost their primacy.

But not everywhere.

Almost exactly a year after the Tibetan Freedom Concert, R.E.M. stepped onstage at the Glastonbury Festival, in England, facing an even larger audience than the one they'd faced the previous June in Washington, D.C. It was the same iteration of the band, Peter, Mike, and Michael, joined by Joey Waronker, Scott McCaughey, and Ken Stringfellow, armed with the same new songs from *Up*. But as the closing act on the storied festival's Friday night, with 95,000 festivalgoers primed and ready for their set, the band delivered a significantly different version of the act they'd presented at RFK Stadium a year earlier. This time "Airportman" was limited to walk-out music, a little textured sound for the audience to listen to while contemplating the neon symbols and pictures that glowed and blinked on the backdrop. A two-headed snake here, a pair of upward arrows there, a fish, a radio tower, and, centered at the very top, a big, shining R.E.M.

When the musicians emerged, the ambient music faded and

Michael took the microphone. He had a band of light blue makeup around his eyes and wore a blue button-up shirt over loose blue athletic pants, white stripes up the sides. "We finally fuckin' made it to Glastonbury," he said, triggering an ovation and then the drum pattern of "Lotus," the most stage-ready of the songs on *Up*. The opening riff spurred another cheer—*Up* was huge in England—and from there the onslaught began. The swaggering decadence of "Lotus" to the multimedia breakdown of "What's the Frequency, Kenneth?" into "So Fast, So Numb," the road warrior smashup from *New Adventures*, then a blisteringly intense arrangement of *Up*'s "The Apologist." Next came "Fall on Me," the first song anyone would think of as an oldie, since it was all of thirteen years old, but the opening notes of "Daysleeper," which had scaled the UK charts just a few months earlier, got a much bigger cheer. When the time came to set up the first hit single they'd scored a dozen years earlier, Michael made certain to establish that they weren't doing it just to be agreeable showmen. "This is technically known as a crowd-pleaser, but we happen to fuckin' like *enjoy* playing it, okay?" He shrugged. "Hope you like it." A short landslide of drums launched a sped-up "The One I Love."

Half an hour into the set, they had the festival crowd electrified, and they'd done it almost entirely with songs that were less than five years old. Nearly half of what they'd played had come from their latest album, released less than a year earlier. Four years after their global superstardom had peaked, in the wake of losing a member and nearly abandoning their group identity, they had emerged strong and sleek, performing a new version of what they'd been doing since they played Kathleen O'Brien's birthday party in the church in 1980. Even after everything, the art and the politics, the videos and the record deals, the headlines and the vast fortunes, it always came down to this. The songs, the performance, the power to do exactly what they wanted at any given moment.

"This is me and Peter's favorite song," Michael declared. "Grab yourself a partner and start to cry." The mournful, elegiac "Sweetness Follows" began a suite of songs that traced the band's tender heart: "At My Most Beautiful," then "Losing My Religion," and then a massive sing-along "Everybody Hurts," the AIDS-era ballad that

had taken on extra resonance in England in the wave of grief following Princess Diana's death in August 1997. On "Walk Unafraid," *Up*'s
darkly inspirational heart, remade from a computer-driven smolder
into a full-band conflagration, Michael sang with fierce intensity,
recalling the child he used to be, stumbling and awkward but determined. *I'll trip, fall, pick myself up, and walk unafraid,* he sang, drag-
ging the microphone stand with him as he staggered one way, then
the other. *Hold me, love me, or leave me high.*

As the band cornered into the set's concluding half hour, the
bangers, "Finest Worksong," "Man on the Moon," alternated with
newer, lesser-known tunes. A stripped-down acoustic-guitar-and-
vocal "Why Not Smile," from *Up*, the nakedly erotic "Tongue" paired
with the sleazy rocker "Crush with Eyeliner," from *Monster*, and, in
an unexpected choice, the lovely if relatively obscure "Cuyahoga,"
from 1986's *Lifes Rich Pageant*. They concluded, per usual, with a
wild "It's the End of the World as We Know It," Michael leaping off
the stage to greet the forest of arms reaching over the barricade. Fans
taking his hand, patting his shoulder, rubbing his glistening bald
head. A communion, the artist and the audience merging into one
sweaty, screaming mass. He went down the line, reaching out and
being touched, holding out the microphone, amplifying other voices,
repeating the chorus until the musicians stopped and it was just the
crowd chanting over and over. *It's the end of the world as we know it,
it's the end of the world as we know it, it's the end of the world as we know
it* . . . When that dissolved, Michael called out a final thank-you and
good night, and it was all over. But something he'd said just before
they started playing that final song hung in the air.

"This is now, now is here, here is where you are, and it's all real
good."

45

The Name of This Band Is R.E.M.

T*wentieth century, go to sleep / Really deep / We won't blink.*
This is how you age when you're a rock star: quickly. You race your way through your twenties, then if you're lucky things get good in your thirties, so you work even harder. The next thing you know you're in your forties and people start to look at you differently. Because rock 'n' roll is supposed to be the music of youthful rebellion. The sound of insurgency, of tearing it all down and standing glorious in the ruins. If you can stay on your feet, you might get a chance to build it back up again according to your own vision. That's when people really start to listen. If you're doing it right, what they hear reminds them of what they've already been thinking. You're still one of them, even after they lift you up and gather in droves to listen to your wisdom. If you're good, and also lucky, you can keep that going for a while. You feel something in the wind, you write it into a song, and people you've never met, people whose lives you can't imagine, hear it and think, *Hey, wow, me too.*

How long can anyone keep that going? Because everything is always changing, and when your job elevates you above the crowd, it's hard to know what's going on around you. You can read the paper, watch TV, keep up with current events, know what's going on. But now you travel in a higher orbit than almost everyone else. Also, familiarity kicks in. Popular music, popular anything, revolves around the next big thing. And there's always someone behind you, someone younger or newer, coming up with a completely different set of followers and shared values and ideas. One of those is aimed at you, and it goes like this: *Fuck those guys.*

The handful of promotional shows they played in the fall of 1998, mixing the new material with songs from the '80s and early '90s, lifted the band out of its post–Bill Berry doldrums. They set up a fifty-three-date European and American tour for the summer of 1999, the first stretch climaxing with that ecstatic evening at Glastonbury. Reacquainted with their powers, R.E.M. paraded across Europe and the UK through the end of July, playing twenty-nine shows in all, then returned to the United States and Canada for twenty-five shows to run through the first half of September. The European concerts were larger, mostly in venues for fifteen thousand or more, all overflowing with cheering fans. The American shows were smaller, almost all in the midsize outdoor amphitheaters promoters call the sheds, five-to-ten-thousand-capacity venues outside major cities. Old-line fans would hire babysitters or else pack up the kids and a picnic, come out, and make an evening of it.

The trend continued when the band released its next single in November. Written as the theme song to a big-budget biopic of Andy Kaufman that had been titled *Man on the Moon*, after the *Automatic for the People* song that reflected on the late comedian's death, "The Great Beyond" sounded like a sequel to the earlier song, employing a similar musical structure and lyrics that played off the images and ideas in the original song. The movie, starring Jim Carrey as Kaufman, underperformed with critics and viewers, which didn't help sell the song in the United States, where it peaked in the mid-fifties on the *Billboard* chart. Away from home, R.E.M. was still popular enough for that not to matter. "The Great Beyond" rose to number eleven on the all-European list, while in Britain it leaped into the top three, the biggest hit they'd ever have in that country.

Eventually the world spins in a different direction. Yesterday's idealism is revealed as naivete or, worse, foolishness. Trusted leaders disappoint or, worse, betray you. In the United States, President Bill Clinton, whose ascent to the White House was concurrent with R.E.M.'s ascent to superstardom and fueled in part by their advocacy, used his power to launch or support laws that did not serve the band's, nor, arguably, anyone's, better interests. While the Clinton administration made long-overdue progress in the fight against AIDS, the president didn't have the will to root out the institutional homophobia of the U.S. armed services. Rather than strip out obviously unconstitutional rules forbidding gay, lesbian, and bisexual citizens from serving in the military, Clinton began a policy known as Don't Ask, Don't Tell, which forbade the military from compelling its members from disclosing their sexual orientation (the Don't Ask part) but also forbade service members from living openly (Don't Tell).

Clinton also oversaw widespread deregulation of the media, allowing a small handful of tycoons to gain control of an overwhelming number of the nation's commercial radio and television outlets. The consolidation of ownership diminished variety among broadcasters, making it even more difficult for non-mainstream artists to find a home on the airwaves. At the same time, the growth of digital music sites and the explosion in file sharing spurred by the Napster site all but ended the need for even the most devoted music fan to actually purchase music. Album sales collapsed, and the recording industry that had supported R.E.M. for two decades staggered.

The current that once picked you up and shot you forward slows, then stops. Then it seems to run in the opposite direction, tugging at your feet, pushing you backward, determined to topple you. No matter: you keep working, writing songs, recording songs, doing your job. You have a recording contract, for one thing. But you also still love the process, finding new chord progressions and melodies, looking for new sounds, new ways to express how it feels to be alive in this way, in these circumstances, in this moment.

As ever, R.E.M. experimented with new ways to make their music. Working in the studio with performance mainstays Scott McCaughey, Joey Waronker, and Ken Stringfellow, the musicians would track a song, then trade instruments and play one another's parts to see if clumsier fingers could add some more interesting textures to the piece. The album they released in the spring of 2001, *Reveal*, was a cornucopia of sound: layers of synthesizers and natural instruments, drum machines, and electronic distortion. Melodically and lyrically more upbeat than the tunes on *Up*, the new songs prompted Michael to write words and melodies full of sun, warmth, and lazy breezes. A summertime album, he decided, and so the songs came back with titles like "Beachball," "The Lifting," and "I've Been High." All had things to recommend them, but none were as striking as "Imitation of Life," which had the urgency and melodicism of mid-'80s R.E.M. and was nearly cut from the album as a result. Too predictable, they worried. And yet it was also a great song, so they not only kept it on the album but released it as the first single, scoring another top ten hit in Europe. American record buyers gave "Imitation of Life" a miss (it topped out at number eighty-three on *Billboard*'s Hot 100). Album sales reflected the disparity, with *Reveal* selling only around 500,000 copies in the United States but more than a million in Europe.

At home they were seasoned entertainers. Overseas they were still conquering heroes. To start 2001, R.E.M. ventured to the Rock in Rio festival, a gathering so immense it made Glastonbury feel intimate, and performed for their largest audience yet: an incomprehensible 195,000. They played to a more fathomable thirty thousand at the Hot Festival, in Buenos Aires, Argentina, a few days later, but felt even more moved at the end of April when they performed at the South Africa Freedom Day celebration in London's Trafalgar Square. The seventh anniversary of free elections in the country also served as a tribute to President Nelson Mandela, who had ascended to his nation's highest office after spending twenty-seven years as a political prisoner of the white apartheid government. A crowd of twenty thousand filled the square, and greeted R.E.M.'s seven-song set, which included three songs from the as-yet-unreleased *Reveal*, with an ovation nearly as rapturous as the one that greeted Mandela's climactic appearance. When Peter picked up his mandolin and played the opening riff to "Losing My Religion," the roar sounded from Hyde Park to the banks of the Thames.

Then came a season of repeats. Another appearance on MTV's *Unplugged,* marking the tenth anniversary of the band's landmark show in 1991, when they were just reaching the height of the *Out of Time* ecstasies. In October they had another go at Neil Young's Bridge School Benefit shows at the Bay Area's Shoreline Amphitheatre. They featured *Reveal* songs at both appearances and were greeted with polite if not rapturous attention, with the exception of "Imitation of Life," whose signature R.E.M. opening of strummed guitar chords tumbling into the chorus earned an immediate ovation. Which served as a pocket illustration of the veteran band's conundrum: How can you move forward creatively when your audience prefers the way you used to sound?

R.E.M. hadn't been officially involved in their first greatest hits collection. *Eponymous,* released in 1988, was entirely a product of I.R.S. Records, whose executives timed its release to coincide with the arrival of *Green* and the mammoth promotional campaign Warner Bros. Records uncorked to herald the first album by its new signing. Given that R.E.M. had scored precisely one hit single during its I.R.S. years, *Eponymous* was more like a best-of, featuring songs that had either played well on college radio or been fan favorites. The band clearly did not begrudge their former record company the chance to piggyback on their new label's promotional campaign: Michael provided his senior portrait from the Collinsville High School yearbook for use in the *Eponymous* artwork (with the plaint THEY AIRBRUSHED MY FACE covering the lower third of his visage), and the unsigned song-by-song sleeve notes were written by Peter.

Fifteen years into their career with Warner Bros., and in the wake of two albums that had not come close to fulfilling anyone's sales expectations, seemed like an excellent time to release a collection of the hits the band had scored over its previous seven albums. Titled *In Time: The Best of R.E.M. 1988–2003* and released in the late fall of 2003, it soon cleared a million copies in the United States, making it the band's first platinum record stateside since 1997, and sold three times that number around the world. The ongoing appeal of the songs obviously had a lot to do with that, but the band also primed the pump by spending the late summer and fall on the road performing old favorites they hadn't pulled out since, in some cases, the 1980s.

"Maybe we're a little defensive about it," Michael admitted during an interview with the TV reporter Adam Weissler when the tour got to Los Angeles in September. "We've always worked really hard as a band not to repeat ourselves or to stagnate." Still, when they thought back to the weeks they'd just spent performing in Europe, it was impossible to overlook the transformative effect the older songs had on the crowd. "People are really excited," he said. "It was phenomenal. And really fun for us."[1]

And yet work on new or at least newish music continued. Preparing to release *In Time*, the band went back into the studio to record three new songs to make the collection feel fresher, and perhaps give fans who already owned all their albums a reason to buy the greatest hits collection, too. Two of the songs were re-recorded versions of oldies. "All the Right Friends" was as old as R.E.M. songs came, a tune Peter and Michael wrote together before they had even met Mike and Bill, performed regularly by the group in 1980 and 1981. "Bad Day," an early and less good draft of "It's the End of the World as We Know It," dated back to 1986. The one truly new song, "Animal," was a lightly psychedelic rocker whose lyrics had a futuristic, even sci-fi theme involving, I think, aliens dropping out of the skies with transcendent knowledge. *The answer landed on my rooftop*, Michael sings, then adds his own commentary: *Whoa.*

Hoping to score a hit with one of the new songs, the band pulled out "Bad Day" and made an elaborate video in which they portray TV news personalities, all of them in blazers, ties, earnest expressions, the whole bit. Michael was the anchorman, and Peter and Mike played correspondents calmly reporting on the various forms of havoc taking place in the world around them, only they're lip-synching the lyrics of the song. They all seemed to be having a ball—even Peter, who usually moved through videos with the evident joy of a man having a tooth extracted, a procedure that was about as fun as the band's attempts to get their new songs played on mainstream radio had become.

All three band members confessed as much that day they were sitting together in Los Angeles waiting to talk about *In Time* with Weissler, the real-life TV reporter, in September 2003. Chatting with the band while the technicians adjusted their lights and levels, the journalist mentioned that he'd already heard "Bad Day" online. It was so great, he enthused, he expected to start hearing it all over the radio, including the city's powerful rock station KROQ-FM. Hearing this, all the members of R.E.M. sighed deeply. "Well, I *hope*," Peter said. "I wouldn't hold my breath," Mike added. When Weissler seemed shocked by their skepticism—it was such a catchy song!—Michael flashed a boyish smile. "Call 'em up and request it, could ya? *Pleeeeeze?*" He continued, more seriously. "KROQ's a very important station that turned away from us at some point." He took a sip of coffee and shrugged. "But maybe they'll love this song. I hope so."[2]

They didn't. "Bad Day" was a top ten hit all across Europe. In the United States it didn't dent the Hot 100.

46

The Murmurers

To the reader: Hello out there. I've been thinking about you, sensing you on the other side of the screen, and I've been wondering about you. It seems like a safe bet that you're an R.E.M. fan, but what *kind* of R.E.M. fan, I wonder, because there are several. Perhaps you discovered the band belatedly, possibly through younger artists who were influenced by them, and you're absorbing their story for the first time. Or maybe you're part of the Great Migration of R.E.M. fans, from when they were all over the radio and MTV, and your memories of the late 1980s or early 1990s all play to the tune of "The One I Love," "Losing My Religion," and "Everybody Hurts" and, ha-ha, "Shiny Happy People."

Or maybe you're the other kind of R.E.M. fan. The OG followers. Let's call them the Murmurers.

If you've spent any time on any of the online fan communities, or if you've read certain critics with an affinity for alt-everything and a vocabulary heavily freighted with words like *indie* and *authenticity* on the one hand and *corporate* and *sellout* on the other, you know who I'm talking about. The guys (and they're almost always guys) who got into R.E.M. during the early Reagan years, when they were still on I.R.S. Records, or perhaps even before that. Who first saw them play in a bar or maybe a pizza parlor. Who have at some point discussed the relative merits of the bands on New Zealand's Flying Nun label with Peter Buck, probably after that show in the bar, and over beers.

The particulars may vary, but one thing doesn't: the conviction that the best album R.E.M. ever made, and it's not even close, is *Murmur.*

I think we all know why. Because that's when they were at their murkiest, when Michael was at his mumbliest. When every note and every word rang out in opposition to mainstream culture. When they weren't just obscure but pointedly so. Not just uncommercial, but proudly, defiantly *anti*-commercial. "That soft-focus, Pre-Raphaelite, dance-barefoot-in-the-kudzu utopian vision," as Sue Cummings wrote about *Murmur* in the savaging of *Lifes Rich Pageant* she published in *Spin* in 1986. Cummings gets bonus points for being so early to the Murmurer game (*Murmur* was only three years old at that point; R.E.M. was still releasing its records on I.R.S.) and even more points for being an actual woman among the legions of indie rock boys. Was she still bending her ear in the band's direction by the time Jim DeRogatis published his *cri de indie R.E.M. coeur* ("It's often noted that the band now regularly breaks promises it made early in its career") ten years later? What would either of them think if they saw Michael, while plugging R.E.M.'s new greatest hits collection, yearning openly to crack the playlist of Los Angeles's KROQ-FM, because it's such an important commercial station? Whatever happened to the Michael who said he didn't even want a hit single, because "I don't think radio deserves me"?[1]

He learned how to make records that millions of people loved, is what. His band had a ton of hit albums and hit singles. So many, in fact, that their sound and vision became not just the sound of mainstream music but also the sound of mainstream culture. Whether you think this is the worst thing that could have happened or the best depends on a few factors. Not the least of them being how highly, when discussing the relative merits of R.E.M.'s albums, you rate *Murmur.*

At first R.E.M. was like an open secret. This band of college-aged guys from a college town, writing and performing rock 'n' roll songs full of big ideas and complicated language. That so much of it seemed to take place among various shades of outsiders (*seemed to* because the lyrics stirred up so many more questions than they provided answers) clarified the signal's amperage. If you were in a position to tune it in and liked what you heard enough to follow the signal, it was like realizing that the thing that once made you unacceptable now gave you entrée into an exclusive club. Another version of the painted, prancing gang Michael joined when he started going to those *Rocky Horror Picture Show* screenings in 1978. The dressing up and dancing were part of a secret language that had a double edge—it seemed to be speaking about satirical movie musicals but was actually about a way of thinking and being. About living outside the lines that society had drawn to govern your life. "This is an excellent movie. It really is," Michael had told that TV reporter, speaking in the first language. "And we're all quite normal, really," he continued, in the second. All of Michael's freaky young friends applauded him that night, and that sound must have gotten under his skin.

The fast, lean sound and scattered imagery of "Radio Free Europe" served as an invitation. The songs on the *Chronic Town* EP and *Murmur*, in all their offbeat tunefulness and lyrical inscrutability, described the pleasures and risks of living outside the lines, while the songs on *Reckoning* and *Fables of the Reconstruction* explained why it was necessary. And when they toured, which was nearly all the time during the first half of the 1980s, the members of R.E.M. found their people, looked into their eyes, and let them know they'd been seen, and understood. And if you knew where to listen, and what you were listening for, you could be a part of that. That's the sound of *Murmur*, and if that was your R.E.M. album back when it was the only R.E.M. album, nothing could ever be more powerful.

Lifes Rich Pageant, Document. The bottom end got punchier, the loose ends tucked and buttoned. The lyrics were still cockeyed, but tighter and brought into focus. "Fall on Me" slipped onto commercial radio, and then "The One I Love" broke big and "It's the End of the World as We Know It (and I Feel Fine)" nearly did the same and it was a new thing. Rock 'n' roll shot through with artistry; pop music invested with a kind of righteousness. *We are hope despite the times* and *Let's begin again* were bracing stuff in the late 1980s, even given the singer's auto-skepticism, and a whole new crowd came in.

This is the point in R.E.M.'s career where the Murmurers start to get twitchy, as if this hadn't been the plan all along. Because even if they'd started as the house band for outsiders, they were never going to be content speaking only to their own people. Hadn't they made that clear when they set out on the road in 1980, taking every show they could possibly book? Anything, anywhere. Rock clubs, of course, but also restaurants, frat parties, roadhouses, gay bars. In New York, New Orleans, Outer New Bunghole, anywhere that had power, lights, and a stage or even just an open piece of floor where they could set up and plug in. They wouldn't play any songs they didn't want to play; it wasn't about making themselves more normal in order to appeal to the normies. On the contrary, it was a matter of projecting their weird vision in such a powerful way that they couldn't be ignored. To be, in Peter's words, the acceptable face of the unacceptable stuff. Which is to say: still unacceptable at heart. Even when they hit the top ten. *Especially* when they hit the top ten.

Then came *Green* and *Out of Time* and the hordes came flooding in. And no wonder: R.E.M. was everywhere. Hit song after hit song after hit song, smash videos, tens of millions of records sold, the band's name on the lips of presidential candidates, tossed around on television as a cultural signifier, shorthand for hip, smart, socially engaged, of the moment. Here the Murmurers wailed with fury. R.E.M. had become so smooth, so mellifluous, so shiny and happy. It was easy for an incredulous Murmurer to miss the weirdness hiding in plain sight. How the beasts jumping the barriers in "Belong" were off to join the fun at the utopian house party of "Shiny Happy People." How the shame and desperation in the lyrics of "Losing My Religion" harmonized with the queer imagery in the song's video. And how this rock band that had started out playing unacceptable music by, for, and about the outsiders had not just dragged the unacceptable into view, and not just put it on a pedestal for the entire world to see, but also made the world love it. Made it *super fucking famous*, in Michael's words. At which point they could, and would, do anything they wanted to do. And get paid $80 million in corporate money to do it.

The freedom held when the media sharks sniffed something about Michael's private life and began implying that he might have AIDS. At which point he felt free to correct them: he was perfectly healthy. And though it was nobody's business, he was also perfectly queer.

Happy to have sex with women and maybe even happier to do it with men. At one time, that kind of admission could be a death knell for a pop star's career. But not for R.E.M. Because they had helped the beasts jump the barricades, and now the old rules no longer applied. And what happened next was *Monster*, was the Monster tour, was R.E.M. at its absolute zenith. Michael could do anything, and none of it was wrong. When he got to his dressing room in Chicago and discovered a gift basket from the venue that included a jersey from the Blackhawks hockey team, he fashioned it into a skirt and wore it onstage.[2] Was it the first time he ever wore a dress onstage? It certainly wasn't the last.

If there was an audience segment R.E.M. could still add to their litany by the mid-1990s, it was the gay men and women who had sensed what Michael's orientation was during the 1980s and either resented his not being public about it or hadn't noticed or cared. Now it was hard to not admire that a pop star of such magnitude could be so out, proud, and often bracingly outlandish. "Michael had an impact on mainstreaming queer culture, I think," says Victor Krummenacher, the bassist for Camper Van Beethoven, who had been among the first out alternative/indie musicians. Krummenacher had no problem with Michael choosing to keep his sex life to himself. The post-punk/alternative rock scene of the 1980s was, like so much of rock 'n' roll, overwhelmingly male, white, and straight, and fame is difficult to navigate under any circumstances. But Krummenacher had plenty of friends who felt differently. Michael changed a lot of minds when he did come out, and the impact, the bassist says, can still be felt. "What's interesting now is how gender ambiguous younger people are," he says. "Everything is more gender fluid . . . and I think Michael is definitely part of that."[3]

You didn't have to be an old-line R.E.M. fan, or even all that invested in the politics of indie-vs.-mainstream culture, to think that *Around the Sun*, the album R.E.M. released in 2004, was more than a little too sleek for anyone's good. If only because that's what the band members thought. And actually said about it, starting not long after the record's release that October. They'd started work in Athens in January 2004 with a relatively big array of new tracks to work on, plus more than enough shared outrage for President George W. Bush, who had leveraged post-9/11 fear into a full agenda of neo-conservative policies that included the invasion of Iraq, to fuel quite a few songs full of jagged political commentary.

The demos they produced were by all accounts bristling with restless energy: guitars, bass, and drums at the center of the mix. Then the band relocated to a recording studio in the Bahamas. Two months of island breezes and tropical sunshine might have been good for the soul, but it also inspired musical torpor. Whatever spiky guitar lines might have existed on the original tracks were either subsumed or replaced by smoother keyboard sounds. Tart sonic missives were rolled in sugar and drizzled in chocolate. Still, some of the songs get their hooks under the skin. The opening track and lead single, "Leaving New York," expertly weaves its dark verses with ringing, tuneful choruses. "Electron Blue" and particularly "The Ascent of Man" pair engaging lyrics with melodies that climb into your pockets and ride around with you all day. But too many of the songs substitute professionalism for inspiration, and lushness for passion. By the time they get to the title track, which pop historians will note is the *first time an R.E.M. album has ever had a title track*, the calls to action (*Hold on, world, 'cause you don't know what's coming*) are overwhelmed by summery metaphors that sound suspiciously like something dreamed up by a man lounging at poolside (*I want the sun to shine on me . . . Let my dreams set me free*).

Critics around the world were less than impressed. *Entertainment Weekly* put it like this: "As arena folk goes, R.E.M. remain cooler than, say, the Wallflowers. Just barely."[4] Which is perhaps another way of saying that *Around the Sun* proved that R.E.M. had joined sex and pizza in the category of Things That, Even When They're Pretty Bad, Are Still Pretty Good. "Leaving New York" hit top tens all across Europe, rising as high as number four on the continental chart. The album topped sales lists all across Europe, though it peaked at only number thirteen in the United States—the first R.E.M. album not to reach the top ten since *Green*, though that record continued selling long enough to go platinum twice, while the new album's visit to the bestseller charts, in every country, was brief. *Around the Sun* moved a million copies overseas,* and a paltry 213,000 during its first year in the United States. If there's one thing R.E.M. fans of every vintage and stripe, and the musicians themselves, can agree on, it's that the lowest point in the band's entire creative history is right here.

The week *Around the Sun* was released, in October 2004, R.E.M. was performing as part of an all-star lineup in the Vote for Change tour. Various acts participated in the forty concerts around the nation, with R.E.M. joining in a six-show whirlwind through five electoral swing states and then, ultimately, at the MCI Center arena, in Washington, D.C. Sharing the bill at most shows with Bruce Springsteen and the E Street Band, John Fogerty, and the neo-folk-rock phenom Bright Eyes, they performed abbreviated sets that began with "The One I Love" and leaned heavily on their most popular material, with just one or two of the new songs tossed in.

The tour, which was intended to raise money and awareness for the political opponents of President George W. Bush, who was running for reelection against the Democratic U.S. senator John Kerry, had a communal vibe that lent itself to cross-act duets. Springsteen played guitar and sang on R.E.M.'s "Man on the Moon" each night, while Michael joined the New Jersey musician on "Because the Night," which he'd cowritten with Patti Smith. Peter and Mike joined the E Street Band for "Born to Run." It looked like a lot of fun. But, as they told every reporter they talked to, they were there to speak truth to power and make a political impact. "The country is going so wrong, we'll do whatever we can to change it," Mike said.[5]

Michael spent so many years distancing himself from the history and traditions of rock 'n' roll that it was astounding to see how excited he was to meet Bruce Springsteen. In the documentary *National Anthem: Inside the Vote for Change Concert Tour*, produced

* Which is a lot of records, obviously, but in the context of everything that had gone before, and also the notoriously enormous Warner Bros. deal, it was a significant step down.

for the Sundance Channel, he's fairly aglow as he makes his way to the venue where the bands will first come together. "To be playing on the same stage as Mr. Springsteen, who is someone I've followed as a fan since I was a teenager, is . . . a little daunting," Michael tells the camera. "I'm nervous," he adds with a laugh. Overhearing Peter working out the guitar part for "Born to Run," the singer goes in to get a closer listen and starts singing along, all the words in place, the intonation just exactly right. Standing on the stage an arm's length from Springsteen during a run-through of "Because the Night," Michael gets so caught up watching the guitarist's solo that he misses the cue to sing his part of the chorus. He regains his poise by the time he calls Springsteen onstage to sing and play with his band during the concert, but when the older musician takes over the vocal for the second verse, R.E.M.'s singer looks like a man whose inner fifteen-year-old is fully and joyously alive.[6]

The failure of *Around the Sun*, which is how you think of a million-plus-selling album by an act that spent a dozen years making albums that sold in the many multiples of millions, spurred a return to R.E.M.'s restless touring habits. After the Vote for Change tour ended (and George W. Bush was reelected), the band toured North America through the middle of December, took the holidays off, then regrouped in Europe just after the New Year, setting out on a long tour that took them across pages of the world atlas they'd never flipped through, all the way into the former Soviet states of Eastern Europe and down through post-apartheid South Africa before returning to the familiar arenas of Japan, New Zealand, and Australia in mid-March. They took most of a couple of months off before returning to Europe for two more months of shows, including a quick set among the world's biggest acts at the Live 8 benefit concert, in London's Hyde Park on July 2, before returning to the city on July 16 to perform a show they'd had to reschedule after the terrorist bombings that tore through London's Underground on July 7, killing fifty-six commuters. Returning to Hyde Park, they played the final show of the tour to 85,000 Londoners for whom "Everybody

Hurts" suddenly had far too much meaning. Nevertheless, the show was a triumph. "Twenty-five years into REM's career, the planets of the band's universe seem to have slid into an especially harmonious alignment," wrote *The Guardian*'s Adam Sweeting in his five-star review. The band, he said, "are currently hitting new peaks as a live act."[7]

47

This Is Going to Be Loud

When the mammoth years began in the 1990s, R.E.M. had all the right attributes to be an award magnet. They were smart but also cool; critics' favorites but also regular guys; edgy but also cooperative. Most importantly, they moved a lot of merchandise. So: Grammys and BRITs. NMEs and Pollstar Concert Industrys. CMJs, Billboards, and Rockbjornens. Song of the Year. Album of the Year. Band of the Year. Best Pop Performance by a Duo or Group with Vocals.* By the time *Out of Time* ran its course, it had started to seem ridiculous . . . The presentation video the band made to hype Warner Bros. Records staff for *Automatic for the People* in the fall of 1992 included a bit with Michael in the band offices, pretending to talk to Lenny Waronker on the telephone while being interrupted by endless messengers handing him trophies, plaques, gold-plated everything. "Oh, it's another award," he says into the phone, considering one for a moment before tossing it aside. "We ran out of doors. We don't know what to do with them."[1]

The gold-plated haul was just beginning. By the middle of that decade, they started getting career-size gongs. MTV's Video Vanguard Award came first, in 1995. Three years later the people behind *Q* magazine's Q Awards handed R.E.M. a Lifetime Achievement

---

* "Awards! They do nothing but give out awards!" Woody Allen's character Alvy Singer grumbles about Los Angeles and/or show business in general in the film *Annie Hall.* "Greatest fascist dictator, Adolf Hitler!" Say what you will about W.A.'s personal life; he was on point there.

Award. It was a start, but you generally need to have been around for at least twenty-five years before the proper halls of fame consider unlocking their doors. For R.E.M. the gilding began in September 2006.

It started with a warm-up at the 40 Watt, in Athens, on the twelfth of September with a community food bank fundraiser called "Finest Worksongs: Athens Bands Play the Music of R.E.M.," a multi-artist show featuring a slate of local acts including Pylon's Vanessa Briscoe Hay, the Drive-By Truckers' Patterson Hood, Five Eight, and a variety of others. All of whom were surprised to discover that the first act to play that night would be the local band R.E.M., including original drummer Bill Berry. The band electrified the crowd with "Begin the Begin" and "So. Central Rain" before leaving the stage to the other acts. The communal vibe from Athens days gone by swept over the evening, and soon the various R.E.M. musicians started getting dragooned onto the stage to help out, adding an additional guitar or backing vocal to whatever tune was coming next. When the whole gang came out for a show-closing "It's the End of the World as We Know It," Michael came back to the front of the stage, mostly to cheer on Five Eight singer Mike Mantione as he sang lead, and to join in on the choruses. By the end there were at least three dozen musicians massed on the stage, with the stars of the show happily subsumed by the crowd.

"This is going to be loud."

Six days later, the four original members of R.E.M. were in front of a few thousand well-dressed folks in a cavernous function room at the Georgia World Congress Center, in Atlanta, about to kick off their mini set at the induction ceremony for the Georgia Music Hall of Fame. The crowd cheered, Michael added his usual introduction, "The name of this band is R.E.M. and this is what we do," and they were off, thundering into "Begin the Begin," then "Losing My Religion," and finally, with a dedication to Texas's progressive governor Ann Richards, who had died earlier that week, "Man on the Moon." Next, Georgia's former U.S. senator Max Cleland inducted the band and Michael made a brief speech, talking about how proud they had

386 | THE NAME OF THIS BAND IS R.E.M.

always been to be from Georgia. Later, his bandmates were just as proud to serve as the backing band for one of their fellow inductees, and Mike and Bill's former neighbor in Macon, Gregg Allman, helping him perform his classic "Midnight Rider."

When they first came to New York, they had been underdressed, underfed, wide-eyed in the streets, sleeping in a van. That was Peter and Michael in March of 1980, on their spring break getaway. They were just a week or two from Kathleen O'Brien's party on April 5, taking their first steps on the journey that would lead them into a head-spinning whirlwind and carry them away for twenty-seven years, until it dropped them back in this city, in this place, standing together at the edge of a ballroom in the Waldorf Astoria hotel, and on the threshold of rock 'n' roll history. Which would be a ridiculous overstatement if it weren't true.

Here was Eddie Vedder, the famously articulate lead singer of the Seattle grunge band Pearl Jam. He stood behind a podium in this formal ballroom in the Waldorf Astoria hotel, talking about those skinny, penniless kids who had wandered these very streets during that long-ago spring break. "The story of how they got together could not be written, especially considering this evening, any more romantic," he proclaimed. "And that is that Michael Stipe and Peter Buck first meet at a record store where Peter is working. Wuxtry Records in Athens, Georgia. Their first conversation, their first discussion, was about Patti Smith's first four records."

The audience, largely middle-aged and older, garbed in ball gowns and tuxedos, whooped and applauded the name of the one-time punk-rock poet of the downtown demimonde. Vedder spoke of R.E.M.'s music, about their influence on as well as their generosity toward other artists. So many people feel so much gratitude to R.E.M., he continued, it was hard for him to imagine that the honor he was about to bestow could begin to repay it. But it was what he had. "And by some strange power invested in me, right now I hereby induct R.E.M. into the Rock & Roll Hall of Fame." It was an industry crowd, top-heavy with chief executives, A&R directors, show business attorneys, power-wielding managers, magazine editors, and program directors. There were friends and family, romantic partners, and a few children around R.E.M.'s tables too, and they all stood up and cheered as the four musicians from Athens came strolling out.

More than a quarter century later, they were pretty much who they always were. Michael came in the lead, looking both cool and dapper in an ivory-colored suit. Peter followed in shirtsleeves, carting a generous glass of red wine. Bill slipped out behind the guitarist, dressed for rock 'n' roll labor in a black blazer and T-shirt. Mike brought up the rear in a more restrained version of his cowboy spangles, a black-and-turquoise affair he set off with his bleached blond mop and rectangular eyeglasses that balanced bookish and stylish. Onstage, Peter and Bill stepped back, letting the others speak for them. The bassist went first, describing how humbled and awed and honored they all were by the "sheer talent of the musicians and non-musicians here tonight." He thanked a few people, his bandmates and parents, then gave a special shout-out to the late Ian Copeland, the concert booker who was so instrumental in the launch of R.E.M.'s career, as well as being, in his words, "the older brother I never had." Michael stepped up next, donning a pair of glasses and graciously calling out each of the four other inductees, Grandmaster Flash and the Furious Five, Van Halen, the Ronettes, and, in an amazing coincidence, Patti Smith. From there he launched into an even longer list, citing a litany of record company executives and staffers, spouses, girlfriends, a boyfriend, promoters, bookers, and the board of the Rock & Roll Hall of Fame. Nearly everyone, it seems, who makes a career as extravagantly successful as R.E.M.'s possible. With the exception, of course, of the band's former manager and partner Jefferson Holt, whose existence went unacknowledged.

Then came the music. They started with "Gardening at Night," the four original members with Scott McCaughey adding a little guitar off to the side. Next came "Man on the Moon," with a joyous Eddie Vedder joining Michael on the lead vocal. Patti Smith came up next for a snarly cover of Iggy Pop's "I Wanna Be Your Dog," ending with a surprising bit of old-school rock nihilism when Peter, infuriated by an ill-performing amplifier, picked the thing up and hurled it off the stage. And nearly into the laps of an elegantly coiffed couple sitting near the front of the stage.

After that came the traditional ending to these high-wattage, high-dollar investitures, one of those enormous jams involving all, or nearly all, of the musicians who had either been inducted or done the inducting. Which in this case included the members of R.E.M., Sammy Hagar from Van Halen, Grandmaster Flash, Ronnie Spector, Stephen Stills, Keith Richards, along with Paul Shaffer's house band, all playing Smith's "People Have the Power." Which was a strange sight to behold, this mash-up of styles and generations, of egos and attitudes, of downtown art and uptown commerce. Of the active construction of temples to worship the memory of rock 'n' roll insurrection.

This is the essential conflict at the heart of the rock 'n' roll industry, in the gear-jamming clash between the core values of rock 'n' roll and industrialized anything. Which only becomes more profound when it's the kind of rock 'n' roll that wields its power in the pursuit of social, cultural, and, especially, political activism. Because if it turns out that someone at a record company hears the chime of cash registers beneath a song, no matter its politics (or theirs), they're going to look for a way to commodify it. And if it turns out, further, that the musicians are, like the MC5's Wayne Kramer, like Bruce Springsteen, and like the members of R.E.M., at least as determined to have their music heard as they are to change the world, you wind up with the bracing spectacle of dissent being transformed into a commercial product: a brickbat affixed with a universal bar code. And given rock 'n' roll's fixation on authenticity, defined by the clear, traceable line between the lived experience of the artist and the content of their art, well, it gets a bit tricky. When dissent becomes commodity, is the protest being corrupted or is the corporate machine being turned against itself?

———

Two months after their night at the Waldorf Astoria, the three active members of R.E.M. gathered in Vancouver, British Columbia, along with McCaughey and drummer Bill Rieflin and the Irish record producer Jacknife Lee, to start work on their new album. Their installation into the rock 'n' roll sarcophagus and, perhaps more to the point, the unhappy response to the languid *Around the Sun* had given the threesome something to prove. That they weren't dead yet; that they could still work up a rage; that they still had the will, and the power, to turn up the volume and rattle the fucking windows. Still feeling burned by the endless studio tinkering and the keyboard-heavy sound on their previous album, Peter asserted himself. This time there would be a lot of guitar, and no Hammond B-3. They were going to work quickly, record live, get the songs on tape, and get out. "Most of that record is just me and Peter on guitar, Mike on bass, and Bill Rieflin on drums and Michael singing," Scott McCaughey says. "All the sessions for *Accelerate* were nothing but fun. Jacknife Lee was the perfect guy for us to meet . . . He was totally on board with keeping things moving and not getting bogged down."[2]

They worked on songs for three weeks, then dispersed. In late June the band went to Ireland for another few weeks of recording. To see how the new material worked, particularly in comparison with the older songs, they decided to try something new. A series of concerts they called "working rehearsals," at the Olympia Theatre, an intimate venue in Dublin. Starting each performance with a tongue-in-cheek announcement that *This is not a show!*, the band played full sets weighted heavily with the new songs, usually eight or nine a night. To measure the fresh material against their classics, they dug deep into their catalog, playing songs like "Letter Never Sent," "1,000,000," "Kohoutek," and "Romance," among other youthful missives they hadn't dusted off in twenty years or more. But the not-a-show shows were mostly about the new material and returning to the practice followed in the years of constant touring: getting the hang of a new song well before they took it into the studio. They played five shows, then spent another three weeks recording, and the new record, minus the mixing and mastering, was finished.

———

On *Accelerate*, R.E.M.'s fourteenth album, the most basic foundation of rock 'n' roll—guitar, bass, drums, vocals—stands almost completely unadorned. A musical construction of brick and steel, raw concrete footings, and rusted metal girding. From the blazing, melodic guitar that kicks off the lead track, "Living Well Is the Best Revenge," to the final shout of the concluding "I'm Gonna DJ"— *You cannot resist! You cannot resist! Yeah!*—it's a barely controlled riot of sound and feeling. "Man-Sized Wreath" distills everything that's right about the album in its first thirteen seconds: a flash of guitar, an explosion of drums and bass, then Michael in brilliantly sarcastic thrall: *Turn on the TV and what do I see? A pageantry of empty gestures all lined up for me—wow!* It's that sardonic "wow" that seals the deal, and it keeps happening, song after song, that good old-fashioned rock 'n' roll kablammo. Distorted guitar, leering insouciance, bulldozing bass, thunderclaps of anger, reassuring jangle, admissions of guilt, the broken wheeze of an organ, halting bursts of sorrow. And still, the glimmer of hope. *Belief has not failed me*, Michael declares in one song. Then, in another: *Where are we left, to carry on.*

Not quite thirty-five minutes from front to back, *Accelerate* plays like a hurricane in a bottle. Everything moves fast. Two of the songs are barely more than two minutes. Only two of the tracks meander past four minutes. Released on March 31, 2008, it performed the precise task the members of R.E.M. hoped it would: restoring the band's critical standing and giving their long-standing fans a reason to buy something new from the band that defined their youth. The growth of streaming music, along with everything else, had diminished record sales across the board, but within the reduced context of the twenty-first-century marketplace, *Accelerate* performed admirably, debuting at number two on *Billboard*'s album list and hitting the top of the charts in Canada, the UK, and seven other European countries. Still, total sales tallied to something less than a million copies.

They set out on a concert tour in late May, mostly playing in arenas and outdoor amphitheaters across the United States and Canada through late June. The company moved to Europe in early July, playing even larger venues, festivals, stadiums, and such, until early October. They took a few weeks off before playing a pair of shows in the South. The second was in New Orleans, for a huge crowd at the annual Voodoo Fest. It was October 26, 2008, the day R.E.M. would perform their last full concert in their home country.

From there they headed to Argentina to kick off a three-week tour of South America before returning north for a sold-out show at the Auditorio Nacional, a ten-thousand-seat venue in Mexico City. There had been some talk about doing a couple of shows in Florida after that, but when the time came to commit to the dates, the road-weariness had already kicked in. "We were like, *Why are we doing that?*" McCaughey recalls. "And then bagged 'em and just finished with Mexico City."[3] The tour had gone very well; the band felt sharp, the audiences were generally large and enthusiastic. They hadn't spoken of breaking up, not in a serious way, but a realization had come into the air. The first hint of autumn that comes at the end of a perfect late-summer afternoon.

The afternoon of the Mexico City concert, sometime between soundcheck and the start of the show, Peter and Michael found themselves together in the empty hall, contemplating the show they were about to perform. The last show in every tour feels like a valedictory, the end of a distinct experience that, having been lived, will never be lived again. But this time the feeling ran deeper than usual. "I went, 'This is kind of sad,'" Peter told *New York* magazine. "And Michael goes, 'Yeah, a little. We're probably never going to play any of these songs again.' And I went, 'You may be right.'"[4]

48

It Was What It Was

A s it ended Michael fell to his knees. The band playing behind him, looping through a few chords, Patti Smith keening up the scale, singing his words. *Oh, over, over, over, baby, over.* His suit was black, and a black beard bristled on his chin, white beneath his mouth, the frost of age. Behind and to his right, Mike worked his bass, and twenty feet to his left Peter strummed guitar. Both musicians also garbed in black suits, over black shirts. They were in Carnegie Hall, before a hushed crowd, maybe that accounted for the formal attire. Maybe the funereal quality is visible only in retrospect, now that we know this was R.E.M.'s final public performance. Which is also why it seems so striking that Michael spent the song's final minute on his knees. An expression of obeisance, or perhaps gratitude, that something so magical took place and that he got to be a part of it.

The Carnegie Hall appearance, an unbilled, one-song shot at the end of an R.E.M. tribute show, was the band's only public performance in 2009. It took place on March 11, at a fundraiser for music education programs for underprivileged students. That was a big night, full of artists who had influenced them (Patti Smith, the dB's, the Feelies) and even more artists who had been influenced by them (Throwing Muses, Darius Rucker, Dar Williams, many others). R.E.M.'s appearance was a surprise, closing the show with "E-Bow the Letter," with Smith reprising her vocal from the original recording.

The closest R.E.M. came to performing during the rest of the year was at the 40 Watt, in Athens, in September, when Peter and Scott McCaughey came to town to play with McCaughey's conceptual group the Minus 5 and the Baseball Project, a band the Seattle musician cofounded with Peter to produce songs about baseball. Mike contributed vocals and tambourine during the encore, and Bill Berry, his face lit by a huge smile, jumped in on drums for a shaggy, high-spirited run through the Beatles' "The Ballad of John and Yoko" and the McCoys' "Hang On Sloopy." Michael was in the house, too, but opted to enjoy the show with the rest of the crowd.

Time moves faster as it passes, then circles back on itself. Patterns repeat and become ingrained. The scenery starts to look familiar. *Haven't we been here before?* Yes, they had, if only because they'd been at it long enough to know what worked. Now the three members of R.E.M. were in their fifties, 2010 marked the thirtieth year of their collaboration. They knew how to make music together. They knew how *they* made music. The critical and commercial success of *Accelerate*, the latter in the reduced terms of the twenty-first century's music industry, and then the across-the-board success of their 2008 world tour underscored the power of their traditional ways and means. Their music was beloved around the world. And so when the time came to do it again, they did it again.

In the early spring of 2010 they got together at their practice space in Athens for five days of songwriting and preliminary recording. Then Peter and Mike met up again in Portland, Oregon, along with Bill Rieflin and Scott McCaughey, to demo more instrumental tracks. They sent the recordings to Michael for his consideration, and in early November the entire band returned to New Orleans for three weeks of studio sessions with Jacknife Lee, to start recording what would be the band's next album.

Circles and patterns. Another Bush had departed the White House (although this one served his full two terms), and the ascendance of another handsome young progressive to the presidency renewed the old sense of hope. Maybe good things were possible after all. Walking the revived streets of post–Hurricane Katrina New Orleans inspired Michael to compose the lyrics to "Oh My Heart," a new version of a song he might've written during the optimistic early 1990s. *The government changed,* he sang over a warm acoustic guitar and accordion. *Hear the song, rearranged.* The power-chord-fueled "Alligator_Aviator_Autopilot_Antimatter" retraced the leering crunch of *Monster,* flirting and insulting in the same breath: *If I didn't like the way you stared at me / I could knock you sideways.* Not all of the music had such direct antecedents, but as the new songs emerged, they came on like old friends. Sounds and textures, narrators that evoked voices from days gone by. Once, the band would have sent the familiar faces away; they'd had no interest in retracing their footsteps. Now the road forward had turned in a new direction, back toward home.

In April 2010, almost exactly thirty years since their first public performance, the members of R.E.M. were back in New Orleans to work on the new record. "All the Best" came on like a tempest, drums pounding, guitar blaring, bass booming, all of them hitting on every beat, *blam blam blam,* while Michael shouted about bad breaks and fuckups. A pie in the face, falling on his ass, making so much noise that blood spilled from his ears. He's a human tornado, hurling furniture and cats as he goes, but here's the punch line: that's exactly what you want him to be. He's a mirror reflecting your dreams back on you. The band keeps blasting away. There's not really a melody here, just a lot of shouting and pounding, and that's not going to stop, even after three decades. *Let's give it one more time,* he yells at his bandmates. *Let's show the kids how to do it!*

R.E.M. first entered Corin Tucker's imagination when she was ten years old. That was in 1983, when her dad, a psychology professor working at the University of North Dakota, in Grand Forks, came home with a copy of *Murmur. This is a great record,* he told his daughter. He had already introduced her to the Beatles, the Rolling Stones, and Queen, among others, and as the new songs played, Corin could tell that R.E.M. belonged in the company of those older bands. It was love at first listen. She followed their career as she grew up, noting the many distinctions between the Athens quartet and the rock bands that filled the commercial airwaves. "They were so different from the hyper-masculine thing that came from the music industry for a while," she says. "They seemed to respect women. Michael was like this romantic poet, and they had an emotional sophistication that was huge."

Tucker started playing piano and then guitar, and when her family relocated to the college town of Eugene, Oregon, she started playing music with friends, forming a band called This That. Graduating from high school in the spring of 1990, Tucker planned to attend the Evergreen State College, in Olympia, Washington, in the fall. She'd done well enough in her classes to feel ready for undergraduate academics. But to prepare for what she already anticipated would be an equally important part of her next few years, Tucker and her friend Tracy Sawyer decided to spend the summer in a college town with a rich music scene.

"I was obsessed with R.E.M., so we went to Athens." Tucker had worked at a restaurant in Eugene and got to Georgia with enough money to spend the summer days hanging out in cafés and the nights in the bars and halls where the local bands played. She and Sawyer, who was also bound for Evergreen, got to know as many musicians as they could, becoming particularly friendly with a band called the Earthworms. And of course they were aware of the town's reigning band, just then in the process of making the album that would project Athens's art-rock ethic into the uppermost reaches of mainstream music and popular culture. "R.E.M. was so smart about how they did things," Tucker says. "They were really conscious of not just the music they made, but the whole business around it. They were thoughtful of how they presented themselves, of being leaders for young people who wanted to be musicians, and not representative of the worst things in capitalist culture. They decided to do it completely differently. And you have to give them credit for building that path."[1]

For Tucker and Sawyer, the path began in Olympia, where they formed a band called Heavens to Betsy and became part of the surging riot grrrl scene, along with Bikini Kill, Bratmobile, and a variety of queercore bands, including Team Dresch and the Third Sex. When Tucker met Carrie Brownstein at a Heavens to Betsy show in the northern Washington college town of Bellingham, they formed Sleater-Kinney and went on to become one of the most popular and influential American post-punk bands of the late 1990s and early twenty-first century.

The riot grrrl bands didn't sound much like R.E.M., but the established band's trademark combination of post-punk fire, folk-rock guitar chime, literate lyrics, and emotive vocals radiated across the pop music spectrum, from the indie bands steering their overloaded vans from one tiny club to another to the vertiginous altitudes where artistically willful superstars like Taylor Swift and Lana Del Rey make whatever music they want to make, whenever they want to make it.

As work on the new R.E.M. album continued through the first half of 2010, there was a growing understanding within the group that it would be their last. After all, it was the fifth of the five albums they owed Warner Bros. The scene they all described later, always with words like "mutual" and "friendly" and "amicable," went like this: At some point during the sessions, Michael looked at his bandmates. "I think you guys will understand, I need to be away from this for a long time." Peter nodded. "How about forever?" Which Mike seconded. "Sounds right to me." And that, according to the account Peter gave *New York* magazine in 2016, was that.

Was it, really?

One of the things that makes R.E.M. unique, particularly among bands that got to be as famous as they did, was how accomplished they were at not talking about themselves. Yes, they'd talk about their work—the joys and challenges of touring, how they wrote these songs, what they tried to capture on the new record. If there'd been trouble along the way, one or more of them would tell that story. About the times they disagreed, how there'd been an argument and maybe they'd even shouted something about breaking up and

stormed off to sulk. But those stories always ended in rapproche-
ment, renewed friendship, a stronger collaboration. When the band
members gave separate interviews, they all tended to tell the same
stories, often using the same language, as if they were reading from
the same talking points. Or maybe they all remembered things in
exactly the same way. It's possible.

But who knows? Go back through all the interviews they gave
between 1981 and 2011 in search of firsthand descriptions of how it
felt to be in R.E.M., from the emotional currents that fueled their
artistry to the forces that resulted in their decision to break up, and
what you'll find is: nearly nothing. It's kind of amazing that they managed to be so very famous for so very long and yet never surrendered
anything beyond the most cursory details of their childhoods, their
families, and their romantic lives. Peter was married twice during the
band's run, both times to women who co-owned nightclubs (the first
in Athens, the second in Seattle), and if he acknowledged his spouses'
existence, he never said much else about them. Bill introduced his
wife Mari to a few reporters during interviews in the mid-1980s but
left it at that. Mike had serious girlfriends, one of whom gave birth
to his son in 1989, but he never spoke of them. Certainly it was easier for the instrumentalists to keep their private lives to themselves.
After all, they had Michael standing in front, absorbing the spotlight.
And also the abuse.

Some of the new songs they were working on in 2010 take zippy
little trips to nowhere. "That Someone Is You" wants to evoke the
40 Watt on a sweaty Saturday night in 1981, but there's not a lot of
there there. It makes juvenilia like Bill's 1980 goof "Narrator" seem
substantive by comparison. Still, the biggest miscue, and perhaps the
most vivid argument that R.E.M. had finally run out of ideas, comes
on the final track. "Blue" began as so many great R.E.M. songs had,
as a studio jam that came out of nowhere, the music emerging less
from the musicians' imaginations than from the murky boil of their
emotions. They picked up their instruments, someone strummed a
chord, and they all followed him into the void.

They'd done it just like that twenty years earlier, when Peter,

Mike, and Bill found their way into "Country Feedback." That time, the process was just as miraculous as the results. According to legend, Michael had come into the rehearsal space as they were banging away, already tuned in to their frequency. He grabbed a microphone, located a melody, and improvised lyrics that were as fucked up and beautiful as the music. *It's crazy what you could have had*, he chanted. *I need this, I need this.* Did he really just make it up on the spot and spit it out fully formed? That's what they said later, and it could be true. What matters more is how perfectly the parts work together. "Country Feedback" was and remains an epic achievement. They played it onstage consistently through the years, and it was not an accident that it was one of their final encores at their last show in Mexico City.

Unfortunately, the attempt to reawaken the "Country Feedback" spell twenty years later falls flat. It doesn't help that the chord progression they came up with for "Blue" is only a slight variation of the one they built into the earlier song. For God's sake, it's even in the same key. This time there was no direct synchronicity with their singer. To get Michael's voice on the piece, Jacknife Lee flew in a recitation the singer had recorded months earlier. *I am made by my times*, part of it went. *I am a creation of now.* Except suddenly it didn't sound like it anymore. To provide some melody, they had Patti Smith sing over the chorus, much like she'd done on "E-Bow the Letter" fifteen years earlier. It would have been a disheartening way for it all to end, were it not for the unexpected reprise of the album's first song, which stands among the most powerful pieces of music they ever recorded.

It was always Michael's burden. Being the voice, and the face, the storyteller. The personification of the music, the animation of the songs. The secret of R.E.M.'s success, the difference between a good band and a great one. They would give him pieces of catchy music and he would turn them into unforgettable songs. Then spellbinding performances. First in recording studios, then on stages all around the world. The world gave him and his band its attention, and then its love. And all the world wanted from him in exchange was everything he had. Which is what he'd given.

By the time they got to Berlin in the third week of June of 2010, the three band members knew they were on their last go-round. But they kept it to themselves, so when the directors Lance Bangs and Dominic DeJoseph came in to film live, in-studio performances of a few of the new songs at Hansa Studio, only the three musicians at the center of the big paneled room knew the significance of the moment. Scott McCaughey and Bill Rieflin were with them too, along with Bertis Downs and a couple dozen friends standing or perching on the packing cases along the edge while they played the new songs. "Oh My Heart," "All the Best," "Mine Smell Like Honey," "Alligator_ Aviator_Autopilot_Antimatter," a couple more. All of it leading to the song they'd use as the album's leadoff track, the one Michael called "Discoverer." This would be the last song R.E.M. ever played.

Here was R.E.M., one last time. Peter in black from head to foot, sawing at the strings of his black Rickenbacker. His hair mostly still dark, but fringed with silver. Mike stood across from him with his blond Fender bass, his hair back to being short, rectangular glasses reflecting the lights. Neither musician was as skinny as he used to be, but such is age, such were the banquets celebrating so many triumphs. Then there was Michael. A charcoal blazer over a striped button-up shirt, over black warm-up pants over worn-in white sneakers. Head shaved, cheeks mossed with salt-and-pepper stubble, thicker and whiter around his chin, horn-rimmed specs completing the look: less the hungry young artist, more the successful gallery owner, nodding his head to the martial blare his bandmates, along with Rieflin and McCaughey, were making. When the verse came around, the singer bore down and let fly.

Hey baby, this is not a challenge, it just means I love you as much as I always said I did . . .

More than three decades since he first stood at a microphone flanked by the other members of R.E.M., fifteen albums into a career that set new standards for creativity, mythmaking, and willful obscurity, "Discoverer" was about laying himself bare. As ever, he was a little vague on the particulars, sketching the sweep of his adulthood in a series of signal moments. A time he made a mistake and was pilloried for his lapse. An evening spent with vodka in one hand and espresso in the other, revelation in the air and disaster dead ahead. Michael regarded it all with equal measures of pride, regret, and awe. Mostly the latter, particularly when he recalled that long-ago spring break in New York, the moment he looked up from a crosswalk and saw the epic city skyline rising from his feet.

Now the song was coming to its climax and he took a step back from the microphone, his head slightly back, throat open as he sang as hard and loud as he could. Singing, finally, about himself. Who he was, who he'd been at the start, who he'd been the entire time.

Discoverer!

Really belting it out, his eyes shut, his throat corded with muscle.

Discoverer!

Again, and again and again, that one word, the truest thing he could say about himself.

Discoverer! Discoverer! Ohhh! Discoverer! Ohh! Discovererrrrrrrrr!

When it was finally over, as the last notes echoed and faded into the ornate wooden ceiling, Michael gripped the microphone with one hand, nodded, and sank to his knees. Head down, reaching for breath, he took a moment to collect himself, then stood up again, his face alight, eyes shimmering with tears. Then he turned to his bandmates and started to applaud.

49

Let's All Get On with It

They kept it a secret for more than a year.

When *Collapse into Now* was released on March 7, 2011, there was no indication that R.E.M.'s fifteenth album would be its last. It earned the usual solid reviews from critics and scaled the world's record sales charts in the usual way, peaking instantly at number five in the United States and the United Kingdom and at various stations of the top tens throughout Europe, Asia, and the antipodes before making a quick descent, finishing its run without notching much in the way of gold, let alone platinum, sales marks. It might have made a bigger splash if the band members had trumpeted its release as R.E.M.'s final word. But of course they didn't do that.

Instead they held off for six months, letting the album run its course before they released their official statement on September 21. There would be no final tour, no climactic performance to pay tribute to their fans, to their career, to who they were when they got together and projected themselves into the music only they could make in quite that way. That, they said, was already over. They had already called it a day and had parted the same way they came together: as friends. In interviews they fessed up to all the clues they'd dropped into, and on the packaging of, the final album, starting with its title. Then there was that line in "Discoverer," the part about *It was what it was / Let's all get on with it.* And how about the cover, which had been the first ever to feature a recognizable portrait of all its extant members. And hadn't anyone noticed that Michael, standing at the center with his hand raised to the camera and thus the world, was waving goodbye?

Being famous, even for a brief period, sticks with you. It changes the way people look at you, and how you look at yourself. The experience of being both larger than life and, in some abstract but painfully obvious way, less than human does strange things to a person's psyche. It's possible to recover, to reconfigure your memories of large-scale notoriety into the fragments of some weird dream you once had. But maybe that's easier said than done. And who really wants to forget how it feels to be that beloved, even if for all the wrong reasons? Or maybe just *some* of the wrong reasons. Because what you did was pretty good, wasn't it? And if it was, then you must not be all that bad, either. It's good to remember this some nights. The long, dark ones that remind you of why you felt so compelled to become so famous in the first place. Because no amount of success ever really chases those away.

For most of the 2010s, Michael Stipe kept his distance from music and from all but the most occasional jaunts into the public eye. He settled down with Thomas Dozol, an art photographer, at some point in the mid-2000s—he's the boyfriend Michael thanked at the Rock & Roll Hall of Fame—and, about ten years later, started wearing a wedding ring and referring to Dozol as "the mister." The couple divide their time between New York City, Berlin, and Athens, where they live in the same house Michael has owned since the 1980s. It's on the same block as his mother and sister, around the corner from Mike Mills, and just a few blocks from R.E.M.'s once and ongoing adviser Bertis Downs.

R.E.M.'s former singer focuses most of his attention on visual art, making photographs, sculpture, and whatever else tickles his fancy. He has published three books of photography in recent years, including one collaboration with author Douglas Coupland. For the first eight or so years after the band separated, he hardly ever sang in public, which seemed particularly sad when he made one of his occasional appearances, because that was when you remembered how great his voice is, and how much you missed hearing it. Then in 2019 he released "Your Capricious Soul," a largely synth-based song that sounded pretty much exactly like what you would have expected a solo Michael Stipe would sound like in 2019. A full album would come eventually, he said, with no promises as to how eventual that would be. A second song, "Drive to the Ocean," came out in 2020, and it was followed a few months later by "No Time for Love Like Now." A collaboration with Big Red Machine, a side project of Aaron Dessner, guitarist for the National, the song emerged a few weeks after the start of the COVID pandemic, and Michael's public performances of the song, all on television, were videotaped solo shots, singing over a recorded backing. Michael says he's still working on his album, but when it will be done is anyone's guess.

For a few years Michael cultivated a long silver beard that gave him a kind of severe Old Testament appearance. It was the face of a shepherd who had steered his flock through decades, perhaps centuries, of pestilence and floods. Then he shaved and his sweet smile reemerged, along with that mischievous sparkle in his eyes. In his early sixties, Michael Stipe has the look of a kindhearted man who has a lot of fun.

Michael's central presence in the public sphere is on Instagram, where he posts frequently, usually putting up batches of photographs he's made to document his most recent meanderings and adventures. A gallery exhibition in Paris, street scenes in London, the annual Pride parade in Athens, Georgia. The shots tend to be artful, demonstrating an exceedingly sharp eye for composition and texture, with an equally acute sense of whimsy. On one recent day he posted images from a junkyard he happened to see. A beat-up piece of plywood with the words DO NOT USE painted on it, another hunk reading NO. A rusty, lichen-coated mailbox only just hanging on to its platform, a corner of what appears to be a piece of junk mail just visible within. Almost all of the pictures are striking. So is the number of self-portraits that usually come with the day's posts. The former

R.E.M. singer, it seems, is still accustomed to the spotlight, and still enjoys presenting his visage for public consumption. So much that in 2024 he made his debut as a model, serving as one of the faces for Yves Saint Laurent's spring collection.

In 2011 Peter Buck moved to Portland, Oregon. His marriage to Seattle club owner Stephanie Dorgan had ended and he'd met another woman who lived in Portland. Maybe most importantly, Scott McCaughey, the Young Fresh Fellows cofounder and R.E.M. utility musician since the 1995 tour, had moved there to be with his new partner. Peter bought a nice old house near the center of town and settled in. He keeps his silver hair long, parting it in the middle, which, along with his generally unsmiling public mien, makes him look a little like Severus Snape, from *Harry Potter*, at his most severe. Until he picks up a guitar or bass and steps onstage somewhere, at which point everything about Peter lightens and something in him takes wing.

During his band's early years, Peter spent so much time and energy working to get the band and their music noticed—he was always the R.E.M. member most likely to be interviewed, speaking at length about his and his bandmates' ideas, tastes, and ideals—that it was surprising to see how dissatisfied, even dismayed, he was when his work began to pay off. For all the dedication, and even joy, he brought to the band's performances, the rest of the success/fame package seemed to grate against his skin. The sparkle he brought to all those early interviews—look at him in that 1984 interview he did for MTV with Mike Mills—has vanished almost completely by 1994. He still answers the questions posed to him, but there's a wariness; he rarely smiles, and it's hard to even imagine him laughing.

Peter's hatred of fame made it all the more excruciating when a brief lapse led to his being arrested and prosecuted for attacking a stewardess on a flight from Seattle to London in 2001, an incident triggered by his mixing red wine with sleeping pills. Peter had already had one strange reaction to sleeping pills in the mid-1980s—it took a long time for the pills to kick in, and sleep was preceded by a period of hallucinatory weirdness during which he painstakingly reduced a stack of newspapers to shreds, leaving knee-deep drifts he had no memory of creating when he woke up the next morning.[1]

When he overdid the sleeping pills again fifteen years later, on the flight to England, his unconscious meanderings turned aggressive, at the expense of British Airways' cabin crew, with whom the sleepwalking musician argued before drenching one with a thing of yogurt he snatched from a service cart. Once again he awoke with no memory of his unconscious actions. But this time he was in trouble. Peter spent the next year battling charges of midair assault, public drunkenness, and damaging the airline's property. He was acquitted in the end—there was enough evidence of the mind-bending powers of sleeping pills, and of Peter's many years of spotless behavior—for the jury to believe that the lapse was the result of a bad combination of substances, rather than the guitarist's bad character. It was the first and last time Peter wound up in the media hot seat, but it did nothing to make him feel comfortable with the public notoriety his music had earned him.

Peter and McCaughey work constantly, writing, producing, and performing for the seemingly endless series of bands and collaborations they form (the Minus 5, the Baseball Project, the No Ones, Filthy Friends, Arthur Buck, and on and on) and producing albums for, and often touring with, the likes of Robyn Hitchcock, the Jayhawks, John Wesley Harding, and Alejandro Escovedo, among others. For several years after R.E.M.'s breakup, Peter ran an annual music festival in the Mexican coastal village of Todos Santos, which boasted performances from Wilco, the Drive-By Truckers, Old 97's, Conor Oberst of Bright Eyes, and many others. Friends like Mike Mills, Steve Wynn, Kevn Kinney, and Led Zeppelin's John Paul Jones would come down to hang out, and most were happy to join in the fun, either adding instrumental or vocal parts for the billed bands or joining one of the unbilled conglomerations Peter and McCaughey pulled together to fill in that night's performance. The festival, which raised money for the Palapa Society, an educational nonprofit supporting local kids, got bigger each go-round until 2016, when it stretched for two weeks, climaxing with a huge concert in the town's central square, attended by thousands. That might have been too much of a good thing: the Todos Santos festival has been on hiatus ever since.

Music continues to be the central organizing factor in his life. When Scott McCaughey suffered a stroke in November 2017, Peter put together a pair of fundraising concerts two months later to help pay for his recovery. Mike Mills and Bill Berry both performed at the shows, along with friends that included Escovedo, the Decemberists, Corin Tucker from Sleater-Kinney, James Mercer from the Shins, and the Drive-By Truckers' Patterson Hood, who had also settled in Portland. McCaughey made a full recovery from his stroke, and by April 2018 he was back onstage with the Minus 5 at Portland's Laurelthirst Public House, Peter at his side, performing the first of what were billed as the Therapy Sessions, a weekly residency that went on for a month.

The COVID pandemic sidelined Peter for a few years, as it did everyone, but he got back to his musical ways once the coast was clear and has been either in the studio, on the road, or on a stage somewhere ever since. As of this writing he's touring with the latest iteration of the Baseball Project, performing songs about the nation's pastime in a combo that includes Mike Mills, Scott McCaughey, Steve Wynn from the Dream Syndicate, and former Zuzu's Petals drummer Linda Pitmon, who doubles as Wynn's wife.

Mike Mills keeps houses in Athens and Los Angeles and has been working most visibly with his childhood church choir friend Bobby McDuffie, now a classical violinist, for whom he composed the 2016 *Concerto for Violin, Rock Band and String Orchestra*. The pair have collaborated on other pieces and shows, including "A Night of Georgia Music," an overview of the work of some of the state's most influential artists, including Ray Charles, the Allman Brothers Band, Otis Redding, the B-52's, Outkast, and R.E.M., and "R.E.M. Explored," featuring classical arrangements of some of his old band's songs. He also performs with original Big Star drummer Jody Stephens in tributes to that great, if largely unheralded, band, as well as on various all-star fundraising shows, for which he is always glad to do "Rockville" or one of the other R.E.M. songs that featured him, such as "Texarkana" or "Superman."

Mike is also a presence on Twitter, where he posts regularly on sports, particularly the exploits of the Atlanta Braves and the University of Georgia football team, and on current events and politics, which is where he really lets fly, unloading frank and often explosive commentary on politics, culture, and particularly Donald Trump, whom he clearly loathes.

Mike is married to Jasmine Pahl, and seems the model of a well-adjusted former rock star, working on projects when and if they capture his attention and spending the rest of his time enjoying himself.

Bill Berry, who left R.E.M. when the band was at the height of its popularity, still spends most of his time on his farm outside Athens, where he has resided for more than thirty years. He never stopped playing music but keeps the vast majority of it to himself. He has made an irregular habit of sitting in with friends, particularly when one of Peter's bands comes through Athens or when Love Tractor performs. Musicians in Athens say he is remarkably generous with his time and attention. During the pandemic, one told me, Bill would call to check in once a week, making certain that things were still okay, that he had everything he needed. They had been friendly before, if not terribly close, and he felt touched by Bill's concern. And even more touched when he realized that Bill was making dozens of calls just like that every week.

In the late 2010s Bill started hosting regular jam sessions with former Five Eight singer Mike Mantione and a few other Athens musicians. They started writing and then recording some original songs, and after a few months they dubbed themselves the Bad Ends and decided to do something with their music. The band's first album, *The Power and the Glory*, was released in late 2022 by the prominent indie label New West. Bill made it clear that he wouldn't tour to promote the album, but he did play a few shows around Athens and, even more amazingly, appeared in the band's videos, playing the drums, riding an ATV, dressing up like a zombie (!) in the clip for "All Your Friends Are Dying," and as a chef in "Thanksgiving 1915."

Still, his appetite for attention is fleeting at best, and as of this writing Bill's most recent appearance with the Bad Ends, in which he played just a part of the band's full set, was billed as his last.

When they ended their collaboration in 2011, the ex-members of R.E.M. vowed they would never reunite. A lot of other bands, including those whose breakups involved great eruptions of rage, mutual hatred, and public trash talking, have gotten back together to tour and even make new music. Breaking up and getting back together now feels almost like a required step in a successful band's journey, which is one of the biggest reasons why the former members of R.E.M. are so determined to do no such thing. Their dedication to never standing on a stage together has remained steadfast, mostly. When Peter got married in 2013, he and the other three members of R.E.M. performed at the reception. Michael sang some songs with other musicians, but when Peter, Mike, and Bill got up to do a short set together, their former singer left the stage. The sole exception, for the length of exactly one song, took place at the band's induction into the Songwriters Hall of Fame on June 13, 2024, when the four original band members performed an acoustic version of "Losing My Religion."

The four ex-members of R.E.M. are, by all accounts, still close friends. When one encounters trouble—a divorce, a bout of depression or any potential digression from a happy, healthy path—the others have stepped in to lend their support, to make sure their friend doesn't steer himself into a ditch. It seems to help. They're all still alive and well, active in their communities and doing things that matter to them.

They're also still part of an exclusive club: only the four of them know how it felt to be in R.E.M. They started out as college kids and ended up as rock 'n' roll superstars. Bill might have missed the last fourteen years, but the die had been cast by then. As Peter has said, Bill never stopped being a member of R.E.M.; he just stopped performing and getting paid.

Do the ex-members of R.E.M., the four of them, ever get together and play some songs just for fun? Back in 1980 they spent months in the back of the church, playing their favorite covers and fiddling with their own ideas because it was the most fun they could imagine having. It's nice to imagine them doing it again, hauling their amps into someone's basement or up to their old Clayton Street clubhouse and cranking it up. Just because they enjoy one another's company, and because they still love the sound only they can make when they line up a tune, count to four, and dive in. Making music in the night, for no reason except that it feels so good to fill the darkness with noise. Gardening at night, they used to say. Gardening at night.

Acknowledgments

Work on this book began, more or less, with the start of the COVID pandemic in the spring of 2020. The ensuing months and then years of near solitude were rough, but also clarifying. In the absence of friends, culture, live music, and virtually everything else at the heart of this story, the music and lives of the men who formed R.E.M. and the people who moved among them became that much more vivid. So much of what pulled them together, inspired their music, and then drew so many millions of people to listen to them began with the simple pleasures of community and art. Happily, R.E.M.'s community proved generous even from afar, and even more welcoming when I got a chance to travel again.

For interviews, background info, fact-checking, comradeship, and other kindnesses:

In and around Athens I am particularly grateful for the help of Grace Elizabeth Hale, whose book *Cool Town* is an essential work for anyone hoping to understand how so many residents of a small academic backwater went on to alter the course of American popular culture. Paul Butchart knows as much about Athens's culture and history as anyone and is remarkably generous and patient. Patton Biddle, aka Pat the Wiz, is an amazing source for information and music, too. I am also grateful for the assistance of Tony Eubanks, Christian Lopez, Armistead Wellford, Mark Cline, Curtis Crowe, Michael Lachowski, Kit Swartz, Dana Downs, Andrew

Carter, Velena Vego, Sam Seawright, Woody Nuss, Rodger Lyle Brown, Sean Bourne, Jay Gonzalez, Patterson Hood, David Barbe, Lance Bangs, Ingrid Schorr, Caroline Wallner, Vic Varney, Mig Hayes, Vanessa Briscoe Hay, Mike Richmond, Johnny Pride, Jonny Hibbert, Mike Hobbs, Terry Allen, Chris Slay, Lauren Fancher, Mark Methe, Spencer Thornton, Jeff Fallis, Debi Atkinson (Montgomery), Maureen McGloughlin, Keith Bennett, Dennis Greenia, Rick Hawkins, Matthew Grayson, and Craig Williams.

At the University of Georgia: Judy McWillie, Robert Croker, Jim Herbert, Art Rosenbaum (RIP), Scott Bellville, Kat Stein, Mary Miller, and the staff of the University of Georgia's Hargrett Rare Book and Manuscript Library.

Also many thanks to: Melanie Herrold (aka Noni Crow), Craig Franklin, Michael Edson, Lori Blumenthal, Mike Doskocil, Danny Gruber, Andy Gruber, Bill Dorman, Jim Warchol, Steven Scariano, Ken Fechtner, Joe Craven, Alan Ingley, David Clark, Mitchell Mills, Mari Berry (Miljour), Don Berry, and Robert McDuffie.

Among R.E.M.'s friends, employees, colleagues, and fellow musicians: Robert Lloyd, Terry Allen, Geoff Trump, Kevn Kinney, Don Braxley, Karen Glauber, Bill Healey, Jeff Wooding, Scott McCaughey, Nathan December, Peter Holsapple, Ken Stringfellow, Mitch Easter, Don Dixon, Joe Boyd, Don Gehman, Scott Litt, Kurt Munkacsi, Peter Jesperson, Mark Williams, Jay Boberg, Cary Baker, Lenny Waronker, Julie Panebianco, Ross Hogarth, Jay Healy, Adam Kasper, Chris Fulton, Gevin Lindsay, Steve Wynn, Corin Tucker, Jason Ringenberg, Jay Gonzalez, Patterson Hood, Jem Cohen, Victor Krummenacher, and Eric Martin.

Legions of other writers and journalists covered R.E.M. before I did. I'm particularly grateful for the help of: Anthony DeCurtis, Rodger Lyle Brown, Tom Carson, David Handelman, Charles R. Cross, and Marc Allan.

Thanks to Andy Leach, Jennie Thomas, and everyone else at the Rock & Roll Hall of Fame Archives.

Jim Desmond goes back nearly all the way with R.E.M., so he was there at the time, saw much of it happen with his own eyes, and paid attention. J.D. has also been a close friend of mine for more than twenty years. His inspiration, guidance, and feedback have been crucial to this project.

Thanks also to Craig Williams for loaning me his collection of R.E.M. materials, and for always being there to draw my attention to the latest wrinkles in the online R.E.M. community.

Thanks to Kristi Colter for her early read and support.

The members of R.E.M. chose not to be interviewed for the book, but they never stood in my way and all found ways to be kind from afar. Peter Buck went out of his way to connect me with people and to confirm certain facts and events. I appreciate Bertis Downs's patience, even from a great remove.

Thanks always to my great friend and agent Dan Conaway, his colleague Chaim Lipskar, and everyone else at Writers House.

I had a dream collaboration with my editor, Jason Kaufman, along with Lily Dondoshansky and everyone else at Doubleday.

Thanks and all my love to my kids, Abe, Teddy, and Max. And a special shout-out to Max, who became a fierce R.E.M. devotee when he was four years old and helped me hear it all again with new ears.

Wier Harman went out of his way to be supportive and share his rock magazine archives. He was an extraordinary light in Seattle's cultural community and I'm sorry I didn't finish this in time for him to read it. Rest in peace, friend.

Claire Dederer lived through this with me, and helped deepen my knowledge of alternative cultures, along with sharpening my thinking and writing. That's not why I love her so much, but it doesn't hurt. Thanks also to Donna Dederer and Larry Jay, and to Lou and Ash Barcott.

To the memory of Dr. Albert S. Carlin.

Notes

Introduction: The Things They Wouldn't Do

1. Catherine Dillon, "R.E.M., One on One," *Athens Night Life*, R.E.M. Special Edition, March 7–13, 1984.
2. Dillon, "R.E.M., One on One."
3. Anthony DeCurtis, *Rocking My Life Away* (Durham, NC: Duke University Press, 1999).
4. *R.E.M. by MTV.*

I. Super Fucking Famous

1. Michael Stipe, interview by Rick Rubin, *Broken Record* (podcast), April 26, 2022.

2. Birdland

1. Bill Dorman, author interview, April 14, 2021.
2. Dorman, interview.
3. Craig Franklin, author interview, January 15, 2021.
4. Curtis Crowe and Melanie Herrold, author interview, May 5, 2022.
5. Crowe and Herrold, interview.
6. Franklin, interview.
7. Christopher Bollen, "Michael Stipe," *Interview*, May 2011.
8. Michael Edson, author interview, May 3, 2022.
9. Johnny Black, *Reveal*, 20.

3. Bad Habits

1. Jim Warchol, author interview, June 26, 2022.
2. Warchol, interview.
3. Craig Franklin, author interview, January 15, 2021.
4. Melanie Herrold, author interview, May 5, 2022.

5. Warchol, interview.
6. Herrold, interview.

4. An Oasis for Artists and Misfits

1. Mark Cline, author interview, July 24, 2020.
2. Sam Seawright, author interview, October 26, 2020.
3. Armistead Wellford, author interview, November 1, 2020.
4. Judith McWillie, author interview, December 14, 2020.
5. Scott Belville, author interview, February 25, 2021.
6. Cline, interview.
7. Curtis Crowe, author interview, October 23, 2021.
8. Art Rosenbaum, author interview, July 24, 2020.
9. McWillie, interview.
10. McWillie, interview.

5. Dance This Mess Around

1. Michael Lachowski, author interview, January 20, 2021.
2. Vanessa Briscoe Hay, author interview, January 5, 2021.
3. Anthony DeCurtis, author interview, September 14, 2021.
4. Glenn O'Brien, review of Gang of Four/Pylon concert, *Interview*, September 1979, quoted in Grace Elizabeth Hale, "The Birth and Death of Pylon, America's Best Rock Band," *Slate*, July 8, 2020.

6. Let's Make a Band

1. Terry Allen, author interview, March 31, 2022.
2. Paul Butchart, author interview, August 18, 2020.

7. Don't Rock 'n' Roll, No!

1. John David Pride, author interview, July 5, 2022.
2. Sullivan, *Talk About the Passion*, 8.
3. Brown, *Party Out of Bounds*, 130.
4. Scott Belville, author interview, February 25, 2021.
5. Belville, interview.
6. Mark Cline, author interview, July 24, 2020.
7. Steve Pond, "R.E.M. in the Real World," *Rolling Stone*, December 3, 1987.

8. A Party in the Church

1. Armistead Wellford, author interview, November 1, 2020.
2. Mark Cline, author interview, July 24, 2020.
3. Kit Swartz, author interview, November 8, 2021.
4. Jeff Wohl, "The Stories That Mattered," *Red & Black* (Athens, GA), May 25, 1990, 4.
5. Wellford, interview.
6. Wellford, interview.
7. Wellford, interview.
8. Paul Butchart, author interview, August 18, 2020.
9. Vanessa Briscoe Hay, author interview, January 5, 2021.

9. Picture James Brown Fronting the Dave Clark Five

1. Curtis Crowe, author interview, October 23, 2021.
2. Crowe, interview.
3. City of Athens police department incident report of raid on Koffee Klub, April 19, 1980.
4. Dennis Greenia, author interview, September 11, 2022; also other published and unpublished accounts.
5. Ken Fechtner, author interview, July 22, 2022.
6. William Haines, "'Underdog' R.E.M. Upstages the Brains," *Red & Black* (Athens, GA), May 8, 1980.
7. Haines, "'Underdog' R.E.M."
8. Sean Bourne, author interview, February 17, 2021.
9. Sullivan, *Talk About the Passion*, 11.
10. Sullivan, *Talk About the Passion*, 11.

10. We Weren't Really Close in a Lot of Ways

1. Quotes and details from Joe Craven, author interviews, January 26–27, 2021.
2. Milano, *Vinyl Junkies*, 59–64.
3. Milano, *Vinyl Junkies*, 59–64.
4. Milano, *Vinyl Junkies*, 59–64.
5. Milano, *Vinyl Junkies*, 62.
6. Craven, interviews.
7. Craven, interviews.
8. Craven, interviews.
9. Craven, interviews.
10. "Eagle Rock Boy on the Firing Line Graphically Described Tough Fight with the Japs: 'It's a Real Job,'" *Eagle Rock (CA) Sentinel*, February 11, 1944.
11. "Injured," *Eagle Rock (CA) Sentinel*, October 6, 1944.
12. "Pretty Wedding," *Eagle Rock (CA) Sentinel*, March 5, 1953.
13. Cohen and Nugent, *Mickey Cohen: In My Own Words*.
14. "Gangsters' Release in Favor Deal for Police, Captain Told," *Los Angeles Times*, October 26, 1949, and other newspapers, 1949–1950.
15. "Gangsters' Release," *Los Angeles Times*.
16. "Pretty Wedding," *Eagle Rock (CA) Sentinel*.
17. Black, *Reveal*, 130.

11. Hey, He Really Knows His Shit!

1. Peter Buck, texts to author, September 6, 2022.
2. Black, *Reveal*, 23.
3. Black, *Reveal*, 23.
4. Black, *Reveal*, 23.
5. Mark Cline, author interview, July 24, 2020.

12. A Certain Amount of Chaos

1. Terry Allen, author interview, March 31, 2022.
2. Mark Williams, author interview, October 12, 2021.
3. Don Braxley, author interview, August 20, 2020.
4. Judith McWillie, author interview, December 14, 2020.

5. Robert Hilburn, "R.E.M. at the Front of the Movement," *Los Angeles Times*, June 2, 1985.

13. Sit and Try for the Big Kill

1. Mitch Easter, author interview, October 7, 2020.
2. Easter, interview.
3. Jonny Hibbert, author interview, September 2021.

14. Lots of Impressive First-Time Songs

1. Sam Seawright, author interview, October 26, 2020.
2. Terry Allen, author interview, March 31, 2022.
3. Jon Young, *Trouser Press*, 1983 interview, published 2013.
4. Peter Buck, texts to author, July 5, 2022.
5. Copeland, *Wild Thing*, 297–98.
6. Fletcher, *Perfect Circle*.
7. Peter Jesperson, author interview, January 6, 2021.

15. Wolves Out the Door

1. Jon Young, "R.E.M.: Really Exciting Music," *Trouser Press*, August 1983.
2. Peter Buck interview in *Trouser Press*, September 1984; quoted in Tim Peacock, " 'Chronic Town': R.E.M. Bids Farewell to the Underground," UDiscoverMusic.com, August 24, 2023.
3. Kurt Munkacsi, author interview, September 9, 2021.
4. Munkacsi, interview.
5. Munkacsi, interview.
6. Mark Williams, author interview, October 12, 2021.
7. Jay Boberg, author interviews, September 16, 2022 and February 2, 2023.
8. Boberg, interviews.
9. Boberg, interviews.
10. Brown, *Party Out of Bounds*, 181.
11. Bill Healey, author interview, November 15, 2022.
12. Fletcher, *Perfect Circle*, 66–67.
13. Jonny Hibbert, author interview, September 11, 2021.
14. Hibbert, interview.

16. Chronic Town, Poster Torn

1. Jay Boberg, author interviews, September 16, 2022, and February 2, 2023.
2. Boberg, interviews.
3. Boberg, interview, February 2, 2023.
4. Craig Lee, "Suburbs, R.E.M. at the Lingerie," *Los Angeles Times*, September 2, 1982.
5. Robert Christgau, "Consumer Guide: R.E.M. Chronic Town," *The Village Voice*, 1982.
6. "R.E.M. Chronic Town," *New Musical Express*, November 12, 1982.
7. Robert Hull, "Chronic Town," *Creem*, January 1983.
8. Review of R.E.M. album *Chronic Town*, *Musician*, December 1982.
9. Andrew Slater, "R.E.M.: Not Just Another Athens, Georgia, Band," *Rolling Stone*, October 28, 1982.

17. Murmuring

1. Jason Ringenberg, author interview, September 8, 2021.
2. Jay Boberg, author interview, September 19, 2022.
3. Boberg, interview.
4. Boberg, interview.
5. Steve Pond, "R.E.M: Murmur," *Rolling Stone*, May 26, 1983.
6. Robert Christgau, "Consumer Guide: R.E.M. Murmur," *The Village Voice*, 1983.
7. Richard Grabel, "R.E.M. Chronic Town," *New Musical Express*, September 3, 1983.

18. R.E.M. Submits

1. Peter Jesperson, author interview, January 6, 2021.
2. David Fricke, "R.E.M. Hits It Big with Murmur," *Musician*, July 12, 1984.
3. Fletcher, *Perfect Circle*, 76–77.
4. "Bob Coburn's Rock Report," *Eyewitness News*, Los Angeles, CA, air date unknown, available on YouTube.
5. Peter Buck, interview (with Mike Mills) by John Gradick, date unknown, aired on Video Music Channel, TV 69, Atlanta, available on YouTube, posted by R.E.M. Video Archive, September 22, 2018.
6. Peter Buck, interview (with Michael Stipe) by Georgia Pine, "Real George's Backroom," October 12, 1983, available on YouTube.
7. Jesperson, author interview.
8. Don Snowden, "The Reckoning of R.E.M.," *Los Angeles Times*, July 18, 1984.
9. Black, *Reveal*, 85.

19. A Collective Fist

1. Jim Herbert, author interview, December 30, 2020.
2. Melanie Herrold, author interview, May 5, 2022.
3. Curtis Crowe, author interview, October 23, 2021.

20. Here We Are

1. Anthony DeCurtis, author interview, September 14, 2021.

21. My Soul Doth Magnify the Lord

1. Black, *Reveal*, 25.
2. Franklin H. Mills obituary, *The Atlanta Constitution*, September 28, 2001.
3. Mills obituary, *Atlanta Constitution*.
4. Mitchell Mills, author interview, March 19, 2021, and Robert McDuffie, author interview, October 6, 2022.
5. McDuffie.

22. Shadowfax

1. Mike Mills, video outtakes from interview (with Mills, Peter Buck, and Michael Stipe) by Debi Atkinson, Journal-TV, April 5, 1984.
2. Mills, interview by Atkinson.

3. Mills, interview by Atkinson.
4. Black, *Reveal*, 25.
5. Alan Ingley, author interview, March 17, 2022.
6. Ingley, author interview.
7. Ingley, author interview.
8. Black, *Reveal*, 26.

23. So You Want to Be a Rock 'n' Roll Star

1. Chris Connelly, "R.E.M.: Reckoning," *Rolling Stone*, May 24, 1984.
2. Joe Sasfy, "Reckoning with R.E.M.," *The Washington Post*, May 10, 1984.
3. Anthony DeCurtis, review of R.E.M. album *Reckoning, Musician*, May 1984.
4. Mat Snow, "American Paradise Regained, R.E.M.'s 'Reckoning,'" *New Musical Express*, April 21, 1984.
5. Don Snowden, "The Reckoning of R.E.M.," *Los Angeles Times*, July 18, 1984.
6. Snowden, "Reckoning."
7. R.E.M. profile by Scott Osborne, *Entertainment Tonight*, July 6, 1984.
8. Mike Mills, interview, aired July 3, 1984, on *The NewMusic*, Citytv, Toronto.
9. Gevin Lindsay, author interview, November 1, 2022.

24. Gravity Pulling Me Around

1. Joe Boyd, author interview, April 16, 2021.
2. Chris Slay, author interview, March 31, 2022.
3. Jude Rogers, "Michael Stipe's Last Stand," *The Quietus*, November 12, 2011.
4. Boyd, author interview.
5. Jesse Thorn, "Michael Stipe on His New Music, Photography and More," *Bullseye with Jesse Thorn*, aired on May 24, 2022, National Public Radio.

25. A Magic Kingdom, Open-Armed

1. Lori Blumenthal, author interview, December 6, 2022.
2. *R.E.M. by MTV.*
3. Fletcher, *Perfect Circle*, 114.
4. Peter Buck, "The True Spirit of American Rock," *Record*, October 1984.
5. *Two at Four*, KATU-TV, Portland, Oregon, July 11, 1985.
6. CBS-TV, *Entertainment Tonight*, August 30, 1985.
7. MuchMusic, interview with Stipe and Buck by J. D. Roberts, 1985.
8. Joe Boyd, author interview, April 16, 2021.

26. What If We Give It Away?

1. All the above from raw video of interview with Peter Buck, Mike Mills, and Michael Stipe by Debi Atkinson, Athens, GA, May 5, 1984.
2. Buck, interview by Atkinson.
3. Buck, interview by Atkinson.
4. Ross Hogarth, author interview, July 16, 2021.
5. Hogarth, author interview.
6. Don Gehman, author interview, February 9, 2023.
7. Gehman, author interview.
8. Gehman, author interview.

9. Jay Boberg, author interview, September 16, 2022.
10. Gehman, author interview.

27. Life's Rich Demand

1. Sue Cummings, "R.E.M., Lifes Rich Pageant," *Spin*, October 1986.
2. Tom Carson, "Sandbox Supermen," *The Village Voice*, September 2, 1986.
3. Geoff Trump, author interview, May 20, 2022.

28. Things We Never Thought Would Happen Have Happened

1. *MTV News: The Year in Rock 1987*, aired December 30, 1987, on MTV, available on YouTube.
2. Scott Litt, author interview, April 15, 2021.
3. Litt, author interview.
4. Bill Flanagan, "R.E.M.'s Double Visionaries," *Musician*, January 1988.
5. Litt, author interview.
6. Don Gehman, author interview, February 9, 2023.
7. Jay Boberg, author interview, February 2, 2023.
8. Cary Baker, letter to Jim Henke, July 7, 1987, in author's collection.

29. Conquest

1. From promotional video made for Warner Bros. Records staff by R.E.M. for the November 8, 1988, release of *Green*, in author's collection, and on YouTube.
2. Jay Watson, "R.E.M. Is Serious About Having Fun," *Red & Black* (Athens, GA), May 6, 1981.
3. Bob Keyes, "Music Pete Buck's Whole Life: Success of REM Won't Change His Life," *Red & Black* (Athens, GA), March 8, 1984.
4. J. D. Considine, "R.E.M.: Subverting Small Town Boredom," *Musician*, August 1983.
5. Jon Young, "R.E.M.: Really Exciting Music," *Trouser Press*, August 1983.
6. Peter Buck, author interview, August 8, 2017.
7. Bill Berry, Warner Bros. Records electronic press kit for *Green*, 1988, in author's collection.
8. Tom Popson, "Interviews: Onward and Upward and Please Yourself," *Chicago Tribune*, October 17, 1986.
9. *MTV News*, aired October 8, 1987, on MTV.
10. Michael Stipe, dollhouse porch interview, aired on multiple dates, 1986, on MTV.
11. *MTV News: The Year in Rock 1987*, aired December 30, 1987, on MTV, available on YouTube.
12. Chris Dafoe, "R.E.M. Tries to Cope with Price of Success from Hockey Arenas to Publicity Bashes," *Globe and Mail* (Toronto), September 1, 1987.
13. Tony Eubanks, author interview, October 2, 2020.
14. Julie Panebianco, author interview, March 1, 2021.
15. Panebianco, author interview.
16. Buck, author interview.
17. Buck, author interview.
18. Jay Boberg, author interview, February 2, 2023.
19. Kit Swartz, author interview, November 8, 2021.
20. Curtis Crowe, author interview, October 23, 2021.

30. Hi, Hi, Hi, Hi

1. Scott Litt, author interview, April 15, 2021.
2. Jay Healy, author interview, July 23, 2021.
3. Black, *Reveal*, 148.
4. *Rockin' in the UK*, aired November 22, 1988, on Super Channel (UK), available on YouTube.

31. Are You Ready to Rock 'n' Roll?

1. Gary Graff, "R.E.M. Keeps Artistry Intact with Theatrics and Music," *Detroit Free Press*, April 6, 1989.
2. Barry Walters, "Simplistic 'Green' May Leave R.E.M. Fans Seeing Red," *San Francisco Examiner*, December 11, 1988.
3. J. D. Considine, "Success Won't Spoil Self-Conscious R.E.M.," *Baltimore Sun*, November 20, 1988.
4. Steve Morse, "R.E.M.'s Latest Is a Long, Lovely Reverie," *Boston Globe*, November 9, 1988.
5. Robert Christgau, "Consumer Guide: R.E.M. Green," *The Village Voice*, December 27, 1988.
6. Peter Buck, interview with Marc Allan, recorded 1989, *The Tapes Archive* (podcast), available on YouTube.

32. The Fever

1. Mari Miljour, author interview, July 15, 2022.
2. Don Berry, author interview, September 18, 2022.
3. Catherine Dillon, "R.E.M., One on One," *Athens (GA) Night Life*, R.E.M. Special Edition, March 7–13, 1984.
4. Gevin Lindsay, author interview, November 1, 2022.
5. Bo Sammons, "Maconite Reflects on Son's Success with Rock Band," *Macon (GA) Telegraph*, July 2, 1984.
6. Miljour, author interview, July 15, 2022.
7. Black, *Reveal*, 172.
8. Fletcher, *Perfect Circle*, 192.

33. A Breath, This Song

1. Mat Snow, "R.E.M.," *Q*, October 1992.

34. Near Wild Heaven

1. Julie Panebianco, author interview, March 1, 2021.
2. Lenny Waronker, author interview, March 27, 2023.
3. Waronker, author interview.
4. *MTV News*, aired November 1990, on MTV.
5. *MTV News*, November 1990.
6. *MTV News*, November 1990.

35. Shiny Happy

1. Jay Boberg, author interview, February 2, 2023.
2. Boberg, author interview.

36. The Most Improbably Successful Group in Music Today

1. Bill Berry, *Villa Lux*, aired March 12, 1991, on RTL4 TV, Luxembourg.
2. Pat Biddle, author interview, November 17, 2020.
3. Jim Sullivan, "R.E.M.: Shadows and Murmurs," *Record*, July 1983.
4. Raw video of R.E.M.'s trip to Paraguay with the Nature Conservancy, 1992.
5. Jim Desmond, texts to author, May 2023.

37. These Are Days

1. Lenny Waronker, author interview, March 27, 2023.
2. Mike Mills speaking with reporter in 1992, for *The New Music*, MuchMusic (Canada).
3. Mills interview, *The New Music*.
4. Mills interview, *The New Music*.
5. Mills interview, *The New Music*.

38. Does Everyone Still Want to Do This?

1. *Lola da musica*, aired October 9, 1994, on VPRO (Netherlands).
2. Mari Miljour, author interview, July 15, 2022.
3. *Live with Regis & Kathie Lee*, aired February 24, 1992, on ABC.
4. Peter Buck and Mike Mills, interview on *The New Music*, aired July 26, 1993, MuchMusic (Canada).
5. Anthony DeCurtis, author interview, September 14, 2021.

39. Enter the Monster

1. *MTV News*, aired January 5, 1995, on MTV.
2. *A Current Affair—Summer Edition*, aired January 13, 1995 (Australia).
3. Fletcher, *Perfect Circle*, 263.
4. *R.E.M.: Rough Cut*, documentary, directed by Jonathan Dayton and Valerie Faris (1995).

40. Did Someone Put a Curse on Us?

1. *All Mixed Up*, aired October 1992, on Super Channel (Europe).
2. *R.E.M.: Rough Cut*, documentary, directed by Jonathan Dayton and Valerie Faris, aired August 19, 1995.
3. "R.E.M.," *Behind the Music*, originally aired December 6, 1998, on VH1.
4. Mari Miljour, author interview, July 15, 2022.
5. Gerrie Lim, "Rapid Eye Monster: R.E.M. and the Reconstruction of New Fables," *BigO*, September 1994.
6. *R.E.M. by MTV*.
7. Fletcher, *Perfect Circle*, 263.
8. Fletcher, *Perfect Circle*, 263.
9. Miljour, author interview.
10. Nathan December, author interview, May 29, 2021.
11. Miljour, author interview.
12. Miljour, author interview.

41. How the West Was Won . . .

1. "R.E.M.," *Behind the Music*, originally aired December 6, 1998, on VH1.
2. Mari Miljour, author interview, July 15, 2022.
3. *1995 MTV Video Music Awards*, aired September 7, 1995, on MTV, available on YouTube.
4. Black, *Reveal*, 44–45.
5. Karen Glauber, author interview, November 21, 2022.
6. Ingrid Schorr, author interview, April 5, 2022.
7. Rosanna Greenstreet, "Michael Stipe: Who Would I Say Sorry To? Everyone I Slept with Before the Age of 27," *The Guardian*, January 11, 2020.
8. Chuck Philips, "R.E.M.'s Former Manager Denies Allegations of Sex Harassment," *Los Angeles Times*, June 21, 1996.

42. . . . And Where It Got Us

1. David Altschul, author interview, May 15, 2023.
2. Barney Hoskyns, "R.E.M.: The Final Act?," *Mojo*, August 1996.
3. Mat Snow, email to author, May 14, 2023.
4. Jim DeRogatis, "New Adventures in R.E.M.," *Request*, Fall 1996.
5. Steve Pond, "R.E.M.: The Ultimate College Rock Band Graduates," *Rolling Stone*, December 3, 1987.
6. Wayne Kramer, author interview, June 22, 2010.

43. I'm Outta Here

1. *Fanning Profiles*, aired October 5, 1992, on RTE TV (Dublin).
2. Mark Cline, author interview, July 24, 2020.
3. Scott Litt, author interview, April 15, 2021.
4. Litt, author interview.
5. Nathan December, author interview, May 29, 2021.
6. Scott McCaughey, author interview, February 24, 2021.
7. "R.E.M.," *Behind the Music*, aired December 6, 1998, on VH1.
8. Mari Miljour, author interview, July 15, 2022.
9. *MTV News: The Week in Rock*, aired October 31, 1997, on MTV.

44. Airportmen

1. Fletcher, *Perfect Circle*, 317.
2. Peter Buck, texts to author, May 20, 2023.
3. "R.E.M.," *Behind the Music*, aired December 6, 1998, on VH1.
4. David Stubbs, "R.E.M. 'Up,'" *Uncut*, December 1998.

45. The Name of This Band Is R.E.M.

1. Raw footage of group interview with Adam Weissler, September 2003.
2. Weissler interview.

46. The Murmurers

1. Michael Stipe, interview, 1986, in *R.E.M. by MTV.*
2. Nathan December, author interview, May 29, 2021.

3. Victor Krummenacher, author interview, August 31, 2021.
4. Doug Brod, "Around the Sun by R.E.M.," *Entertainment Weekly*, October 8, 2004.
5. *National Anthem: Inside the Vote for Change Concert Tour*, directed by D. A. Pennebaker et al., aired October 11, 2004, on Sundance Channel.
6. *National Anthem*.
7. Adam Sweeting, "R.E.M. Hyde Park London," *The Guardian*, July 18, 2005.

47. This Is Going to Be Loud

1. WEA presentation video for *Automatic for the People*, 1992.
2. Scott McCaughey, author interviews, 2021–23.
3. McCaughey, author interviews.
4. Dee Lockett, "Peter Buck Explains the Casual Way R.E.M. Broke Up," *Vulture*, March 14, 2016.

48. It Was What It Was

1. Corin Tucker, author interview, December 2021.

49. Let's All Get On with It

1. Sullivan, *Talk About the Passion*, 97.

Bibliography

Books

Black, Johnny. *Reveal: The Story of R.E.M.* San Francisco: Backbeat, 2004.

Brown, Rodger Lyle. *Party Out of Bounds: The B-52's, R.E.M., and the Kids Who Rocked Athens, Georgia.* 25th anniv. ed. Athens: University of Georgia Press, 2016. First published 1991.

Buckley, David. *R.E.M. Fiction: An Alternative Biography.* London: Virgin Books, 2002.

Cohen, Michael Mickey, and John Peer Nugent. *Mickey Cohen: In My Own Words; The Underworld Autobiography of Michael Mickey Cohen, as Told to John Peer Nugent.* Hoboken, NJ: Prentice-Hall, 1975.

Copeland, Ian. *Wild Thing: The Backstage, on the Road, in the Studio, off the Charts Memoirs of Ian Copeland.* New York: Simon & Schuster, 1995.

DeCurtis, Anthony. *R.E.M.: The Rolling Stone Files.* New York: Hyperion, 1995.

Fletcher, Tony. *Perfect Circle: The Story of R.E.M.* London: Omnibus, 2013.

Gray, Marcus. *It Crawled from the South: An R.E.M. Companion.* London: Guinness, 1992.

Hale, Grace Elizabeth. *Cool Town: How Athens, Georgia, Launched Alternative Music and Changed American Culture.* Chapel Hill: University of North Carolina Press, 2020.

Lurie, Robert Dean. *Begin the Begin: R.E.M.'s Early Years.* Portland, OR: Verse Chorus, 2019.

Milano, Brett. *Vinyl Junkies: Adventures in Record Collecting.* New York: St. Martin's Griffin, 2003.

Niimi, J. *Murmur.* New York: Bloomsbury Academic, 2005.

Sullivan, Denise. *R.E.M.: Talk About the Passion; An Oral History.* Updated ed. New York: Da Capo, 1998. First published 1994 by Underwood-Miller.

Documentaries and Video Collections

Bangs, Lance, Peter Care, Jem Cohen, Jonathan Dayton, Dominic DeJoseph, Nigel Dick, Katherine Dieckmann, et al., dirs. *The Best of R.E.M.: In View 1988–2003.* Burbank, CA: Warner Reprise Video, 2003.

Care, Peter, dir. *Road Movie*. Burbank, CA: Warner Reprise Video, 1996.

Care, Peter, Jem Cohen, Jonathan Dayton, Valerie Faris, Spike Jonze, Mark Romanek, Jake Scott, Randy Skinner, and Jodi Wille, dirs. *R.E.M. Parallel*. Burbank, CA: Warner Reprise Video, 1995.

Cohen, Jem, Tom Corcoran, Jonathan Dayton, Valerie Faris, Kevin Flaherty, Tony Gayton, James Herbert, et al., dirs. *When the Light Is Mine: The Best of the I.R.S. Years 1982–1987*. Hollywood, CA: Capitol Records, 2006.

Gayton, Tony, dir. *Athens, Ga.: Inside/Out*. 1987; Oaks, PA: Music Video Distributors, 2003.

Knowles, Julia, dir. *R.E.M.: Perfect Square*. Burbank, CA: Warner Reprise Video, 2004.

Leach, Blue, dir. *R.E.M. Live*. Burbank, CA: Warner Bros., 2007.

McKay, Jim, and Michael Stipe, dirs. *Tourfilm: R.E.M.* Burbank, CA: Warner Reprise Video, 1990.

Menotti, Gary, dir. *R.E.M.: Live from Austin, TX*. Los Angeles: New West Records, 2010.

Moon, Vincent, and Jeremiah, dir. *This Is Not a Show: Live at the Olympia in Dublin*. Burbank, CA: Warner Bros., 2009.

Young, Alex, dir. *R.E.M. by MTV*. Burbank, CA: Rhino Entertainment, 2015.

Index

ILLUSTRATION CREDITS

ABOUT THE AUTHOR

PETER AMES CARLIN is a writer and the author of several books, including *Homeward Bound: The Life of Paul Simon*, published in 2016, and *Bruce*, a biography of Bruce Springsteen published in 2012. Carlin has also been a freelance journalist, a senior writer at *People* in New York City, and a television columnist and feature writer at *The Oregonian* in Portland. A regular speaker on music, writing, and popular culture, Carlin lives in Portland.